FUNK & WAGNALLS

The Great Composers

Their lives and times with program notes for the recordings

CONTENTS

The Great Composers

In addition to the records themselves, one of the features that makes your Family Library of Great Music the superior collection it is, is the treasury of information contained in *The Great Composers*. Fully illustrated for your greater enjoyment, all 22 chapters of *The Great Composers* are an integral part of your record library. In their entirety, the 264 pages of this book present the complete biographies of the world's greatest composers—their lives, the times in which they lived, and most importantly, their music.

The final pages of each chapter of *The Great Composers* contain the Program Notes for the selections contained in the 22 albums. All 60 pre-selected masterpieces are explained in a straightforward, understandable manner, to help increase your knowledge and comprehension of them.

For your convenience, this binder has been especially manufactured so that each chapter can be inserted periodically with the greatest facility. You will notice that Beethoven is covered in three chapters of *The Great Composers*; Tchaikovsky, Mozart, and Brahms in 2 chapters each.

Not only will this valuable, informative book become a treasured addition to your book-shelves, but it will serve as an interesting conversation piece displayed anywhere in your home.

Ludwig van Beethoven

His Life and Times 1770-1804

PROGRAM NOTES FOR THE SIXTH SYMPHONY
By Robert Jacobson

FUNK & WAGNALLS, INC.
NEW YORK, NEW YORK

Youth in Bonn

Johann van Beethoven gave his eldest son Ludwig his first music lessons at an early age. Remembering the success the Mozart children had had some years before, Beethoven senior was quite determined to exploit the boy's skill while he was still young enough for it to be unusual. However, it was not until 1778 that Ludwig made his first public appearance, as a pianist; but so that as much profit as possible might be made from the occasion he was described in the concert announcements as 'six years old'. It soon became normal practice for Johann to subtract a year or two from his son's age to make him appear even more precocious, and for many years afterwards Beethoven himself believed that he had been born in 1772.

Ludwig van Beethoven was in fact born on 15th or 16th December 1770. The roots of his family are still fairly obscure. They were of Flemish origin, and the somewhat slender information we have suggests that they were tradesmen and artisans (the Dutch prefix 'van' has not the noble associations of the German 'von' and originally indicated merely that its bearer was the owner of a plot of land).

In 1733 Louis van Beethoven, the composer's grandfather, settled in Bonn, which had since the 13th century been the seat of the Archbishop-Electors of Cologne (called Electors because with other ecclesiastical and lay rulers they were responsible for the election of the Holy Roman Emperor). At the beginning of the 18th century the Elector Joseph Clemens endowed a musical chapel which was enlarged and improved by his successor, and it was here that Louis van Beethoven, a bass singer, obtained employment. He married a German, Maria Josepha Poll, who took to drink and had to be taken into care, and it was presumably her weakness in this direction that was inherited by her son, Johann. Like Louis, Johann was a singer, but a tenor, employed at the same chapel, and he augmented his income by teaching violin and clavier. In 1767 he married a cook's daughter, Maria Magdalena Keverich, rather against the will of his father who felt that his son was marrying beneath him. Maria Magdalena soon became, however, the mainstay of the Beethoven family, for Johann proved himself to be a dissipated man, chiefly interested in drink and in the exploitation of his eldest son's musical talent. Three children of this marriage survived infancy, Ludwig, Kaspar Karl (born 1774), and Nikolaus Johann (born 1776).

Beethoven quickly learned all that his father could teach him. It is possible that he had some lessons from van der Eede, the aged court organist, and he was taught by Tobias Friedrich Pfeiffer, a good musician who was, however, one of Johann van Beethoven's drinking companions. The two men,

returning from a drinking bout, would turn Ludwig out of bed for a lesson regardless of the time of night. Music took up every minute of the boy's time and his schooling was forced to take second place—he attended several primary schools, including the Tirocinium, which prepared pupils for the gymnasium; but instead of entering the gymnasium at the age of eleven, as was usual, he abandoned his studies altogether. At this time he was described as 'a shy and taciturn boy, the necessary consequence of the life apart which he led, observing more and pondering more than he spoke, and disposed to abandon himself entirely to the feelings awakened by music and (later) by poetry and to the pictures created by fancy.'

At about the time that Ludwig left school he began to take lessons from the most important of his masters, Christian Gottlob Neefe, who had come to Bonn in 1779 as musical director of a theatre company and who had subsequently been appointed court organist. Neefe gave his pupil a thorough musical training, teaching him in particular to play Bach's *Well-tempered Clavier*, and his influence was acknowledged by Beethoven in 1793 when he wrote to Neefe, 'If I ever become a great man, yours shall be a share of the credit.' During Neefe's absence abroad in 1782 Beethoven, then only $11\frac{1}{2}$ years old, deputised for him as court organist, and the following year he acted as cembalist (or director) of the court orchestra—an extremely responsible position, for the cembalist guided the orchestra's performance, playing by sight from the score.

This work gave Beethoven an opportunity to put his lessons into practice, and while he was at the theatre he also became well acquainted with the popular operas of the day. But his work was not officially recognised until 1784, when he was appointed assistant court organist at a salary of 100 thalers a year. Beethoven was by this time already skilled in the improvisations which were to make his name in Vienna: in 1785, while accompanying the singer Ferdinand Heller, he asked leave to try and put Heller off his note. Heller agreed, thinking that it would be impossible for so young a performer to do this; but he soon found that he was wrong, for Beethoven's accompaniment became so complicated that Heller was unable to find the closing notes.

In 1787 Beethoven visited Vienna. Who sponsored the visit or how he obtained money for his journey is not known, but it was at this time that he met Mozart, for whom he played. Mozart at first received the playing rather coolly, thinking that the piece had merely been well prepared; but when Beethoven improvised on a theme of Mozart's suggesting Mozart was visibly impressed and told the distinguished

gathering of musicians, 'Some day this young man will make a great noise in the world.' Beethoven's stay in Vienna was however abruptly cut short when he received news that his mother was seriously ill. He hurried back to Bonn, but on 17th July she died.

After his wife's death Johann van Beethoven began to go steadily downhill: he drank more and more, and on one occasion Stephan von Breuning recollects seeing Ludwig 'furiously interposing to rescue his drunken father from an officer of police'. These years were very hard ones for the Beethoven family and Ludwig was forced to apply for help to Franz Anton Ries, with whom he had formerly studied the violin. He also gave music lessons and it was as a music teacher that he entered for the first time the house of the von Breuning family, with whom he was to become very close friends. Frau von Breuning was a widow with four children (Stephan, her second son, had studied with Beethoven under Ries): Beethoven soon became a member of their family circle, and this first contact with a cultured society so different from the hard world in which he had grown up had a markedly softening effect on his character. At their home he also met Franz Gerhard Wegeler, a young doctor who married Eleonore von Breuning, and who was later to write a biography of Beethoven.

Another friend Beethoven made at this time was Count Ferdinand Waldstein, an enthusiastic amateur musician, who was to be one of his most generous benefactors—among other works the so-called 'Waldstein' Piano Sonata is dedicated to this patron, who gave the composer a piano and numerous gifts of money (which he usually pretended had come from the Elector!); Beethoven on his side com-posed the music for a *Ritterballet* performed in March 1791, and which purported to be by Count Waldstein.

In 1788 the Elector Max Franz decided to revive the theatre and opera at Bonn. A new orchestra was engaged including both Beethoven, who played viola, and Franz Anton Ries, who played violin. The four years during which Beethoven was a member of this orchestra gave him a knowledge of all the best schools of the day (except that of Berlin), and ex-perience as an active member of an orchestra. By 1789 Johann van Beethoven had become incapable of carrying out his work properly. He was dismissed from the chapel choir and Ludwig now became legally, as well as in fact, head of his family: Johann continued to receive half his salary, but the other half was paid to Ludwig in addition to his own. After Johann's dismissal his general decline continued, and in 1792 he died.

In 1790 Haydn passed through Bonn on his way to England and when he visited the town again on his return journey in 1792 the musicians gave a big dinner in his honour. Beet-hoven, who was present on this occasion, showed Haydn a cantata he had composed, and perhaps Haydn suggested that Beethoven should come and study with him in Vienna. Wherever the idea came from, it was not long before Beet-hoven acted on it. By August he had left Bonn, never to return. Among his luggage was his autograph album, in which Count Waldstein had inscribed: '. . . The Genius of Mozart is mourning and weeping over the death of her pupil. She found a refuge but no occupation with the inexhaustible Haydn; through him she wishes to form a union with another. With the help of assiduous labour you shall receive Mozart's spirit from Haydn's hands.'

3

Arrival in Vienna: Life 1792-1802

When Beethoven arrived in Vienna in 1792, turning his back on Bonn and the Rhineland for the last time, the city was the musical capital of Europe. It was dominated by the personalities of Haydn (now sixty) and Mozart (who had died the previous year) but there was also a constant demand for new music which was met by a host of minor composers, most of whom have been forgotten today. Opera flourished in two state-controlled theatres and at the newly-formed Theater auf der Wieden, but public concerts were seldom given and even subscription series – the normal form of concert-giving at the time – were few. Some members of the nobility maintained permanent musical establishments and chamber music was very popular; most music-lovers played with, and even composed for, chamber ensembles. Pianists were judged above all by their ability to improvise, but in 1792 Mozart's supremacy in this art had not yet been challenged.

It was as a student that Beethoven came to Vienna, and he was soon taking lessons with Haydn – an arrangement which did not prove to be very satisfactory, as Beethoven was far too strong-willed for his easy-going master. By the time Haydn left for England in 1794 the lessons were at an end, and when publishing his first composition Beethoven refused to call himself 'pupil of Haydn', for he insisted that although he had had some instruction from Haydn he had

never learned anything from him. He subsequently studied with Albrechtsberger, court organist and an authority on contrapuntal and church music, and with Antonio Salieri, Mozart's former rival, who was court Kapellmeister and director of the Opera. Franz Anton Ries's son Ferdinand recalls: 'All three valued Beethoven highly, but were also of one mind touching his habits of study. All of them said Beethoven was so headstrong and self-sufficient that he had to learn much through harsh experience which he had refused to accept when it was presented to him as a subject of study.' This is very revealing of Beethoven's character – until his meeting with the von Breunings and Count Waldstein he had never learned to practise self-control, and he was subject throughout his life to ungovernable fits of temper.

When Beethoven first arrived in Vienna he was very short of money, for although he was still in theory employed by the Bonn court his salary was soon discontinued, in spite of Franz Anton Ries's efforts on his behalf. There were, however, many ways for a musician to earn a living in Vienna. Piano-playing in the salons of the aristocracy was very remunerative, and was also a means of gaining well-to-do pupils. Publication of compositions could bring in a little money, but it was more profitable to sell the sole rights in new works for a limited period before publication, or to sell the dedications of works. Concert-giving was another source of income, but Beethoven did not give a concert for his own benefit until he had been in Vienna for eight years.

With the help of introductions which he had been given by his friends in Bonn, Beethoven was soon established in Viennese society. His first lodgings were in the same house as those of Prince Lichnowsky, a patron of the arts and amateur musician, and before very long he had moved into the Prince's apartment and was living with him as an honoured guest. Beethoven became quite a dandy – although the unaccustomed necessity of keeping up appearances began to be rather a strain. Dinner at Prince Lichnowsky's house was served at four o'clock. 'Now,' said Beethoven, 'it is desired that every day I shall be at home at half past three, put on better clothes, care for my beard etc. – I can't stand that.' Besides Lichnowsky, at this time Beethoven met and became intimate with other Viennese nobles including Prince Lobkowitz (another musical amateur and patron), Baron van Swieten (the friend of Haydn and Mozart) and Freiherr Zmeskall von Domanowetz (an official in the Royal Hungarian Court Chancellery); as well as many of the city musicians, among them the violinist Schuppanzigh, the pianist Hummel, and Amenda, a theology graduate who had become a music teacher. His circle of friends was also increased by the arrival in Vienna of Wegeler and two members of the von Breuning family.

But despite the glamour of his new life Beethoven did not forget his brothers. After his father's death they too came to Vienna. Kasper Karl became a teacher of music, while Nikolaus Johann took a job in an apothecary's shop and was eventually able to set up on his own account. And Beethoven was always ready to help them with gifts of money, or with advice if necessary.

In 1795 a young singer, Magdalene Willmann, came to Vienna, where she appeared in several productions of the Court Opera. She so entranced Beethoven that he proposed marriage, but was refused, according to the girl 'because he was so ugly and half crazy'. His sorrow does not seem to have lasted very long and, besides, the year was marked for him by a number of other important events: for the first time he appeared in public as composer and pianist; and best of all was the appearance of the first of his works to be published in Vienna, the three Piano Trios, which Beethoven himself distinguished as the first of his compositions deserving attention when he designated them 'opus 1'. From this time he composed steadily – often working on several pieces at once – and each work added to the foundations of his new fame as a composer. By 1801 he had written the first three Piano Concertos, the First Symphony and an enormous amount of chamber music, including the 'Pathétique' and 'Moonlight' Sonatas.

Although he was never a keen traveller, in 1796 Beethoven visited Prague and Berlin, where he played several times at court and, according to Ries, received a gold snuff-box filled with money of which he was very proud. But although he did not go abroad very often, he preferred to spend the summer months in some quiet country retreat near Vienna. He was always a great lover of the country – a love that was later to be revealed in the 'Pastoral' Symphony.

Acclaimed as a pianist and well on the way to making his name as a composer, at the end of the 18th century Beethoven appeared to be poised on the threshold of a brilliant career. But already he was threatened by the disaster which was to change his life. It was in 1798 or 1799 that he first noticed symptoms of deafness, and although they had not yet become serious he visited innumerable doctors during the next few years in an attempt to find a cure. But nothing worked, and by 1801 Beethoven could no longer pretend to the world that his hearing was normal. On 1st June he wrote to Amenda: 'I wish that you were with me, for your Beethoven lives most unhappily, in discord with nature and with the Creator. More than once I have cursed the latter for ex-

A 19th-century print of St Peter's Square in Vienna, where Beethoven lived in 1799 and 1802 (Austrian National Library, Vienna)

A bust of Countess Giulietta Guicciardi—although little is definitely known about her friendship with Beethoven it seems likely that he fell in love with her in 1801 (Beethovenhaus, Bonn)

posing his creatures to the slightest accident, so that often the loveliest blossoms are destroyed and broken by it. You must be told that the finest part of me, my hearing, has greatly deteriorated . . . Whether it can ever be cured, remains to be seen.' His hopelessness increased as his hearing gradually grew worse – 'the unhappiest of God's creatures', he called himself – and on 29th June he wrote to Wegeler: 'My ears . . . whistle and roar incessantly, night and day. I can say that I am leading a miserable life; for two years, almost, I have been avoiding all the social functions, simply because I feel incapable of telling people I am deaf.'

However, by November Beethoven again had cause for happiness: he was in love, as he told Wegeler. 'Now my life is a little more agreeable again, because I spend more time with others. You would hardly believe how dreary, how sad my life has been in the last two years: my bad hearing haunted me everywhere like a ghost, I fled from men, had to appear a misanthropist, though I am far from being one. This change has been brought about by a charming fascinating girl, who loves me and whom I love. At last, after two years, there have been some moments of complete bliss, and this is the first time I have ever felt that marriage could make one happy . . .' It seems most likely that this letter referred to Countess Giulietta Guicciardi, to whom Beethoven had previously given piano lessons. But nothing came of his love, perhaps because of the difference in their social positions, and in 1802 Giulietta Guicciardi married Count Gallenberg. With his love affair at an end and the prospects for his future increasingly grim in 1802 Beethoven left Vienna to spend the summer in nearby Heiligenstadt.

A stroll in the Prater *—a 19th-century print showing members of Viennese society at leisure (Albertina Print & Drawing Collection, Vienna)·*

A view of Vienna in the early 19th century (Austrian National Library, Vienna)

Crisis: Life 1802-04

In 1802 Beethoven told the composer Johann Krumpholz, 'I am not satisfied with my works up to the present time. From today I mean to take a new road.' His first two symphonies and three piano concertos were behind him, as well as the highly original piano sonatas of op. 27 and op. 31 (the second of op. 27 is the famous C sharp minor, so-called 'Moonlight', of lasting popular appeal; and op. 31, no. 2 in D minor is his most dramatic work to date). The three sonatas of op. 31 may well have been completed after his remark to Krumpholz and may have been in his mind when he made it – already they are on the new road. The *Eroica* was not far off, and he was on the threshold of a period of unparallelled power and fecundity.

To see the true immensity of this achievement (or, rather, to get some idea of the will-power that made it possible) we must consider Beethoven's state of mind in 1802. His hearing had been worrying him, and his doctor had been far from reassuring; the verdict, indeed, was that there was already little hope of an improvement and every possibility of deterioration. No kind of cure could be imagined. Beethoven was plunged into despair. The thought of suicide gripped him more than once. To be faced at the age of thirty-two with such a nightmare was almost too much – and Beethoven at this time thought he was only twenty-eight, since his father, anxious to exploit him as a boy prodigy, had falsified his age. His friend Stephen Breuning, writing to another

admirer of the composer, said, 'You could not believe the indescribable, I might say *horrible* effect, which the loss of his hearing has produced on him.' Beethoven spent the summer of 1802 in the country resort of Heiligenstadt, near Vienna, and his darkest (and some of his noblest) thoughts are expressed in a letter, now famous, to his brothers, known as the Heiligenstadt Testament, and clearly intended as a form of will. The following translation is by Constance S. Jolly, and is quoted in Schindler's *Beethoven as I Knew Him* (Faber, 1966):

For my brothers Carl and . . . . Beethoven:

O ye men who consider or declare me to be hostile, stubborn, or misanthropic, how unjust you are to me! You do not know the secret cause of what seems so to you. From childhood my heart and mind were filled with the tender feelings of goodwill; I was ever ready to perform great things. But consider that for six years I have been afflicted with an incurable complaint, made worse by my incompetent physicians, deceived year after year by the hope of an improvement, forced at last to accept the prospect of a lasting infirmity, whose cure may take years or indeed be impossible.

Born with an ardent, active temperament, ever inclined to the diversions of society, I was forced at an early age to seclude myself, to live in loneliness. If at times I tried to

Count Rasumovsky (above) and Prince Lobkowitz (below), joint dedicatees of the 'Pastoral' Symphony. Both were invaluable patrons to Beethoven. Rasumovsky was the Russian ambassador to Vienna, Lobkowitz an Austrian nobleman (Austrian National Library, Vienna)

ignore all this, how harshly was I driven back by the doubly sad experience of my poor hearing, yet I could not say to people, 'Speak louder, shout for I am deaf!' Alas, how was it possible for me to admit to an infirmity in the one sense that in me should be more perfect than in others, a sense that I once possessed in the greatest perfection, a perfection, indeed, such as few in my profession enjoy or have ever enjoyed – oh, I cannot do it.

Forgive me, then, if you see me draw back from your company which I would so gladly share. My misfortune is doubly hard to bear, since because of it I am certain to be misunderstood. For me there can be no recreation in the company of others, no pleasures of conversation, no mutual exchange of thoughts. Only just as much as the most pressing needs demand may I venture into society; I am compelled to live like an outcast. If I venture into company I am overcome by a burning terror, for I fear that I may be in danger of letting my condition become known.

Thus has it been during the last half year, which I have spent in the country. Ordered by my wise physician to spare my hearing as much as possible, he almost encouraged my present instinctive mood, although, often moved by the urge for companionship, I have let myself be tempted into it. But how humiliating it was when those standing near me heard a flute in the distance that I could not hear, or someone heard a shepherd singing and again I heard nothing.

Such experiences brought me to the depths of despair – a little more, and I would have put an end to my life. Art alone stayed my hand; ah, it seemed impossible for me to quit the world until I had brought forth all that I felt under an obligation to produce. And so I endured this wretched existence – wretched indeed, with so sensitive a body that a progressing change can transport me from the best condition to the worst. Patience, I am told, I must choose as my guide. This I have done; my determination, I hope, will remain firm until it shall please the inexorable Fates to break the thread. Perhaps my condition will improve – perhaps not – I am content. To be forced at the early age of twenty-eight to become a philosopher is not easy, less easy for the artist than for any other.

O Divine One, thou lookest down into my innermost soul, thou seest into my heart and knowest that love of mankind and a desire to do good dwell therein. O men, when some day ye shall read these words, reflect that ye wronged me, and let the child of misfortune be comforted that he has found one like himself who, despite all the obstacles that Nature has thrown in his way, yet did all that lay within his power to be received into the ranks of worthy artists and men.

You, my brothers Carl and . . . . . . , as soon as I am dead, if Professor Schmidt be still living, request him in my name to describe my malady, and to this document that you now read attach the account of my ailment so that, at least as far as possible the world may be reconciled with me after my death. At the same time, I declare you two to be the heirs of my small fortune (if so it can be called). Divide it fairly; bear with and help each other. What you have done to harm me, that you know was long since forgiven.

To you, brother Carl, I give special thanks for the affection you have shown me of late. It is my hope that your life may be better, more free from care, than mine. To your children, recommend virtue, for that alone, not money, can give happiness. I speak from experience: it was virtue that sustained me even in my affliction; to it, next to my art, I must give thanks that I did not end my life by suicide. Farewell, and love one another.

I thank all my friends, particularly Prince Lichnowsky and Professor Schmidt. It is my wish that instruments from Prince L. be preserved by one of you, but let no quarrel arise between you because of them. If they can serve a better purpose for you, just sell them – how happy I shall be if, even in my grave, I can be of help to you.

So let it be. Joyfully I hasten to meet death. If it comes before I shall have had the opportunity to develop all my artistic capabilities, then, in spite of my hard fate it will still come too soon, and I shall probably wish that it had been delayed. Even so, I should be content, for will it not release me from a state of endless suffering? Come when thou wilt: I shall meet thee bravely.

Farewell, and do not wholly forget me in death. This much I deserve from you, for in life I have often given thought how to make you happy. Be ye so.

Ludwig van Beethoven

(seal)

A few days later, Beethoven adds a postscript:

Thus I take leave of you, and indeed sadly. Yes, the fond hope that I brought hither with me, that at least to a certain degree I might be cured, this hope I must abandon entirely. As the autumn leaves fall withered to the ground, so is my hope blighted. I leave here almost as I came; even that buoyant courage that often animated me in the beautiful days of summer has left me. O providence! grant me but one day of pure joy! It has been so long that true joy has been but a stranger to me. When, oh when, Divine Power, can I once more feel it in the temple of Nature and of men? Never? No, that would be too hard.

It is a salutary experience to listen to the music that followed this sad document, the magnificent brilliance of the Second Symphony, and the wonderful continuous expansion of the spirit that leaped into being in the works that came after – the next four symphonies, the 'Waldstein' Sonata, the Fourth Piano Concerto, the Violin Concerto, the Razumovsky Quartets, *Fidelio*. The 'new road' became the greatest highway in music, cut through a fearsome terrain against all odds. No one can tell whether the renewal of music Beethoven achieved was the result of his conquest

Above: *The countryside near Bonn. Beethoven's love of the countryside, as we see in the 'Pastoral', was very strong; even after he went to Vienna he used to spend every summer in the country*

of misfortune, or whether his resolve to continue was because of the forces that were already seething in his imagination, making suicide impossible. At first it was probably the latter, though it must have given him a new sense of strength in coping with the hard fact of deafness. His will must have been taken over by his imaginative power. The Heiligenstadt Testament shows the gulf between the artist and the man.

(Continued in Beethoven Album II)

Was Beethoven a Romantic?

The Romantic view of Beethoven dies hard, and to see why this is so we must first define our terms. Romanticism was a very real force in the 18th century in the form of a rebellion against the existing order. It began in literature and painting rather earlier than in music; already in the middle of the century the French writer Jean-Jacques Rousseau was advocating a return to 'nature', regarding forms and conventions as humanly stultifying. There was a stirring of spiritual unrest, and it could be made explicit in words. Music, however, usually waits to see what the world is up to before it appears to comment; there is nearly always a delay between trends in the other arts and their counterparts in music. It might be true, for instance, to say that the real composer of the French Revolution was Berlioz – but he was not born for a decade afterwards! During the French Revolution Beethoven was in his teens; what he heard of it must have affected him deeply, for he was at heart a democrat. Later its aftermath and the behaviour of Napoleon bitterly disappointed him, the more so as Vienna was the capital of a completely autocratic empire.

But we must not attribute the fire of Beethoven's music to a romantic frenzy born of social frustration. Beethoven, like Shakespeare, was the complete artist, capable of an almost universal range of expression. For every work of Beethoven that is obviously dramatic there are a dozen that are expressive in profoundly different ways, more often than not subtle and seemingly relaxed. There is scarcely a human feeling that he cannot express; and many of them, of course, are not expressible in words. His range and the untranslatability of music itself make him the most difficult of all composers to write truthfully about, simply because it is so easy to jump to the obvious conclusions about his fiercest works. We cannot in truth say that the powerful Fifth Symphony is 'typical' any more than we can say that *Hamlet* is 'typical' of Shakespeare, who also wrote the 'typical' *A Midsummer Night's Dream*. Beethoven also composed profound comedies, and many other works that are neither comedies nor tragedies. In this sense Beethoven is objective – the reverse of Romantic.

Before Beethoven there were already Romantic composers.

There was *Sturm und Drang*, the so-called 'storm and stress' movement to which Goethe's earlier plays belonged; one can find ripe examples of it in, for instance, the work of Bach's son Carl Philipp Emanuel, written when Beethoven was a small boy; and it even touched the middle-period symphonies of Haydn. The deliberate cultivation of what was known as *Empfindsamkeit* (the exploitation of 'sentimental' moods) was the real origin of the massive 19th-century Romantic movement, which would have happened if Beethoven had never existed. The later Romanticism of which Beethoven is so often supposed to be the father was in reality a development of the move towards conscious personal individualism that had begun much earlier. It produced many masterpieces, but like all trends it had to reach a point of no return, when self-regarding individualism became obsessive at the end of the 19th century. It is Beethoven's unparalleled range of objective expression that makes him bigger than any trend; the Romantics, however great, could absorb only a little of his influence, and that the more obvious kind.

During the 19th century a composer had to produce heroic symphonies or tone poems if he was to be taken seriously; most took this idea as a starting-point. Beethoven, on the other hand, did not write the 'Eroica' Symphony until he himself had grown up to it. This marks him as a realist, not a romantic, and it also emphasises his unique position as a Classical master with exceptional powers of expression – the climax, indeed, of a vast process of musical development that had begun as a reaction against the polyphony of Bach and Handel, who themselves were the culmination of an era. But both these eras saw the growth of purely *musical* ideas: Romanticism was chiefly concerned with *extra-musical* thought, and the musical changes that took place as a result of it were almost incidental, and essentially a loosening of discipline. It may very reasonably be argued that Romanticism introduced into the arts a new dimension, and so it did; but when the whole range of Beethoven's achievement is considered it is clear that, while he was not unaware of this dimension and did not fail to explore it, he penetrated many others. He could not have done this without maintaining a type of artistic discipline alien to the characteristic Romantic.

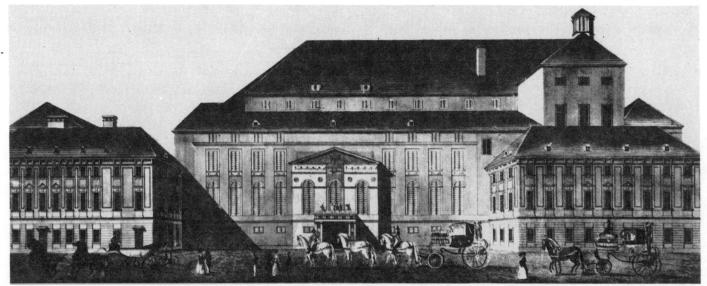

The Theater an der Wien – scene of the remarkable concert at which the 'Pastoral' Symphony was first performed (Meyer Collection, Vienna)

Ansicht des k.k.priv. Theaters an der Wien von der Jägergasse.

PROGRAM NOTES FOR THE RECORD

by R O B E R T   J A C O B S O N

The Sixth Symphony

Throughout music history, composers of every nationality have been fascinated by nature and, in turn, by imitating or portraying nature through music. In *Israel in Egypt* Handel managed to relate all the plagues suffered by the Egyptians, and Haydn did similar tonal painting in his oratorios *The Seasons* and *The Creation*. Vivaldi evolved a tone portait of the yearly cycle in his *Seasons* for string orchestra, and Schubert often sought such descriptive effects in his songs, such as the swimming fish in 'The Trout.' Even Rossini had his moments, such as in the last-act storm interlude of *The Barber of Seville*. The gallop of horses' hoofs, the rustling of leaves, the jingling of sleighbells, the singing of birds, falling rain or snow, and leaping fish or bounding animals all have been fodder for the composer's mill. In the 19th century the programmatic symphony had no greater document than Ludwig van Beethoven's Symphony No. 6, the 'Pastoral.' Its five movements were characterised by the composer as 'The Awakening of Joyful Feelings on Arrival in the Country,' 'Scene by the Brook,' 'Jolly Gathering of Country Folk,' 'Tempest/Storm' and 'Shepherd's Song, Glad and Thankful Feelings after the Storm.'

Beethoven, however, was by no means wholly innovative in this conception. In 1796, when his first three piano sonatas were published in Vienna, the printed edition carried an advertisement for a 'Grand Symphony,' subtitled 'A Musical Portrait of Nature,' by a minor Swabian composer named Justin Heinrich Knecht. The work had been published nearly a dozen years earlier, and it is possible that the younger composer knew of Knecht's suggestive titles and then, in 1808, welded them into his own noble symphonic conception. Knecht's five movements were highly detailed in their description of the countryside and its shepherds, the coming of a storm, the noise and winds of a tempest, the clearing of the sky and finally, 'Nature, in a transport of gladness, raises its voice to heaven, and gives thanks to its Creator in soft and agreeable song.' Beethoven abhorred such literalness in a piece of music and noted on his score: 'More an expression of feeling than a tonal painting.' In his sketch-books he warned, 'The hearers should be allowed to discover the situations . . . All painting in instrumental music, if pushed too far, is a failure . . . Anyone who has an idea of country life can make out the intentions of the author without many titles.'

Beethoven was drawn to nature's setting during his Vienna days, for he liked best to compose during long walks through the local countryside. His mystical feeling for the fields and forests verged on pantheistic worship — he once exclaimed, 'The trees in the forest worship God,' and another time, 'I love a tree more than a man' — and when this materialised in a work such as the 'Pastoral' Symphony, it was more an expression of love than awe.

On the outskirts of Vienna he could see shepherds and enjoy the tunes they played on their pipes. By the time he came to write this Symphony, however, he had become too deaf to hear them. He wrote in his Heiligenstadt Testament of his growing despair.

Beethoven wrote the Symphony No. 6 in F relatively quickly between the summer of 1807 and the following year. It was completed some time about June of 1808 at Heiligenstadt, on the outskirts of Vienna. The work has been considered miraculous by biographers: i.e., that Beethoven could conceive a large-scale work redolent of such love and happiness at a time when his own life was beset by grave problems and tensions. But his powerfully dramatic style — he composed his Fifth Symphony (op. 67) in this same period (1803-1809), as well as the 'Waldstein' Sonata (op.53), the 'Eroica' Symphony (op. 55), the 'Appassionata' Sonata (op.58), the Violin Concerto (op.61), *Fidelio* (op.72) and the 'Emperor' Concerto (op.73) — was rechannelled into music of classic perfection and optimistic Romanticism. The Symphony No. 6 (actually fifth in the sequence) was premièred in Vienna's Theater an der Wien on 22nd December 1808, as part of a gargantuan program that included the aria 'Ah, Perfido!,' the Fourth Piano Concerto, the Fifth Symphony, the Choral Fantasy and the Gloria and Sanctus from the C major Mass. Beethoven himself conducted and was soloist in the Fourth Concerto and the Choral Fantasy.

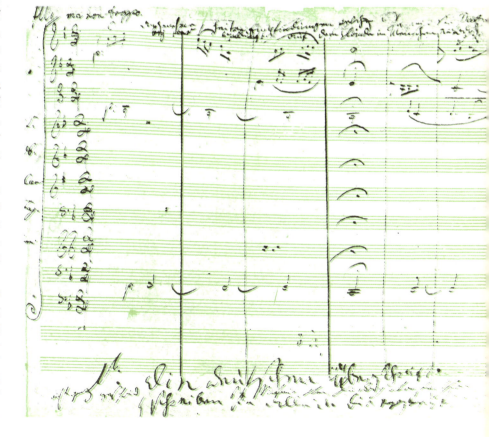

Beethoven's handwriting: the manuscript of the opening of the 'Pastoral' Symphony (Beethovenhaus, Bonn)

Hector Berlioz, who brought 19th-century Romantic fervour to soaring heights, was not to be dissuaded by Beethoven's own warnings apropos of his Symphony's program, and he wrote a highly personal and imaginative description of the 'Pastoral' Symphony, remarkably capturing its mood and character. The first movement he calls 'an astonishing landscape . . . as if it were the joint work of Poussin and Michelangelo. The composer of *Fidelio* and of the "Eroica" wishes in this symphony to depict the tranquillity of the country and the peaceful life of shepherds . . . Ravishing phrases caress one's ears deliciously, like perfumed morning breezes. Flocks of chattering birds fly overhead; and now and then the atmosphere seems laden with vapours; heavy clouds flit across the face of the sun, then suddenly disappear, and its rays flood the fields and woods with torrents of dazzling splendour.' Of the contemplative second movement, Berlioz observed: 'Beethoven without doubt created this admirable scene while reclining on the grass, his eyes uplifted, ears intent, fascinated by the thousand varying hues of light and sound, looking at and listening at the same time to the scintillating ripples of the brook that breaks its waves over the pebbles of the shores. How delicious this music is!' The third movement takes us into 'the midst of a joyous reunion of peasants.' Their dance becomes animated and noisy. 'There is a clapping of hands, shouting; the peasants run, they rush madly . . . when a muttering of thunder in the distance causes a sudden fright in the midst of the dance. Surprise and consternation seize the dancers, and they seek safety in flight.'

Berlioz despairs of trying to describe the fourth section: 'It must be heard in order to appreciate the degree of truth and sublimity which descriptive music can attain in the hands of a man like Beethoven. Listen to those gusts of wind, laden with rain; those sepulchral groanings of the basses; those shrill whistles of the piccolo, which announce that a fearful tempest is about to burst. The hurricane approaches, swells; an immense chromatic streak, starting from the highest notes of the orchestra, goes burrowing down into its lowest depths and seizes the basses, carries them along and ascends again, writhing like a whirlwind which levels everything in its passage . . . It is no longer merely a wind and rain storm; it is a frightful cataclysm, the universal deluge, the end of the world.' The last movement, Berlioz writes, 'ends with a hymn of gratitude. Everything smiles. The shepherds reappear . . . the sky is serene; the torrents soon cease to flow; calmness returns, and with it the rustic songs whose gentle melodies bring repose to the soul after the consternation produced by the magnificent horror of the previous picture.'

The opening movement (*Allegro ma non troppo*) begins with a sunny melodic phrase in the strings, the very essence of simplicity. Beethoven did not proceed with an elaborate working out of the material here; instead, little melodic fragments keep repeating themselves with a joyous naïveté, revelling in their own beauty and charm. There are slight variations in instrumental colours along the way, akin to the play of light and shade in nature itself. As the renowned musicologist Sir George Grove has said: 'I believe that the delicious, natural, May-day, out-of-doors feeling of this movement arises in a great measure from this kind of repetition . . . When the sameness of fields, woods and streams can become distasteful, then will the 'Pastoral' Symphony weary its hearers. The way the composer worked this modest material shows an incredibly fertile imagination and reflects his own joy in the presence of nature.'

The second movement (*Andante molto mosso*) is filled with serenity and soft murmuring sounds like a flowing brook, portrayed in a rippling figuration. (Beethoven observed in his sketch-book, 'The more water, the deeper the tone.') The little trills in the violins suggest the chirpings of insects, and the flute arpeggio in the second theme was intended to imitate the call of the bird known as the yellowhammer — so Beethoven told his biographer Anton Schindler. Near the end there is the unmistakable call of the cuckoo (clarinet), preceded by a quail (oboe) and a nightingale (flute). Just as Beethoven felt at peace while wandering beside the rustic brook, so this music conveys a feeling of happiness and relaxation.

The Scherzo (*Allegro*) has a middle section recalling the country bands Beethoven heard outside Vienna — with a croaking two-note bassoon player set against the piping oboe tune. The rest is made up of rustic dance music, with heavy-footed stomping alternating with phrases of grace. This leads directly into the memorable storm music (*Allegro*). There is a moment of suspense just before the storm breaks, a quiet that is broken by rustling winds and the first drops of rain. Then the tempest breaks out in earnest, and is made more ominous by the growling of the lower strings. Now come crashes of thunder, lightning and high-powered winds. This violent episode vanishes almost as quickly as it had blackened the bucolic scene, leading into the radiant hymn of thanksgiving of the Finale (*Allegretto*). This opens with a yodelling shepherd's song (on the clarinet), which is taken up by horns, violins and the full orchestra in a set of variations that increase in exhilaration. The whole universe seems to celebrate the return of the sun and the freshly washed earth in this tumultuous but sublime fifth episode, one of the most majestic musical pictures ever painted — a creation eons beyond portraying any specific 19th-century landscape, for, like Shakespeare, Beethoven transcended reality through his grandeur and incomparable poetic sensibility.

His Life and Times 1840-1877

PROGRAM NOTES FOR THE SIXTH SYMPHONY
By Robert Jacobson

fw

FUNK & WAGNALLS, INC.
NEW YORK, NEW YORK

Tchaikovsky: Autobiography in Music

It is impossible to understand Tchaikovsky's music fully without understanding something of the man. All Romantic art is a conscious expression of the artist's emotions and an extension of his dream-world; but in Tchaikovsky's case the emotions ranged between such violent extremes and the dream-world was so vivid and real to the composer, that his music is autobiographical to a quite unusual if not a unique degree.

This autobiographical, nakedly emotional character of Tchaikovsky's music at one time told against its success, especially with individuals or civilisations (like the French) that regarded such lack of reticence as distasteful or simply barbaric. Now, however, in the middle of the 20th century—when music has been opened to huge new audiences composed of people with no tradition of emotional reticence—Tchaikovsky has achieved a huge popularity such as he could never have enjoyed in his lifetime. On the other hand an extremely sophisticated musician like Stravinsky proclaims his admiration and affection for Tchaikovsky's melodic gifts, his handling of small forms and the strong 'period' flavour of his music. In fact Tchaikovsky's music appeals to two quite different kinds of listeners: to the non-specialist for its all-too-human emotionalism and sense of nostalgia, and to the professional musician for its aristocratic elegance and distinctive bouquet.

There was already a strain of mental or nervous disease in Tchaikovsky's family—his maternal grandfather, a French émigré named Assier, was described as 'epileptic', though in those days when so little was known of mental illness, this was no doubt a vague, general term. Tchaikovsky himself showed as a child a morbidly acute sensibility, a feverish attachment to his mother in particular and to his family in general and an emotional instability that was already neurotic in character. As he grew up, his attachments were all to members of his own sex; and since homosexuality was regarded with horror in the society in which he moved, his life was made even more miserable than that of the ordinary neurotic by acute feelings of guilt and inferiority, desperate attempts to conceal his real feelings and tragically unsuccessful efforts to lead a normal emotional life. He was haunted by fear of death and by hallucinations (that his head would fall off, for instance, when he was conducting one of his own works), and he attempted suicide when his marriage failed.

His only lasting emotional tie with any woman outside his own family was with the widow Nadezhda von Meck, with whom he corresponded for fourteen years—though he carefully avoided meeting her—and who made him an allowance. On the other hand he frequently became emotionally, and in some cases physically, involved with young pupils or students, and in one case with the singer who played the leading male part in one of his operas. The hopelessness and frustration of these relationships, and the secrecy and deception that they involved, took a directly physical toll of Tchaikovsky, who aged very early: when he died at the age of fifty-three he was described as looking like a man of seventy.

This agonising interior life—clearly reflected in much of his music, especially his symphonies and two chief operas *Eugene Onegin* and *The Queen of Spades*—was to a great extent concealed behind the conventional facade which the composer took care to elaborate. He was born in comfortable circumstances, the son of a successful engineer, and he seems never to have seriously questioned the social and political system in which he grew up. When his music brought him success and Nadezhda von Meck's allowance a certain amount of financial ease, he visited Germany, France and Italy and his whole style of living (as can be seen today by visitors to the museum at Klin, which was his country house) was that of a cultivated, cosmopolitan Russian such as we meet in Turgenev's novels. In fact this Turgenev exterior concealing a Dostoevsky-like interior world of emotional instability and nervous illness gives Tchaikovsky's music its particular charm.

Nineteenth-century Russian culture was still to a very great extent cosmopolitan, continuing the debt to Germany which dated back to the days of Peter the Great and the debt to France first incurred by Catherine II. It was, for instance, quite essential for anyone with pretensions to social elegance to speak French fluently and with a good accent, and to have at least a nodding acquaintance with French literature. A knowledge of German was equally important for those studying for the professions or engaged in research; and family holidays in Germany were a commonplace among the wealthier members of the middle class or minor gentry.

This state of affairs was something of a controversial matter. The Slavophil movement, which aimed at minimising the influence of western Europe on Russian life and returning as far as possible to the patriarchal patterns of Russian life before Peter the Great, was a form of neo-conservative nationalism and confined entirely to the educated classes. The strong revolutionary element provided by the intelligentsia (significantly enough a word that we have borrowed from the Russian) was almost wholly in favour of the westernisation of Russia, a process that logically involved the disappearance of the theocratic monarchy of the Tsars and the Orthodox Church, which was intimately allied to the monarchy. Tchaikovsky, though confessing a purely emotional allegiance to Orthodoxy, was a loyal subject of the Tsar and not seriously concerned with public affairs or intellectual movements.

Tchaikovsky's only important connection with the Slavophil movement was in the field of music, and there he occupied a borderline position. By the St Petersburg composers who were grouped round Balakirev (namely, Mussorgsky, Cui, Rimsky-Korsakov and Borodin), Tchaikovsky was regarded as an arrant westerniser, because he wrote western-style symphonies instead of symphonic poems on Russian themes and did not commit himself to any specific allegiance to Russian folk music. In fact, however, there are countless echoes of Russian folk music all through Tchaikovsky's work: the slow movement of the Violin Concerto and the finales of the Second and Fourth Symphonies are obvious examples.

More important than this, Tchaikovsky's music perfectly reflects the Russian society of his day precisely by reason of its international character. The strains of French ballet music, Italian opera and the German symphony are combined with memories of Russian folk music or church music in a way that is not only personal but deeply characteristic of late 19th-century Russia. The Slavophils, and their musical counterparts the so-called 'nationalist' composers of the St Petersburg school, were attempting to recall or re-create an idealised Russian *past*, as we see in Mussorgsky's *Boris Godunov*, Borodin's *Prince Igor* or Rimsky-Korsakov's *Kitezh*. Tchaikovsky, on the other hand, gives expression to the superficially cosmopolitan, yet deeply Russian society of his own day; and his *Eugene Onegin* and *The Queen of Spades* introduce us to Russian characters belonging if not to Tchaikovsky's own day, yet to only a generation or so earlier. Stravinsky's deep affection for Tchaikovsky's music, and his lack of interest in the Russian 'nationalist' composers, is easily explained by this fact: that with Tchaikovsky he re-enters the world in which he himself grew up, while the Nationalists' music belongs either to a museum of the Slavonic past or to that naturalism which Stravinsky regards as a late-19th-century aesthetic aberration.

What were Tchaikovsky's greatest gifts as a composer? First of all a rich and extraordinarily original gift of melody. In his great tunes it may be possible to trace French,

German or Italian elements yet—even when they have no affinity with Russian folk song—we feel them at once to be unmistakably Russian. The big D flat melody in his overture *Romeo and Juliet*, which is one of the great tunes of the world, has a sinuous self-recreating quality that bears the mark of the fine craftsman (as you will find if you try to hum it) yet the emotional immediacy and catchiness of a pop tune. In his ballet music Tchaikovsky could invest the smallest fragment of melody with a haunting, evocative quality that makes the listener quite forget the French model which is often in the background.

It is in the ballet music, too, or the ballet-like movements of the symphonies, that we find most clearly Tchaikovsky's second great gift—that of colourful instrumentation. There it is delicate and formed of the simplest yet subtlest contrasts and blends, as we find also in the slow movement of the Violin Concerto. In the first and last movements of the symphonies and the finales of the concertos, on the other hand, Tchaikovsky achieves an extraordinarily buoyant and physically exciting brilliance, quite unlike Wagner's and closer in character to that of Berlioz. Although he considered himself deficient in the specifically symphonic art of 'developing' a single idea, yet the cumulative effect of his artfully varied repetitions and quasi-repetitions is unquestionably symphonic. His handling of dance rhythms, which play a large part in his music, reveals a strength of instinctive animal vitality astonishing in a man so tortured nervously. Once again it is perhaps this apparent contradiction in Tchaikovsky, like his Turgenev exterior and Dostoevsky interior, that forms part of the fascination that this music exercises over the mid-20th century an age full of similar contradictions and instinctively attracted both by mental or emotional suffering and by animal vitality.

Tchaikovsky's Early Life

Tchaikovsky did not think seriously about becoming a professional musician until he was about twenty—unusually late for a composer. So a description of his childhood—unlike, for instance, Mozart's—is not a continuous narrative of musical precocity and early fame. Rather, we have to search among the details of a very ordinary childhood for the few odd facts and events that, in retrospect, can be seen to have been the seeds of later developments.

He was born on 7th May 1840. His father, Ilya Petrovich Tchaikovsky, was a mining engineer and at the time was employed by the Government managing a mine at Votkinsk, about 700 miles east of Moscow. He belonged to the upper middle class, and this was an important job, so at the time of Tchaikovsky's birth the family was well-off and socially prominent in the district. They lived in the style of the great landowners in a large house with a large staff; the father was also the commander of a troop of a hundred Cossacks.

His first wife died after bearing him one daughter; in 1833 he married Alexandra Andreyevna Assier, who came from a family of French Huguenot descent. Their first child was Nikolai (born 1838); then came Piotr, the composer (1840);

later followed Alexandra (1842), Ippolit (1844) and the twins Anatol and Modest (1850). Modest later produced a three-volume *Life and Letters* of his composer brother.

Tchaikovsky's father, though fond of music, had no gift for it. His mother sang well, and she had a brother and sister who were noted amateurs. But there are no other traces of music in Tchaikovsky's ancestry, and none of his brothers or sisters shared his inclination for it.

The first signs of anything unusual in Tchaikovsky appeared at the age of $4\frac{1}{2}$ when a young Frenchwoman called Fanny Durbach joined the family as governess to his six-year-old brother Nikolai. On the very first day Piotr burst into tears and begged to be allowed to join in the lessons. By the time he was six he was fluent—if inaccurate, as early poems show: '*Toi, oh Russie aimé vien! vien! aupré de moi . . .*' —in French and German. Years later Mademoiselle Durbach described her young pupil to his brother Modest: 'When we read together none listened so attentively as he did, and when on holidays I gathered my pupils around me in the twilight and let them tell tales in turn, no one could improvise so well as Piotr. . . . His sensibility was extreme, therefore I had to be very careful how I treated him. A trifle

3

wounded him deeply. He was brittle as porcelain. With him there could be no question of punishment; the least criticism or reproof, that would pass lightly over other children, would upset him alarmingly.'

Fanny Durbach did not teach music, and so—as Modest Tchaikovsky wrote—'the place of music master to the future composer fell to the lot of an inanimate object—an orchestrion [musical box] which his father brought back with him after a visit to St Petersburg.' This instrument played melodies by Mozart, Bellini and Donizetti, and it was not long before Tchaikovsky was picking the tunes out on the piano: 'He found such delight in playing that it was frequently necessary to drag him by force from the instrument. Afterwards, as the next best substitute, he would take to drumming tunes upon the window-panes. One day, while thus engaged, he was so entirely carried away by this dumb show that he broke the glass and cut his hand severely.'

At the same time it became clear that music had a particularly strong emotional effect on the boy. One day his parents gave a musical party. Tchaikovsky went to bed early, but when Fanny Durbach went to his room she found him sitting up in bed, crying feverishly. She asked him what was the matter and was told: 'Oh this music, this music! Save me from it! It is here, here'—pointing to his head—'and will not give me any peace.'

When Tchaikovsky was eight, in 1848, his father retired and the family moved to Moscow. Now he was often taken to the opera and was able for the first time to hear an orchestra and to get to know more music than he had heard in the drawing-room at Votkinsk. He also now had piano lessons, at which he made good progress. But—perhaps as a result of this sudden exposure to music—a reaction set in in his character. Instead of the cheerful, charming boy he had been he became nervous and irritable. After an attack of measles and a six-month convalescence he recovered to some extent; but it is to this period that much of his later nervous trouble can be traced.

In 1850 Tchaikovsky was sent to the preparatory section of the St Petersburg School of Jurisprudence. Clearly his parents had in mind for him the kind of career that most boys of his class normally followed: after law school he would become a civil servant and remain for ever a mere cog in the vast bureaucratic machine of Tsarist Russia. A story related by Modest Tchaikovsky—relevant because it indicates his strong attachment to his mother and underlines the importance to him of her subsequent death—tells how when she left him at the school 'he completely lost his self-control and, clinging wildly to her, refused to let her go.... It became necessary to carry off the poor child by force, and hold him fast until his mother had driven away. Even then he broke loose, and with a cry of despair ran after the carriage, and clung to one of the wheels, as though he would bring the vehicle to a standstill.'

Two years later the family moved to St Petersburg. In the same year Tchaikovsky passed into the School of Jurisprudence proper. He was to stay there until 1859. 'There is reason to believe,' writes his biographer Edwin Evans, 'that the seeds of his homosexual tendencies were sown at the school.'

Musically, Tchaikovsky's years at the School of Jurisprudence were not eventful. He continued to have private lessons with a succession of teachers; he broadened his acquaintance with the music of others, developing especially a passion for Mozart that lasted all his life—surprisingly, perhaps, for there is little musical affinity between the two. Non-musically, the main event of these years took place in 1854 when his mother died of cholera. As we have seen, he was particularly attached to his mother, in characteristically homosexual fashion, and her loss left a deep scar on his sensitive soul. Scholastically, though not a brilliant success he did well enough, and there was still no indication that he would not follow the humdrum career planned for him in the civil service.

Indeed in 1859, when he was nineteen, he left school and entered the Ministry of Justice as a clerk. Again he performed his duties adequately if without enthusiasm, becoming meanwhile something of a gay young man-about-town, Only one incident from his official career—indicative perhaps of the nervous temperament beneath the bureaucratic surface—survives. Modest Tchaikovsky relates: 'He had been entrusted with a signed document from the chief of his department, but on his way to deliver it he stopped to talk with someone, and in his absence of mind never noticed that, while talking, he kept tearing off scraps of the paper and chewing them—a trick he always had with theatre tickets or programmes. There was nothing for it but to re-copy the document, and, however unpleasant, to face his chief for a fresh signature.'

But underneath, to the disapproval of nearly all his relations, his thoughts were now leading irresistibly towards music. A series of letters to his sister Alexandra (known as Sasha), who had to some extent replaced his mother as his confidante, charts the progress of events:

March 1861: *They have made me an official, although a poor one; I try as hard as I can to improve and to fulfil my duties more conscientiously, and at the same time I am to be studying thorough-bass!*

December 1861: *I think I have already told you that I have begun to study the theory of music with success. You will agree that, with my rather exceptional talents (I hope you will not mistake this for bragging), it seems foolish not to try my chances in this direction.*

September 1862: *I have entered* [part-time] *the newly opened Conservatoire. . . . As you know, I have worked hard at the theory of music during the past year, and have come to the conclusion that sooner or later I shall give up my present occupation for music. Do not imagine that I dream of being a great artist. . . . I only feel I must do the work for which I have a vocation.*

Finally, April 1863: *My musical talent—you cannot deny it— is my only one. This being so, it stands to reason that I ought not to leave this God-sent gift uncultivated and undeveloped. For this reason I began to study music seriously. So far my official duties did not clash with this work, and I could remain in the Ministry of Justice. Now, however, my studies grow more severe and take up more time, so I find myself compelled to give up one or the other. . . . In a word, after long consideration, I have resolved to sacrifice the salary and resign my post.*

So, at the age of twenty-two, Tchaikovsky abandoned his official career and the prosperous if unexciting future that it offered and entered upon a life exclusively devoted to music.

Tchaikovsky's parents. His musical talent came from his mother's side of the family (Tchaikovsky Museum, Klin)

Tchaikovsky's Life 1863-77

The St Petersburg Conservatoire, which Tchaikovsky entered full-time in 1863, had only opened the previous autumn. It was an offshoot of the Russian Musical Society, a joint foundation of the German Grand Duchess Elena Pavlovna and the pianist Anton Rubinstein, who directed it. The teaching staff included, besides Rubinstein himself, the Polish violinist Henri Wieniawski and the Polish pianist Theodor Leszetycki (later a world-famous teacher under the German version of his name, Leschetizky).

Tchaikovsky, when he joined part-time in September 1862, was one of the first pupils to be enrolled. He was still continuing his legal studies, but he applied himself furiously to the course in strict counterpoint given by Nikolai Zaremba as well as studying composition with Rubinstein, and piano and flute. Rubinstein remembered later that, when asked for some dozen variations on a theme, the young Tchaikovsky produced two hundred. Little wonder that he soon abandoned his legal studies and devoted himself whole-heartedly to a musical career. Neither Rubinstein nor Zaremba approved of any music later than Mendelssohn's; but Tchaikovsky had already heard and been fascinated by compositions by Liszt and Berlioz at the Russian Musical Society's concerts, and Wagner's visit to St Petersburg in 1862, when he conducted concerts of his own music, was a revelation. In Herman Laroche, who was later to make his name as a music critic, he had a sympathetic fellow-student. Much of his spare time was spent in the circle of his married sister, Alexandra (Sasha) Davidov, either in St Petersburg or at the Davidov country house at Kamenka, which was to be a second home to him all his life.

In the autumn of 1865 Tchaikovsky's first orchestral composition, *Dances of the Serving Maids*, was conducted at an out-of-doors concert by Johann Strauss the younger; and almost at the same time he was invited to teach theory at the newly founded Moscow Conservatoire. The invitation owed its origin to Anton Rubinstein's brother, Nikolai, who was having difficulty in finding a teaching staff – as can be imagined from the fact that Tchaikovsky had not yet completed his musical training in St Petersburg. In fact, although he accepted the offer and had a student quartet performed that autumn, as well as making his very nervous debut as a conductor with an overture of his own, he still toyed with the idea of entering the government service. However, in January 1866 his graduation cantata – a setting of Schiller's *Ode to Joy* – was performed, and although Tchaikovsky could not face the statutory public viva voce examination, he was awarded his diploma and given a silver medal. The official verdict on his work ran as follows: 'Theory of composition – excellent. Instrumentation – excellent. Orchestration – good. Pianoforte – very good. Conducting – satisfactory.'

Tchaikovsky's first year as a teacher at the Moscow Conservatoire was largely coloured by his nervousness about lecturing (though he proved to be a good teacher) and by his inability to escape the round of late nights and heavy drinking in which Nikolai Rubinstein, with whom he lodged, expected him to share. He spent the summer months with the older generation of Davidovs, his sister Sasha's parents-in-law, near Peterhof, where at the end of July he suffered his first nervous breakdown. This was the result of over-

Late 19th-century Moscow—this photograph shows the river Moskva and the Kremlin (Bibliothèque Nationale, Paris)

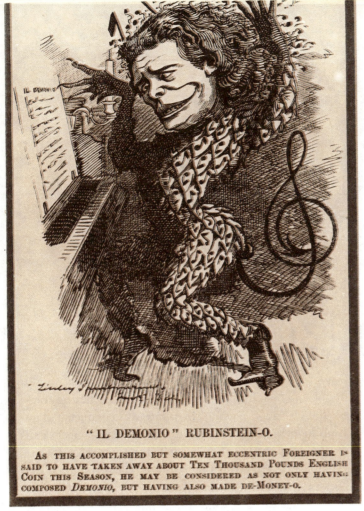

" IL DEMONIO " RUBINSTEIN-O.

AS THIS ACCOMPLISHED BUT SOMEWHAT ECCENTRIC FOREIGNER IS
SAID TO HAVE TAKEN AWAY ABOUT TEN THOUSAND POUNDS ENGLISH
COIN THIS SEASON, HE MAY BE CONSIDERED AS NOT ONLY HAVING
COMPOSED *DEMONIO*, BUT HAVING ALSO MADE DE-MONEY-O.

working on his First Symphony combined with his Moscow way of life and, probably at least, his inability to avoid emotional involvement with his pupils at the Conservatoire. To hallucinations and phobias were now added what he described as 'apoplectic strokes' and 'heart cramps' which, whatever their actual nature, were serious enough to make the local doctor forbid all work for the time being.

He was able to be back in Moscow, however, in time for the re-opening of the Conservatoire in September. His old teacher Anton Rubinstein had severely disapproved of what Tchaikovsky had shown him of the First Symphony, and even when revised it failed to satisfy; so that it was not until February 1868 that the work had its first complete performance, in Moscow under Nikolai Rubinstein. Meanwhile Tchaikovsky was working on his first opera, *The Voyevoda* (based on Alexander Ostrovsky's play *Dream on the Volga*), which occupied much of his summer holiday of 1867, spent again with the older Davidovs at Hapsal in Estonia. The opera had its première in February 1869 at the Bolshoi Theatre, where it was well received.

Meanwhile Berlioz's visit to Moscow in December 1867 was the occasion not only of a public speech by Tchaikovsky at the banquet in his honour, but also of a rapprochement with the group of St Petersburg composers – Balakirev, Rimsky-Korsakov, Mussorgsky, Borodin – and their champion, the critic Stassov. Tchaikovsky had hitherto believed them to be his enemies, owing to their very vocal hostility to the Rubinsteins and the latter's cosmopolitan, 'Western' conception of music. Now, he found them on the contrary appreciative and even admiring, though clearly anxious to convert him to their own nationalist musical creed. He himself made his debut as a critic in defending Rimsky-Korsakov's *Fantasia on Serbian Themes* when it was performed the following March in Moscow.

In June 1868 Tchaikovsky paid his second visit to Western Europe, including Berlin and Paris, in the company of two Moscow friends and the young step-son of one of them, Vladimir Shilovsky, who was a pupil – and, it seems probable, the lover – of Tchaikovsky. His enthusiasm for the operatic performances that he heard in Paris may have contributed to his infatuation the following September with a Franco-Belgian prima donna, Désirée Artôt, who sang Desdemona in an Italian company's performance of Rossini's *Otello* at the Bolshoi. She was a pupil of Pauline Viardot-Garcia, with whom she shared a not immediately prepossessing appearance offset by a brilliance of personality and a wealth of artistic endowments that made conquests wherever she went. Tchaikovsky may well have been infatuated by the artist rather than the woman. How seriously Désirée Artôt herself contemplated marriage to Tchaikovsky is not known. Her mother, who travelled with her, was against the idea – and when a Spanish baritone, Mariano Padilla y Ramos, supplanted Tchaikovsky and married her in Warsaw, Tchaikovsky did not take long to recover from the shock, and continued to see her on friendly terms when she returned to Russia.

The première of *The Voyevoda* in February 1869 caused Tchaikovsky to break with his friend Laroche, whose criticism of the work was unfavourable though (as we now see) penetrating. A symphonic poem, *Fate*, was hardly more successful – though a private criticism by Balakirev was equally perspicacious – and the work remained unpublished. He was already at work on a new opera, *Undine*, which he finished in the summer of 1869 at Kamenka. The friendship with Balakirev ripened during the autumn of this year, which Balakirev spent in Moscow. Balakirev gave his younger friend the idea of a *Romeo and Juliet* overture and attempted to play a detailed part in its composition. In fact the work failed completely at its first performance in March 1870, though it confirmed Nikolai Rubinstein's high opinion of Tchaikovsky as a composer. It is strange today to think that in Vienna, Paris and Dresden this most popular of all Tchaikovsky's symphonic poems (for, though called an overture, it is in fact a symphonic poem) should have been actually hissed.

Meanwhile lodging, as he continued to do, with Nikolai Rubinstein became an increasing strain and in May 1870 Tchaikovsky described himself in a letter to Balakirev as 'an unbearable hypochondriac, as the result of serious nervous disorders'. He had started a new opera, *The Oprichnik*, and though his first set of songs (including 'None but the weary heart') had a success at this time, the rejection of his *Undine* by the St Petersburg opera depressed him. When news came that his beloved Vladimir Shilovsky was desperately ill with consumption in Paris he hurried there and later, when the boy's condition improved, accompanied him to the German resort of Soden, from where he visited Mannheim for a performance of Beethoven's *Missa Solemnis* ('one of the most inspired of musical creations') and Wiesbaden, to find Nikolai Rubinstein 'in the act of losing his last rouble at roulette'. Surprised by the outbreak of the Franco-Prussian War in July, he fled to Switzerland, where he spent six weeks doing little but revise *Romeo and Juliet*. By the middle of September he was back in Moscow.

March 1871 saw the first all-Tchaikovsky concert, with a programme consisting mostly of salon trifles but including the D major String Quartet, which contains the popular 'Andante cantabile' movement. The celebrated writer Turgenev graced the occasion with his presence and the press, including the faithless Laroche, was favourable. Work on *The Oprichnik* went badly this autumn and Tchaikovsky seized an opportunity to join Vladimir Shilovsky in Berlin, Paris and Nice during January 1872, telling his brother to give out that he had gone to join their sister Alexandra. The summer was spent partly at Kamenka and partly with Vladimir Shilovsky, who had returned to Russia. At Kamenka he began his Second Symphony, which had its first performance in Moscow in the following February (1873); this time Laroche's enthusiastic notice healed the old breach, and the Nationalist composers hailed him as a brother. *The Oprichnik* was accepted by St Petersburg, though not performed until a year later, in April 1874. His next opera, *Vakula the Smith*, was composed as an entry for a competition organised by the Russian Musical Society. The summer of 1873 was spent first at Kamenka and then abroad – in Switzerland with the music-publisher Jürgenson and his family, and then in Milan and Paris, returning to Russia in mid-August. Compositions of this year included two sets of Six Piano Pieces (opp. 19 and 21) and the symphonic poem *The Tempest*, which he entrusted to Vladimir Bessel, who became his publisher. This had a successful first performance in Moscow towards the end of December.

The year 1874 opened with the composition of the F major String Quartet, and in April Tchaikovsky went to St Petersburg to supervise the production of *The Oprichnik*, a work that the composer knew to be poor, though Laroche praised it. Immediately after the performance he fled to Venice – which he hated – and from there to Rome and Naples. In the mistaken idea that his competition opera had to be finished by August 1874 (the actual date was twelve months later) he completed the score in a month and then tried to get it performed at once, without success. He was infuriated by Laroche's criticism of *The Tempest:* 'How tenderly he points out that I imitate Litolff, Schumann, Glinka, Berlioz and God knows who else. As if I could do nothing but compile from any old source!' By December, however, he described himself as 'wallowing with my whole soul in the composition of a piano concerto' – and the following year the First Piano Concerto in B flat minor was finished.

Tchaikovsky's first meeting with the violinist Leopold Auer, which took place in 1875, prompted the composition of the *Melancholy Serenade* for violin and orchestra; but apart from this and another set of songs, the rest of the year was taken up with two major compositions – the Third Symphony and the ballet *Swan Lake*. The first Russian performance of the Piano Concerto, in November, was a failure, but now Nikolai Rubinstein, who had earlier rejected it, was to change his mind (and Tchaikovsky to adopt some of his suggestions) and the work embarked on its career of unbroken popularity.

Early in 1876 Tchaikovsky accompanied his brother Modest to Berlin, Geneva and finally Paris, where the composer was delighted by a performance of *Carmen*. Back in Russia he attended the première of his Third Symphony in February and completed his Third String Quartet a month later. The spring and summer were spent largely abroad, in Vichy (where he took a cure), Vienna, Lyons and Bayreuth, where he attended the first performance of *Das Rheingold* ('as music it is incredible nonsense . . . with occasional flashes of extraordinary and amazing beauty'). Writing from Kamenka in August he announced his intention of marrying, a project which haunted him all the autumn; and in December *Vakula the Smith* had its première at the Maryinsky Theatre in St Petersburg.

(Continued in Tchaikovsky, Album II)

A painting by A. Benois of the river Neva at St Petersburg, seen from the suburb of Okhta. When Tchaikovsky started his career in the Ministry of Justice he took part-time lessons at the St Petersburg Conservatoire and it was owing to these lessons that he decided to give up the civil service for music (Collection of Anna Tcherkessoff, Paris)

Russia in the Mid-19th Century

Nineteenth-century Russia was still, in some ways, stuck in the Middle Ages. Scarcely touched by the Industrial Revolution, insulated from the political and social upheavals that infected western Europe after the French Revolution of 1789, the Tsarist empire maintained a strict political system that was more or less incapable of peaceful change. In consequence it went in perpetual fear of violent revolution—which of course had to come and in 1917 did come.

Socially, the system was literally feudal. The Tsar was the 'little father' of all his people, an autocratic and often cruel ruler. All the land was owned by the aristocrats, who were mostly extremely wealthy. There was a managerial middle class, to which Tchaikovsky's father belonged, and from whom the enormous number of bureaucrats (such as Tchaikovsky himself was educated to be) needed to run this vast, centralised empire were drawn. And at the bottom there were the serfs, until 1861 literally enslaved to their masters. Tchaikovsky's father, being a landless official, had only one serf. But landowning aristocrats had hundreds or even thousands, all their personal property.

It was thus a very stable society that Tchaikovsky was born into. But to maintain the stability a system of illiberal repression was needed—often reminiscent of Russia later. Foreign travel was discouraged; foreign visitors were suspect; censorship governed the arts and the dissemination of news. One field where Tsarist Russia was usually freer than the succeeding regime was music. Nowadays, the government generally decides what sort of music is acceptable: Tchaikovsky, though he brushed with the censors over the literary content of some of his operas, could at least write the notes he liked.

One reason for this, perhaps, was that music—or at least Russian music—was simply not taken seriously. Tchaikovsky's desire to become a professional musician was mocked by most of his friends and relations not only because they doubted his talent but also because it was inconceivable to them that anyone should devote his life exclusively to music. His only noteworthy predecessors as Russian composers, Glinka and Dargomyzhsky, had been in effect amateurs; of his nationalist contemporaries Borodin was also a chemist, Cui a military engineer, Rimsky-Korsakov a naval officer, Mussorgsky a soldier. None of them had received a formal musical education—and when Rimsky-Korsakov late in life decided to remedy this the others felt that he had let the side down.

This state of affairs is not altogether surprising, for it was only in 1862 that Anton Rubinstein (later Tchaikovsky's teacher) founded Russia's first conservatoire in St Petersburg. Before that, musical education could only be obtained from visiting foreigners or by going abroad. And it was this same Rubinstein who once had to fill in a form which demanded to know his profession. He put 'musician'—but this was rejected on the grounds that there was no such profession. Eventually, after much discussion, it emerged that his father had been a merchant. So he wrote in 'merchant's son' and the officials were satisfied. Such was the bureaucratic system of Tsarist Russia and the esteem in which native musicians were held!

This is not to say that there was no music in Russia—only that, rather like England at the same period, to be taken seriously it had either to be imported or to be written by foreign-trained Russians in a foreign style. Thus there were flourishing opera houses in Moscow and St Petersburg; but the operas were nearly all Italian—Rossini, Bellini, Donizetti—or at least in the Italian style. Symphonic music was less widespread: at the age of twenty Tchaikovsky did not know how many symphonies Beethoven had written.

A Russian winter scene by Kustodiev (Russian State Museum, Leningrad)

Music in Russia

Tchaikovsky once described Russian music as 'tied to the tail of the more cultured Europe', and infuriated Slavophils and musical nationalists by doing so.

Before 1731, when the Empress Anna introduced the first Italian operatic troupe, music in Russia had consisted of church music and folk music, both unusually rich. Between 1735 and 1840 there was a kind of dynasty of Italian composers at the Russian court, including such famous names as Galuppi, Traetta, Paisiello and Cimarosa; and, under Catherine the Great, French *opéra comique* was introduced and became popular with the educated classes. Russian composers soon began to imitate Italian opera (Bortnyansky, Fomin and Matinsky were all trained in Italy between 1770 and 1790) and the last of the Italians, Catterino Cavos, reformed Russian operatic singing. Boieldieu's visit to Russia (1803-10) popularised the new French light opera, and this had its influence on the operas of Alexis Verstovsky (1799-1862) – though his *Askold's Tomb* (1835) was nearer in style to Weber's *Der Freischütz*.

Despite inclusions of folk-song fragments or liturgical quotations there was no real Russian opera, let alone orchestral or chamber music, until a gifted, half-trained amateur, Mikhail Ivanovich Glinka, returned from listening to opera in Italy and studying counterpoint in Berlin and wrote his *Life for the Tsar* (now renamed *Ivan Susanin*) in 1836. Both this and the later *Ruslan and Lyudmila* are an amalgamation of French and Italian grand opera, Russian folk-song and oriental pastiche; and it was this very amalgamation, with its cosmopolitan components, that Russians

immediately recognised as a true, intimate reflection of their own culture. All Russian composers up to and including Stravinsky have been deeply influenced by Glinka's music and feel an incommunicable affection and respect for it – though this has not always been shown in the same way.

Some ten years younger than Glinka, Alexander Dargomyzhsky was a pioneer in a different musical vein. Realism and humour play a large part in his songs, which are in many cases vignettes of the Russian state-official types caricatured by Gogol. In his two chief operas, *Rusalka* and *The Stone Guest*, Dargomyzhsky introduced a new form of melodic recitative which had a great influence on Mussorgsky; and he also developed the style of oriental pastiche found in Glinka's *Ruslan and Lyudmila*.

In St Petersburg, the northern capital without a medieval past, there sprang up soon after Glinka's death in 1857 a school of consciously nationalist composers, in love with their idea of the Slavonic past and hostile to Western European musical influences. The men, grouped round Mili Balakirev, were Nikolai Rimsky-Korsakov (an ex-sailor), Modest Mussorgsky (an ex-Guards officer), César Cui (a lecturer on fortification at the Staff College) and Alexander Borodin (a distinguished chemist). This group of amateur musicians, who learned their trade largely by composing, included at least one genius (Mussorgsky) and three outstanding talents, and their works made Russian musical history during the years when Tchaikovsky was himself at the height of his powers.

In Moscow, on the other hand, where the Rubinstein brothers had set a new, western standard of musical values and professional workmanship, the 'Mighty Handful' of St Petersburg – the nickname given them by their champion, the critic Stassov – were regarded as eccentrics and amateurs. Tchaikovsky's personal relations with them were friendly, and his Second Symphony and some of his operas show that in fact he could compose in their style with just as much conviction as, and often with more skill than, they themselves. But, with the exception of the professorial Rimsky-Korsakov, Tchaikovsky rated them rather low as composers.

In a letter to Madame von Meck he sums them up: 'Borodin? Greatly talented, but he is already fifty . . . and cannot write a line without somebody's help . . . Cui? his music is elegant, coquettish and meticulous but what can you expect of a Professor of Fortification? . . . Mussorgsky . . . revels in crudeness for its own sake, flaunts his musical ignorance and boasts that his genius is richer because he has refused training . . . Yet he has flashes of real talent, not without originality . . . Balakirev is the greatest personality of the circle. Unfortunately he stopped before accomplishing much . . . In spite of his great gifts he has done much harm. He ruined Rimsky-Korsakov by assuring him that study was harmful...'

In their turn the circle nicknamed Tchaikovsky 'Sadyk-Pasha', after a notorious bandit chief of the day. However, Rimsky-Korsakov appealed to him for technical advice. It is interesting that, apart from Mussorgsky, the Nationalists' music has faded more than Tchaikovsky's, the museum element in all Slavophil art being no match for the sheer human eloquence, the melodic wealth and the craftsmanship of Tchaikovsky's best works.

PROGRAM NOTES FOR THE RECORD

by R O B E R T   J A C O B S O N

The Pathétique: Sixth Symphony

The descriptive title of this symphony—'Pathétique'—is one way of describing Tchaikovsky's own life, begun at Votkinsk in 1840. It was for the most part an existence of torment, doubt, disappointments, anguish and confusion. So it was appropriate that he should end his composing career with this pessimistic Sixth Symphony in B minor, filling it as he did with premonitions of death, with a sense of inner torture and inordinate sadness. The work was premièred on 28th October 1893, only ten days before the composer's death. Tchaikovsky himself conducted the first performance with the Russian Musical Society in St Petersburg. It was only moderately successful, and both the critics and the orchestra members responded with decided coolness and confusion—much more so than at the première of his Fifth Symphony five years earlier.

The morning after the concert, Tchaikovsky's brother Modest found the composer with the score of his symphony, which was to be sent to the publisher Jurgenson that very day. He seemed reluctant to send it with no title other than 'Symphony No. 6', but the idea of calling it 'Program Symphony' did not satisfy him, nor did Modest's suggestion of 'Tragic.' Modest remembered later: 'I had left the room before he had come to a decision. Suddenly, I thought, *"Pathétique."* I went back to the room—I remember it as though it was yesterday—and I said the word to Peter. "Splendid, Modi. Bravo, *Pathétique!"* And he wrote in my presence the title that will forever remain.' The term *pathétique* denotes a type of drama and theatrical music concerned with the emotions, particularly those of suffering and sorrow.

Three days after his brother had named the new work, the composer was with friends for dinner and the theatre, and in good spirits. The next day at lunch he drank only a glass of water—but one that had not been boiled beforehand. By nightfall it was clear that he was seriously ill with cholera, which was then prevalent in St Petersburg. 'I think this is death,' he said to his brother. The next day he was dead

Nearly all of Tchaikovsky's music impresses as dramatic and dance-oriented, and the Pathétique Symphony is his ultimate statement as far as drama and theatrical contrasts are concerned. It should be noted, too, that the last three years of his life were spent composing two of his greatest stage works, the opera *Queen of Spades* and the *Nutcracker* ballet, as well as the Sixth Symphony. The most potent influences on his writing were Liszt, Berlioz and Schumann, all commanding figures in the forefront of Romantic emotionalism and fervent orchestral coloration.

Tchaikovsky dedicated his Sixth Symphony to his nephew Vladimir Davidoff, to whom he admitted that the work did have a program. 'But a program of a kind that remains enigmatic to everyone. Let them guess it who can,' the composer wrote. Only in the years between the two World Wars was there revealed among Tchaikovsky's sketches a sheet of music paper with this pencilled note: 'The ultimate essence of the plan of the Symphony is LIFE. First part—all impulsive passion, confidence, thirst for

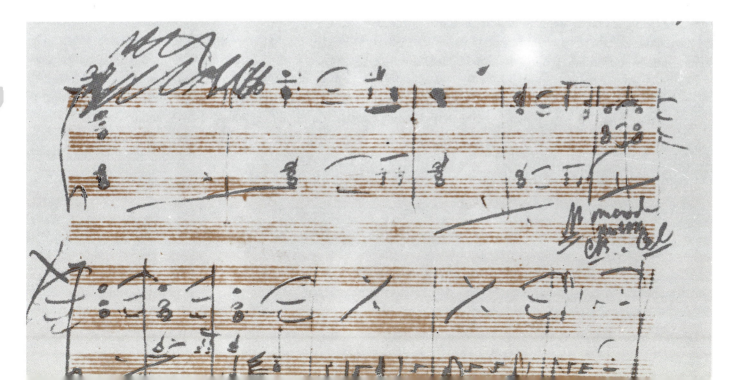

The manuscript of part of Tchaikovsky's 'Pathétique' Symphony (Tchaikovsky Museum, Klin)

activity. Must be short. (Finale DEATH—result of collapse.) Second part, love; third, disappointments; fourth ends dying away (also short).' The year of this note appears to have been 1892, when Tchaikovsky had begun a Symphony in E flat that he soon set aside as 'an empty pattern of sounds.' This work had no relation to the life-and-death pattern he had outlined. The sketch, thus, did represent an early program for the Sixth Symphony. 'I am now wholly occupied with the new work (the Sixth Symphony),' he wrote his brother Anatole on 22nd February 1893, 'and it is hard for me to tear myself away from it. I believe it is being born as the best of my works. I must finish it as soon as possible, for I have many affairs to wind up, and I must also go to London soon. I told you that I had completed a symphony which suddenly displeased me, and I tore it up. Now, I have composed a new symphony, *which I certainly shall not tear up.*'

On his return from London, Tchaikovsky wrote Modest that he was head-over-heels in his new symphony: 'The orchestration gets more difficult, the farther I go. Twenty years ago, I let myself write easily without much thought, and it was all right. Now I have become cowardly and uncertain. I have sat all day over two pages. What I wished for has constantly come to nothing. In spite of this I do make progress.' By 24th August 1893, he was writing his publisher that he had finished the orchestration: 'I give you my word of honour that never in my life have I been so contented, so proud, so happy, in the knowledge that I have written a good piece.'

Tchaikovsky's symphonic writing spans twenty-six years, from his Symphony No. 1 in G minor of 1866, to this last major work, the Pathétique. But he was continually troubled by personal doubts: 'All my life I have been much troubled by my inability to grasp and manipulate form in music . . . what I write has always a mountain of padding: an experienced eye can detect the thread in my seams and I can do nothing about it.' He once said he would be sorry if his symphonies only meant a progression of harmonies, rhythms and modulations: 'Should not a symphony reveal those wordless urges that hide in the heart, asking earnestly for expression?'

The Pathétique Symphony opens with a funereal introduction (*Adagio*), in which the dark voice of a solo bassoon introduces what later becomes the main theme of the first movement. It is a grieving figure that slithers over the ghostly double bass chord. The tempo quickens, and the theme becomes fragmented and is tossed about from instrument to instrument (beginning with the violas, then the flutes) with increasing agitation. This excited dialogue dies down in preparation for the famous melody of the second theme in the violins and cellos, which seems like a sweet remembrance of the happy past. Tchaikovsky marked it to be played 'tenderly, very *cantabile* and expansive.' The development begins with a crash, becoming more torturous and nervous and eventually approaching a hysterical pitch. There is another powerful climax, followed by a repetition of the opening themes. The movement closes solemnly in the trumpets and trombones, then the woodwinds, against the resigned falling scale of plucked strings.

In place of the traditional slow movement, Tchaikovsky conceived of a strangely graceful dance, a waltz that has an almost sinister gait, which is then clouded over by the Trio (middle section) with its repeated drumbeats. The third movement (*Allegro molto vivace*) begins softly with indistinct, whirling figurations that quickly appear and vanish. Then in the distance a marching theme is heard, gradually approaching and growing louder and louder in defiance. Despite this vitality, there is a foreboding of terror, building to a mighty climax that warns of imminent catastrophe. The Finale (*Adagio lamentoso–Andante*) is a bleak ending, a veritable outcry of pain and futility. The opening phrase in the strings sighs pathetically at the nothingness ahead. The melodic second theme, a simple flowing line for the violins, seems to bid farewell to life. This is climaxed by a tone of despair as the music dies away to the tolling of a gong. The melodic second theme again returns, now transformed into a gloomy minor mode. Its falling line seems to symbolize descent, as it grows darker in colour and finally dies away to a hushed stillness.

Of this apotheosis of human suffering, one of the most celebrated symphonies in all of Russian music, critic Donald Francis Tovey has written: 'Nowhere else has he [Tchaikovsky] encountered so great a variety of music within so effective a scheme; and the slow Finale, with its complete simplicity of despair, is a stroke of genius which solves all the artistic problems that have proved most baffling to symphonic writers since Beethoven. The whole work carries conviction without the slightest sense of effort; and its most celebrated features . . . are thrown into their right relief by developments far more powerful, terse and highly organised than Tchaikovsky has achieved in any other work . . . All Tchaikovsky's music is dramatic; and the Pathétique Symphony is the most dramatic of all his works.'

Wolfgang Mozart

His Life and Times 1756-1782

PROGRAM NOTES FOR THE PIANO CONCERTO IN B FLAT,
OVERTURES: COSI FAN TUTTE, THE IMPRESSARIO,
THE MAGIC FLUTE, DON GIOVANNI
By Robert Jacobson

FUNK & WAGNALLS, INC.
NEW YORK, NEW YORK

Mozart the Child Prodigy

On 21st November 1747 Leopold Mozart, the fourth violinist in the court orchestra of the Archbishop of Salzburg, married Anna Maria Pertl, daughter of the steward of the convent of St Gilgen. Five children of their marriage died in infancy, but two survived. One was a daughter, Maria Anna, born on 30th July 1751; the other was a son, born on 27th January 1756. The boy's baptismal names were impressive – Joannes Chrysostomus Wolfgangus Theophilus. But to the world he was and is known as Wolfgang Amadeus.

His musical talent showed itself early and spontaneously – at the age of three he was picking out by ear on the harpsichord passages from pieces his sister, known to the family as Nannerl, played at her music lessons. His father, seeing this but not really taking it very seriously, began to teach the boy simple little minuets. But soon things developed: at the age of five Wolfgang began to compose short pieces in the same style. At first his father wrote them down, but quickly the boy learned to do it himself.

Wolfgang, as pictured for us by the court trumpeter and friend of the family, Johann André Schachtner, was 'tender and affectionate' and obsessively devoted to music: 'As soon as he began to give himself up to music his mind was as dead to all other concerns, and even his childish games and toys had to be accompanied by music.' The only other subject that took his interest was arithmetic. His ear was incredibly acute, and his independence and self-confidence are shown by the story of the clavier concerto that he is said to have written at the age of four, and which looked like 'a daub of notes, for the most part written over ink-blots'. His father, looking it over, could see beneath the smudges that it made sense, but said, 'It is so extraordinarily difficult that no one in the world could play it' – to which the boy replied, 'That is why it is a concerto; it must be practised till it is perfect; look! this is how it goes.' So saying, he proceeded to play it himself.

His first public performance took place when he was $5\frac{1}{2}$, in a comedy by the local court organist. But his father's ambitions were not so localised: he realised that in his children's precociousness – for the girl too, though she faded out later, was no mean musician – he had a valuable property that was worth exploiting beyond the confines of the cultured but small town of Salzburg.

So father and the two children set out on the first of many trips which, if they had some of the features of a circus, were also of great value to the boy Mozart, who could not but gain from impressions and influences of the outside world. Encouraged by the success of three weeks spent in Munich, where brother and sister were well received by the Elector of Bavaria, the family next set out for Vienna, the musical and social centre of Austria. Entering Vienna, Leopold tells how Wolfgang's charms enabled them to avoid paying customs duty: 'For he made friends at once with the customs officer, showing him his clavier, invited him to visit us and played him a minuet on his little fiddle. Thus we got through.'

In Vienna the Emperor was delighted with the 'little magician' and invented games to test his abilities: playing the clavier with one finger, and with the keyboard covered by a cloth – a trick which became an important part of the 'show'. However, the boy was not interested in mere exhibitionism and the adulation of amateurs: he wanted to be recognised by a real connoisseur and so insisted that Wagenseil, the court composer and very famous in his day, should be present – for, as Mozart said, 'I am playing a concerto of yours: you must turn over for me.' All the ladies of the court fell for him – he would spontaneously jump into the lap of the Empress, throw his arms round her neck and kiss her. When the little Princess Marie Antoinette picked him up after a fall on the polished floor, he said, 'You are good – I will marry you.' Asked why by the Empress, he replied, somewhat priggishly, 'From gratitude – she was good to me, but her sister stood by and did nothing.'

Love and presents were showered on the children. 'Everyone,' wrote Leopold, 'is amazed, especially at the boy, and everyone whom I have heard says that his genius is incomprehensible.' Unfortunately their triumph was cut short by scarlet fever. Wolfgang was in bed for a fortnight; his admirers expressed their sympathy but refused to come near for fear of infection. This was bad for business: 'My boy's illness has meant a setback of about four weeks for although since his recovery we have taken in twenty-one ducats, this is a mere trifle, seeing that we only just manage every day on one ducat, and that daily there are additional expenses.'

But Leopold had proved the boy's powers and popularity, and after a brief return to Salzburg he thought the time was ripe for a 'European Tour'. So father, mother and the two children set off on a journey that was to last from 9th June 1763 until 30th November 1766. The voyage began inauspiciously: they had not gone far when their carriage broke down. But the mishap was turned to good account. They visited the organ in a nearby church and Leopold explained the use of the pedals – 'whereupon Wolfgang pushed the stool away and played standing at the organ, at the same time working the pedals and doing it all as if he had been practising for several months.'

The journey was littered with successes. At Frankfurt, on 30th August 1763, the following advertisement appeared:

The boy, who is not yet seven, will perform on the clavecin or harpsichord; he will also play a concerto for the violin, and will accompany symphonies on the clavier, the manual or keyboard being covered with a cloth, with as much faculty as if he could see the keys; he will instantly name all notes played at a distance, whether singly or in chords on the clavier, or on any other instrument, bell, glass, or clock. He will finally, both on the harpsichord and the organ, improvise as long as may be desired and in any key, thus proving that he is as thoroughly acquainted with the one instrument as with the other, great as is the difference between them.

On 18th November the Mozarts arrived in Paris, where they were to stay for five months. With the help of the well known man of letters Friedrich Melchior Grimm they gained the entrées they required. Leopold wrote: 'He has done everything – opened the court to us, managed the first concert, and is going to manage the second . . .' They caused a great stir at Versailles with their concerts, even though when Madame de Pompadour refused to kiss Mozart, he said indignantly: 'Who is this that does not want to kiss me? – the Empress kissed me.' He astonished both the court and other noble circles by his performances on clavier and organ, sight-reading and improvising accompaniments to various songs. Leopold thought it time to publicise the boy as a composer, and accordingly had four sonatas for pianoforte and violin engraved and dedicated to members of the court.

On 10th April 1764 the Mozart family left Paris for London. Leopold was very impressed by the friendly naturalness of the King and Queen, who received the prodigy with great enthusiasm. For King George III was a lover of music – he passionately admired Handel – and put the 'invincible' Wolfgang through his paces. The boy sailed through some difficult pieces by Wagenseil, J. C. Bach and Handel at sight; he made an even greater impression by accompanying the Queen in a song and a flute player in a flute solo, and improvising a charming melody on a bass by Handel. He also made a great impression on J. C. Bach, the great Johann Sebastian's youngest son, who was a fashionable London composer at this time and the Queen's music master. It was while in London that Mozart composed his first symphonies.

There were two public concerts, of which the second was arranged on the King's birthday, 'taking advantage of the fact that the nobility and gentry would be up for the birthday'. Mozart was advertised as 'the greatest wonder of which Europe or the world can boast'. The concert was a success; Leopold netted to his surprise a hundred guineas and wrote proudly: 'My boy knows in this his eighth year what one would expect only from a man of forty.'

Although more of Mozart's music was published at this time the public eventually tired of the prodigy and were not so keen as Leopold hoped to test the boy's talents in private 'every day from 12 to 3, admittance 2/6 each person'. So the Mozarts decided to cut their losses and repair to the Hague. Then, after being delayed by an illness which came near to killing both Nannerl and Wolfgang, they reached Amsterdam, where two concerts of the boy's own music were given, including the first performance of a symphony. Although, because it was Lent, concerts were forbidden, an exception was made in this case because the 'exhibition of the marvellous gifts of these children redounds to the glory of God'.

They returned to the Hague, where Mozart wrote much music to order; from there they all went to Paris again, and finally they travelled through Switzerland back to Salzburg, fêted everywhere.

At home in Salzburg, the brilliant success of their tour astonished the Archbishop, their own patron. In order to prove for himself that Leopold had not been exaggerating his son's talents, the Archbishop had Wolfgang locked in a room and made him write, under strict surveillance, a sacred cantata. This was performed on 12th March 1767. Meanwhile Leopold concentrated on Wolfgang's technical

Mozart playing to the Emperor and his family at Schönbrunn. It was here that he invented his popular trick of playing on a keyboard covered with a cloth (Austrian National Library, Vienna)

training, which had been neglected on tour, putting the boy through a course in counterpoint.

On 11th September they all left again for Vienna, where Leopold hoped that the celebrations of the betrothal of the Archduchess Maria Josepha to King Ferdinand of Naples would offer profitable scope. However, the Archduchess died of smallpox; the Mozarts fled from Vienna, but all the same both Nannerl and Wolfgang caught the disease, and Wolfgang was blind for nine days.

Returning to Vienna in January they found that things had changed. Money was tighter, and little profit accrued – 'none whatever,' wrote Leopold, 'save a medal, which is, it is true, beautiful, but so worthless that I do not even care to mention its value.'

The boy was, however, commissioned to write an opera, *La Finta Semplice* (The Pretended Simpleton); but its scheduled performance was called off owing to intrigues, petty jealousies and squabbles. The public cold-shouldered the prodigy who, now twelve, was gradually ceasing to seem such a miracle. None the less, his operetta *Bastien und Bastienne* was given a performance at a private theatre and some occasional music was commissioned and performed. Mozart even conducted some of his works in public in the presence of the Emperor.

By this time the Archbishop of Salzburg had seen that all the attention paid to Mozart could be turned to his advantage. Wolfgang was given an official – but unsalaried – post and had his rejected opera performed; he was commissioned to write a good deal of music. However, Leopold's feet and pocket were itching again. He decided to put into practice a long-cherished desire to try their fortunes in Italy, and so in December 1769 they left for the 'golden land of music and the one gateway to operatic fame'.

Mozart's Life: 1769-81

On 13th December 1769, leaving Mozart's sister Nannerl and his mother in Salzburg, Wolfgang and Leopold embarked on a journey which not only increased Mozart's reputation but also, even at such a tender age, acted as a kind of finishing school. Italy at this time was the musical centre of the world, and although Mozart would already have heard the latest Italian music in Salzburg this would only have increased his interest in visiting its source. In a letter to his sister from Verona, dated 7th January 1770, he wrote: 'Here ends the German booby, and the Italian one begins.' The letter then continues in Italian.

In Italy the Mozarts visited Rovereto, Verona, Milan, Parma, Bologna, Florence, Rome and Naples. Wolfgang's fame spread like wildfire – a chain reaction of emissaries, messengers, noble recommendations and newspaper reports – and, as expected, the young composer's charm and the impression made everywhere by his skill opened wide every door. Wolfgang now made his mark more because of his serious intentions and accomplishments than as a side-show exhibit – even though this element still remained: in Rovereto and Verona he was mobbed by admiring crowds when he tried the organs in the main churches.

On 16th January 1770 this 'most highly skilled Youth' performed a 'series of musical compositions' at the Philharmonic Academy in Mantua – a concert in which he pre-

sented two of his own symphonies, played a harpsichord concerto at sight and improvised a fugue. At the end of the month they arrived in Milan, where Mozart met the popular – and then famous – Italian opera composer, Niccolò Piccinni, at a rehearsal of the latter's *Cesare in Egitto* (Caesar in Egypt). He also struck up a friendship with two young castrati for whom he composed two Latin motets, and appeared at masked balls and composed three songs for a gala soirée in the presence of royalty. All this, however, brought him fame rather than money, as Leopold was keenly aware: 'But on the whole we shall not earn much in Italy. The main thing is that there is the greatest enthusiasm and understanding here and that the Italians see how much Wolfgang knows. Otherwise one must generally accept admiration and bravos as payment.' Nevertheless, as a result of the soirée Wolfgang was commissioned to write an opera for the next Milan season.

The Mozarts then travelled via Parma to Bologna, arriving on 24th March. Bologna was something of an artistic centre, and the impression Wolfgang made on the town in general and in particular at a concert at Field-Marshal Count Pallavicini's – which lasted from 7.30 p.m. until midnight, and had an audience of 150 guests including the highest nobility – was perhaps more important than his impact anywhere else in Italy.

Armed with this praise the Mozarts descended on Florence, where Wolfgang composed a number of fugues. Leopold wrote: 'Everything went off as usual and the amazement was the greater as Marquis de Ligniville, who is the finest expert in counterpoint in the whole of Italy, placed the most difficult fugues before Wolfgang and gave him the most difficult themes, which he played off and worked out as easily as one eats a piece of bread.'

On Wednesday 11th April, in the middle of Holy Week, they arrived in Rome, where they were 'received like grand people with a discharge of artillery'. They dashed at once to the Sistine Chapel, where the choir was singing a *Miserere* by Allegri, a 'secret' piece whose written text was not allowed outside the chapel. Mozart heard the work, wrote it down from memory, and went back two days later on Good Friday to check his manuscript against another performance. He had only to correct a few minor errors.

It is not surprising that this feat caused a great stir in the city and considerably augmented the interest shown in the boy by the high society circles in which, as usual, he and his father moved.

After an equally successful visit in the middle of May to Naples, where they met the Italian composer Niccolò Jommelli and Dr Charles Burney, the English diarist, composer and musical historian, the Mozarts returned to Rome. Here, on 8th July, Wolfgang was awarded the Order of the Golden Spur by the Pope, a great honour which had only previously gone to two other musicians – Lassus and Gluck. The Order carried with it the title of *cavaliere* – knight – and in fact impressed Leopold much more than his son; for although Wolfgang enjoyed using it for a while he soon treated it with the indifference with which he eventually came to regard most worldly advantages.

On his return to Milan on 18th October, Wolfgang set about the composition of his commissioned opera *Mitridate, re di Ponto* (Mithridates, King of Pontus). There was as usual a little trouble with the singers, but the boy worked very closely with them to make sure that what he wrote was completely suited to their tastes, accomplishments and personal idiosyncrasies. Many people declared that, great virtuoso though he was, it was impossible for so young a composer – and, what was more, a German – to write an Italian opera, and to grasp and apply the principles of composing for the theatre. However, the work was enthusiastically received and given twenty times to overflowing and enthusiastic houses. As a result of this success Mozart was commissioned to write another opera for the Milan carnival of 1773.

Very pleased with their Italian successes, the Mozarts set off for Salzburg. On the way back they visited Turin, Venice, Padua, Vicenza and Verona, finally arriving home at the end of March 1771. For a short time the family was reunited; but very soon Leopold received a letter telling him that Mozart had been commissioned by the Empress Maria Theresa to compose a dramatic work for the marriage

Hieronymus von Colloredo, Prince-Archbishop of Salzburg, painted by F. X. König. Both Mozart and his father were employed by the Archbishop, but they suffered from the oppressive and illiberal atmosphere at his court, and received little appreciation or financial recompense for their work (St Peter's Monastery, Salzburg)

A 17th-century print of the inside of Salzburg Cathedral (Charles Augustus Museum, Salzburg)

of Princess Maria Ricciarda Beatrice of Modena to the Archduke Ferdinand. On 13th August they set off for Milan to attend the wedding.

Mozart's contribution to the festivities, which was called *Ascanio in Alba*, was received with the enthusiasm he was by now accustomed to, and completely put Hasse's opera *Ruggiero* in the shade. According to one witness the Archduke and Archduchess not only applauded two of the songs until they were repeated but, leaning from their box both during and after the performance, they bowed towards Wolfgang and emphasised their approval by cries of 'Bravissimo maestro' and by clapping – an example followed by all present.

By mid-December Mozart was back in Salzburg and had been commissioned to write an opera, *Il Sogno di Scipione* (Scipio's Dream), to celebrate the festivities accompanying the installation of the new Archbichop of Salzburg – Hieronymus Joseph Franz von Paula, Count of Colloredo. The performance took place early in May, and relations with the new Archbishop were at first cordial, though a stricter regime was expected. 'For the time being' Mozart was appointed court *Konzertmeister* (director of the court orchestra) at a small salary and also given leave to go to Italy again in the autumn.

On 4th November 1772 Leopold and Wolfgang were again in Milan, when the boy began to prepare his new opera *Lucio Silla*, which had been commissioned on his first visit. Once again he worked in close collaboration with the fine singers and his opera absorbed him completely. In a letter to his sister he wrote: 'I do not know what I am writing, for I can think of nothing but my opera and am in

danger of writing down not words but a whole aria.' The first performance, on 26th December, was, however, not a great success, owing to a certain amount of confusion on the stage; but the opera was afterwards given twenty times to very full houses with many encores. On this visit to Italy Leopold attempted to secure a court position for Wolfgang in the court of Grand Duke Leopold at Florence, but this fell through and in March 1773 they returned to Salzburg.

On their return their position in Salzburg looked far less promising. The new archbishop was not popular with his people, and besides he took Mozart's musical gifts as no more than what was due from servant to master – an attitude which was hardly likely to please the much-fêted Mozarts. In July Leopold took Wolfgang to Vienna to renew their acquaintance with Maria Theresa but, again, no court appointment was forthcoming. They stayed for only two months, during which time Mozart wrote a second series of string quartets, and returned to Salzburg in the autumn.

For over a year their travels were suspended and Wolfgang settled down to work. His first String Quintet, the Piano Concerto in D major, the Bassoon Concerto, nine symphonies, two Masses and other works were written at this time. He was also busy with a new comic opera, *La finta giardiniera*,(The Pretended Garden-Girl) commissioned for the Munich carnival of 1775, whither they travelled on their ninth journey.

After this great success they returned to Salzburg to face the future hopefully. But there were soon problems of personal relationships both between the archbishop and the Mozarts and between father and son – problems which eventually caused a permanent rift.

The Mozart family in 1780, painted by Johann-Nepomuk della Croce. Wolfgang and his sister are at the keyboard, and Leopold holds a violin; the portrait on the wall is of the mother, who had died in 1778 (Mozarteum, Salzburg. Original in Mozart's House, Salzburg)

Mozart's Salzburg: the garden of the Schloss Mirabell, one of the Archbishop's residences

After the cosmopolitan glitter of Mozart's concert tours Salzburg must have seemed unbearably provincial. In September 1776 he wrote to Padre Martini: 'I live in a country where music leads a struggling existence . . . as for the theatre, we are in a bad way for lack of singers . . . Meanwhile I am amusing myself by writing chamber music and music for the Church.' Although Mozart's first official commission was for an opera, *Il re pastore* (The Shepherd King), part of the celebrations when Maria Theresa's youngest son, the Archduke Maximilian, visited Salzburg, the Archbishop was really only interested in church music – during 1776 Mozart wrote four masses, organ sonatas for church use and only a little light orchestral music for the court. The atmosphere seemed very confined after their tours: Salzburg was limited socially, for the Archbishop treated his musicians as domestic servants and even seemed to be uninterested in Mozart's talent – the young composer's work met with churlish criticisms and unnecessary restrictions. There were, however, other outlets for his compositions – for instance the well-known 'Haffner' Serenade (K.250) was written for the wedding celebrations of the daughter of the wholesale merchant and burgomaster, Siegmund Haffner.

At the beginning of 1777 it still looked as if no permanent appointment would be forthcoming in Salzburg. Mozart's relations with the Archbishop became increasingly strained, and in the same letter to Martini he adds that his father 'has already served this court for thirty-six years, and as he knows that the present Archbishop cannot and will not have anything to do with people who are getting on in years, he no longer puts his whole heart into his work.' The Archbishop, however, did not seem to favour youth either, and Leopold

and Wolfgang – lured by the glint of gold and the possibility of gaining some appreciation – were soon keen to make another concert tour.

They applied for permission to the Archbishop but met with a blank refusal – he was not having his servants 'going on begging expeditions'. A formal petition from Leopold resulted in the dismissal of father and son, but Leopold was afterwards ungraciously reinstated on the understanding that he would not leave Salzburg, although Wolfgang was free to do as he liked. And so Wolfgang – who was probably very relieved to escape for a time from his father's possessiveness and the unpleasant atmosphere of the Salzburg court – set out with his mother on 23rd September 1777. Leopold had briefed them carefully about what they should do, who to see, how to look after themselves, how much to spend and, more important, how much money to make: 'The object of the journey is, was, and must be the acquirement of a fixed position and the making of money.'

From the beginning the tour was a disappointment – Mozart was used to making an immediate hit wherever he went and he found no pleasure in 'doing the rounds', seeing people on his father's recommendation, searching for patronage or discussing plans, and receiving nothing in return but advice and praise. At Munich he offered his services to the Elector, who had no vacancy for a composer; he then tried to become resident composer at the opera, or to organise ten people to provide him with a ducat a month each to keep him in Munich – but all without success.

So rather gloomily Mozart and his mother left Munich for Augsburg, Leopold's home town, where they met some of Leopold's relations: with one cousin, Maria Anna

Thekla, Mozart had soon become close friends. It was a great relaxation not to be under his father's eye all the time, though Leopold could not resist ordering his family's progress in a series of very detailed letters. In Augsburg Mozart visited Johann Andreas Stein, the piano manufacturer, to whom he introduced himself incognito, though his superlative piano-playing soon gave him away. He was much impressed by the mechanical efficiency and the quality of Stein's instruments. Both his improvisations on the organ and his violin-playing made a great impact in Augsburg, but the concert which he gave on 22nd October was only a moderate success, and he had to work very hard for little financial return. He played a symphony, several concertos and an improvised fugue and sonata – and all with the Augsburg orchestra, which he found laughably bad. When Mozart and his mother left for Mannheim on 26th October all he was sad to leave behind was his pretty little cousin.

Mannheim was perhaps the most important musical centre in Germany, boasting a very fine and justifiably famous orchestra and an important school of composition. Leopold wrote to his son: 'I hope you will get something to do in Mannheim, where they are always performing German operas. Perhaps you will get a contract to compose one.' Christian Cannabich, one of the leading composers, and his family befriended the Mozarts, and Wolfgang gave lessons to Cannabich's talented daughter, Rosa, for whom he wrote the Sonata in C, K.330. For a change he had a thoroughly good time, meeting writers, musicians and composers – among them the flautist Wendling.

It was Wendling who introduced Mozart to the Webers, a large family, not very well off, and he seems immediately to have fallen in love with sixteen-year-old Aloysia. She was a very accomplished singer, and Mozart was so affected by her sorry plight that according to his mother 'he immediately wants to give his life and property for them'. What was more, he proposed a trip to Italy to promote the girl. Leopold was horrified and – partly to keep the peace – Mozart eventually relented: after several months in Mannheim sighing after Aloysia he and his mother set off for Paris.

Leopold was convinced that once again his son would take Paris by storm. But this time the not-so-youthful genius

Part of the 17th-century facade of Salzburg Cathedral

was overshadowed by the operatic battle raging between the Gluck and Piccinni camps. Although he was welcomed by the Duc de Guines, formerly French ambassador in London, and wrote the Flute and Harp Concerto for the duke and his daughter, the rest of society was not very interested. While in Paris he also composed some ballet music, *Les Petits Riens*, two pieces for the Concert Spirituel (an institution founded for the production of sacred vocal works), a Sinfonia Concertante for four wind instruments, the Piano Sonata in A minor, K.310, and the so-called 'Paris' Symphony, K.297, for the second performance of which he wrote a new slow movement. He was not so avid for employment, however, that he would take any job offered – he turned down the position of organist at Versailles because the salary was not high enough. Then in July, after a short illness, his mother died. While Wolfgang was still suffering from the shock of her death news reached him of a possible job in Salzburg. Glad of an excuse to end his solitary stay in Paris he soon started his journey home.

But Wolfgang's enthusiasm was not great enough to send him straight back to Salzburg. He stayed for some time in Mannheim – to the consternation of Leopold, who had by now definitely committed him to the Salzburg job, and who was running out of cash. But the prospect of the Archbishop was not very appealing and Leopold's pestering took a long time to get Mozart on the move again. Even when he left Mannheim he only travelled as far as Munich, where many of his Mannheim friends – including the Webers – were staying. But Aloysia had fallen out of love and, disillusioned, Mozart left for home.

Back in Salzburg Mozart started work as organist in court and cathedral, but his relations with the Archbishop had soon deteriorated badly. He composed a great deal – amongst other works is the Sinfonia Concertante (K.364). However, he was frustrated by the lack of an opera company, although he did manage a few minor stage works before his next big chance – a commission to compose an Italian opera for the Munich carnival. The resulting opera, *Idomeneo, re di Creta*, is the first of Mozart's operas still in the repertory: it represents the consummation of the *opera seria* style which by then was already becoming old-fashioned. The opera was performed in Munich two days after Mozart's twenty-fifth birthday and Mozart himself was present at the rehearsals and the first performance, which his father and sister were also able to attend. But while there he received a peremptory summons to Vienna, where the Archbishop was staying, and had to set off at once. He was treated worse than ever before and prevented altogether from following his own inclinations. Finally, having been subjected to a torrent of abuse, he handed in his resignation. The Archbishop, unwilling to acknowledge that it was possible for his servant to resign ignored the application and when Mozart presented it in person for a second time he was kicked out of the door by the steward, Count Arco.

Despite the insult this was ideal for Wolfgang, who wanted to stay on freelancing in Vienna. For Leopold in Salzburg it made the atmosphere fairly unpleasant, though he did manage to keep his job. So at twenty-five Mozart was at last free and alone in the magically promising city of Vienna, having delivered an irrevocable blow for the independence of composers.

Marriage and Independence: 1781-82

1781 was perhaps the most momentous year in Mozart's all-too-brief life. It began with the performance of his most important work to date, the *opera seria Idomeneo*, and half way through the year the composer found himself a free man. Alone in Vienna, with his down-to-earth dreams, his genius and with over three hundred and fifty works to his credit, liberated from the restricting servitude of both Archbishop and joyless Salzburg, he was free to set up in 'business' for himself, still young, but no longer the child prodigy and independent of his possessive father-manager, who considered his son had been foolish in his severing connections with his former employer, the Archbishop. Mozart wrote to his father: 'I shall be able to prove to you how useful Vienna is going to be to us all. . . . Apart from my health, I now think there is nothing so indispensible as money. . . . Do have confidence in me; I am no longer a fool, and still less can you believe that I am either godless or an ungrateful son. So rely absolutely on my brains and my good heart. . . . Why, where could I have learnt the value of money, when up to the present I have had so little to handle. . . . Necessity alone teaches one to value money.'

Mozart moved into lodgings with the Weber family, who were now in reduced circumstances, owing to the death of the head of the family, Fridolin, and were pleased to take in a lodger. Indeed the mother, Maria Cäcile, seemed to have her eye on Mozart as a possible husband for one of her daughters. The previous object of Mozart's affections, Aloysia Weber, was now married to an actor but Mozart made light of the affair in his letters to his father for he knew how displeased Leopold had been about the friendship, although the composer admitted: 'It is fortunate for me that her husband is a jealous fool, and never lets her go anywhere, and I therefore seldom have a sight of her.'

Owing to some unfortunate gossip concerning Mozart's position in the Weber household, he was forced to move to another place of lodging. It was rumoured that he was interested in one of the daughters, Constanze, also a singer, who was eighteen years old. Of the matter Mozart wrote: 'Because I am living with them, therefore I am going to marry the daughter. There has been no talk of our being in love. They have skipped that stage.' But he swore he was not interested in marriage: 'God has not given me my talent that I may attach it to a wife and waste my youth in idleness' – a poignant statement, considering the 'youth' was twenty-five and had only another ten years to live. However, he *did* fall in love with Constanze, much to the delight of the mother, although it is probable the attachment was hastened not a little by the attentions of one of Mozart's pupils who had fallen in love with him. The news, broken in December, was a great shock to Leopold and Mozart attempted to soften the blow with praise of his fiancée, albeit with a certain amount of enviable down-to-earthness: 'She is not ugly, but at the same time far from beautiful. . . . She has no wit, but she has enough common sense to enable her to fulfil her duties as a wife and mother.'

He was fully aware that there were to be no great prospects ahead: 'All that I desire is to have a small assured income. . . .' But even his courtship did not run smoothly. For a certain amount of malicious talk from a rival composer about Mozart's unreliability caused the girl's guardian to draw up a marriage contract which insisted 'that I bound myself to marry Mlle Constanze Weber within the space of three years and that if it should prove impossible for me to do so owing to my changing my mind, she should be entitled to claim from me three hundred gulden a year.' As it happened, in order to free themselves from the interferences of Constanze's mother, who seems to have been a woman of low principles, low breeding and also addicted to the bottle, they married in haste on 4th August 1782, without Leopold's blessing, though this, in fact, came the next day.

Ever since his withdrawal from the Archbishop's service in the May of the previous year, which has previously been detailed, Mozart had been tackling the problem of earning a living. He started by taking pupils, but although he could have had as many as he wanted he chose not to – 'I intend to be paid better than others, and so I prefer to have fewer pupils.' He also published six violin and piano sonatas by subscription. But his chief interest was in the stage: 'In

A view of the house in the Singerstrasse, Vienna where Mozart lived in 1781 (Austrian National Library, Vienna)

9

Vienna my sole amusement is in the theatre', and he was in fact commissioned to write an opera, a German *opéra comique*, of the then still new type called *Singspiel*, which combined spoken dialogue with sung passages – *Die Entführung aus dem Serail* (The Abduction from the Seraglio).

He began the work in July 1781, and worked quickly and with great enthusiasm and insight as originally the production was planned for the autumn. But it was put off till the next year.

In December of 1781 there took place the famous pianistic 'duel' between Mozart and Clementi, arranged as an entertainment at court for some Russian visitors by Joseph II. Clementi, who was twenty-nine, had a great reputation, and the two competitors improvised, played their own works, and sightread. Mozart is generally considered to have 'won', and he had a low opinion of the Italian: 'He has not a farthing's worth of taste or feeling; he is a mere *mechanicus*.' But Mozart did grant that 'his star passages are thirds'. He had hopes of obtaining a position at the court, but these came to nothing.

At the end of 1781 the two giants, Mozart and Haydn, met for the first time, and began a famous and lasting friendship. On 5th March 1782 Mozart gave his first concert in Vienna, with great success, and another at the Augarten, a fashionable open air pleasure garden. His group of pupils was gradually enlarged, but he was still occupied with *Die Entführung aus dem Serail*, which was being delayed through libretto changes, the preparations at the theatre and the usual management/artists arguments. However, by royal command, the first performance took place on 16th July 1782, to a packed house and, despite an organised opposition, was a huge success, justly deserving the many encores and tumultuous applause with which it was greeted. The emperor, who was proud of his conservative tastes, liked it and considered the music new and ambitious; indeed he told Mozart that it was too good for the Viennese and had too many notes in it, receiving the reply from Mozart that the composer considered he had put into it just as many notes as he deemed necessary.

With this spectacular success, Mozart had really established himself as a composer in Vienna, and could understandably expect to look forward to reasonable prosperity. However, troublesome times lay ahead.

(*Continued in Mozart Album II*)

by ROBERT JACOBSON

Piano Concerto in B flat

Weariness and detachment, yearning and fatalism, introspection and vigour flavour many of the last works of Mozart, composed during 1789-1790. These include the Piano Sonata in D (K.576), several quartets (K.575, 589, 590), the Clarinet Quintet (K.581), and the String Quintet in D (K.593). In contrast to earlier compositions that convey self-assurance and a joyous optimism about the future, these works are pervaded with a mood of weariness and melancholy resignation. Even the moments of humour occasionally present resolve ultimately into bittersweet yearning or renunciation. Thus, an air of gentle philosophical acquiescence and an autumnal atmosphere envelops the B flat Piano Concerto (K.595), Mozart's last work in this form, dating from late 1790. Notable in its reserve, it has indeed the intimacy of chamber music. The Concerto was first performed on 4th March 1791, at a benefit concert given by the clarinetist Joseph Beer at the home of the court caterer to the Emperor of Austria.

Cuthbert Girdlestone, in his analysis of the full complement of Mozart piano concertos, writes concerning this final example: 'The resignation and nostalgia which infuse the works of these two years are present in all three movements, even in the 6/8 rondo. It spreads not only a veil of sadness over the whole concerto; it also casts on it at times, as it were, an evening light, announcing the end of a life . . . Needless to say, we do not look upon this as a forewarning of Mozart's own death; even if he had not been destined to pass away eleven months later, his mood at the close of 1790 would have inspired him with these strains . . . This resignation is not present all the time; now and again, his soul remembers its rebelliousness of former years and more passionate notes are sounded, but they do not last and weariness soon reigns supreme again . . .'

The writer also comments that B flat is a favourite key with Mozart, particularly in his mature period; besides in this concerto, the composer used it for two quartets, a trio, two piano sonatas, two violin sonatas, a wind serenade and a symphony. 'It expresses before all a state of serenity, as absolute a calm as Mozart's restless soul can experience. It calls up a benedictory spirit; applying to it what has been written of an andante of Beethoven, we would say that its mildness is like "grace falling on the soul of a saint." A typical B flat work of Mozart's leaves behind it a feeling of moral well-being, the expression of which is accompanied by playfulness in the first movements and gaiety in the finales.'

This last Piano Concerto in B flat opens with an *Allegro*, its first subject in the violins setting the mood for what is to come in the ease and freedom of Mozart's rhythms. The second theme has a graceful melodic arch, sweeping downwards over a two-octave span and darkening the landscape much as the composer did with Donna Elvira's music in *Don Giovanni*. There is the sheer sensuous melody, beauty and grace of his earlier concertos; yet there is a more sophisticated tone as well — not unlike the unique blend Mozart achieved in *Così fan tutte*, a work of the same period. The piano, when it enters with the opening theme again, does nothing to disturb the mood already created by the orchestra in the long introductory passage, though it occasionally turns more dramatic and emotional. The piano writing is distinguished by its lack of virtuosity purely for its own sake; and there is none of the sense of conflict or competition between orchestra and soloist that typifies many piano concertos. The feeling is instead one of expressive unity, with sorrow and resignation held firmly in hand by the composer's classical restraint. One of Mozart's contemporaries noted, ' This music, so harmonious and so lofty in inspiration, so pure, both soft and sorrowful . . . made me forget as I listened to it my past woes and those that the future perhaps held in store for me . . . '

The second movement (*Larghetto*) continues this same mood, opening with an elegaic song of farewell on the piano. The music has an unearthly serenity, both tender and noble. The third and final episode, the rondo (*Allegro*), offers a late example of Mozart's 'hunt' music, outwardly joyful as in his earlier works yet with an intense yearning, too. This graceful but strong music has the character of an operatic aria. Here the piano rises to virtuoso heights, and Mozart's keyboard writing is brilliant. Alfred Einstein writes that this finale 'breathes a veiled joyfulness, as if blessed children were playing in Elysian fields, joyful but without hate and without love.' Einstein described Mozart's final piano concerto as 'a work of the highest mastery of invention — invention that has the quality of that "second naïveté," of which we have spoken, welding the solo and *tutti* parts into the richest, closest relation, speaking in the most transparent sonority, and fusing perfectly the *galant* and "learned" styles. It is so perfect that the question of style has become meaningless. The very act of parting from life achieves immortality.'

The frontispiece of the first edition of Mozart's B flat Concerto 'for harpsichord or forte-piano', published soon after its composition in 1791 (Society of the Friends of Music, Vienna)

Così fan tutte

Così fan tutte was composed in the years 1789-90 and first performed in Vienna on 26th January 1790 under the composer's direction. The opera is in two acts to a libretto by Lorenzo da Ponte; the sparkling story concerns Don Alfonso's bet with two young men, Ferrando and Guglielmo, that their much-enamoured ladies would not remain faithful to them under temptation. Accordingly the two young men leave their beloveds, ostensibly to go to war, but return disguised as Albanians. Each attempts, and eventually succeeds, to seduce the other's beloved and Don Alfonso wins his wager. The many intricacies of the plot are too numerous to be detailed here, but the title, Così fan tutte, can be freely translated as 'All women do it'.

One Berlin critic, in 1805, noted of the opera: 'That this evidence of the infidelity of all women was regarded merely as a jest is precisely the delicate charm of the whole opera, and that this infidelity, on the other hand, is let off so easily is proof of the playful sense of beauty on the part of the composer. Everything is only masquerade, playfulness, jest, dallying and irony.' Set in 18th-century Naples, Così is a true opera buffa, or old-fashioned Italian comic opera. Although it was favourably greeted at its Vienna première, not until this century has Così fan tutte become a consistent feature of the international repertory.

The ebullient wit that abounds throughout the opera marks the Overture as well, which has a mock sentimental tune in the oboe just after the opening chords. The phrase 'così fan tutte,' as sung in Act II by the men, is then stated in the low strings, and the Overture whirls to an effervescent presto conclusion with sparkling woodwinds and strings.

Don Giovanni

Mozart's collaboration with Da Ponte on Don Giovanni, just three years earlier, produced quite a different work. They called it a 'dramma giocoso,' or gay drama; and, to be sure, it does have generous measures of both tragic emotion and comedy. Don Giovanni was written on commission from the Italian opera company in Prague, where the composer and librettist had triumphed in 1786 with The Marriage of Figaro. The form of this masterwork is almost undefinable, because of the many and diverse elements the collaborators poured into it. As Einstein says, 'Where material like this is concerned, in which, as in Faust, such dark, primeval, demonic forces are inextricably combined, analysis can never be complete. The work is sui generis, incomparable and enigmatic from the evening of its first perfomance to the present day.'

All these unique qualities are present in the Overture, which opens with sombre chords for the trombones, repeated three times; this motif is associated with the Commendatore (Donna Anna's father), whose ghost appears before Don Giovanni at his dinner. Subdued

drum rolls heighten the ominous atmosphere and suggest the opera's fateful conclusion, when the Don is dragged off to hell. The fast section of the Overture, which has nothing to do with any motifs in the opera proper, suggests the buoyant lighter side of the work. After the three main ideas are presented and expanded, the Overture is rounded off with a string and woodwind coda.

The Magic Flute

Mozart called his Magic Flute a comic opera; yet, although it has undeniably comic elements, it also has a serious, spiritual thread running through it simultaneously. Actor, stage director and poet, Emanuel Schikaneder organised a company for the Theater auf der Wieden in Vienna and asked his composer friend to write for him a Singspiel, a new sort of comic opera with music and spoken dialogue. It was completed on 28th September 1791 and was presented two days later, with tremendous success. Both the collaborators were Masons, so the magical fairy-tale core of the libretto is filled with all kinds of obscure Masonic references, symbols and figures. The basic struggle is between good and evil, as personified by Sarastro and the Queen of the Night. Pamina and Tamino, the idealistic young lovers, can come together only after trials by fire and water. The three solemn chords that begin the Overture evoke Sarastro, the awesome priest of high ideals. Then follows a lively tune that is elaborated upon, giving a foretaste of the charming birdseller Papageno and his comic mate Papagena.

The Impresario

Mozart wrote The Impresario, a one-act 'comedy with music' in 1786, four years after the composition of Il Seraglio and in the same year as The Marriage of Figaro – in fact The Impresario interrupted the writing of the latter. It is a satire on the theatrical conventions of the time, epitomising the rivalry which existed between prima donnas and the casting problems which beset a theatre manager. Written in the Italian style, the overture is considered by some to be a parody of the typical Italian opera overture of the time.

The action takes place in the impresario's room at the opera house. Two singers have applied to sing the same role, and both give superb displays of their art. The impresario likes them both, and the singers squabble. Eventually a compromise is reached whereby the character in the opera is split into two and both the singers enact the part on the stage at the same time.

Commissioned by Emperor Joseph II of Austria, The Impresario was first performed in the Orangery at Schönbrunn on 7th February 1786, at festivities in honour of the governors of the Netherlands. Like most of Mozart's other overtures, the Impresario Overture is a single movement in sonata-form. Its festive, bustling tone well sums up the opera's action.

Johannes Brahms

His Life and Times 1833-1872

PROGRAM NOTES FOR THE PIANO CONCERTO NO. 2 IN B FLAT
By Robert Jacobson

f&w

FUNK & WAGNALLS, INC.
NEW YORK, NEW YORK

Brahms's Early Life

Johannes Brahms was born on 7th May 1833. His mother, a hard-working spinster until 1830, was already forty-four at the time, but his father was only twenty-seven. Everyone was surprised at their marriage – not least Brahms's mother herself – because of her age and the speed with which Jakob Brahms proposed. But as a happy-go-lucky double-bass player (he could also tackle a flute or horn) working in pleasure gardens and theatre bands, who had always lived from hand to mouth, a week of lodging with this neat little seamstress and her married sister at their haberdashery shop was enough to convince him not only that Johanna Henrike Christiane Nissen came originally of better stock than his own (his father was an inn-keeper), but that she had a real gift for running a home. All he could offer her was a three-roomed first-floor apartment in a dark and squalid dock-side quarter of Hamburg. But she brightened it with pot plants and birds in cages, which together with her excellent cooking, her love of birthday and Christmas celebrations and her general goodness of character, transformed poverty into happiness and reasonable content for her husband and her three children, Elise (born 1831), Johannes, and Fritz (born 1835).

The parents had to make sacrifices for the two boys' education. At six Johannes went to a private school kept by Heinrich Voss. Five years later he moved on to a still more progressive establishment directed by Johann Friedrich Hoffman, which he always remembered with gratitude. But it was his father's world of music that really kindled his imagination. By 1840, when he was still only seven, his passion for the piano had grown so strong that he was allowed to start lessons with Otto Cossel. Even though Jakob Brahms was not a high-minded musician himself, at least he had the intelligence to choose someone for his son who was: Cossel, detecting the boy's exceptional talent, developed it so wisely and well that when Brahms took part in a concert at the age of ten an impresario who happened to be passing through Hamburg immediately proposed a highly lucrative American tour. It was stopped by the wise Cossel, who not only called in his own former teacher, the formidable Eduard Marxsen, to help point out the folly of such a project for a child, but also with self-sacrificing generosity persuaded Marxsen to accept Johannes as his own pupil in view of such remarkable promise. Marxsen would take no money for the task: his own richest reward came many years later when given the dedication of the B flat major Piano Concerto. As a teacher he not only developed the pianist in Johannes, but also encouraged his increasing desire to compose, balancing his Romantic susceptibilities with a strong respect for Classical form such as he himself had inherited from teachers directly linked with Mozart, Beethoven and Schubert.

But money had to be earned somehow, even if not in America; for the Brahms family was often in very straitened circumstances indeed when Jakob's attempted short cuts to prosperity went awry, as they usually did. In time Johannes found publishers willing to pay him for hack work, such as arranging and even ghost composing, and he also gave a few cheap music lessons. But his initial plunge into the professional maelstrom at the age of thirteen was a good deal less salubrious: there was plentiful work at night playing popular songs and dances in the taverns and clubs around the docks, and it was here, among the sailors and prostitutes of Hamburg, that Brahms learned the facts of life in the crudest possible way. By the spring of 1847 the strain of this squalor, on top of serious work for Marxsen, had gravely undermined his health. But salvation arrived in the nick of time: Adolf Giesemann, a patron of the Alster Pavilion where Jakob played in the six-piece band, invited Johannes to stay at his home in the village of Winsen all the summer to give piano lessons to his daughter Lieschen.

Here, amidst congenial friends and in the open air, Brahms grew well, strong and happy again, especially as the fields, woods and river seemed to intensify his urge to write music. In later life it was always the same: many of his greatest works grew from holidays in the countryside he loved so well. The village of Winsen had its own male-voice choir for which Brahms arranged folk-songs and wrote part-songs as well as conducting it both on this stay and another the following summer. He never forgot the joy of these visits. Forty years later he referred to his memory of Adolf Giesemann as 'of the most beautiful kind that the human heart can treasure'. Back in Hamburg, of course, there was all the old drudgery again, though already Romantic literature was beginning to offer another source of imaginative escape. And in 1848 and 1849 he had the spur of working for recitals of his own.

The year 1850 brought the forty-year-old Schumann to Hamburg in the course of a tour with his eminent pianist wife Clara. Brahms dared to send him a small packet of compositions for perusal: to his chagrin they were returned unopened. But consolation was not long in coming in the person of the brilliant young Hungarian violinist, Reményi, born just three years before Brahms, and in exile from his own land for activities against Austria during the 1848 uprisings. They quickly struck up a friendship – Brahms was particularly interested in the Hungarian gypsy music

Reményi liked to play – and when after a visit to the United States Reményi eventually returned to Hamburg, the two set out to give a few recitals together in not-too-distant towns. The date was April 1853.

The first stop was Brahms's beloved Winsen; the second was Celle, where he amazed everyone by transposing the piano part of Beethoven's C minor Violin Sonata at sight into C sharp minor because the piano was a semitone flat. In Hanover, before playing to the King, they first called on the King's Konzertmeister (who had secured their royal invitation) – none other than Reményi's old Hungarian schoolfriend, Joachim, already a famous violinist at the age of twenty-two. Shy as Brahms was, he could not help noticing that as soon as he played some of his own compositions all Joachim's sympathy and admiration were directed towards him, not the flamboyant Reményi. Discreetly, Joachim – who was to become one of Brahms's greatest friends and helpers – also assured him of a warm return welcome should anything disrupt the tour. And trouble was not long in coming, for availing themselves of Joachim's introduction to the 42-year-old Liszt, reigning in splendour as leader of the progressive New German School in Weimar, attention was again focused on accompanist rather than soloist, as Reményi liked to imagine himself. Worse still, Brahms neither seemed to appreciate the compliments showered on his compositions by Liszt, nor found himself able to summon up any comparable enthusiasm for Liszt's own music. A break was inevitable: Reményi stayed on to try to ingratiate himself with the avant-garde, while Brahms rejoined Joachim for the summer. Eventually they gave a concert together, on the proceeds of which Brahms set off on a solitary walking tour by the Rhine, armed with the strictest instructions from Joachim to forget all about his 1850 rebuff and visit the Schumanns in Düsseldorf.

It was on the last day of September 1853 that he eventually took the plunge. Whispers from Joachim had gone ahead: this time Schumann, although far from well, received him with open arms. As for Clara Schumann, her diary records: 'Here again is one of those who comes as if sent straight from God. He played us sonatas, scherzos etc. of his own, all of them showing exuberant imagination, depth of feeling, and mastery of form. Robert says that there was nothing that he could tell him to take away or add. It is really moving to see him sitting at the piano, with his interesting young face which becomes transfigured when he plays, his beautiful hands, which overcome the greatest difficulties with perfect ease (his things are very difficult), and in addition these remarkable compositions.'

For just over a month Brahms's happiness knew no bounds: the warmth, sympathy and encouragement of this simple yet wholly dedicated family was the haven he had unconsciously sought all his life. Other friends joined their enthusiastic evenings of music-making, with joy reaching its height at Joachim's arrival. Schumann, Brahms and another young musical friend called Dietrich even decided to write a violin sonata together for Joachim – Brahms's Scherzo from it is still very often heard. Finally, on 2nd November, Clara's diary sadly notes that Brahms played his F minor Sonata in the evening as a farewell. But to assist the 'young eagle in his flight through the world', Schumann broke a very long silence in his old paper, the *Neue Zeitschrift für Musik*.

Life 1853-1862

In November 1853, at the age of twenty, Brahms arrived in the great musical centre of Leipzig armed with eulogistic introductions from Schumann to the leading music publishers. It was not entirely easy for him being dubbed 'Schumann's young Messiah', but his unaffected modesty and sincerity won over even the cynical. Liszt and Berlioz were among the eminent musicians who came to hear him play his C major Sonata at the Gewandhaus. And when he returned to Hamburg and his family, from whom he had never before in his life been parted at Christmas, he was able to delight them with the news that all three of his Piano Sonatas and his E flat minor Scherzo for piano had been accepted for immediate publication. When the new year brought an early reunion in Hanover with Joachim and the Schumanns (there to hear Joachim conduct Schumann's D minor Symphony), life began to seem almost too good to be true. But Brahms was still with Joachim in Hanover when he read a newspaper report that on 27th February 1854 Robert Schumann had suffered a mental breakdown and attempted to drown himself in the Rhine. Brahms's immediate reaction was to go to Düsseldorf to help. Little could he have guessed that it was a decision destined to influence the rest of his days.

Clara, still only thirty-five, was distraught. Already she had six children, and a seventh was expected within a few months. Her devotion to her husband and her unquestioning belief in his genius in the face of all difficulties and doubts were already legendary. But she desperately needed a friend, and she turned to Brahms – now approaching his twenty-first birthday – without reserve. On his part, Brahms had received greater kindness and encouragement from Schumann than from any other great artist he had encountered. No one tried to bring Schumann, in the isolation of his Endenich asylum near Bonn, greater comfort or more genuinely hoped for his recovery. But proximity to Clara, the leading woman pianist of her generation as well as a devoted wife and mother, imposed strains too great for such impressionable young shoulders to bear. It was not long before friendship on his part had grown into engrossing love. All he wanted was to be at Clara's side, asking for nothing but to comfort her when news from the asylum was bad, and to rejoice with her if any day brought a temporary gleam of hope.

His family and friends, hearing of only a few smaller new piano works like the Variations on a theme by Schumann, op. 9, and the Ballades, op. 10, were dismayed that his

3

Brahms as a young man, painted by Maria Fellinger (Museum of Local History, Hamburg)

Clara Schumann and Joseph Joachim playing together—a picture painted in 1854 by A. Menzel. Brahms first met Joachim, who was to be his life-long friend and helper, in 1853 and it was on the insistence of the violinist that he visited the Schumanns later the same year (Schumannhaus, Zwickau)

career no longer seemed to matter. They were unaware that the tumultuous conflicts of feeling through which Brahms was passing were in fact overflowing into sketches for several works destined to win him a place amongst the immortals – works like the D minor Piano Concerto, the C minor Piano Quartet and even the C minor Symphony. His parents seemed less worried after Brahms brought Clara to meet them in November 1854 when she was in Hamburg for a concert; later, in 1855, Clara herself eased Brahms's financial situation by finding a way of inviting him to share in the recitals she was giving with Joachim as part of her battle to support her husband and family. When the situa-

tion worsened at Endenich in 1856, Brahms took up residence at Bonn to be within call. He took Clara to see her husband for the last time and, with Joachim, walked ahead of the coffin when Schumann was eventually buried in Bonn on 31st July 1856. Almost immediately afterwards Brahms and his sister Elise set off with Clara and two of her children to ease their sorrow in a tour of Switzerland. Presumably they faced up to the reality of the situation for the first time at this moment in their lives. For, back in Germany, Clara Schumann returned to Düsseldorf to prepare to move to Berlin to take up a teaching appointment, while Brahms went home to Hamburg.

For Brahms, too, there was soon some professional solace. After a preliminary Whitsuntide visit instigated by one of his pupils, he was invited to the court of Detmold in the autumn of 1857 to spend three months there giving piano lessons to the Princess Friederike, playing the piano at court concerts and conducting the choral society – the court orchestra already had its own aged conductor whom the Prince of Detmold felt unable to dislodge. The salary was generous, there was plenty of time for composition, and the surrounding forests were most beautiful – a factor of major importance to such a lover of nature and the open air as Brahms. He valued it enough to return for the same period in 1858, and yet again in 1859, producing his two orchestral Serenades in D, op. 11, and A, op. 16, as prime tribute to Detmold's almost 18th-century calm and seclusion.

For the rest of the time Brahms lived in Hamburg, at first in the rather better apartment his parents were able to afford after his father's promotion to the theatre band, but later, when he needed more quiet for composition, on his own in a garden flat rented from friends in the suburb of Hamm. And, back in the bigger world again, life had many ups and downs. A holiday at Göttingen in the summer of 1858 brought unforeseen emotional complications when he found himself as strongly drawn to the daughter of a professor of medicine there – a young girl called Agathe von Siebold, with striking black hair and a lovely voice – as she was to him. When Clara joined the party he was torn in half by his feelings towards the two women, the one as spirited and carefree as the other was preoccupied and serious. Eventually he abandoned Agathe – out of fear of hurting Clara as much as of forfeiting his own freedom. But it was Agathe who inspired his Songs, opp. 14 and 19, and, as if to make amends for causing her pain, he dissolved the letters of her Christian name into a theme sung out by the violins in the first movement of his Second String Sextet in G, op. 36.

His biggest musical achievement was nevertheless the completion of his First Piano Concerto in D minor; first projected as a two-piano sonata, then as a symphony, its ideas all grew direct from his own *Sturm und Drang* during the darkest days of Robert Schumann's illness. When Brahms gave the première under Joachim's baton, in Hanover in January 1859, the reception was respectful. In Leipzig two days later, the work proved a total disaster: the public was unprepared for so symphonic a conception of a concerto. Though its warmer welcome in Brahms's native city in March helped to restore some of his confidence, the experience was a distressing one – sowing seeds of self-doubt never wholly overcome for the rest of his life.

The year 1860 brought a different crisis. Incensed at an

article in the *Neue Zeitschrift für Musik* claiming that all musicians who mattered were devotees of the progressive new German school headed by Liszt and Wagner, Brahms drew up a manifesto condemning this 'so-called' new German school as 'contrary to the innermost spirit of music, strongly to be deplored and condemned'. Unfortunately the article was published in the Berlin *Echo* with only the signatures of Joachim, Julius Otto Grimm and Bernhard Scholz in addition to Brahms's own, instead of with the very long list of names originally envisaged. Since Brahms and Joachim were still under thirty, the protest carried no weight: it merely caused much ill-feeling, and drove Brahms himself to take up a far more extreme anti-Romantic pose than was compatible with his own innermost heart.

In Hamburg itself he was finding considerable enjoyment in conducting a ladies' choir which he had gradually developed into a group of about forty voices. Choral conducting had always appealed to him ever since his teenage experiments in the village of Winsen, followed up, of course, by much more extensive experience at Detmold. For all three choirs he arranged folk-songs, besides composing a large number of quartets and part-songs. But secretly he hoped his work in this direction might lead to something more. Friedrich Wilhelm Grund, conductor of the Hamburg Philharmonic Society and of the Singakademie, was a very old man, within sight of retirement: might the city fathers think of him, Johannes Brahms, when it came to appointing a successor?

In the course of 1862 the decision was made. The job went to his singer friend Stockhausen. To Clara he at once confessed, 'This is a much sadder business for me than you think, or can perhaps understand. As I am altogether rather an old-fashioned person, so I am in this, that I am not a cosmopolitan, but love my native town as a mother . . . And now this hostile friend comes and ousts me . . . perhaps forever. How rare it is for one of us to find a permanent niche, and how glad I should have been to find mine in my native town! Happy as I am here, with so much that is beautiful to rejoice me, I nevertheless feel, and shall always feel, that I am a stranger and can have no peace.' The 'here', it should be noted, was Vienna, where he had come on a short visit in September 1862. By 1863 it had become his new headquarters and before long he was to adopt it as his home for the rest of his life.

The Prince of Detmold's castle, where Brahms was employed as piano-teacher

Success in Vienna: Life 1862-72

In spite of the fact that prophets are never accepted in their own land, Brahms, at twenty-nine,, was still devoted to Hamburg and his parental home. When he went to Vienna in September 1862, it was only for a short visit. Not even amidst the tremendous disappointment of learning, in November, that he had not been appointed conductor of the Hamburg Philharmonic Society, the post he had set his heart on, did he as yet envisage the possibility of settling in the Austrian capital. None the less, it was a city teeming with music and musicians, not nearly as hidebound in atmosphere as many major centres in his native Germany, its arms wide open in welcome to interesting visitors. Professionally, he was persuaded to present his visiting card in two chamber concerts during November, at which he himself played the piano part in his G minor and A major Quartets as well as some solos, followed early in 1863 by further programmes of piano works, songs and female choruses. Furthermore both Dessoff and Herbeck, conductors of the Opera and Gesellschaft der Musikfreunde respectively, showed interest in his two Detmold serenades. Personal friendships proved yet more rewarding. He was still young, with a relish for food and drink and amusement, and particularly enjoyed himself in the company of the composer Peter Cornelius, the pianist Tausig, and the musicologist Nottebohm. He also met Wagner, twenty years his senior, for the first time. Though he was wary of further close emotional entanglements, there were always several attractive female singers in the offing, notably Luise Dustmann, Bertha Porubszky, and most important, Ottilie Hauer, whose personal charm no less than her voice inspired him to write several more beautiful songs – just as he had done for Agathe von Siebold not so long before.

Later in 1863, he had the immense satisfaction of being invited to become conductor of the Wiener Singakademie, and scored an enormous success with his opening programme, on 15th November, of Bach, Beethoven, Schumann (the *Requiem for Mignon*) and some of his own folk-song arrangements. As the winter progressed he was sometimes criticised by the public for over-serious, high-brow programmes. Vienna was a pleasure-loving place. But after the first season's last concert on 17th April 1864, the singers themselves were happy enough under his baton to invite him to continue for the next three years. Surprisingly, Brahms declined. As he wrote to a friend, 'While in any other city a regular position is desirable, in Vienna one lives better without it. The many interesting people, the libraries, the Burgtheater, and the picture galleries, all these give one enough to do and enjoy outside one's own room.'

At this moment he had, in fact, come to feel an increasing need for freedom to compose, to undertake concert tours at will, and to visit his friends, whether Joachim (as at the time of his engagement early in 1863) or Clara Schumann, near whom he chose to spend some days in the autumn of 1863 and the whole summers of 1864 and 1865 in the Lichtental suburb of the spa of Baden-Baden, where she had bought a holiday house and was surrounded by a stimulating international circle of friends including Pauline Viardot, the great singer; Turgenev, her devoted admirer; Johann Strauss, the waltz king; and Anselm Feuerbach, the painter.

Last but not least, Brahms could foresee that he might need some free time to settle ominous family problems in Hamburg. On returning home for his thirtieth birthday in May 1863, he found his father and mother sorely strained by the seventeen years between them. Johanna was now 74, and ailing. By February 1864 Jakob had achieved his life's ambition: no more pleasure-garden and theatre bands, but a regular place in the double-bass desks of the Hamburg Philharmonic Orchestra. When old Frau Brahms complained at the noise of the extra practice involved, even Johannes – who loved both parents deeply – realised that they would have to part, and personally arranged separate accommodation, at his own expense, for his mother and sister. On 2nd February 1865 Brahms's mother died. The blow struck him to the heart. He himself was sufficiently good and true to appreciate her own fundamental goodness and the tragedy of her position in having loved a husband so much younger than herself. But when, in the following year, his father married again – this time a widow eighteen years his junior, a certain Caroline Schnack, at whose restaurant he had become accustomed to taking his meals – Brahms was completely understanding. His relations with his step-mother were of the friendliest. And he even invited his father to Vienna, and also to accompany him on a walking tour of Austria, the Rhineland and the Swiss mountains in the course of the next couple of years.

Switzerland, incidentally, was steadily increasing its hold on Brahms at this time, and not only for holidays. He made important concert tours to its centres, both alone and with Joachim, during 1865 and 1866, and soon numbered Mathilde Wesendonck (immortalised by Wagner in *Tristan und Isolde*) among his own personal friends. And it was after a period of comparative seclusion high up on a mountain overlooking the lake of Zurich that he arrived at Clara Schumann's Baden-Baden home, on 17th August 1866, with the almost completed manuscript of a work far more ambitious than any of the chamber music (including the F minor Piano Quintet, the Horn Trio in E flat and the C minor String Quartet) in which he had recently been engrossed, a work which was in fact to change his whole position in the eyes of the world – the German Requiem.

This had been gestating in his mind ever since the Schumann tragedy – its funeral march movement was in fact salvaged from a symphony he had projected in his very early twenties. The death of his mother intensified his desire to complete it, and though as a seven-movement work it did not reach the world till 1869, in Leipzig, its first three movements had a try-out (only partially successful owing to a bad performance) in Vienna in December 1867, and the official première (except for the subsequently added extra movement) took place in Bremen Cathedral in April 1868 with Brahms himself conducting. Many of his closest friends came long distances for the performance, but it was Clara Schumann's presence that gave him the deepest pleasure. Her diary for Good Friday records: 'The Requiem

7

has taken hold of me as no sacred music ever did before. . . . As I saw Johannes standing there, baton in hand, I could not help thinking of my dear Robert's prophecy, "Let him but once grasp the music wand and work with orchestra and chorus", which is fulfilled today. The baton was really a magic wand and its spell was upon all present, even upon his bitterest enemies. It was a joy such as I have not felt for a long time. After the performance there was a supper in the Rathskeller, at which everyone was jubilant – it was like a music festival. . . . Reinthaler made a speech about Johannes which so moved me that (unfortunately!) I burst into tears. I thought of Robert, and what joy it would have been to him if he could have lived to see it. . . . Johannes pressed me to stay in Bremen for another day. . . . I wish I had not given way to him. . . .' Clara at this time was in her forty-ninth year, Johannes in his thirty-fifth.

In spite of the several offers of permanent teaching posts in Germany that followed this great success, by Christmas 1868 Brahms at last decided to make Vienna his permanent home. As tribute to its charms, he wrote what was always one of his favourite works, the *Liebeslieder* Waltzes for vocal quartet and piano duet, amidst a spate of choral works that between 1868 and 1872 included *Rinaldo*, the Alto Rhapsody, the *Song of Destiny* and, as a tribute to Bismarck and the German Emperor during Brahms's intense fit of patriotism (shared by Clara) during the Franco-Prussian War, the *Song of Triumph*. Behind the Alto Rhapsody of 1869 there was a rather more personal story, for while spending the summer at Baden-Baden with the Schumanns his susceptible heart had started to beat rather more fast whenever he found himself in the presence of Clara's third daughter, Julie. When Julie announced her engagement to an absent Italian count, Clara's diary records that Johannes was 'quite altered . . . he seldom comes to the house and speaks only in monosyllables when he does come'. Immediately after the wedding Clara wrote: 'Johannes brought me a wonderful piece a few days ago, the words from Goethe's *Harzreise im Winter* [Journey through the Harz in winter] for alto, male chorus and orchestra. He called it his bridal song. It is long since I remember being so moved by a depth of pain in words and music. . .This piece seems to me neither more nor less than the expression of his own heart's anguish. If only he would for once speak as tenderly!'

The buffetings of fate were by this time beginning to tell: Brahms was developing a brusqueness in personal relationships that not everyone could understand. Even Clara herself was a frequent sufferer. And there was another blow to come. At the end of January 1872, only a few weeks after he had settled into the modest new apartment at Karlsgasse No. 4, which was to remain his life-long Viennese home, he heard that his father was critically ill with cancer of the liver. Rushing to Hamburg he was not too late – as was unfortunately the case with his mother almost exactly seven years earlier. Eleven days were granted him by his father's bedside before yet another chapter in his life came to an end.

(Part 2 of Brahms continued in Album 17)

The staircase leading to Brahms's rooms at his house in Vienna, where a splendid housekeeper called Frau Truxa solved all his domestic problems

Two 19th-century silhouettes by *Bithorn*. Left: Johannes Brahms and the beggar Right: Brahms conducting (*Austrian National Museum, Vienna*)

Brahms: Classic or Romantic?

Classic or romantic: what do the terms really mean? Goethe was one of the first to try and explain how and why they came into being. Discussing his *Walpurgisnacht* with Eckermann he observed: 'The distinction between classical and romantic poetry, which is now spread over the whole world and occasions so many quarrels and divisions, came originally from Schiller and myself. I laid down the maxim of objective treatment in poetry, and could allow no other; but Schiller who worked quite in the subjective way, deemed his own fashion right . . . The Schlegels took up this idea and carried it further, so that it has now been diffused over the whole world; and everybody talks about classicism and romanticism – of which nobody thought fifty years ago.'

Musicians were not long in recognising a similar distinction between the 'objective' and 'subjective' approach, to borrow Goethe's key words, in their own sphere of activity, and indeed by the mid-19th century few of them thought or talked about anything else. They went farther than their literary and artistic colleagues in refusing to foster peaceful co-existence. Sides had to be taken for one faction or the other, the 'objective classicists' rallying behind Brahms, and the 'subjective romanticists' behind Liszt, Wagner, and their lesser camp followers of the New German School.

Why was Brahms so intransigent a die-hard in his contemporaries' eyes? For this he himself was partly to blame. In a fit of youthful pique at the way too many of the progressivists took their superiority for granted, he published a manifesto in the *Berlin Echo* condemning the ideals of the New German School as 'contrary to the innermost spirit of music, strongly to be deplored and condemned.' He very soon deplored and condemned his own folly in putting such words into print. But the damage was done; henceforth he was type-cast.

And taken at its surface value, there is little to suggest that his own music flowed from any but classical springs. He genuinely venerated the past, seeing himself as the heir of traditions perfected by Beethoven rather than a musical redeemer to whom new truths had been vouchsafed. The logic inherent in classical forms like passacaglia, fugue, variation, rondo, and most of all, sonata form, seemed to him more sound than anything Liszt, for instance, had to offer in his symphonic poems, pledged first and foremost to evoke atmosphere and tell stories. Moreover Brahms felt well able to make his works cohere as wholes without systematic recourse to the 'leitmotivish' trick of thematic metamorphosis, and to express every shade of meaning that

9

he wanted without introducing new chords into the harmonic vocabulary. Even the kind of orchestra Beethoven used did not seem to him in any way inadequate. Though no sybarite, he was by no means insensitive to sheer sensuous beauty of sound *per se*. But he could get all the opulence he wanted without demanding the outsize orchestras Berlioz favoured, as also all the required shades of colour without recourse to exotic new instruments like the cor anglais, tuba or celeste. His refusal to supply his works with descriptive titles was the final proof, in his contemporaries' eyes, that his music was objective craftsmanship rather than a sublimated slice of his emotional life.

But that is where they were wrong. Today we can see that in many ways Brahms was infinitely more subjective than many arch-romantics who looked outwards for inspiration, no matter whether to literature, art, landscape or whatever, rather than drawing on their own personal experience. Brahms's life is written into his work, but it is wholly dissolved into musical terms. Only once, in the slow movement of his youthful Piano Sonata in F minor completed at the time of his first encounter with the Schumanns, did he ever supply any 'programme' – a Sternau poem about moonlight and loving hearts. After that, he never let outsiders into his secrets again. But the story is there all the same. That the *Sturm und Drang* of the D minor Piano Concerto, the C minor Symphony and the C minor Piano Quartet (even though completion and publication of the last two were long delayed) was directly attributable to Brahms's own anguish (when he was torn between love for Clara and loyalty towards her dying husband), was confirmed when, in a letter to Simrock, at the time of the Quartet's eventual publication, he identified himself with Goethe's Werther, who shot himself on realising he was irretrievably in love with the wife of his best friend. And in Joachim's copy of the D minor Piano Concerto Brahms wrote the words 'Benedictus qui venit in nomine Domini' over the slow movement knowing that Joachim was one of the inner circle

who knew that 'Domini' referred to Robert Schumann, and that the music enshrined Clara's image. More than a few of the songs of op.14 and op.19 tell of Brahms's passing infatuation (after Clara had dedicated herself to her husband's memory and perpetual widowhood) for Agathe von Siebold: the musical letters from her name are even woven into the fabric of his G major Sextet. In 1869, when a growing interest in Clara's daughter, Julie, was abruptly halted by Julie's engagement to an Italian count, Brahms chose a passage from Goethe's *Harzreise im Winter* – the cry of the man for whom the cup of life invariably turned to bitterness each time he took it up – to set as his Alto Rhapsody. His attachments to various singers always produced a further outpouring of solo song. His patriotism in the Franco-Prussian War gave rise to the *Triumphlied* of 1870. His violin Concerto stands as a permanent memorial to his friendship, at its peak, with Joachim – the Double Concerto for violin and cello and the two last Sonatas for violin and piano could all be seen as part of a deep longing for reconciliation with Joachim after the painful break. Personal contact with Richard Mühlfeld and his superb artistry sparked off the clarinet works just when everyone – and even the composer himself – was beginning to feel that his life-mission was nearly completed. And just as his mother's death had inspired his Requiem, so Clara Schumann's approaching end, after a severe stroke, was directly responsible for the *Vier ernste Gesänge*. His FAF motto (a 'frei aber froh' retort to Joachim's early 'frei aber einsam') crops up in arpeggio-type themes throughout his entire output. And he even made his personal farewell to music, and to life itself, through a set of eleven Chorale Preludes for the organ.

Many other examples could easily be found. These are the more obvious ones, providing overwhelming evidence of the wholly subjective approach of this most stalwart guardian of tradition. Brahms, in fact, was both classic and romantic, a man who wrote music with his heart's blood while refusing to wear his heart on his sleeve.

Brahms as 'maestro'— pencil sketches by Willy von Beckerath. Brahms's three-year stint as conductor of Vienna's Gesellschaft der Musikfreunde made him more at ease when writing for orchestral instruments (Friends of Music Society, Vienna)

PROGRAM NOTES FOR THE RECORD

by ROBERT JACOBSON

Piano Concerto in B flat

Johannes Brahms wrote four concertos during his lifetime—each a masterpiece of its kind—beginning with the First Piano Concerto in D minor, dated 1861 (the composer was then twenty-nine), followed by the Violin Concerto in D major in 1879, the Second Piano Concerto in B flat major in 1882 and, finally, the Double Concerto in A minor for Violin and Cello in 1888. As he carried on the great Central European symphonic tradition in his own four symphonies, Brahms conceived these concertos symphonically as much as he did soloistically. Indeed, they might be considered powerful symphonies with soloists.

Brahms's position as a composer of concertos, symphonies and other works was superbly summed up by critic James Gibbons Huneker: 'A Classicist and a Romanticist, he led music in her proper channels by showing that a phenomenal sense of form and a mastery of polyphony second only to Bach are not incompatible with progress, with a faculty of uttering new things in a new way ... Brahms reminds one of those medieval architects whose life was a prayer in marble; who slowly and assiduously erected cathedrals, the mighty abutments of which flanked majestically upon mother earth, and whose thin, high pinnacles pierced the blue; whose domes hung suspended between heaven and earth, and in whose nave any army could worship, while in the forest of arches music came and went like the voices of many waters ... Whatever he wrought, he wrought in bronze and for time, not for the hour. He restored to music its feeling of form. He was the greatest symphonist in the constructivist sense since Beethoven ... Brahms is the first composer since Beethoven to sound the note of the sublime ... A pure musician, a maker of absolute music, a man of poetic ideals is Brahms, without thrusting himself forward in the contemporary canvas. Not Berlioz, not Wagner, but the plodding genius Brahms was elected by destiny to receive upon his shoulders the mantle dropped by Beethoven as he ascended the slope to Parnassus, and the shoulders were broad enough to bear the imposing weight.'

In the spring of 1877, with his friend Dr Theodor Billroth, Brahms journeyed to Italy for the first time—to Rome, Naples and Sicily. Returning to Austria and the town of Pörtschach, while still imbued with the flavour of Italy, he sketched the themes of his titanic Piano Concerto No. 2. He then seems to have put these sketches aside until three years later, when he again visited Italy in the spring—this time Venice, Florence, Siena, Orvieto, Rome, Naples and Sicily. Back in Vienna, he resumed work on the Concerto once more with this Italian sojourn in mind. Two months later, on 7th July 1881, the score was completed. That same month he wrote in a letter to Elisabeth von Herzogenberg: 'I don't mind telling you that I have written a tiny, tiny *pianoforte concerto* with

a tiny, tiny wisp of a *scherzo*. It is in B flat, and I have good reason to fear that I have worked this udder, which has yielded good milk before, too often and too vigorously.'

This 'tiny' concerto turned out to be nothing less than the monumental Second Piano Concerto in B flat major, and the 'tiny' wisp of a scherzo is the monumental *Allegro appassionato* section Brahms inserted between the opening and slow movements, thus giving the Concerto a four-movement symphonic form of spaciousness and breadth. The critic Hanslick was to dub the piece 'a symphony with piano obbligato.' And in the early years after the Concerto was premièred (9th November 1881, in Budapest, with Brahms as the soloist), the presence of this scherzo section puzzled its audiences. The English musicologist Donald Francis Tovey brilliantly answered the question of the relevance of the scherzo to the other three movements: 'Of all existing concertos in the Classical form this is the largest. It is true that the first movement is shorter than either that of Beethoven's E flat Concerto or that of his Violin Concerto; shorter also than that of Brahms's own First Concerto. But in almost every Clas-

Brahms with a group of friends (Society of the Friends of Music, Vienna)

11

sical concerto the first movement is as large or larger than the slow movement and finale taken together, and there is no scherzo. Here, in his B flat Concerto, Brahms has followed the first movement by a fiery, almost tragic *Allegro* which, though anything but a joke, more than fills the place of the largest possible symphonic scherzo; the slow movement is easily the largest in any concerto, while the finale, with all its lightness of touch, is a rondo of the most spacious design. We thus have the three normal movements of the Classical concerto at their fullest and richest, with the addition of a fourth member on the same scale.'

Tovey goes on to say that the first movement with its stormy episodes is perfectly complemented by this stormy second movement—and that the Andante third movement, brimming with poetry, brings with it a calming, safe feeling. 'And now we have the finale. What tremendous triumph shall it express? Brahms's answer is such as only the greatest of artists can find; there are no adequate words for it (there never are for any art that is not itself words—and then there are only its own words). But it is, perhaps, not misleading to say here, as can so often be said with Beethoven, something like this: "We have done our work—let the children play in the world which our work has made safer and happier for them".'

The first movement of the B flat major Concerto (*Allegro non troppo*) begins quietly and dreamily with a beautiful, mellow horn solo, the theme of which dominates the entire section. This is echoed by the solo piano arpeggios and then lyrically continued by woodwinds and violins. The piano then plunges heroically into a jagged solo cadenza, followed by a return to the original theme by the full orchestra and the first appearance of a second, more lyrical theme in the violins. Both themes are elaborated upon before still another melody is offered by the lower strings, horns and bassoons. The central section of the movement is a stormy development of all these ideas, but with primary emphasis on the opening horn call; this ultimately ushers in the brilliant closing material, consisting of flashing octave trills for the solo piano set against fanfare-like reiterations of the horn call.

Composers have rarely included a scherzo movement in the piano concerto form, but Brahms conceived one of symphonic proportions, richness and tragic vitality. This section (*Allegro appassionato*) begins with a massive, crashing theme in the piano, while in the depths of the

orchestra the lower strings and horns pull in the opposite direction. In contrast to this cresting excitement, a plaintive melody for the violins is introduced and eventually taken up by the piano and developed in a typically Brahmsian rocking, see-saw figure. Both themes are developed, culminating in a heroic middle section, after which the opening material returns for a stormy close.

A solo cello launches the noble third movement (*Andante*) with a nostalgic melody, almost as if in counterbalance to the warmth of the French horn opening in the first movement. This melody, too, dominates the songful line of the movement, returning frequently with poetic effect. The violins repeat the material, and then the piano enters with a kind of variation on the theme. There follows a second variation, with fragments of the theme exchanged between orchestra and solo piano, the latter with dramatic figurations of trills and downward arpeggios. An episode of new material is heard in a dialogue between the clarinets and piano. Tovey has described it this way: 'The pianoforte is accompanied by two clarinets. The melody consists of a few notes spaced out like the first stars that penetrate the sky at sunset. When the strings join in, the calm is as deep as the ocean that we have witnessed in the storms of this gigantic piece of music.' The solo cello theme returns, embellished with delicate trills on the piano that rise higher and higher till they fade off into silence.

The genial rondo Finale (*Allegretto grazioso*) is an example of the Brahms who, in Robert Haven Schauffer's phrase, 'emitted music at a rate that reminds one of Caesar crossing the Alps while dictating letters to a dozen secretaries at once.' This begins with the brightly skipping principal theme played by the solo piano in octaves. It is repeated by the violins and then further extended in the solo part. When both sections have been worked over, the piano introduces two new contrasting themes (one a sprightly Hungarian-like tune), which are then taken over by the woodwinds. All these ideas—mainly branches from the trunk of the main theme—are developed and extended. The piano writing is extremely brilliant, particularly in the final return of the main theme, where the tempo grows faster. The Concerto concludes with glittering arpeggios for the piano and then a sudden, surging crescendo for full orchestra. Tovey rightly called this a 'great and child-like finale' for a Concerto filled with monolithic power and intense poetry.

Printed in the United States of America

His Life and Times 1810-1849

PROGRAM NOTES FOR THE POLONAISES, NOCTURNE, ETUDES AND MAZURKAS

By Robert Jacobson

fw

FUNK & WAGNALLS, INC.
NEW YORK, NEW YORK

Early life: 1810-30

Perhaps it is not surprising that early writings obscured biographical facts of Chopin's life behind a tangle of myth and invention, if only because these seemed to harmonise with the romantic and mysterious aspects of his music. Even the date of birth has only quite recently been established as 1st March 1810 in place of a previously accepted 22nd February. This was at Zelazowa Wola, a small village near Warsaw, and the house, now a Chopin museum, can still be seen. The composer's father was French yet had so completely identified with his adopted country that he never spoke of relatives in France. Later Chopin was to live 20 years in Paris without knowing that two aunts dwelt nearby. They in turn were unaware that their nephew was among the greatest musicians of the day.

Soon his family moved to Warsaw, and before long the boy grew intensely attracted to music. Piano lessons began in 1817 and he made the exceedingly rapid progress we should expect; indeed, his first composition, a polonaise, was written that same year and Chopin made his first public appearance in 1818, in a Gyrowetz concerto. A few other compositions followed, and his improvising began to lead towards that unique appreciation of the piano which was to be the basis of his art. By 1822 further keyboard instruction had become unnecessary, and the G sharp minor Polonaise was written. Chopin entered Warsaw High School the following year, was by now teaching himself harmony, and began attending closely to the peasants' music when on holiday. In 1825 he played to Tsar Alexander I and his opus 1, a rondo, was published. The 1826 Variations on *Der Schweizerbub* showed a great advance on previous compositions despite academic studies having lately taken precedence over music.

That same year Chopin entered the Warsaw Conservatoire to pursue, with Joseph Elsner, studies which had already begun privately. In 1826, too, came the *Rondo à la mazur*, the first work displaying genuinely personal qualities, and during his 1827 holiday he began the Variations on Mozart's *Là ci darem*, his earliest piece for piano and orchestra. While the Sonata op.4 is dully academic, other items, such as his Mazurka op.68 no.2 and Nocturne op.72 no.1 (both published posthumously), also sound an individual voice.

Hummel's brilliant playing was a source of inspiration in 1828, as was that of Paganini, who visited Warsaw the following year; indeed, it was soon after hearing the latter that Chopin began composing his own studies. In 1828, too, he got a first look at the outside world, visiting Berlin with a colleague of his father's, where they attended first-rate operatic performances. Back in Warsaw formal exercises were pursued at the Conservatoire while, besides taking a full part in the city's social life, Chopin worked at his own pieces, like the Fantasia on Polish Airs op.13 and the Krakowiak op.14, both for piano and orchestra, besides smaller items.

It became evident that Poland could offer Chopin little more in terms of musical education and that he must venture abroad. Money was, of course, lacking and on petitioning the Minister for Public Instruction in April 1829, his father was told, 'Funds cannot be used for the support of this class of artist.' Chopin, then, had to face the world without outside help, yet he could do so with a certain confidence. When he left the Conservatoire a few months later his final report said: 'Chopin, Frédéric (3rd-year student); outstanding abilities, musical genius, etc.'

Vienna was the obvious place to go first, being second only to Paris as a musical centre. Chopin's first concert, in August 1829, was extremely successful, the press waxing so enthusiastic over 'the indescribable perfection of his technique' that a second concert had to be given. He was drawn back to Warsaw, however, partly by his love for Constantia Gladkowska, a charming singer, once his fellow student, and partly by the thought of his unfinished F minor Concerto. Perhaps because he expected to be abroad for a number of years and still had his name to make, that love was never declared, but the completed F minor concerto was heard, with full orchestra, in a concert at the Warsaw National Theatre the following March (1830). Despite some of the reviews of his Vienna concerts being misleadingly translated in the Warsaw papers, public curiosity had been aroused and the theatre was sold out three days in advance. Besides the Concerto, he played his Fantasia on Polish Airs, everyone being delighted except Chopin himself, who had perhaps made a mistake in performing on his own quiet-voiced piano. The press notices, however, were long and appreciative, showing real understanding. For instance: 'His gayest melodies are tinged with a certain melancholy by the power of which he draws the listener along with him . . . The land which gave him birth gave him also her melody, which forces its way to the surface again and again in the works of this artist. More than once these tones seem to be the happy echo of our native harmony; Chopin knows what sounds are heard in our fields and woods, he has listened to the song of the Polish villager, he has made it his own, and has united the tunes of his native soil in skilful composition and elegant execution.'

So many were turned away from this concert that, as in Vienna, another had to be given, these two events marking the climax of Chopin's success in his native land. But much remained to be done before he could leave. His other concerto, the E minor, had to be finished, and he found it hard to begin sustained work. Besides some of the op.10 Etudes, the Nocturnes, op.9 and the first two of op.15, were now in existence and prove that by this time Chopin was perfectly sure of his true path as a composer, however uncertain his material future seemed. Finally the E minor was completed and heard at his final Warsaw concert. That was in October 1830, and the following month Chopin left Poland forever.

Recognition in Paris: Life 1830-37

With Poland behind him forever, Chopin arrived at Vienna for the second time on 24th November 1830. On the 29th, Warsaw revolted against the Russians. Little sympathy was to be had in Vienna, for Austria had taken its share of the spoils resulting from the partitions of Polish territory, and Chopin experienced the greatest anxiety over the fate of his family and friends. His moods were, however, extremely variable, as is shown by his letters, and these fluctuations – despair succeeded by nonchalance, enthusiastic outbursts alternating with cynicism – remained characteristic. Actually, the family was safe, and his father urged him to stay in Vienna for a while.

Concerts were hard to arrange because of the unrest, and Chopin did not finally appear in public until the following April, when he played his E minor Concerto without attracting much attention. It is difficult to guess why he remained indecisively in Vienna for so long, unless he felt reluctant to move further still from home in such troubled times. The defiant, strife-torn Scherzo op.20 hints at his state of mind, especially when the Trio's peaceful atmosphere, based on an old Polish lullaby, is suddenly obliterated by the battle's return.

An intended visit to Italy was now impossible, so in June Chopin decided finally to try Paris. Temporarily stranded in Munich through a delay in funds arriving from home, he gave a successful concert on 28th August before passing to Stuttgart. There he learnt that Warsaw had fallen on 8th September, and this disaster to Polish hopes again threw him into despair. Yet by the middle of the month he was in Paris, which was to be his second home and the city from which his fame would spread over the whole civilised world.

Paris as Chopin found it that autumn is described later on, but he may well initially have felt bewildered by the sheer quantity of artistic and intellectual activity, unparalleled in Vienna, let alone Warsaw. Fortunately he carried letters of introduction and so quickly met well-known musicians. Their prompt recognition of his genius was confirmed by Chopin's first Paris concert on 26th February of the following year (1832), and this placed him in the front rank of pianists. Liszt and Mendelssohn applauded furiously, and the *Revue Musicale* wrote: 'Piano music is generally written in certain conventional forms that may be regarded as basic and that have been continually reproduced for over thirty years. It is one of the defects

Kwiatkowski's watercolour of a Polish dance (National Museum, Warsaw)

of this type of music, and our most skilful artists have not succeeded in ridding their works of it. But here is a young man who, surrendering himself to his natural impressions... has found, if not a complete renewal of piano music, at least a part of that which we have long sought in vain, namely an abundance of original ideas of a kind to be found nowhere else.... I find in Chopin's inspirations the signs of a renewal of forms which may henceforth exercise considerable influence upon this branch of the art.'

Besides his musical friends, Chopin turned to the numerous Polish emigrés living in Paris. He had first come to the attention of the Czartoryskis, Potockis, Radziwills and other aristocratic families long ago during 1818 when he appeared in Warsaw as a child prodigy, and these now provided the key to his material success. Prince Valentin Radziwill introduced Chopin to the extremely powerful Paris Rothschilds; and his acceptance by the fashionable world of which they were a centre soon led to his being asked to give piano lessons to the daughters of aristocratic families. Before long his income from teaching was very considerable, the envy of his less fortunate fellow exiles. After his death most of Chopin's furniture was sent to Warsaw, there to be destroyed by the Russians in 1863, but a few surviving items give a vivid impression of the atmosphere of elegance and distinction in which he lived once established in Paris.

Chopin still occasionally appeared in public, as in December 1833 when, together with Hiller and Liszt, he took part in movements from Bach's Concerto for three pianos (written for harpsichords) at the Conservatoire, or when he played his E minor Concerto at Rouen with great success. But he was temperamentally as unsuited to public performance as was his style of playing and, secure in his teaching, he was not sorry to leave the virtuoso's life behind.

Now that he was settled, Chopin began systematic publication of his works. The Mazurkas opp.6 and 7 appeared in December 1832 and the B flat number of op.7 enjoyed great popularity. Chopin was capable of driving a hard bargain in business matters yet had no difficulty in finding publishers, and his compositions were generally well received by critics in France and Germany.

Only rarely did Chopin leave Paris during this period, but in May 1834 he accepted Hiller's invitation to visit the Lower Rhineland Festival at Aachen, the only event of this kind he ever attended. The following year his parents went to Carlsbad and he journeyed there to meet them – for the last time. By now Chopin was in love again, and far more seriously than with Constantia Gladkowska a few years before. He had known Maria Wodzińska as a child in Poland and had given her piano lessons. Besides being an excellent pianist, she had grown into an extremely attractive girl who had made a considerable impression on the poet Slowacki and on the future Napoleon III. At first her aristocratic family seemed to favour their friendship and Chopin and Maria eventually became engaged. Already his health was giving cause for concern, however, a rumour of his death even circulating in 1835, and chiefly for this reason the engagement was broken off in 1837. But this was done in a cold, heartless manner that wounded Chopin deeply. After his death twelve years later, a packet was found among his effects containing all his letters from the Wodzińskis; he had labelled it *Moja Bieda* (My Misery).

Mediterranean Romance: Life 1837-39

By the time his engagement to Maria Wodzińska was broken off in 1837 Chopin had already met Aurore Dudevant – or George Sand, to give her the name under which her books were published and by which she is usually known. Indeed, they had met the previous year, being introduced by Liszt. The composer was by then a rather different person from the eager, naive youth who had reached Paris in 1831, having grown into one of the most original musicians of the day, his confidence in his own powers fully justified by a distinguished list of works. In the year he and George Sand met, for example, Chopin published his F minor Concerto op.21, the Andante spianato and Grande Polonaise op.22, his first Ballade op.23, the four Mazurkas op.24, his two Polonaises op.26 and the pair of Nocturnes op.27.

In April 1837 George Sand invited him, together with Liszt and the Countess d'Agoult, to stay at Nohant, her country house near Châteauroux in the Berry province of France. He did not go, but once he knew, later that year, that all hope of a happy marriage to Maria was lost he had no reason to hold back. Soon a warm friendship became something very much more.

There were several reasons for their leaving Paris quickly. First, George Sand was threatened by one Mallefille, a former lover whom she had cast aside for Chopin. Secondly, the composer's health continued to give cause for anxiety. They were misled by friends who had never been there into believing Majorca to be an ideal retreat, full of sunshine and fresh air, and they resolved to pass the winter and spring of 1838–39 there. Preparations were made in great secrecy, Chopin selling his Preludes op.28 to a publisher for 2000 francs to provide funds. George Sand left Paris on 18th October to be joined by Chopin at Perpignan on the 29th or 30th. He arrived, she wrote, looking 'as fresh as a rose and as pink as a beetroot – *and* in good health, having stood up like a hero to his four nights in a stage-coach.... Our trip is beginning "under the happiest auspices", as the saying goes: the sky is wonderful.' Chopin took along his unfinished manuscripts, his Bach volumes which he never tired of studying, lots of music paper, and was, we may be sure, already thinking about all the music he would write.

At first everything seemed to go well, and Chopin wrote to a friend in Paris:

'Here I am at Palma, among palms, cedars, cacti, olive trees, oranges, lemons, aloes, figs, pomegranates, etc. – everything that is to be found in the hot-houses of the Jardins des Plantes. The sky is like turquoise, the sea like lapis lazuli, the mountains like emerald and the air like Heaven. In the daytime, sunshine; everyone goes about in summer clothes and it's hot. At night, guitars and songs for hours on end. Enormous balconies with overhanging vines: Moorish ramparts. Everything, including the town, has an African look. In a word, life is marvellous.'

After staying in Establiments, a village near Palma, they moved to the deserted monastery at Valldemosa, in those days a wild and remote place. George Sand wrote during November:

'I have also reserved a cell, i.e. three rooms and a garden, for 35 francs a year in the monastery of Valldemosa – a huge and splendid deserted place in the mountains. Our garden is strewn with oranges and lemons; the trees are cracking beneath their burden.... Vast cloisters of the most beautiful architecture, a delightful church, a cemetery with a palm tree and a stone cross like the one in the Third Act of *Robert le Diable*. The only inhabitants of the place, besides ourselves, are an old serving-woman and the sacristan, our steward, doorkeeper and major-domo rolled into one. I hope we shall have some ghosts. My cell door looks on to a huge cloister, and when the wind slams the door it rumbles like gunfire through the monastery. You see that I shall not lack poetry and solitude.'

But when the weather broke and there were frequent storms, Chopin's health soon deteriorated alarmingly and local doctors were little help. Due, no doubt, to their gossip, the rumour circulated that the composer was a consumptive, and he was regarded by the local population with horror. Yet as so often when his condition gave rise to despair, Chopin rallied surprisingly. As George Sand wrote: 'His goodness and patience are angelic. We are so different from most of the people and things around us ... our family ties are only more strengthened by it and we cling to each other with more affection and intimate happiness.'

In fact their stay must have included many good days. In January 1839 Chopin's piano finally arrived and he finished the Polonaise op.40 no.2 and began the Scherzo op.39.

In February he sent to Paris fair copies of the Ballade op.38 and both op.40 Polonaises. But they were glad to leave Majorca as soon as weather permitted. Despite his recovery, anxiety over Chopin's health had continued and the primitive conditions, combined with the poor climate so different from what they had expected, led them to detest the place. As George Sand confessed, their venture had been a 'complete fiasco.'

A view of Valldemosa from the Carthusian monastery in a print by Laurens (Frederyk Chopin and George Sand Museum, Valldemosa)

The Return to France: Life 1840-49

After leaving Majorca thankfully behind, Chopin and George Sand stayed for a while at Marseilles. The composer had had a bad crossing, yet again recovered quickly. They paid a short visit to Genoa before going on to Nohant, George Sand's country home, for the rest of the summer of 1839. She wrote of Chopin, 'He has a splendid piano and delights us from morning to evening. He has written some ravishing things since he has been here.' Chopin had indeed found a productive mood again and during that summer composed three of his op.41 Mazurkas, the Impromptu op.36, his Nocturne op.37 no.2, and the opening movement, scherzo and finale of his Sonata op.35 – the funeral march for which had been written in 1837.

With the autumn it was time to return at last to Paris and his pupils. Among his first visitors was the distinguished pianist and composer Moscheles, for whom Chopin played his new Sonata among other things. Moscheles said it was the first time he had understood Chopin's music – a hint, perhaps, of the misinterpretations to which it was subject even then.

Although Chopin and George Sand did not go to Nohant in 1840, their routine during their remaining years together until 1846 did not change. Once the concert and teaching season was finished they went to Nohant until October or early November, with friends arriving to stay with them for a few weeks at a time. During this period, therefore, Chopin's life was outwardly almost without incident. His two recitals in 1841 and 1842, his father's death in 1844 and a visit by his

A drawing of Chopin at the piano in 1838 (Polish Library, Paris)

sister Louise that same year are virtually the only events to be recorded. Yet it was during these peaceful days, with nothing to disrupt his mental and spiritual equilibrium, that his genius reached its height in a virtually unbroken sequence of masterpieces. Writing in 1842, the great painter Delacroix gives us an idea of the tranquillity amidst which they were created:

'When you are not assembled for dinner or lunch or billiards or for walks, you can go and read in your room or sprawl on your sofa. Every now and then there blows in through your window, opening on to the garden, a breath of the music of Chopin, who is at work in his room, and it mingles with the song of the nightingales and the scent of the roses . . . I have endless conversations with Chopin of whom I am really very fond and who is a man of rare distinction. He is the truest artist I have ever met, one of the very few one can admire and value.'

The summer of 1844 probably marked the highest point of Chopin's and George Sand's happiness together. From that time onwards the situation began to deteriorate, just as the composer's health weakened as consumption increased its hold on him. George Sand's children, Maurice and Solange, were growing up and beginning to assert themselves. The story of her break with Chopin is too complex to be retold here, but is a tangle of acrimonious family quarrels in which both Solange and Maurice played extremely discreditable parts. Even on his last visit to Nohant, in 1846, he found it difficult to compose. The Barcarolle op.60 and Polonaise-Fantasy op.61, two of his greatest pieces, were finished then, but never again, after November 1846, did Chopin find the right working conditions and the final three years of his life were almost wasted.

His health continued to decline yet he was as busy as ever in Paris, where he stayed, alone, throughout 1847. It was during October of this year, too, that he published his last significant works, the Mazurkas op.63, his Waltzes op.64 and the Cello Sonata op.65. In February 1848, a week before the revolution erupted in Paris, Chopin gave his last concert there. Despite his physical weakness, his playing held listeners as spellbound as ever, yet this event may be taken as the virtual close to his career. More than that, with the revolution's success an epoch had ended. Just as the break with George Sand removed the only human contact that could give stability to his so highly strung nerves and emotions, the removal of Louis-Philippe from the throne of France destroyed the only society in which Chopin could exist.

He must have felt that Paris, his home for half of his lifetime, no longer had any place for him, and he readily accepted an invitation from his Scots pupil Jane Stirling to visit England and Scotland. The story of that melancholy sojourn is told in his despairing letters. When he returned to Paris during November 1848 Chopin was a dying man. His decline did not follow a regular course and there were days when he seemed stronger. While these periods grew rarer and more brief, he was still able to compose a little. The Mazurkas op.67 no.2 and 68 no.4 were written at this time, the second, his actual last composition, still bearing witness to his harmonic adventurousness. Now, also, came his final song, *Melodia* ('From the hills, where they carried the load of nightmarish crosses, they saw from a distance the promised land').

Chopin died on 17th October 1849 at about two o'clock in the morning. Later that day casts were taken of his face and hands, and Kwiatkowski made several sketches of his head. There was a post-mortem and his heart was sent in an urn to Poland, where it rests at the church of the Holy Cross in Warsaw. The funeral at the Madeleine was not until 30th October but was of exceptional splendour. A packed church heard Mozart's Requiem, which had not been performed in Paris since Napoleon's remains were brought from St Helena to the Invalides in 1840. From the Madeleine a long procession passed along the Grands Boulevards to the Père-Lachaise cemetery. Contrary to the custom of that time, there was no oration at the graveside, and when all was finished the large crowd departed in silence.

Chopin and George Sand

Aurore Dudevant was 32 when she met Chopin, and already, for that time, a woman of unusual experience. Married at 18, she had soon grown tired of her boring husband and the provincial existence he led. She went to Paris in 1831 – the same year as Chopin, as it happens – determined to lead that life of total freedom which was the young Romantics' ideal. It stands to reason that this entailed a series of love affairs, yet Mme Dudevant became equally involved in the city's very flourishing literary and artistic life. For a time she wore men's clothes, ostensibly to be able to join more freely in male society but in fact, surely, to draw attention to herself. Yet that was only a temporary phase because she discovered she could write. Most of her books might be unreadable now, but novels like *Indiana* (1831) or *Lélia* (1833) quickly won her a European reputation due to their attacks on such social institutions as marriage. She adopted the pseudonym of 'George Sand' for the publication of *Indiana* and that name soon became synonymous in the conventional mind with socialism, revolution and, perhaps worse, the break-down of family life. Needless to say, she was regarded with particular horror in England.

By 1836 the process of legal separation from her husband was complete, and George Sand was left with a considerable fortune, the custody of her two children, Solange and Maurice, and an estate at Nohant. She had met Liszt and his mistress the Countess d'Agoult, and, as we saw above, in the autumn of 1836, just after he had become engaged to Maria Wodzińska, she was introduced to Chopin. His first impressions were apparently not favourable. This would be partly because his mind was naturally full of Maria, yet partly also because of George Sand's rather notorious adventures. Chopin had at times an exaggerated regard for social conventions that might be seen as a counterbalance to his disregard for musical rules and regulations. But his aversion did not last, for George Sand was a woman of very considerable charm and accomplishment. For example, one of the finest existing portraits of Chopin is by her, and her interest in music was genuine. An engaging description of her appearance and behaviour at a soirée given by Chopin not long after they had met is written by Joseph Brzowski:

'Madame G. Sand, dark, dignified and cold . . . regular features, calm, or rather inanimate in their expression, in which one could only perceive intelligence, reflection and pride. Her dress fantastic (obviously proclaiming her desire to be noticed), composed of a white frock with a crimson sash and a kind of white shepherdess's corsage with crimson buttons. Her dark hair parted in the middle, falling in curls on both sides of her face and secured with a ribbon around her brow. Nonchalantly she took her place on the sofa near the fireplace and, lightly blowing out clouds of smoke from her cigar, answered briefly but seriously the questions of the men sitting beside her. ∴ . . After Liszt and he had played a sonata, Chopin offered his guests ices. George Sand, glued to her sofa, never quitted her cigar for a moment.'

UN HIVER

A

MAJORQUE

PAR

GEORGE SAND.

1

BIBLIOTHÈQUE ROYALE

I

PARIS,

HIPPOLYTE SOUVERAIN, ÉDITEUR

de F. Soulié, H. de Balzac, A. Luchet, J. Lecomte, Paul de Kock, A. Brot, etc.

Rue des Beaux-Arts, 5.

1842

She may have seen Chopin's polite reserve as a challenge to her own powers, yet she quickly succumbed to the fascination of his personality and music. That reserve was impenetrable except to a very few Polish intimates, as George Sand eventually realised, but part of his attraction for her may have lain in the impression he conveyed, and which was remarked on by many who saw him, of a fiery, passionate spirit dwelling in a frail body. He was of unusually slight physique, yet his whole being was characterised by distinction and refinement. This implies no effeminacy or ineffectualness, for Chopin was perfectly capable of getting his own way – that side of his nature being apparent, for example, in his hard bargaining with publishers. The idea that George Sand was the dominant partner is at best a simplification, as is shown by a remark of the poet Mickiewicz, who often saw them at close quarters: 'Chopin is her evil genius, her moral vampire, her cross; he tortures her and will probably end by killing her.'

That is an exaggeration, no doubt, but she revered him as a musician besides looking after him with great devotion. For how long Chopin was her lover in the usual sense of that term is uncertain, yet his life was bound up with George Sand's almost until the end. Once her support was withdrawn his composing stopped and, as we shall see, his life went to pieces. This was not just because only she knew what steps were necessary to preserve his health, but because he needed somebody near to provide companionship and security, and to love him and understand him so far as anyone could.

However much she may later have misrepresented events in her *Histoire de ma vie* or have fictionalised them in her novel *Lucrezia Floriani*, our debt to Aurore Dudevant is a considerable one. From 1839-46 Chopin was shielded from all material stresses, his day-to-day life was smoothly organised and he was free to devote himself to composition and teaching. Each summer (with the exception of 1840) was spent quietly in the country at Nohant, where much of his composing was done. He had the sunniest room in the house and the routine was arranged to suit his wishes – compare this to the struggles of Berlioz or Wagner! The ending of this relationship caused Chopin much pain, and was brought about largely through intrigues by George Sand's malicious offspring, Maurice and Solange. But for several years conditions were maintained in which his art could flower in untroubled freedom, and it was then he wrote his greatest works. When hearing them we ought surely to remember with gratitude the woman without whom they might not have been composed.

9

PROGRAM NOTES FOR THE RECORD

by ROBERT JACOBSON

As one critic has written, 'Chopin was a phoenix of intimacy with the piano.' Moreover, Frédéric Chopin revelled not only in the piano per se but particularly in brief solo pieces, poetically working the various forms of etudes, polonaises, nocturnes, and so on, into a new carat of artistic gold. Because of his uniqueness as a composer for the piano, he was to influence almost everyone else who came after him; yet his inventiveness and originality at the very height of the Romantic movement demonstrated that he bore few ties with what had come before.

As a pianist and a composer for the piano sans pareil, Chopin revolutionised piano technique by introducing new dynamics and sonorities, brilliant and daring virtuosity, and new modes of composition. Through his hundreds of piano pieces he created a new era in piano music and keyboard playing—one that was to lead to Liszt and his school, to Debussy, and on to the modern school of

pianism as we know it. What typifies his work is an innate elegance and perfection in the structuring of a piece, as well as striking originality of musical thought. Unendingly beautiful, his melodies were influenced, as he himself admitted, by the sensuous unfolding bel canto lines of Bellini, Donizetti and Rossini. In the manner of the singers of his time, he added exquisite embellishments and ornamentation to enhance the simple, affecting melodic line. To this he further contributed a revolutionary sense of harmony, tonality and dissonance. As a pianist, he strove for ease, suppleness, grace, colour, a singing liquid tone and a smooth keyboard touch. He also made new use of the pedal to achieve haunting sonorities and coloration.

The salons of the period influenced Chopin in the dance forms he adopted; he turned out dozens of waltzes, mazurkas, and polonaises. And fused with this choice was

19th-century print of a harvest festival in the district of Sandomir (Polish Library, Paris)

his deep Polish nationalism which, besides impassioned political sentiment, left its mark on much of his music through Polish dance forms and the distinctive tonalities of Polish folk music. Composer Anton Rubinstein summed it up when he said: 'The piano bard, the piano rhapsodist, the piano mind, the piano soul is Chopin. . . . Tragic, romantic, lyric, heroic, dramatic, fantastic, soulful, sweet, dreamy, brilliant, grand, simple; all possible expressions are found in his compositions and all are sung by him upon his instrument. . . . In all of his compositions we hear him relate rejoicingly of Poland's vanished greatness, singing, mourning, weeping over Poland's downfall and all that, in the most beautiful, the most musical way.' A later biographer, James Huneker, commented: 'Chopin's music is the aesthetic symbol of a personality nurtured on patriotism, pride and love; that it is better expressed by the piano is because of that instrument's idiosyncrasies of evanescent tone, sensitive touch and wide range in dynamics. It was Chopin's lyre, the "orchestra of his heart"; from it he extorted music the most intimate since Sappho. Among lyric moderns, Heine closely resembles the Pole.'

The Polonaises

Huneker calls Chopin's polonaises 'heroic hymns of battle. Along with the ballades, scherzos, etudes and some of the preludes, these works brought forth some of Chopin's most masculine writing, and gave vent to the fiery side of his nature. 'Chopin put his patriotism, his wrath and his heroism into his polonaises,' the biographer has written. Along with the mazurkas, the polonaises are the composer's most Polish works. And they reveal his two sides: the objective, martial character versus the moody, morose one. As a dance, the polonaise originated towards the end of the 16th century as a courtly procession of aristocratic couples to the sound of music; it came to symbolize war and love, a pageant of martial splendour involving fierce warriors and noble women. In Chopin's hands the polonaise became an ode to ancestral glory, a grand tapestry of emotions. Franz Liszt wrote, 'In this form the noblest traditional feelings of ancient Poland are represented. The polonaise is the true and purest type of Polish national character. . . . They belong to the most beautiful of Chopin's inspirations.'

Opus 44

Chopin wrote some 18 polonaises for the piano and other instruments between 1817 and 1846. Liszt called the F sharp minor Polonaise (op. 44) a dream poem, the 'lurid hour that precedes a hurricane,' with a 'convulsive shudder at the close.' It opens impressively, and the first theme has defiant power. The middle section is a ghostly mazurka, separating the other two tempestuous sections and

ending like an agitated nightmare. Huneker says it is 'a confession from the dark depths of a self-tortured soul.'

Opus 53

One writer described the A flat Polonaise (op. 53) as 'the story of Chopin's vision of the antique dead in an isolated tower of Madame Sand's chateau at Nohant.' Though less feverish than its predecessor, this one is nicknamed the 'Héroïque' and thrills with the thunder of horses' hoofs and strident challenges. Its sonorous picture of battles and martial glory fairly brims with excitement and brilliant effect.

Opus 40 no.1

Probably the most celebrated of the polonaises is the A major (op. 40), the so-called 'Military,' a work of great pianistic brilliance and muscularity, with massive chords and a forceful main subject. To Anton Rubinstein this composition was a tone portrait of Poland's centuries-old greatness. The story is told that, after composing it, Chopin was terrified in the dreary watches of the night by the opening of his door and the entrance of a spectral procession of richly robed Polish nobles and ladies. Startled by these ghosts of the past conjured up by his music, the composer is said to have fled the apartment.

Nocturne

Opus 27 no. 1

The nocturne, or 'night piece,' originated with an Irish composer of sentimental genre music named John Field, but Chopin raised the form to a new plateau by infusing it with dramatic breadth, passion and a characteristic poetic grandeur. His compositions in this vein are true nocturnal reveries, filled with agitated or faint whispers and poignant remorse. The Nocturne in C sharp minor is one of the greatest examples of this form. In it one commentator finds 'a description of a calm night at Venice, where, after a scene of murder, the sea closes over a corpse and continues to serve as a mirror to the moonlight.' A persistent melody builds in fervour, only to move into a more positive theme and then return to the plaintive opening. It is marked by a psychological tension and dramatic spirit that are quite beyond the bounds of the traditional nocturne.

The Etudes

The word 'etude' actually means a study, and Chopin's predecessors wrote such compositions mainly for piano students to perfect specific aspects of their keyboard technique. Through his constant inventiveness and pianistic magic, however, Chopin raised the prosaic etude to new artistic heights. In this form as well, he revealed a titanic temperament that was often obscured by the Romantic softness of his appearance and the attitudes prevalent at the time.

Opus 10 no. 3

Chopin began writing etudes quite early; his Opus 10 was composed between 1829 and 1832. The dozen études of this opus were dedicated to Franz Liszt. Chopin conveys great intimacy in No. 3 in E, which is considered one of his choicest. The critic Niecks wrote that it 'may be counted among Chopin's loveliest compositions,' since it combines 'classical chasteness of contour with the fragrance of romanticism.' Chopin himself told a friend that he had never in his life written another such melody and once, on hearing it, raised his arms and cried out, 'Oh, ma patrie!' (Oh, my country!). A study in expressivity, it recalls the nocturne style in its softly poetic evocation of atmosphere.

Opus 10 no. 5

The fifth etude of Opus 10 is generally known as the 'Black Key,' since it is mainly played on the black keys of the piano. Combining grace and wit, archness and invention, it is full of Polish elegance. The pianist needs a particularly smooth, velvety touch for this ingeniously conceived work.

Opus 25 no. 1

Opus 25 opens with the familiar study in A flat, commonly referred to as the 'Aeolian Harp.' After hearing Chopin play it, Robert Schumann wrote: 'Imagine that an aeolian harp possessed all the musical scales, and that the hand of an artist were to cause them all to intermingle in all sorts of fantastic embellishments, yet in such a way as to leave everywhere a deep fundament tone and a soft continuously singing upper voice, and you will get the right idea of his playing. . . . After the etude a feeling came over one as of having seen in a dream a beatific picture which when half-awake one would gladly recall.'

Opus 25 no. 5

The Etude No. 5 in E minor is a sonorous piano piece, richly embroidered in the middle section. Kullak has noted that it is most important for the pianist to master the deep rhythmic life of this work. 'If, in addition, he possesses a fine feeling for what is graceful, coquettish, or agreeably capricious, he will understand how to heighten still further the charm of the chief part.'

The Mazurkas

Huneker called Chopin's mazurkas 'dances of the soul.' And Liszt observed: 'Coquetries, vanities, fantasies, inclinations, elegies, vague emotions, passions, conquests, struggles upon which the safety or favours of others depend—all, all meet in this dance.' The mazurka was a Polish women's dance, a sort of female counterpart to the more heroic strains of the masculine polonaise. It began as the local dance of the province of Mazovia, where it was called the *mazurek*, and conveys at once a sense of intoxication, humour, poetry and melancholy in its subtle shifts of tone.

As with the polonaise, Chopin took the framework of this ethnic dance, developed and enlarged it, and endowed it with choice melodies and piquant harmonies. Still, his mazurkas strongly retain the recognisable flavour of his native land and culture. 'The latent and unknown poetry which was only indicated in the original Polish mazurkas,' wrote Franz Liszt, 'was divined, developed and brought to light by Chopin. Preserving their rhythm, he ennobled their melody, enlarged their proportions; and—in order to paint more fully in these productions, which he loved to hear us call "pictures from the easel," the innumerable and widely differing emotions which agitate the heart during the progress of this dance . . . he wrought into their tissues harmonic lights and shadows, as new in themselves as were the subjects to which he adapted them.' Chopin produced some 50 mazurkas between 1825 and 1849, all showing intense concentration and conciseness in skillfully blending often widely diverse components.

Opus 7 no.1   Opus 41 no.1
Opus 24 no.4   Opus 68 no.4

The exotic flavour of the Mazurka in B flat major that opens Opus 7 is a familiar delight. This work is marked by expansiveness, elegance and ease. The Mazurka No. 4 in B flat minor (op. 24) carries intimations of the grandeur of Chopin's large-scale work yet to come. The Mazurka No. 1 in C sharp minor (op. 41) is a statement of unfailing courage, with a slight tinge of sadness. Here Chopin works the main theme in various ways and to startling effect; rhythmically, it is a fascinating study. The Mazurka No. 4 in F minor (op. 68) is said to be Chopin's final composition, and its spirit is one of decay, faltering weakness and dissolution. One of the 19th century's great musical geniuses, a significant innovator and memorable performer, the Polish composer died in Paris at the tragically early age of thirty-nine.

Printed in the United States of America

His Life and Times 1685-1750

PROGRAM NOTES FOR THE BRANDENBURG CONCERTOS NO. 2, NO. 6, AND THE CLAVIER CONCERTO IN D MINOR
By Robert Jacobson

fw

FUNK & WAGNALLS, INC.
NEW YORK, NEW YORK

Bach's Early Life

Grove's Dictionary of Music and Musicians lists separately thirty-eight Bachs, all related and all but the first three known to have been professional musicians. Number 32 of these, and by far the greatest, is Johann Sebastian Bach, born at Eisenach on 21st March 1685.

Little is known about his childhood. In 1692 or 1693 he entered the Gymnasium at Eisenach: the school provided the choir for St George's Church and sang at weddings and funerals. Sebastian also took part in the Currenden (processional singing through the streets) which had been famous in the neighbourhood for more than fifty years. He had no formal music lessons until after he left Eisenach, but his skill as a string player can be attributed to his father, who taught him to play the violin and viola.

In 1694 Sebastian's mother died, and after the death of his father the following year he was sent to Ohrdruf to live with his eldest brother, Johann Christoph the younger, who was then organist of St. Michael's Church there. Johann Christoph had been taught for three years by Johann Pachelbel, a famous organist, and was well qualified to continue Sebastian's musical education. From him Sebastian received his first music lessons: he learned quickly and eagerly, and no sooner had his brother given him one piece to learn than he would ask for something more difficult.

While Sebastian was at Ohrdruf he attended the Lyceum. When Sebastian entered the Ohrdruf Lyceum tuition there was still of a very high standard. He was usually near the top of his class, although he was considerably younger than the average age, and it seems likely that he was also a member of

Johann Ambrosius Bach, the composer's father. When his son was born Johann Ambrosius was town musician at Eisenach and he probably taught Sebastian to play the violin and viola (German State Library, Berlin)

the choir. In 1697 Elias Herder, a young musician, joined the staff of the Lyceum. He had been a member of the school of St Michael's Convent at Lüneburg for six years, and it was probably on his recommendation that Sebastian set out for Lüneburg with Georg Erdmann in 1700 when the increasing size of his brother's family forced him to leave Ohrdruf.

There had been a school attached to St Michael's at Lüneburg from the time of its foundation, and music was an important part of the curriculum even before the office of Cantor (director of music) was instituted in 1555. By the time Bach entered the school it consisted of two choral bodies: the 'Chorus Symphoniacus' and the Mettenchor (whose scholars received free board and lodging and were paid for their work). In April-May 1700 Bach's name, together with that of Erdmann, appears on the list of the Mettenchor. Although his voice broke soon afterwards and he was no longer able to sing in the choir, he remained at Lüneburg for three years, possibly maintained there by his skill as an instrumentalist.

Some sixty miles from Lüneburg was the Court of Celle – a miniature Versailles where French music was very popular. More than once Bach walked to Celle to hear the Court Orchestra – his first introduction to French music and to French instrumental technique – and it is even possible that he was temporarily employed there, for the orchestra never performed publicly, and it is otherwise uncertain how he obtained admittance.

Bach was not yet eighteen when he left Lüneburg, but he was already an accomplished musician and had discovered a natural talent for composition. Above all he was conspicuous for his promise as an organist, and it was in this field that he tried to obtain his first employment. A new organ was being built in the church of St Boniface at Arnstadt, a town with which the Bach family had been connected for many years, but it was not completed until the summer of 1703 and in the meantime Bach tried to find similar work elsewhere. It was probably at this time that he competed for the organistship at Sangerhausen which, although he was originally chosen by the selectors, he eventually failed to obtain owing to his youth. It was therefore his skill as a violinist which gained him his first appointment: on Easter Day 1703 he was enrolled in the household of the younger brother of the Duke of Weimar as a member of his chamber orchestra. It is possible that while at Weimar Bach deputised for Johann Effler, the organist; but he did not stay there long. By July the organ at Arnstadt had been completed, and the fact that Bach was called from Weimar to inspect it gives some indication of the height his reputation had already reached. The following Sunday, according to custom, Bach played the organ at an inaugural recital, and was immediately offered the post of organist. He received formal notice of his appointment on 9th August 1703.

In the late autumn of 1705 Bach decided that the time had come to achieve an unfulfilled ambition – a visit to

Lübeck to hear the great organist Buxtehude. He had saved enough money to face the three-hundred-mile journey with confidence, and he boldly asked for a month's leave.

When Bach returned to Arnstadt he had been away three months instead of one. This was reprehensible, but in addition the authorities soon discovered that their young organist had returned with revolutionary ideas about the accompaniment of hymns that dismayed and confused the congregation. On these points, and on the perennial question of choir-training, he was brought to book. The only result was that Bach, reacting like a very young man, went to the other extreme in his chorale playing, and remained obdurate about the choir. After leaving him alone for several months with extreme forbearance, the authorities tried once more to force him to deal with the choir and added an entirely new complaint of a personal nature. A 'stranger maiden' had been heard singing in the empty church to Bach's accompaniment – a highly improper proceeding in a building in which no woman should raise her voice except as a member of the congregation. The gossip behind this petty accusation finally made up Bach's mind for him. He determined to marry the musical 'stranger maiden', his second cousin Maria Barbara Bach, who was a grandchild of Old Heinrich like himself, and to look for a post elsewhere.

He found that an organist was required for the church of St Blaise at Mühlhausen, another of the free Imperial cities, and it would appear that he was in fact invited to apply for the post. He was unanimously appointed and his prospects appeared rosy. A legacy from a maternal relative came to hand just when he needed a little extra money, and on the strength of this he married Maria Barbara and set up a home of his own in October 1707.

At first things went well. Bach was very flatteringly invited to compose the official cantata for performance in the civic church of St Mary in celebration of the beginning of the town council's year in February. He produced *Gott ist mein König* (God is my King), scoring the work for all the available resources, and impressing the Council to such an extent that they ordered its publication. He also induced the authorities to have the St Blaise organ thoroughly overhauled, and enlarged by adding a third manual. But the pastor and congregation of his own church did not approve

An 18th-century print of the market place at Eisenach where Bach lived until he was ten years old (Thüringer Museum, Eisenach)

A 19th-century print of the Bach family tree (Bachhaus, Eisenach)

3

of the high-baroque style of church music, however suitable it might be for an official function; the new anti-formalist and Puritan spirit of Pietism had taken hold and the enthusiastic young composer found his activities curtailed.

Bach decided to resign. Mühlhausen was sorry to lose him, but the situation was so generally appreciated that he was released without any ill-feeling on either side, and he maintained contact with the many friends he had made there. As at Arnstadt, he was succeeded by a cousin, Johann Friedrich Bach.

During his short spell at Weimar in 1703 as chamber musician to Johann Ernst, Bach evidently had a chance to display his skill as organist as well as violinist. When in 1708 the reigning Duke Wilhelm Ernst required a new chamber-musician and organist, he was reminded of the brilliant young man who had been in his late brother's employ, and invited him to fill the vacancy. This flattering offer came at the right moment, enabling Bach to resign from his now untenable Mühlhausen post with dignity, and promising a full use of those talents which he was so anxious to employ to the glory of God.

His new employer, of whom he already knew something, was a remarkable and eccentric man. His life was founded on a sincerely held religious faith, which caused him to be a

Arnstadt: detail of the organ-pipes

most conscientious though thoroughly despotic ruler of his people. He imposed a strict regime on his household. Life in the moated Renaissance palace of Wilhelmsburg revolved round the services of the court chapel, known as 'Himmelsburg' (the City of Heaven), which everyone had to attend, and the music of which was the principal concern of the Kapell.

Meanwhile the new regime suited Bach admirably: with Salomo Franck at hand to provide the words, he set himself joyfully to fulfilling the conditions of his new appointment. He was also becoming very much the family man. Maria Barbara bore seven children at Weimar, of whom four survived infancy; two were to become famous in their own right, Wilhelm Friedemann and Carl Philipp Emanuel. His household also included apprentices, one of whom, Schubart, had lived with the young couple from the time of their marriage, and was to succeed as organist to the Court of Weimar. Bach had achieved a home in the true tradition of his family.

Apart from his journeys to test new organs, for which he had apparently no difficulty in securing approval at any time during his career, Bach seems to have begun at this time the habit of taking a period of leave in the early autumn to visit places where there was something of musical interest to attract him. He was certainly in Cassel in September 1714, when he played the organ before Friedrich of Hesse-Cassel (later to become King of Sweden), who was so impressed by a dazzling pedal-solo that he presented the player with a ring from his own princely hand.

In time, however, Bach was to find the undercurrents of Court life as unpleasant as the small-minded strictures of town councils or the bickerings of rival churches. When Leopold of Anhalt-Cöthen, a young and highly musical prince, came to visit his sister and her husband, Bach was there to make music. Leopold immediately fell under his spell, and when in August 1717 he needed to replace the Kapellmeister of his own recently formed Kapell, he invited Bach to fill the post. This was a most tempting offer to the unhappy Konzertmeister, but Bach did not decide immediately. He was awkwardly placed; resignation from a Court appointment was impossible, and his release depended on the whim of the Duke. In the existing state of affairs he could not count on goodwill from that quarter.

At first the Duke flatly refused to release him. It was bad enough to lose a valued servant, but to lose him through the agency of his despised nephew was altogether too much. A second application infuriated him to such a degree that he had Bach placed under detention in the Schloss. Bach spent the time by beginning the compilation of the 'Little Organ Book' of chorale preludes. But it was not to be completed; after a month the Duke told Bach that he was free to go elsewhere. In December 1717 he departed for Cöthen and a very different life.

Cöthen and Prince Leopold

It is tempting to think of Bach's time at Cöthen as a harmonious interlude in an otherwise 'troublous life'. His situation there was as congenial and productive as Haydn's was to be at Eszterháza, and he had no thought when he embarked on it but that he would end his days in Leopold's service. This is interesting in that Bach's declared bent had hitherto been towards church music, for which there was no official opportunity at Cöthen. The fact that he could cheerfully give up his chosen career for a branch of music on which he had so far made little impact is indeed surprising. Either Bach was heartily weary of the constant difficulties that had hampered him on his chosen path from Arnstadt onwards, or Prince Leopold was a very remarkable young man indeed. It was probably a mixture of both.

One member of the Cöthen Kapell is of special interest to us – Christian Ferdinand Abel, violinist and virtuoso viola-da-gambist, whose son Carl Friedrich, in partnership with Bach's youngest son Johann Christian, ran successful concerts in London for many years. Including Bach, the total number of the members of the Kapell was sixteen, offering a balance between wind and strings of the normal baroque standard with the trumpets (and their accompanying drums) as the only brass. For this body, as a whole, as individuals and in small groups, Bach wrote the greater part of his instrumental music, and all in under six years. It seems probable that he produced for Cöthen considerably more music than has survived, writing as he did for a prince whose admiration and devotion he reciprocated. But even so it is an impressive achievement.

In May 1718 Leopold took six members of the Kapell, including Bach, to Carlsbad when he went to take the waters in fashionable style. He was proud to display their abilities before the assembled aristocracy, and it may have been on this occasion that the Margrave of Brandenburg, a relative of the Elector, extracted a promise from Bach to provide him with some music for his own Kapell.

Life at Cöthen, congenial in every way, was given added pleasure by the realisation that the young family growing up round him was showing musical talent. On 22nd January 1720 Bach wrote the very first clavier exercises for his oldest son Friedemann in a 'Little Clavier-Book' which, added to from time to time as the pupil made his rapid progress, was to pass through the hands of all his brothers, down to the youngest, Johann Christian. But this happy domesticity was not lasting. In May 1720 Leopold took his Kapell to Carlsbad as before, but this time he kept them there till July. When Bach returned to his family after this long separation, he found to his great grief that Maria Barbara had died only a few days before, and was already buried. To his own distress was added anxiety about his

A print of 1757 showing Gisela Agnes, mother of Prince Leopold. It was due to her influence on Leopold's father that the Calvinist severity of Cöthen was relaxed enough for Bach's music to be played there

young children. He remembered all too vividly his own parents' death when he was Friedemann's age, and that in his own case the move to a new life with his elder brother at Ohrdruf had helped him.

As no other suitable posts offered themselves, Bach settled down to normal routine, bearing his widowerhood and coping with his motherless family as well as he could. He remembered his promise to the Margrave of Brandenburg, and began to collect together a set of six concertos to present to him. It is not known how many of these, if any, were specially composed for the purpose, or whether Bach even knew what were the resources of the Margrave's establishment. But they were all suited (except No. 1, which requires horns) to the Cöthen Kapell, and were frequently played by them. Even No. 1 was probably heard on one of the recorded occasions when visiting horn virtuosi came to Cöthen. The presentation score which Bach sent to the Margrave in March 1721 bears no signs of use, and the concertos may never have been heard by the dedicatee.

Until 1720 the Cöthen Kapell had not included singers, but during that year a young soprano, Anna Magdalena Wilcken, the daughter of a trumpeter at the court of Weissenfels, was appointed. During 1721 Bach became strongly attracted, and, in spite of the wide difference in age, he began to think that here was the wife and mother needed by the Bach household. He had no difficulty in obtaining

Leopold's permission; the Prince himself was contemplating marriage with his cousin Friederica Henriette of Anhalt-Bernburg, and in December first the Kapellmeister and a few days later the Prince were married. After the gay celebrations of the royal wedding were over, Bach and Anna Magdalena settled down to a life of mutual contentment, which was to remain undisturbed through all the difficulties which lay ahead.

Occupied with his official work and happy in his home, Bach did not at first realise that the atmosphere of Cöthen was changing. He was also busy during 1722 in composing and compiling not only the 'Well-Tempered Clavier', but also the French and English Suites and the Inventions and Sinfonias, all useful in the instruction of his sons and pupils. But he could not avoid noticing that since Leopold's marriage to a girl whom Bach later described as an 'amusa' his interest in the music that his Kapellmeister produced was lessening. Doubtless his affectionate nature gave in quite understandably to the fancies of a frivolous bride. A move

A plan of the town of Cöthen in a print of 1730

from Cöthen appeared inevitable, if Bach's abilities were to continue to find adequate expression. There was also anxiety about the education of his children. The small Lutheran school in Cöthen was hardly adequate, and a position in a town that could provide better schooling for his sons, and the hope of a university career to follow, seemed desirable. When Bach heard in June 1722 that Kuhnau, Cantor of St Thomas's in Leipzig, had died, he decided to apply.

The negotiations were protracted, and, as the delay was due entirely to conditions in Leipzig they will be discussed later on. Leopold put no difficulties in Bach's way, and though his young bride died on 4th April 1723, it was too late to beg his Kapellmeister to remain. Bach was by that time fully committed to Leipzig, where he was installed on 22nd April. He and Leopold parted with heavy hearts, but they kept in touch, and the Prince welcomed Bach and Anna Magdalena to his court on many occasions until his own early death in November 1728.

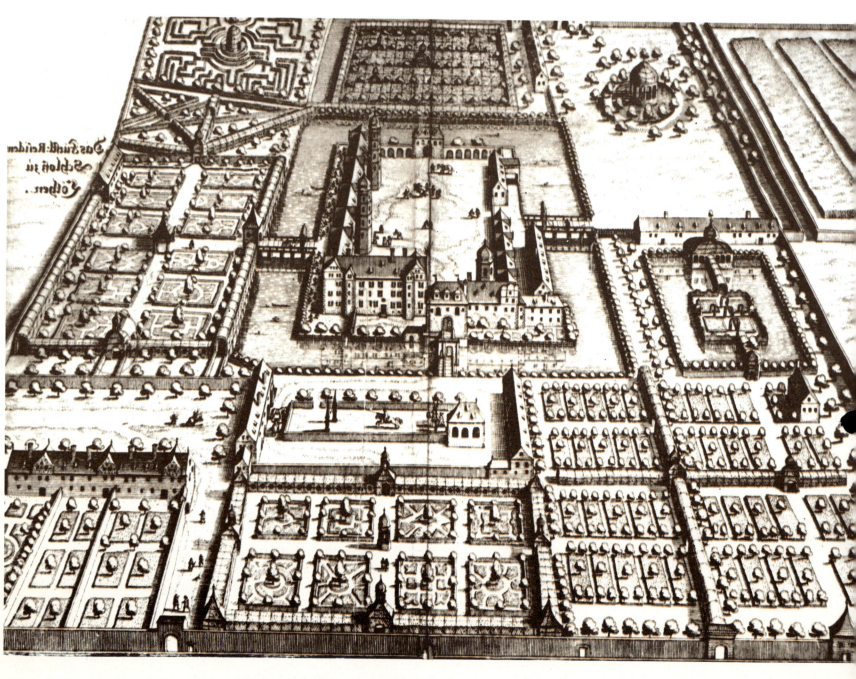

Accolades and Arguments

The Cantor's duties were demanding. As a member of the school staff, third in seniority after the Rector and Conrector, he was required to train the singers and instrumentalists, to teach the Catechism and Latin, and for one week in every four to take his turn of full-time duty as Inspector in charge of the discipline of the school.

The school was unfortunately going through a bad period. The Rector, Johann Heinrich Ernesti, was elderly and no longer in effective control, a serious matter in a school constituted as was the Thomasschule. It was still basically a choir school; the fifty-five foundation scholars, all boarders, selected for their musical ability chiefly from among the poorer families, had to provide all the voices from treble to bass which were needed for the various church choirs.

Bach threw himself immediately and with enthusiasm into the composition of music for the church services. Cantatas were required for every Sunday, except in Lent and Advent, and for the various festivals of the church's year, amounting to fifty-nine in all. Music was also called for at Vespers four times a year – Passion Music on Good Friday and a Magnificat on the three high festivals. Bach's aim – and according to tradition his achievement – was to compose a five-year cycle of cantatas, two hundred and ninety-five in all; of these about two hundred still exist. It was thought for many years that the composition of this large output was spread out at the rate of one new cantata a month, as had been officially required of him at Weimar, but recent research suggests that it was concentrated within his first few years at Leipzig, and that, for example, he wrote or adapted from earlier works some one hundred and fifteen cantatas during his first two full years of residence there, in addition to the Magnificat for Christmas 1723 and the *Passion according to St John* for Good Friday 1724.

The musical climax of Bach's first years at Leipzig was the performance on Good Friday 15th April 1729 of the *Passion according to St Matthew* in the Thomaskirche. This, his largest-scale work, was designed to make full use of all available resources; the 'chorus primus' and 'chorus secundus' provided the double choir and the soloists; the town musicians, the school instrumentalists and the University students supplied the two orchestras, and the small organ high above the chancel arch was brought into use as well as the large organ in the west gallery, where all the performers were crowded.

Meanwhile Bach's domestic life had its compensations. The three musical sons of his first marriage were making good progress in the school. The eldest and most brilliant, Friedemann, was given every opportunity to develop his gifts, and was even sent for one year to Merseburg to study the violin with J. Gottlieb Graun, before taking his place as a law student in Leipzig University in 1729. Emanuel, being markedly left-handed, excelled at the keyboard, for which he needed no better instructor than his father.

With the death of the old Rector Ernesti in October 1729 there came a glimmer of hope that conditions in the Thomasschule might improve. The following June, Bach was cheered to learn that his old Weimar acquaintance and admirer, Johann Mathias Gesner, had been appointed to fill the vacancy, although he was not to take up the post until September. Meanwhile Bach had to face strong criticism from an unsympathetic Council.

April 1731 saw the beginning of the enlarging of the building in which the Thomasschule, its Rector, and its Cantor had been housed since 1553. Two main storeys, as well as further accommodation in the steeply pitched roof, were built above the sturdy but inadequate three storeys of the older building. For a year the Rector, Cantor and pupils had to be housed elsewhere, and the normal running of the school was considerably disrupted. Less was expected from the Cantor in the way of new music for the churches, and Bach had time to engrave a sixth Partita to add to the series he had been bringing out since 1726, and to publish them all together in a volume of *Clavierübung* (Keyboard Exercises), the first of four with the same title, of which the last appeared in 1742.

The refurbished Thomasschule was opened in May 1732, and the benefits of the rule of the new Rector could be fully felt. Gesner, though progressive in his educational ideas, managed to reconcile them with the necessary maintenance of the school's musical duties, and his kindly but firm rule restored the order and discipline which had been so lacking under Ernesti.

An 18th-century print of a religious service in the Thomaskirche in Leipzig

Life was certainly more agreeable now, but its normal routine was again broken early in 1733. In February, the King-Elector died, and throughout Saxony no elaborate church music was to be heard during the official mourning. In June, Bach applied on behalf of his 23-year-old son, Friedemann, for the organistship of the Sophienkirche which had fallen vacant, and had the great pleasure of his son's appointment against considerable competition. He accompanied Friedemann to Dresden when he took up his position in August, and at the same time presented his music along with a letter in which he quite openly begged for a court appointment, and frankly stated the reasons for his request.

It was not a propitious moment. Poland was resisting the succession, and the Elector had an unwelcome war on his hands. It is hardly surprising that Bach's appeal was ignored. Undeterred, the loyal Cantor saw to it that his Collegium Musicum marked every possible royal occasion with musical celebrations, which came to a climax when Augustus and his queen came to Leipzig on an official visit at the end of the war, in October 1734, and were regaled with two festive cantatas in three days. By this time Bach was becoming seriously alarmed about his future prospects, since his friend Gesner, disappointed at not obtaining a

A. C. Platz, one of the Council at Leipzig who finally decided to accept Bach as Cantor to the Church of St Thomas in 1723 (Stadtarchiv, Leipzig)

university post in addition to his Rectorship, had decided to leave Leipzig in November. His successor was another Ernesti, unrelated to the previous one; he had been Con-rector for three years, and Bach knew only too well that he could expect no support on the musical side from him. Ernesti was all for a complete reorganisation of the curriculum in favour of wider academic study. But Bach still received no communication from the Court.

However, there were other pleasanter things to occupy his mind. Friedemann was satisfactorily settled in Dresden; Emanuel went to Frankfurt University in 1734; the following year Bernhard secured the organistship of the Marien-kirche at Mühlhausen, where his father still had a number of friends. Also, the children born to Anna Magdalena in the refurbished Cantor's apartment were flourishing; the building was definitely healthier. 1735 saw the publication of Volume Two of *Clavierübung* containing the Italian Concerto and the Overture in the French Style, both for a two-manualed harpsichord, and the addition of a Credo, Sanctus, Benedictus and Agnus Dei to the already composed Kyrie and Gloria, thus completing the work now known as the B minor Mass.

The reign of the new Rector Ernesti began peaceably enough, though Bach soon missed the encouraging support of his friend Gesner. He knew enough of his superior to be aware that no chance would be missed of belittling the study of music at the expense of what Ernesti considered the only real function of the school.

No clash occurred until July 1736, when a crisis arose over a question of prefectorial appointments, a delicate business where musical ability was as important a consideration as other qualities.

Meanwhile the King-Elector at long last appointed Bach as Court Composer, and Count Kayserling, the Russian envoy, was instructed to summon Bach to Dresden to receive his patent. The Count, who suffered from insomnia, employed as harpsichordist Johann Gottlieb Goldberg, a pupil of Friedemann and of Bach himself, to play to him when he could not sleep. In gratitude for his share in the appointment Bach presented Kayserling with the work now known as the 'Goldberg Variations' to while away the wakeful night hours. He made public acknowledgement by giving a recital on the Silbermann organ in the new Liebfrauenkirche, an occasion which must have been both architecturally and musically an apotheosis of Baroque art.

In 1738 Bach received into his household Johann Elias Bach of Schweinfurt, who at the age of thirty-three had raised sufficient funds to enable him to study theology at Leipzig University. In return for board and lodging Elias undertook the education of the three remaining sons, and acted as his cousin's secretary. To this kindly, affectionate man, who lived as a member of the family until 1742, we owe an attractive picture of Bach's home life. His letters describe

in intimate detail those small happenings which are so illuminating, and so lacking for Bach's life as a whole.

Meanwhile, the publication of the *Clavierübung* proceeded; in 1739 Volume Three was issued, consisting of the great organ preludes on the Lutheran Catechism hymns, in which the Greater Catechism is represented by preludes for manuals and pedal and the Lesser by preludes for manuals alone, framed by the Prelude in E flat and the Fugue in the same key (which since the days of Mendelssohn have been played together and are known in England by the name 'St Anne', from the fugue subject which resembles the first line of the hymn-tune of that name by Dr. Croft). The final volume came out in 1742, and contained the 'Goldberg Variations' 'for harpsichord with two manuals', for which Bach had obtained Count Kayserling's permission to publish.

After the 'Battle of the Prefects' the Leipzig authorities evidently decided that the only thing to do was to accept Bach's own interpretation of his duties; thenceforward they left him in peace. In 1740 they even went so far as to appoint another member of staff to relieve him of what remained of his pedagogic duties. Having long ago supplied the liturgy with an adequate supply of cantatas and Passions, Bach devoted his last years to composing music which, though it all had an ostensible purpose in true 18th-century fashion, was in reality an exploration towards the furthest limits to which canon and fugue could be taken within the tonal limits of contemporary musical language.

While his health remained sound – and it did not begin to fail seriously until 1749 – he travelled around in his usual fashion, examining and reporting on organs, giving recitals and visiting Dresden. He no longer had the comfort of his cousin's presence in his home; Johann Elias left in 1742 to begin a career which very soon took him back to his home town of Schweinfurt as Cantor.

The gap in Bach's family circle was soon partly filled by the arrival in Leipzig in 1744 of Johann Christoph Altnikol to be his pupil and assistant and also a bass singer in the choir. Apparently boys were tending to leave school earlier, and the supply of mature broken voices was poor. This promising young musician was of great use as copyist and amanuensis to his master, and Bach soon felt able to leave his family with Altnikol to keep an eye on them while he went farther afield. He was eager to pay a second visit to Emanuel in Berlin, but the military escapades of Frederick the Great made this inadvisable for some time. In 1745, Frederick invaded Saxony, capturing Leipzig in November and Dresden in December, but a sort of peace was patched up at the end of the year.

Meanwhile Bach completed the Second Book of the 'Well-Tempered Clavier' in 1744, intending the pieces for the instruction of his two youngest sons, just as the previous collection had been made for the three eldest. He also prepared, in 1746, for the publisher Schübler, a set of six chorale preludes for organ 'with two manuals and pedal', which are not in fact original compositions but transcriptions of movements from various church cantatas which, in their turn, were based on chorale melodies and treated in 'prelude form'. Bach evidently had little hope of their being heard again in their original setting, and was

9

sufficiently attached to them to wish to prolong their life in a more practicable medium.

In 1747, Bach made his last and most remarkable journey. Travelling by way of Halle where Friedemann, now organist there, joined him, he proceeded to Berlin, and on Sunday 7th May, he arrived in Potsdam where the Court was in residence. Frederick's evening concert was about to begin, but when the new arrival was announced, he abandoned his preparations, and exclaiming, 'Gentlemen, old Bach is here', welcomed his court accompanist's famous father with genuine enthusiasm.

Such 'condescension' required a due acknowledgment, and Bach set to work to explore the possibilities of the royal theme more thoroughly than he had been able to do extempore. He first used it as the subject of a three-part fugue, and then of a magnificent six-part fugue, demonstrating its suitability for such treatment despite his modest withdrawal from the attempt in the King's presence. He also wrote a number of canons on the subject, and added, for the King's own performance, a trio-sonata for flute, violin and cello (with continuo) into which ingenious references to the theme are woven. A manuscript copy of the complete collection, which Bach called 'A Musical Offering', was sent to Frederick the Great, and later in the year the work was engraved and published.

During the course of 1748 Bach had the satisfaction of securing a good appointment for Altnikol at Naumburg, and though sorry to lose him, the affection that had blossomed between Altnikol and Bach's beloved 'Lieschen', his daughter Elisabeth Juliane Friederike, secured him a devoted son-in-law. The marriage took place in January 1749.

Though 'fugue' in its wide sense formed the essence of Bach's language, and the composition of fugues of every kind was second nature to him, he had never attempted a systematic pedagogic study of the subject. This he now proceeded to do, not in the text-book form, but characteristically by practical demonstration. The 'Art of Fugue' on which he now embarked, and which he was destined not to complete, exhibits every known device of fugue and canon, all based on one simple yet malleable subject, set out in open score for clarity, but nevertheless keyboard music. Like Bach's other instructive works, the ostensible intent does not prevent him from writing music of the highest possible aesthetic value, though it has taken longer for this to be generally realised than is the case with any other of his works.

During 1749 Bach had a serious illness, probably a stroke. His recovery was evidently very doubtful, because in June the Dresden Prime Minister recommended his personal Kapell-Direktor, Gottlob Harrer, to the Leipzig authorities on the eventual occasion of the decease of Herr Bach. He rallied, and when early in 1750 his eighteen-year-old son Johann Christoph Friedrich left home to serve in the Court

at Bückeburg, he actually took into his home a last pupil, Johann Gottfried Müthel. He was already nearly blind, and in January he underwent an operation at the hands of the English eye-surgeon John Taylor, who was later to treat Handel. But the operation was not successful, and the necessary confinement in darkened rooms reduced his resistance to the strain of 18th-century surgery.

The last months were spent in an attempt to complete a final collection of preludes for the organ, with the help of Altnikol and Müthel as amanuenses. These, now known as the Eighteen Chorale Preludes, are largely re-workings of earlier pieces: a touching example of Bach's sensitivity to words induced him to change the attribution of the final prelude from 'When we are in deepest need' to 'Before Thy throne I come', both hymns being commonly sung to the same tune. This was his very last music; after an attack of apoplexy he was unconscious for ten days, and in the evening of the 28th July, he died.

His simple funeral in the churchyard of the Johanneskirche was thus announced from the pulpit of St Thomas on the 31st July: 'There has passed to his rest, and now sleeps blessedly in God, the right worthy and esteemed Herr Johann Sebastian Bach, composer to His Majesty the King in Poland and Prince-Elector of Saxony, Kapellmeister to His Highness of Anhalt-Cöthen, and Cantor of St Thomas's School in the Thomaskirchhof. With the rites of Christian usage his body has this day been committed to the earth.'

Clavier Concerto in D minor

The concerto in Germany of the early eighteenth century was under the influence of the Italian and French Baroque models of the day. From Italy, there was the classic example of Antonio Vivaldi, who wrote literally hundreds of works for solo instrument (frequently the violin) and ensemble playing—although the creation of the modern solo concerto can be traced, among others, to Albinoni and Torelli. From France there were the works of Leclair, Couperin, and Rameau, but these resembled suites of dances rather than actual concertos.

It was Johann Sebastian Bach in Germany who took the prevailing forms of the day and summed them up in brilliant concertos, particularly for harpsichord and violin, producing some 24 instrumental concertos. In this collection are certain arrangements or transcriptions of concertos, from one instrument to another, or for chamber ensembles. In these works Bach mixed both the strict three-movement concerto style with the longer suite form of multiple movements, to give an architectural solidity to the melodic Italian style.

While Bach's violin concertos were in the traditional line of contemporary composing styles for strings, the seven solo harpsichord and orchestra concertos are among the first works of their kind. They show signs of an important musical revolution in Germany: the slow decline of the church as the center of musical life and the emergence of the self-sustaining public concert hall in its place. With this came the development of the keyboard concerto in German music. As conductor of Leipzig's Collegium Musicum between 1729-36, Bach programmed much of his own music—and here was the motivation for composing his seven harpsichord concertos. These were by and large transcriptions of his earlier works, primarily violin concertos, or occasionally inspired by works of other composers. Bach was under constant pressure to turn out new pieces, and this was an expediency.

The concept of a harpsichord concerto in Bach's time was considerably different from the piano concerto of Mozart's and Beethoven's day, when the solo instrument was pitted against and contrasted with the ensemble. In the earlier era, the harpsichord formed an essential part of every concerto as a basic instrument, serving to support and accompany the solo instrument, and operating as a unifying force in the orchestral sections. In Bach's concertos, the harpsichord is not so much the solo instrument as it is the predominant instrument, involved in intricate, magnificently crafted interplay.

The first time Bach employed the clavier for a concerto was in the well-known D minor, whose origins have been traced back to an early viola d'amore and another violin concerto. Composed in the standard three-movement form of fast-slow-fast, the overall character is solemn and tragic. A driving relentlessness typifies the first movement *(Allegro),* which moves along irresistibly in unison as the solo harpsichord picks up the basic musical materials and transforms them. The poignant *Adagio* beautifully unravels as the harpsichord soars in a richly decorated version of the initial melody. This is followed by a highly spirited, brilliant dance-like *Allegro* finale, full of vigor and rich figurations.

A print, dated 1743, of the Opera House in Berlin. In 1747 Bach went via Berlin to Potsdam where he played at the Court of Frederick the Great (Kunstbibliothek, Berlin)

Brandenburg Concertos Nos. 2 and 6

Several years before this sequence of harpsichord concertos, Bach—then Kapellmeister to Prince Leopold of Anhalt-Cöthen—set down his famous, masterful set of Six Brandenburg Concertos. Christian Ludwig, the Margrave of Brandenburg, commissioned composers to write works for his court orchestra. He met Bach in 1719, was impressed and asked him to write a set of concertos. Bach finished this assignment early in 1721, and called them 'Six Concertos for divers instruments.' He submitted them 'humbly' to his benefactor with the plea that he not judge 'their imperfections too harshly,' and that he try to find in them 'the profound respect and the very humble allegiance that they seek to convey.' Again, Bach made use of the Italian form of the concerto grosso he inherited from Vivaldi and others; and they stand as Bach's earliest essays in absolute music on a grand scale, a remarkable expression of an adventurous mind.

To contrast the *ripieno* (large instrumental group) with the *concertino* (small cadre of solo players) he had the felicitous idea of using a different set of solo instruments for each of his concertos—except in No. 3 where the orchestra is divided into three parts (violins, violas, cellos) to replace the solos. No. 1 is scored for a wind ensemble of horns, oboes and bassoon added to the strings, while the violino piccolo is prominent. No. 2 has a flute, oboe, trumpet and violin in solo positions; No. 4 features a violin and two flutes (or recorders); No. 5 the flute, violin and harpsichord; and No. 6 only the strings as in No. 3. They are audacious statements of a genius full of variety, originality, vigor and glorious melody.

The prime feature of the perfectly proportioned Brandenburg Concerto No. 2 is the unique colour achieved by the quartet of high-pitched instruments: trumpet, recorder, oboe and violin. The latter appears first in the initial movement *(Allegro)*, followed by the others. The theme and its variants are combined with fascinating complexity and wealth of invention, embellished by the trumpet's brilliant,

fanciful figurations. The middle *Andante* is a beautiful trio of a religious nature and tenderness, with the trumpet remaining silent. A trumpet theme, however, begins the light-hearted final movement, *Allegro assai,* with the oboe, violin and recorder following in succession. Later the ensemble takes up the theme and all combine in the dashing closing.

The more somber Brandenburg Concerto No. 6 was probably the first of the set to be composed. Prince Leopold was a capable viola da gamba player, so this concerto might very well have been intended for him. It is scored for two violas, two viola da gambas and a cello in the solo department (the two violas are of the variety to be held in the ordinary arm position, while the violas da gamba are held, like the cello, upright between the legs). The first movement *(Allegro)* begins with the mellow violas introducing the main theme, which is then altered slightly in rhythm and interspersed with new ideas before returning to the original statement. A lovely nostalgic melody, again for the violas, begins the expressive second movement *(Adagio ma no tanto),* while the gambas remain silent; its ending has a sorrowful quality. But the energetic finale *(Allegro)* is full of driving gaiety with rhythmic and melodic variants of the opening theme, the soloists imitatively and competitively vying with one another.

As Karl Geiringer has written in his expert study of Bach, 'The Brandenburg Concertos seem to embody the splendor and effervescence of court life at Cöthen, and, moreover, they reveal the composer's delight in writing for a group of highly trained instrumentalists. There is an exuberance and abundance of inspiration in this music which only a genius, aware of his newly achieved full mastery, could call forth. Craftsmanship and richly flowing melodic invention, logic and zest for experimenting, counterpoise each other here to an extent rarely equaled again even by Bach himself.' And Ernest Newman summed up Bach's position in declaring him far ahead of his own time in his luxuriance of melody, his intensity in harmony 'or the way he could force the most complex polyphony into the service of the profoundest emotional expression, or the freedom and variety of musical speech to which he could attain even while he fettered himself with seemingly the most crabbed forms. ... Within the ... older forms that lay ready to his hands ... he could indulge himself to his heart's content in the sounding of the very depths of the human soul. ... There is hardly an emotion that is not expressed, and with a poignancy that remains undiminished even after three generations of post-Tristan developments.'

An old wood-cut of Ohrdruf where Bach lived with his brother, Johann Christoph, organist of St Michael's Church (German State Library, Berlin)

Printed in the United States of America

Grieg

His Life and Times 1843-1907

PROGRAM NOTES FOR THE PIANO CONCERTO IN A MINOR AND PEER GYNT SUITÈ NO. 1

By Robert Jacobson

fw

Funk & Wagnalls, Inc.
NEW YORK, NEW YORK

Early Life: 1843-68

The proud and picturesque old town of Bergen, crowded between the North Sea and the mountains of western Norway, holds many memories of Edvard Grieg, who was born there on 15th June 1843. The composer's birthplace at 152 Strandgaten was destroyed during the last war, but his charmingly situated villa at Troldhaugen is open to visitors and close beside it, behind a precipitous rock-face, is the resting-place of his ashes. A fine collection of his manuscripts, sketch books and early editions can be inspected in the Bergen Public Library.

But even more evocative are the living reminders of the ancestry and environment that went to the making of one of the most original among the 19th-century national Romantic composers. Grieg once said that the smells of the Bergen waterside fishmarket had been an inspiration to him and one may remember, when buying a fresh lobster there today, that it was the fishing trade that brought the founder of the Norwegian branch of the family, Alexander Greig, over from Scotland at the end of the eighteenth century. (The next generation was to alter the spelling of its surname in conformity with Norwegian pronunciation.)

Leaving behind the ancient wooden warehouses that line the fish-quay and turning towards the centre of the town, one comes across statues not only of Grieg himself but also of other notable Bergen citizens: the dramatist Ludvig Holberg, sometimes called the Molière of the North, for whose bicentenary in 1884 Grieg was to write the *Holberg Suite;* the romantic poet J. S. Welhaven; and the spell-binding violinist and artistic visionary Ole Bull, to whom the young Grieg was to owe encouragement, practical advice and above all his first acquaintance with Norwegian folk-music. Perhaps the strongest link between Grieg, Bull and the more remote musical past of Bergen is the still flourishing Harmonien, one of the oldest musical societies in Europe, nowadays with its professional Symphony Orchestra. Edvard Grieg's grandfather had been among the founder members of Harmonien in 1769, and his mother Gesine Grieg sometimes appeared as solo pianist at its concerts.

It was from his mother that Edvard Grieg received his first piano lessons and it was Ole Bull who, after hearing the boy extemporise, recommended that he should be sent to the best institution of higher musical education that could then be found, the Leipzig Conservatory. Grieg was only fifteen when he went to study in Germany. He suffered mentally from homesickness and physically from the chest complaints that were to handicap him for the rest of his life, and he also found much of the Conservatory teaching distasteful and unsympathetic. The brilliance of Mendelssohn, who had founded the Leipzig Conservatory in the year of Grieg's birth, and the imaginativeness of Schumann, who had been one of its first professors of composition, had given place to a solid academic regime whose inflexibility Grieg was prone to exaggerate in later life, even to the extent of maintaining that he had learnt nothing from it. But at least it furnished him with a piano technique sound enough to ensure him a career as concert performer of his own works, and among his

composition teachers Moritz Hauptmann seems to have done much to help his originality to blossom into the harmonic individuality that was to prove one of the leading traits of his style.

Outside the formal curriculum of the Conservatory, Leipzig offered wonderful opportunities. Artists like Clara Schumann and Wilhelmine Schröder-Devrient were giving authoritative performances of Robert Schumann's piano works and songs, and the flood of Wagner's genius was beginning to envelop the great centres of European music – Grieg, while a student in Leipzig, heard fourteen successive performances of *Tannhäuser*. There were interesting fellow-students too, among them Arthur Sullivan and the Dane, C. F. E. Horneman, with whom Grieg was to be in close contact in the early days of his career. Another contemporary, Edward Dannreuther, pianist and writer on Wagner, remembered Grieg as 'a slightly built youth, of a typical Northern physiognomy, with flaxen hair and large dreamy blue eyes, very quiet, self-absorbed and industrious. As a pianist he never laid much stress on technique, but his playing was always delicate and intelligent.'

On graduating from the Leipzig Conservatory in the spring of 1862 Grieg took part in a students' concert, when two of his works were performed. They were the Four Piano Pieces, op. 1 and the Four Songs for Alto Voice, op. 2 – the earliest published examples of the two genres in which Grieg was to excel, namely the short characteristic piano piece and the solo song with piano. The songs are to German texts, while the piano pieces look back to Schumann and Chopin, although by no means without clear indications of stylistic independence. Before long, as we shall see, Grieg was to come under a number of influences which to an increasing extent emancipated him from the more obvious German traits derived from his Leipzig studentship. After leaving Germany, Grieg spent about a year in his native Bergen, where at a concert on 21st May 1862 some of the op. 1 pieces and the op. 2 songs were again performed, together with a D minor String Quartet which is no longer extant. Another lost work, *Rückblick* for chorus and piano, was specially composed for Harmonien. During this year when he was centred in Bergen, Grieg travelled to London and Paris in the summer months, returning to Bergen again for the winter. He left again in April 1863, this time for Copenhagen, apparently to study with the Danish composer Niels Gade.

Copenhagen provided further inspiration for song-writing, for it was there that Grieg became acquainted with the greatest living Danish man of letters, Hans Christian Andersen, and set four of his *Melodies of the Heart*, op. 5, including 'Two brown eyes' and 'I love thee' – the latter destined to become the most popular of all Grieg's songs, though regrettably too often through a German translation. He drew upon Andersen's verses again for several of the Romances op. 18. In Copenhagen also the young song-composer found his ideal interpreter and his life-long companion. Nina Hagerup, an eighteen-year-old cousin on his mother's side, had been born in Bergen but had been brought to Denmark by her parents while she was still a child. She trained as a singer, and although her voice was restricted in power – the effect, it was said, of a childhood ailment – it was beautiful in quality and was controlled by a thoroughly musical temperament. In spite of the misgivings of Nina's parents, who feared young Edvard had no prospects and wrote a kind of music no one wanted, Nina and Edvard were married in Copenhagen in the summer of 1867.

At various stages in his life, Grieg came into contact with a number of musicians who were engaged like himself in the propagation of a national music. Among these were the organist Ludvig Lindeman; the violinist Ole Bull; the pianist – of some international standing – Thomas Tellefsen; Halfdan Kjerulf, a composer of piano pieces and songs. But the man who made the greatest impression on Grieg at this stage in his career was another composer, Rikard Nordraak. A Norwegian by birth, he had studied in Berlin and eventually returned to his native country full of nationalist sympathies. Grieg and Nordraak met in Copenhagen, probably for the first time in the summer of 1863, and again a year or two later. Kjerulf made the comment that it must have been a meeting of extremes. Red-haired, impulsive, brilliant in conversation, a natural musician with little academic schooling, Nordraak was in every way a complete contrast to Grieg, and their friendship may well have begun as an attraction of opposites. Grieg himself remarked: 'We were infinitely unlike each other in spite of our mutual sympathy.' But through his conversations with Nordraak, and perhaps even more by hearing him play his incidental music to plays and stories by Björnson (to whom Nordraak was related), Grieg was helped to discover himself, to feel his way towards a more strongly emphasised national idiom, and, in his own words, 'to express something of the best in me that lay a thousand miles away from Leipzig and its atmosphere'. More precisely, in terms of musical expression,

this revelation pointed towards development along three lines: by making closer contact with Norwegian romantic literature, of which Björnson was now the leading exponent, and taking subject-matter from national legend and history as well as inspiration from mountain scenery and peasant life; secondly, by absorbing the scales, intervals and rhythms of folk music into his own musical language; and thirdly, by working mainly on the small scale of the impressionistic genre picture rather than within the organically more complex sonata forms hallowed above all by the prevailing German tradition.

Although Grieg later in life described the effects of his meeting with Nordraak as a sudden demisting of the eyes, the process must in fact have been more gradual, with Bull, Kjerulf, Gade, Hartmann (a prolific Danish composer) and Horneman each contributing in his own way to his artistic development. The magnetic attraction of Copenhagen was to remain powerful for some time to come. Even the ardent Nordraak was half Danish by birth, and showed no reluctance to join with two of the younger Danish composers, Horneman and Matthison-Hansen, and with Grieg to found a society known as Euterpe, dedicated to the performance of works by Danish and Norwegian musicians alike. Grieg's own compositions at this period of transition are ambivalent. The four piano Humoresques, op. 6, which he dedicated to Nordraak, show how far he had already gone towards shedding the influence of Schumann and Mendelssohn; Nordraak joyfully recognised in them a strong Norwegian element and praised the second piece of the set characteristically by saying he might have written it himself. But there is also an affinity between the Humoresques and the more reticent nationalism of Gade's Scandinavian Dances. There are strong indications of Grieg's debt to Gade and Hartmann in the Piano Sonata, op. 7. The first of the three Violin Sonatas (in F, op. 8) likewise is dedicated to a Dane, the author Benjamin Feddersen, and has been aptly des-

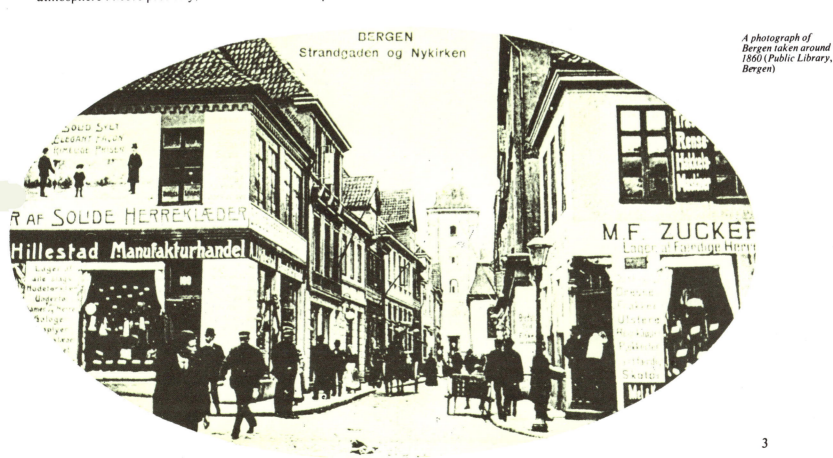

BERGEN
Strandgaden og Nykirken

A photograph of Bergen taken around 1860 (Public Library, Bergen)

cribed by Walter Niemann: 'Its background is the Danish landscape . . . Denmark's beech-woods, blue lakes and gentle twilight are felt as an undertone to the whole work.' Yet the primitive heterophony of the Hardanger fiddle (a national instrument of the violin family with specially tuned strings) resounds through more than one movement of these 'Danish' works, and Grieg's familiar fingerprints of falling sevenths, bare fourths and fifths and pedal-supported dissonances can already be found in them.

Poor Nordraak had little time left to him. A victim, like so many of his gifted contemporaries, of the tuberculosis bacillus, he died early in 1866, ironically neither in Denmark nor in Norway but in a Berlin lodging. Nordraak and Grieg had both planned to visit Germany towards the end of 1865, intending to go on to Italy together. But Nordraak's desperate illness meant that Grieg had to decide whether to abandon his tour and stay at his friend's bedside (thereby probably endangering his own precarious health) or to go on alone. He took the latter course, an action for which Nordraak reproached him bitterly in a last letter.

When Nordraak's death occurred (on 20th March 1866) Grieg had been in Rome for nearly three months. He had been writing one of the last of his 'Danish' works, the concert overture *In Autumn*, op. 11, and he had met for the first time his most famous compatriot, Henrik Ibsen. He expressed his sincere grief for Nordraak in a poignant and prophetic Funeral March which might almost, with its grave modality, be taken for an early work of Ravel, although in reality it owes much to the stage funeral music of Hartmann. It is by far the most daring, and appropriately the most Norwegian, of Grieg's compositions up to this date and forms a worthy tribute to Nordraak, who had bequeathed to Norway two great gifts: his setting of Björnson's magnificent verses beginning 'Yes, we love this land . . .' (now the national hymn) and his liberating influence on Grieg. Björnson himself spoke of Nordraak with matchless eloquence: 'Here were clarity and force, a full, round sum of Norse melodies and patriotism, Norse characterisation, Norse dreams and fairy-tales and a wealth of plans for Norse operas and symphonies. Here Grieg listened and learnt, here he was born anew.'

On returning from Italy, Grieg set about establishing himself as an all-round professional musician in Christiania. He took lessons in organ-playing in the hope of obtaining a secure church appointment and applied for the post of conductor at the theatre where Björnson was now director; even Ibsen's support, however, did not avail him in this project, though the author of *Peer Gynt* consoled him with the thought that he might be reserved for a less monotonous round than that of the theatre pit. On 15th October 1866 Grieg gave a public concert with the help of his fiancée Nina Hagerup and of Wilhelmina Norman-Neruda, the violinist who was later to become Lady Hallé. The all-Norwegian programme included some of the Humoresques, the Piano Sonata, the first Violin Sonata and songs by Nordraak and Kjerulf as well as by Grieg himself. The success of this concert led to his being appointed conductor of the Philharmonic Society—an amateur orchestra—and also to the growth of his reputation as a teacher. In conjunction with Otto Winter-Hjelm, a pupil of Kjerulf's who had written helpful reviews of Grieg's compositions, an attempt was made to found an Academy of Music in Christiania.

All these promising activities seemed to justify marriage and a permanent home in the Norwegian capital, although for the summer holidays, when freedom from routine tasks left time and energy for composition, the Griegs continued to prefer the softer climate and more congenial society of Denmark. And thus it was at Søllerød, in the countryside a few miles north of Copenhagen, that they spent the summer of 1868 and there Grieg's most popular large-scale work, the Concerto in A minor for Piano and Orchestra, came to be written.

A landscape in Telemark, painted by Erik Theodor Werenskiold (National Gallery, Oslo)

Inside the poster:

L'ŒUVRE : 22, Rue Tu

PEER GYNT

Poème dramatique en 5 act

d'HENRIK-IBSEN, Musique de E. GRIEG
Traduction de M. le Comte PROZOR.
Orchestre conduit par M. GABRIEL MARIE
Solo de Violon par M. HOLLFELDER

Aase	Mᵐᵉ BAUDIERI.
Peer Gynt	M. DEVAL.
Solveig	Mˡˡᵉ SuZANNE AUCL.
La Femme en vert . . .	Mᵐᵉ RÉGINE MARTI.
Ingrid	Mᵐᵉ REYNOLD.
Le Fondeur	
Le Passager	
Le Tortueux	M. ALBERT-MAYER
Aslak	
Anitra	Mˡˡᵉ JANE AVRIL.
Le 1ᵉʳ Troll de Cour . .	M. JARRY.
Chœur arabe.	Mᵐᵉ BERTHILDE.
Le Vieux de Dorre . . .	M. KOBOLD.
Le Capitaine	M. ROCHEFORT.
M. Eberkopf	M. FLANDRE.
M. Ballon	M. NANDOUTPA.
Une Fille de Troll . . .	Mˡˡᵉ ISAAC.
Pilote	M. MIGNAUN.
Une voix dans la coulisse	Mˡˡᵉ MEZANO.
Chef des Chœurs . . .	M. BRETONNEAU.

Poster for Peer Gynt
*by Edvard Grieg
designed by Edvard
Münch (1863-1944)
(Grieg's House,
Troldhaugen)*

Work with the Dramatists: Life 1866-74

With the completion of the Piano Concerto in the summer of 1868, Grieg attained the peak of his creative talent, revealing himself as a national romantic of the first order. In the eyes of Europe he was worthy to be ranked beside his great fellow-countrymen, Henrik Ibsen and Björnstjerne Björnson, as a representative of the vitality of a small nation that had not only justified its political independence but had already made notable contributions to the world's artistic heritage. The life of a young musician in Christiania still had its frustrations: concerts were not always adequately supported and the Academy founded by Grieg and Otto Winter-Hjelm soon fell into decline. But when Grieg received an unsolicited letter from Franz Liszt, praising his Violin Sonata, op.8, in the warmest terms and inviting him

to Weimar, the Norwegian Government willingly awarded him a bursary to defray his travelling expenses. Another year was to pass, however, before he could start on the journey – a year filled with personal sorrow, for his only child Alexandra died soon after her first birthday.

By the time he was ready to take up the invitation Liszt had moved on to Rome and was in residence at a monastery near the Forum. There he received Grieg with the greatest kindness and with the unfeigned interest he always showed in any manifestation of creative talent and originality. He listened while Grieg played through the Second Violin Sonata (in G, op.13) and the works particularly associated with Nordraak — the Humoresques and the Funeral March; and at a subsequent meeting Liszt himself read the Piano

5

Concerto at sight from the manuscript, with many spontaneous expressions of approval at its bold independence, a quality he had already hailed in another nationalist composer, Bedřich Smetana. Grieg's response to Liszt's generous and powerful support was to dedicate to him a cantata for female voices and organ, *At a Southern Convent's Gate*, op.20, a work deserving of mention not so much for its intrinsic importance, which is comparatively slight, but because it marks the beginning of a period of fruitful collaboration with the second greatest Norwegian author of the day, Björnstjerne Björnson.

A man of striking physical presence, huge and rugged, with a gift of fluent oratory and a prolific pen, Björnson might have been the personification of a youthful vigorous nation with deep ancestral memories. In later years he was to turn to the dramatisation of problems of contemporary life, but when Grieg first knew him he was full of enthusiasm for Norse history, legend, scenery and folk culture in all its forms, around which he wove his novels of an idealised peasantry, interspersed with lyric poems of haunting beauty. For his dramas he chose episodes from the Norse sagas or, as in *Mary Stuart in Scotland*, subjects from the romantic past of other nations. Needless to say, he was an admirer of Norwegian folk song and dance; and two of his stories, *Arne* and *The Bridal March*, include vivid descriptions of peasant musicians. His lyrics were written expressly for musical setting and had already inspired Kjerulf and Nordraak to produce some of their best songs. Now that these men were no longer alive (Kjerulf had died in 1868, two years after Nordraak) Björnson turned to Grieg as his chief collaborator. The partnership was a fortunate one on both sides; Björnson's strong, extrovert personality had a beneficial effect on Grieg's natural diffidence and shyness, while as a composer Grieg was never more successful than when his imagination was kindled by Björnson's poetry. His *Four Songs from 'The Fishermaiden'*, op.21, include 'The First Meeting', one of the loveliest short songs of the century and one that could only have been created by two great Norwegian artists working in complete sympathy. *The Princess*, another magical lyric, had been set to music by Kjerulf, was re-set by Grieg and was later to attract Delius, always an admirer of Norwegian literature. In *From Monte Pincio*, op.39 no.5, Björnson and Grieg unite in a more elaborately constructed picture from the Mediterranean. An interesting experiment, seldom heard today, was the melodrama *Bergliot*, based on the saga of Harald Haardraada and set by Grieg for declamation by a woman's voice with piano accompaniment which he later orchestrated. For another of Björnson's saga-dramas, *Sigurd Jorsalfar* (Sigurd the Crusader), Grieg composed songs, choruses and entr'actes. When poet and composer watched a performance of it together on Independence Day, 17th May 1872, Grieg sank disconsolately into his stall at the efforts of an unmusical actor to sing his role and had to be revived by a thump in the back from the less sensitive Björnson. On the same day another of the fruits of their collaboration, the cantata *Landsighting* (Recognition of Land), dealing with the return of Olav Trygvason to claim the throne of Norway, was first performed in aid of the restoration of the ancient cathedral of Trondhjem.

Grieg and Björnson next planned to work together on a full-scale opera on some Norse legendary or historical subject. This idea would have pleased Ole Bull, who had dreamed of founding a national lyric theatre and ballet, and had even, at Bergen in 1850, arranged for the production of a ballad-opera, a folk dance ballet and a Hardanger fiddle recital on the stage. Further development of the national theatre under the young and then unknown Henrik Ibsen met with little tangible success, but had the indirect result of bringing dramatist and musicians together and establishing in Norway the concept of a stage-play liberally supplied with incidental music. Björnson's first proposal was for an opera to be based on his drama *Arnljot Gelline*, and Grieg even made sketches for the music. This subject, however, was quickly abandoned in favour of a new text dealing with the story of Olav Trygvason from which Björnson had already taken an episode for the cantata *Landsighting*. The opera would unfold in three acts the introduction of the Christian faith into Norway under Olav's militant proselytising, and the overthrow of paganism. The opportunities which such a theme would provide for dramatic situations, character-conflicts, ceremonial and crowd scenes and even ballet (in the heathen temple), were attractive; and although Grieg had had little experience of writing for the stage and there were no Norwegian precedents, the spectacular operas and opera-ballets of the Danish national romantics, Gade and Hartmann, would serve very well as models. Grieg's incomplete score of *Olav* is in fact strongly indebted to Hartmann.

Unhappily Björnson failed to keep his side of the bargain: after sending the text of the first three scenes, promising the rest after a short interval, and urging Grieg to aim at completing the whole work by the autumn of 1873, he suddenly became absorbed in something quite different – the writing of realistic prose dramas of contemporary life – and Grieg was unable to get from him even a synopsis of the remainder of the libretto. When eventually Björnson was prepared to revive the project he was characteristically annoyed to find that Grieg in his turn had cooled off and was engaged in another major score – nothing less than the *Peer Gynt* music commissioned by Ibsen. Björnson never finished *Olav* and Grieg, after keeping his drafts of the music in his desk for many years, brought them to light in 1889, orchestrated them and published them as a suite for concert performance by soloists, chorus and orchestra, dedicating the score (with some generosity, one would have thought, under the circumstances) to the author of the text. The portion completed includes the pagan temple scenes and shows a flair for barbaric colour that might have made it very effective on the stage. For long after the breakdown of the enterprise Grieg kept returning to the idea of writing a full-length opera – at one time collaboration with Ibsen was proposed – but he never fulfilled his ambition. In a letter to his friend Frants Beyer in 1886 he expresses his admiration for *Tristan* and *Parsifal*, and adds: 'Now you will realise why I often go out and stare up at the clouds as if I could find there the Norwegian drama in Norwegian music that I have dreamt of, which I have always believed I could create some day, but which I now begin to think is fated to come from another.'

By the age of thirty Grieg had become one of the most distinguished artists in Norway, a recipient of the Knighthood of St Olav and of a state pension of 1,000 Kroner. A similar award was made to Johan Svendsen, the composer and conductor to whom Grieg had dedicated his Second Violin Sonata. For a time Grieg and Svendsen shared the conducting of the Christiania Philharmonic concerts and they were on the warmest terms of friendship. Grieg's capacity for making and keeping friends was, indeed, one of the most attractive sides of his personality. His correspondence was voluminous and his letters in Norwegian and German are among the most winning and elegant ever written by a musician: several collections have been published but many others are filed away in libraries and museums in various parts of Europe. They give a lively picture of the cultural life of the second half of the 19th century, especially during the period when the Griegs were making concert tours and paying social visits in Germany, Holland and England. One of their most intimate acquaintances from these later years, Julius Röntgen, paid this tribute: 'Grieg was just as original in his personal relations as in his music. He possessed in high degree the gift of self-expression, his fund of reminiscence was inexhaustible and his words brought everything to life'.

These years in Grieg's life saw the composition of some of the most important works in his nationalist music as well as the Piano Concerto which, for one reason and another, has become the best loved of all his music in the international repertoire. Owing to Grieg, the nationalist movement was established and future years were to see further developments.

Portrait of Ibsen painted in 1895 by E.T. Werenskiold (National Gallery, Oslo)

Peace and Prosperity:Life 1875-1907

Ibsen's invitation to Grieg to write the incidental music for *Peer Gynt* turned out to be a much lengthier commitment than Grieg had originally imagined. Having managed to obtain another grant from the government he had left Christiania in the summer of 1874 and gone to Sandviken in the west of the country. There he worked on the *Peer Gynt* score throughout the summer and autumn. The orchestration was not completed however, until the summer of 1875 and the first performance of the revised version of Ibsen's play with Grieg's music took place in February 1876.

Back in Bergen in the spring of 1876 he wrote the Six Songs, op.25, to words by Ibsen and the Five Songs, op.26, to words by Julius Paulsen. Apart from these songs the only work of importance which he wrote in 1876 – a year marred by the death of both his parents – was the *Ballad in the Form of Variations*, op.24, for piano. In August of that year Grieg was in Bayreuth to hear the first performance of Wagner's *Ring*, but this summer also took him on holiday into the Norwegian mountains. It is from this date that his music begins to show increased signs of the influence which his native country was having on him. In June 1877 he went for the summer months to Børve in Ullensvang in the Hardanger district. It was there that he composed 'Along the River', the earliest of his songs to words by the peasant-poet O. A. Vinje. So stimulated was he by the surroundings that he stayed on at Børve through the winter and well into the following year, returning home only in the autumn of 1878. During this prolonged stay in the country he produced the String Quartet in G minor, *Albumblade* (Album Leaves) and the 'Improvisations on Norwegian Folk-Songs'.

The return to civilisation seemed to bring a sudden halt to the flow of inspiration of the previous year, for Grieg wrote nothing for eighteen months. He always believed that these periods of artistic aridity were caused by ill-health, and although they became more frequent as he grew older he was able to profit from them by increasing his fame as an exponent of his own works both at home and abroad.

In the spring of 1880 Grieg's creative powers returned and he was able to complete the set of songs to words by Vinje which he had started some three years previously at Børve. It was also in this year that he took on the post of conductor of Harmonien for a period of three years. Indeed in the early 1880s Grieg became more closely identified than ever with the Westland and with Bergen, the town of his birth. In company with Björnson he took a leading part in the funeral ceremonies of Ole Bull, conducting Bull's famous melody *The Herdgirl's Sunday* and his own 'Elegiac Melody' *The Last Spring;* the close kinship of these two lovely melodies with their cadences of rising thirds or fourths – a marked characteristic of Norwegian folk-music, possibly derived from language intonations – must have given added poignancy to the occasion.

The Cello Sonata, op.36, belongs to the same period and is dedicated to the composer's brother, John Grieg, who like Edvard had studied in Leipzig, though he never took up music as a profession. A national celebration that gave rise to a work of lasting interest was the bicentenary of Holberg's birth: Grieg was commissioned to write a cantata and a suite of pieces in the dance-forms of the Baroque age, in which Holberg flourished as a dramatist. It is not certain whether the *Holberg Suite*, op.40, was originally written for piano and later arranged for string orchestra or vice versa, but it is the orchestral version that is best known, helping to fill in the awkward 19th-century gap in the repertory of the string orchestra. The writing for strings is brilliantly effective and Grieg manages to preserve the spirit of the old dance-forms while stamping them clearly with the imprint of his own personality.

In the same year, 1884, the Griegs began to build the villa they named 'Troldhaugen' (Trolls' Mound) a few miles outside Bergen. This house, which still remains as an intimate memorial to the composer, was to become the centre of the Griegs' warm hospitality and the starting-point for many an excursion into the mountains. Frants Beyer, a neighbour and Grieg's regular correspondent during his travels abroad, often shared in these expeditions. Others who took part in them were Julius Röntgen, Frederick Delius and Percy Grainger. The Griegs were by now in fairly comfortable circumstances, for in addition to the state pension, royalties from sales of publications and fees from concert tours, was a retaining fee willingly paid by the Leipzig firm of Peters, who bought up all rights in Grieg's works from other German, Norwegian and Danish publishers and immediately accepted anything new he cared to send them. Grieg's mounting reputation as a composer, both in the Scandinavian countries and in the world at large, together with state support, had enabled him to shed his teaching and other routine commitments and to devote himself to writing and concert-giving. He no longer needed to spend much time in Christiania, but could live for months at a time either in Denmark or, as he and his wife came to prefer, in the more beautiful regions of the Westland. For the holidays of 1869 the Griegs had had the use of the pleasant country house at Landaas which was still in the

A corner of Grieg's house at Troldhaugen outside Bergen. Here he spent the last years of his life

family's possession, and while there Grieg was able to make a close study of Lindeman's great book of Norwegian folk-music, *Mountain Melodies Old and New*. In its complete form this is a veritable treasure-house of more than five hundred songs and instrumental pieces, although representing but a third of the material Lindeman actually collected. These tunes are harmonised with a skill which, in a remarkable way, combines simplicity with musicianly distinction. Features commonly associated with Grieg's harmonic idiom, such as his use of chromatic chords, pedal notes and canonic imitation owe not a little to Lindeman's settings. As for the melodies themselves, their abundant variety was a revelation to Grieg, whose knowledge of folk-music had up to this time been limited in extent, being derived mainly through other educated musicians like Kjerulf and Nordraak. He at once re-set seventeen of Lindeman's tunes for piano in his opus 17, enriching them still further with modal or chromatic harmonies and laying them out pianistically. The whole of this set was dedicated to Ole Bull.

From this time onwards Grieg returned again and again to Lindeman. The *Ballad in the Form of Variations*, one of his few compositions for piano in extended form, is based on a splendid minor tune from Valders, 'I know so many a lovely song . . .' The 'Improvisations on Norwegian Folk-Songs', op.29, the Norwegian Dances for piano duet and the *Old Norwegian Melody with Variations* for two pianos are all indebted to Lindeman for their themes: the two-piano work indeed takes not only its theme (*Sigurd and the Troll-Bride*) from that source but also a great deal of Lindeman's striking chromatic harmony. The dozen songs freely arranged for men's voices (op.30) can all be found in Lindeman's collections, of which a modern reprint has been edited by O. M. Sandvik and Øystein Gaukstad. (Incidentally, the researches of Dr Sandvik and others have shown that the immensely rich vein of Norwegian folk-music first tapped by Lindeman was by no means worked out a hundred years later. The archives of Oslo University Library contain more than 10,000 melodies collected up to the present time.) Two later books of folk-music arranged by Grieg come under rather a different category. 'Norwegian Folk-Tunes', op.66, uses melodies collected in the Jotunheim mountains by Grieg himself in company with Beyer and Röntgen in the 1890s: Delius borrowed from this set not only the tune of *In Ole Dale* but also some of Grieg's harmony as the basis of his short tone-poem *On Hearing the First Cuckoo in Spring*, and Percy Grainger's transcriptions of English folk-tunes are modelled on such pieces as Grieg's setting of the Norwegian *In Deepest Thought I Wander*. With the *Slåtter*, op.72, which are free piano transcriptions of Hardanger fiddle tunes, we arrive chronologically and stylistically in the 20th century: their uncompromising harshness has caused them to be neglected unjustly in an age that has welcomed Bartók's Hungarian works.

Concert engagements, combined with invitations from their many friends, constantly took the Griegs abroad. In 1883, for example, there was a series of Grieg concerts in numerous centres in Germany and Holland, followed by a Christmas holiday with their Dutch hosts, the Röntgens, and in the spring another journey to Rome. In Vienna they were guests of Heinrich and Elisabeth von Herzogenberg, the close friends of Brahms, and it was in their home that

Grieg and Brahms first met. Brahms expressed his admiration for Grieg's *Ballad in the Form of Variations*, a work that shared some of the massive, quasi-orchestral features of Brahms's own larger keyboard compositions. For Tchaikovsky, whom they also met, the Griegs never lost their sincere personal regard and he, in his turn, has left a word-portrait of Edvard Grieg as he appeared in the days of his widest renown: 'Into the room came a very little middle-aged man, very thin and with shoulders of unequal height. His fair hair was brushed back high and he had a thin, almost youthful-looking beard and side-whiskers . . . He had uncommonly attractive blue eyes of medium size – irresistibly fascinating – like the gaze of an innocent, noble child.'

Tchaikovsky and Grieg, with Boito and Max Bruch, were made honorary Doctors of Music of Cambridge University in 1894. The occasion was one of many visits which Grieg made to England, where he was always assured of an enthusiastic welcome, though he dreaded the vagaries of the climate and, most of all, the industrial fogs. He took part in orchestral and chamber concerts in London in the spring of 1888 and returned to England in August for the Birmingham Festival, where he conducted his *Autumn* Overture and the *Holberg Suite*. The next spring he joined three famous violinists – Lady Hallé, Joseph Joachim and Johannes Wolf – in performances of his three Violin Sonatas, the third of which (in C minor, op.45) was to be his last venture into the larger Classical forms. After this work, he wrote only songs and instrumental miniatures.

In the autumn of 1891 the twenty-fifth anniversary of Grieg's first public concert in Christiania was celebrated with choral and orchestral performances, a banquet at which Ibsen was the principal speaker and a torchlight procession. The following year the silver wedding of Edvard and Nina was the occasion for lavish festivities in Bergen, with telegrams and gifts pouring into Troldhaugen from all over the world. Even stronger tokens of affection and admiration accompanied the celebration of Grieg's sixtieth birthday, when the round of concerts, excursions and banquets culminated in a speech from Björnson, who with his usual magnificent rhetoric unfolded the composer's life-history against the background of Norwegian traditions.

Ardent nationalist though he was, Grieg despised any form of artistic or intellectual parochialism, a fault Ibsen

9

had warned the Norwegian against in some of the satirical parts of *Peer Gynt*. He was a musician first and foremost, and when the first national Music Festival was held at Bergen in the summer of 1898 he insisted that one of the best orchestras in Europe, that of the Amsterdam Concertgebouw under Mengelberg, should be invited; regional interests were affronted but Grieg's courageous attitude gave his country a new revelation of international standards of orchestral playing. His inborn love of freedom and justice likewise transcended the boundaries of his own country. He took a firm line during the Dreyfus affair in 1899, refusing an invitation to conduct in Paris as a mark of disapproval of the action of the French government in this notorious case. Through a misunderstanding, his letter to the director of the concerts got into the newspapers of various countries and when, three years later, he accepted another invitation to Paris there were interruptions in the theatre where the concert took place and the Griegs had to be given a police escort out of the building. The tension between Norway and Sweden that accompanied the proposal to separate the crowns (the two countries having been under a single monarchy since 1814) affected Grieg strongly and his letters show the enormous relief that followed the bloodless achievement of complete Norwegian independence in 1905.

In the last two decades of his life Grieg composed comparatively little, though he constantly made arrangements and revised earlier work. Two of his finest sets of folk-music arrangements belong to this period. The Hardanger fiddle tunes of *Slåtter* taken down first of all by Johan Halvorsen from the playing of a peasant musician, Knut Dale, and adapted by him for the modern violin were thence freely arranged by Grieg for the piano. For the Four Psalms, op.74, Grieg turned once more to Lindeman's collection, selecting from it four ancient chorales of the Norwegian church in the forms to which they had evolved in the mountain communities: these he arranged for mixed voices, with a harmonic and contrapuntal freedom such as had seldom, if ever, before been applied to folk-tunes. 'I count this set of Four Psalms,' wrote Dr Edmund Rubbra in 1948, 'as among the finest choral music of the 19th century and it should be far more widely known, not only for its intrinsic qualities, but because it reveals a facet of the composer that has remained largely unrecognised.'

The manuscript sketch of Guten *(The Youth) —the first of the Six Songs, op. 33, which are settings of poems by Vinje (Public Library, Bergen)*

Although his output of compositions diminished and the chronic ill-health that had dogged him since his student days gave him little respite, Grieg maintained an active professional and social life almost up to the end of his days, and the volume of his correspondence continually increased. Early in 1907 his Dutch friend Julius Röntgen came to Norway and at a concert given in Christiania in the presence of the King and Queen Grieg and he played the Norwegian Dances for piano duet and Nina sang some of her husband's songs: it was the last time that they were to appear together on a concert platform. When, later that summer, he saw Röntgen off by boat from Bergen, he felt a presentiment that it was a final parting. Yet he was already planning his usual autumn journey to England, this time to conduct scenes from *Olav Trygvason* and the Piano Concerto, with Grainger as soloist, at the Leeds Festival. Prepared for the voyage, the Griegs were about to embark at Bergen when it became evident that Edvard was too ill to go on. He was ordered into the Bergen hospital and died there two days later, in the early hours of 4th September. Some time before he had written prophetically in his diary: 'The Westland is a love that costs me dear, for it robs me of my life. But it was the Westland that gave me life . . . the thrill of life, the desire to reproduce it in sound. The gift has really been a loan. I must repay it when it falls due.'

At the funeral an orchestra under the leadership of Adolf Brodsky, the Russian-born violinist who had settled in Manchester and become one of the Griegs' intimate friends, played Nordraak's Funeral March, as the composer had desired, and 'The Last Spring' from the *Elegiac Melodies:* and a choir with Ingolf Schiøtt as soloist sang his arrangement of the chorale *The Great White Host*. Grieg's ashes were placed in the grotto at Troldhaugen a few months later; those of Nina, who lived until the end of 1935, now rest beside them.

Measured beside the output of some other famous nationalist musicians of his time – Tchaikovsky for example, or Dvořák – that of Grieg is small both in quantity and, for the most part, in scale: he completed no symphony or opera, and only one concerto and one string quartet. Yet everything he wrote, down to the most unpretentious piano piece. is unmistakably his own. His style is unique; it can be parodied but not imitated. His influence on the music of his age was, nevertheless, more extensive than is sometimes realised. A whole generation of British composers came under the spell of his harmonic invention – Delius, Moeran, Warlock and Bax among them. French music is not untouched by him, especially round the turn of the century – both Debussy and Ravel acknowledged this, the former tacitly, the latter with openly expressed gratitude. Until the rise of Carl Nielsen and Sibelius to full maturity, Grieg was the dominant musical figure in the northern countries, and there are echoes of Grieg in the early work of Sibelius. Unfortunately a handful of Grieg's works tended to be over-performed, both in the concert room and still more by amateurs, and a reaction set in. Yet, some of his best music is still comparatively little known. The time has now come when a new generation of students, artists and music-lovers may be glad of an opportunity to reappraise Grieg's contribution to the music of the Romantic century.

PROGRAM NOTES FOR THE RECORD

by R O B E R T   J A C O B S O N

The A minor Piano Concerto

The name of Edvard Grieg is synonymous with Norwegian music; together with the Finn Jan Sibelius and the Dane Carl Nielsen, Grieg represents the true flowering of a Scandinavian musical renaissance. Like Smetana and Dvořák in Bohemia, and Mussorgsky and Borodin in Russia, Grieg helped to establish a national consciousness of a native musical tradition, basing many of his works on Norwegian folk tunes and dances. Although he grew up with the German Romantic style of Schumann and Mendelssohn and was schooled in Danish musical culture through the teaching of Niels Gade, Grieg's career was to take a decisive turn in 1863. In that year he met and befriended young Rikard Nordraak, a fervent Norwegian nationalist who wrote his country's anthem. It was Nordraak who introduced the youthful composer to the Norwegian folk music and peasant culture that ultimately inspired him to champion musical nationalism in his homeland.

'It was as if the scales fell from my eyes,' Grieg later reflected. 'From Nordraak I learned for the first time what the Norwegian folk-song was, and learned to know my own nature.' The composer declared that from this time onward he would react 'against the effeminate Mendelssohnian-Gade Scandinavianism, turning with enthusiasm into the new, well-defined path along which the Northern School is now travelling.' From then on, Grieg sought to shape his writing around the idioms of local folk-songs and dances. In addition, he helped to found the Norwegian Academy of Music, which sponsored concerts of Norwegian music, and he became conductor of the Harmonic Society in Christiania (now Oslo), where he helped greatly in performing works by Norwegians.

During his lifetime, Grieg became best known for his piano pieces, numerous songs and other small works, in which he revealed his genius as a lyrical miniaturist rather than as a titan of the symphony, concerto or sonata forms (although a string quartet, three sonatas for violin and piano and a cello sonata by him do exist). Great success came to him finally—and ironically—with the world première of his A minor Piano Concerto in Copenhagen in 1869, followed by equal recognition for his incidental music to *Peer Gynt* in 1876.

A government stipend Grieg received in 1869 provided him with the means to travel to Rome to visit the great virtuoso-composer Franz Liszt, who had praised his F major Violin Sonata. At his home in Villa d'Este, Liszt tried out the manuscript of the A minor Concerto at the piano. Grieg wrote his parents a letter about this meeting: 'I admit that he took the first part of the Concerto too fast, and the beginning sounded helter-skelter, but later on, when I had a chance to indicate the tempo, he played as only he can play. It is significant that he played the cadenza, the most difficult part, best of all. . . . In the Adagio, and still more in the Finale, he reached a climax, both as to his playing and the praise he had to bestow. . . . Toward the end of the Finale the second theme is, as you may remember, repeated in a mighty *fortissimo*. In the very last measures, when in the first triplets the first tone is changed in the orchestra from G sharp to G, while the piano part, in a mighty scale passage, rushes wildly through the whole reach of the keyboard, he suddenly stopped, rose up to his full height, left the piano and with big, theatric strides and with arms uplifted walked across the large cloister hall, at the same time literally roaring the theme. When he got to the G in question he stretched out his arms imperiously and exclaimed, "G, G, not G sharp! Splendid!" In conclusion, he handed me the manuscript, and said in a peculiarly cordial tone: "Keep steadily on; I tell you, you have the capability, and—do not let them intimidate you".'

At its première later that year the new concerto triumphed, and soloist Edmund Neupart (to whom it is dedicated) reported to the composer: 'Even as early as the cadenza in the first movement the public broke into a real storm. The three dangerous critics—Gade, Rubinstein and Hartmann—sat in the stalls and applauded with all their might.' With the immediate popular reception of his concerto, Grieg was dubbed 'the Chopin of the North' by one great pianist. And, indeed, the music does recall Chopin (Grieg's favourite composer) in passages, as well as Robert Schumann (to whose music he was exposed through concerts by Clara Schumann in Leipzig). Both in their spirit and music, Grieg and Chopin have much in common. Just as in Chopin's mazurkas and polonaises there is the voice of his native Poland, lamenting and exulting, so in Grieg there is the outdoor atmosphere of the North and its spectacular scenery joined with a spirit of brisk independence.

The first movement of the buoyantly optimistic A minor Concerto (*Allegro molto moderato*) is introduced by a crescendoing roll on the kettledrum, followed by a crash from the full orchestra and pounding octaves on the solo piano, all based on a descending three-note pattern. A march-like theme follows more softly, led by the woodwinds and punctuated by the strings. This is continued by the clarinet and bassoon, and then by the full orchestra. The piano picks up this theme and then breaks out into

11

a fresh idea of its own, a kind of whimsical subject or humoresque. The mood turns quiet, and then a second melody is heard in the cellos and winds before the piano takes it up poetically. This nocturnal passage becomes more impetuous before the full orchestra returns with the three-note motto. The development of these themes leads into the solo piano cadenza, and the movement ends majestically.

Muted strings open the atmospheric second movement (*Adagio*), with bassoons and horns underpinning this beautiful melody. The piano eventually enters with a rippling theme that is expanded. Orchestra and piano blend in a repetition of the opening theme, and the movement ends peacefully with more piano ripplings and a dying horn. A few bars link this with the Finale (*Allegro moderato molto e marcato*). The piano returns with a lilting *halling*, a popular Norwegian dance in double time.

strongly accented. After the full orchestra has taken up this theme, the solo instrument goes on to a bold chordal idea. The orchestra returns to the first theme and builds to a mighty climax, breaking off suddenly to allow the piano to emerge with a brief solo passage. The *halling* is taken up again with even greater vigour by both piano and orchestra, and once again this subsides to make way for a new theme stated by the flute, accompanied by strings. The piano rhapsodises on this leisurely; the *halling* is then resumed in slightly quicker tempo, and the whole first section of the movement is repeated. The orchestra builds up a lengthy climax, and the piano has another cadenza. After a dramatic pause, the original theme is transformed into the triple time of the *springdans*, and the work rushes to an exhilarating finish, summing up the joy of life and youthful fire that Grieg poured into this music.

Peer Gynt Suite No. 1

Henrik Ibsen's allegorical, poetic drama *Peer Gynt* was first produced in 1867; the playwright had drawn on Norse folk legend to create his vain, boastful hero, who is also a chronic liar. Peer lives with his aging mother Aase. On the wedding day of his former beloved, Ingrid, he abducts her and takes her off to the mountains. After she deserts him, he becomes an outlaw and is involved in various adventures, including one with the troll king's daughter in the Hall of the Mountain King. When the trolls (supernatural beings in Scandinavian mythology) attack him, Peer is saved by the ringing of church bells, which frightens away the trolls. He then goes to live in the woods, and is followed there by the faithful Solveig, who is in love with him. But he soon deserts her to return home in time for his mother's death, after which he is off again for America, Morocco and Egypt. When he comes home for the last time, he is a feeble old man, who finds redemption for his wasted life in the constancy and devoted care of Solveig.

Six years after its première, Ibsen revised his play and asked Grieg to write incidental music for it. At first Grieg lacked interest in the undertaking, for he felt the subject would not stimulate his creative powers. But, as his wife recorded, 'The more he saturated his mind with the powerful poem, the more clearly he saw that he was the right man for a work of such witchery and so permeated

with the Norwegian spirit.' His only other theatre music had been that written for Björnson's *Sigurd Jorsalfar*. He had also begun work on an opera, *Olav Trygvason;* but when he and Björnson had a falling-out, Grieg accepted Ibsen's invitation to compose music for *Peer Gynt*. The play with his music was premièred in Oslo in 1876 and was a great success. Soon after, Grieg divided his score into two orchestral suites, the first of which (op. 46) is the composer's most popular symphonic work.

The opening section, 'Morning,' is a nature painting rendered in the form of a barcarolle. Its lovely melody has suggestions of yodelling in the mountains and cow-bells. This is followed by the poignant elegy for muted strings which accompanies Aase's death in the play. The third movement is the well-known 'Anitra's Dance,' a rhythmically exciting oriental dance in a mazurka tempo; its exotic air is accentuated by the use of a triangle, and the overall mood is one of Eastern sensuality. The final section of the first suite, entitled 'In the Hall of the Mountain King,' conjures up the land of the trolls and gnomes; it is based on a single, rather grotesque motif, which begins in the bassoons and is passed on through the orchestra as intensity builds up to a furious climax. This collaboration between Norway's greatest playwright and its leading composer, then, firmly established that country's claim to a full-scale artistic nationalism, as well as its place in the mainstream of world culture.

Printed in the United States of America

His Life and Times 1797-1828

PROGRAM NOTES FOR THE UNFINISHED SYMPHONY
AND THE FIFTH SYMPHONY
By Robert Jacobson

f&w

FUNK & WAGNALLS, INC.
NEW YORK, NEW YORK

Scholarship: Life 1797-1813

Schubert's father, Franz Theodor, was a schoolmaster. He lived and taught in an apartment-house situated in a suburb to the north-west of the City of Vienna. The dwelling was a typical Viennese structure, two storeys high, built round three sides of an oblong courtyard. The front of the building abutted on the street, the Nussdorferstrasse, and contained the main entrance. The open side, beyond the courtyard, was fenced, with a small gate. By this back entrance one could reach a series of steep, stone steps which led to the parish church, the Liechtenthal Kirche. Tenants who occupied an apartment in the dwelling had the use of one large room and a small kitchen. Franz Theodor rented two apartments and in these cramped quarters he conducted his school; there were two sessions per day to accommodate the large and growing number of pupils. During these years, 1786-1802, his wife, Elisabeth, bore twelve children. Only four sons and one daughter survived infancy; Franz, the fourth son, was born on 31st January 1797.

When Schubert was five years old his father moved into a nearby house in the Säulengasse. It was actually a smaller building than the one he had left, but he was able to occupy more rooms in it and so cope with a school then numbering three hundred boys. Schubert received early instruction in music from his father and an older brother, Ignaz. He was gifted with an exceptionally sweet voice and sang in the parish church choir. The organist, Michael Holzer, taught him organ-playing and composition. By the time he was eleven years old he was a skilful violinist and pianist, and had already begun to compose. In October 1808 the young Schubert entered a competitive examination for a place in the Imperial Court Chapel Choir (the forerunner of today's Vienna Boys Choir). He was successful. His voice was the

prime factor, but as the announcement of the competition made clear, a high standard of attainment in music and academic subjects was required as well. Schubert met these requirements with ease. The choral scholars were instructed in all general subjects as well as in music at an institution of recent foundation, educational in function but administered by a religious order. It was known as the 'Stadtkonvikt' (City College) and became, in effect, the leading boarding school in Vienna for the sons of commoners; other students, in addition to the choral scholars, attended there. Rules were strict, hours of study and music-practice were long, food was scanty and, in the winter, rooms were poorly heated. But for a boy of Schubert's potentials the College was an incomparable source of encouragement and nurture. Chamber music he was acquainted with from his earliest days since the Schubert family, in common with many other Viennese families, could muster its own string quartet. At the City College he played in the students' orchestra, graduating quickly from a modest place in the second violins to principal first violin and then to deputy conductor. In his capacity as a Court 'Singknabe' he grew familiar with the major choral music of the day. He was instructed in music theory and composition by extremely able music-teachers headed by the internationally famous Antonio Salieri. At the end of his five years in the College he emerged an accomplished musician and with a substantial body of youthful compositions as the fruit of those adolescent years. Nearly a hundred works have survived from that period. Many are juvenile and of limited interest, but others proclaim in unmistakable terms the incipient genius and one of them, the String Quartet in E flat (D.87), is in the standard repertory. His first symphony, in D major, was finished in October 1813, a few days before he left the City College.

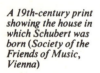

A 19th-century print showing the house in which Schubert was born (Society of the Friends of Music, Vienna)

The young Schubert
carrying his violin -
a painting by Larwin
(*Austrian National
Library, Vienna*)

Escape to Freedom: Life 1814-21

Soon after leaving the City College, Schubert enrolled as a student in a teachers' training college. The building was situated near St Stephan's Cathedral in the heart of the Inner City. To him the year's study seemed merely another stage in his preparation for the life of a schoolmaster, his aim being to take a position in his father's school. But we, who can look back on 1814, see it as a critical year in his progress as a composer. The capital was *en fête* for this was the year of the Congress of Vienna, and the diplomatic services of all Europe were represented there. At his parish church, the Liechtenthal Kirche, Schubert's first Mass, in F major, was performed as part of the festivities and although this full-length religious work is not without significance, the year 1814 is more notable in the Schubert annals for the composition, on 19th October 1814, of his first masterpiece in song, the initiation of the German *Lied*. It was the setting of Gretchen's plaint from Goethe's *Faust*, known as 'Gretchen am Spinnrade' (Gretchen at the Spinning-wheel). The despairing words of the girl are given melodies so deeply expressive and the hum of the wheel so transmuted into a magical murmur of sound on the pianoforte, that the song remains today after a century and a half as fresh and moving as when Schubert first wrote it.

He entered his father's school in the autumn of 1814 and remained there for two and a half years. In spite of the gruelling duties of a long teaching day, the number of works composed during those years almost staggers belief. In O. E. Deutsch's *Thematic Catalogue* (to which we owe the 'D' numberings of his works) we find that they exceed four hundred. Four symphonies, two masses and some half-a-dozen operatic works represent the output of larger compositions; numerous pianoforte solos and chamber works were also composed during the period. But it is the immense number of songs which swells the total, for he wrote over 250 between the autumn of 1814 and the end of 1816. A few of these songs are in the front rank of his masterpieces – 'Erlkönig', 'Der Wanderer' and the Harper's songs from Goethe's novel *Wilhelm Meister*. Many more are lyrical gems, among the world's favourites, and include 'Heiden-röslein' (Hedge Rose) and 'Die Forelle' (The Trout).

One day in the autumn of 1815 a visitor entered Schubert's classroom – a dramatic moment in the composer's life had he but known it. He was Franz von Schober, a young law student who, because of his friendship with Spaun, had become acquainted with Schubert's songs and was now determined to meet their author. He was, even then, in his

late teens, an assured and eloquent man of the world, and Schubert was greatly impressed. Schober urged him to abandon teaching and devote his life to composition. This was pushing at an open door and after a year of indecision Schubert made up his mind. He took his new friend's advice and left his father's school and the parental home. He was given lodgings in the home of Schober's mother, a wealthy widow, and for the first time tasted freedom. For eight months in 1817 he gave himself wholeheartedly to composition. A series of pianoforte sonatas and many of his most popular songs, among them 'An die Musik' (To Music) and 'Der Tod und das Mädchen' (Death and the Maiden) were written in this period. But the freedom was shortlived and he was obliged to return to his old task. The only work of note to come from his pen in the months which followed was his Sixth Symphony in C. Then, in July 1818, a second opportunity to escape presented itself. He obtained the position of music-master to the family of Count Johann Esterházy and went with them to their summer residence in Zseliz, Hungary. His pupils were the two young countesses, Marie and Karoline. It was not an entirely successful venture, and when Count Esterházy returned to Vienna Schubert gave up the post. Those summer months at Zseliz had seen the production of several pianoforte duets, the first of his mature

works in this medium, including the Variations on a French Air, which, when published as his op.10, were dedicated to Beethoven by 'his admirer and worshipper, Franz Schubert'.

While he lived in the Schobers' home, Schubert met the well-known operatic baritone Johann Michael Vogl. An impressive figure, somewhat of a poseur, but with genuine vocal and interpretative gifts, Vogl at first took a patronising attitude. It quickly changed. He came to venerate the young composer and was soon a close companion and an outstanding singer of his songs. After the spell of work at Zseliz had finished, Vogl took Schubert with him on holiday in Upper Austria. The two men, always ready to give a recital of the songs, were welcomed everywhere they went and for Schubert it was a period of unmixed delight. Towards the end of the holiday he composed the celebrated 'Trout' Quintet in A major, for pianoforte and strings. Its name is due to the fact that one movement is a set of variations on the song of that name.

On his return to Vienna there was no thought of a return to teaching. Instead Schubert took lodgings with Johann Mayrhofer and decided to try to live by his pen. His efforts to achieve success in the Viennese opera world were now begun. It is fortunate that intensive work on music for the stage did not silence his song-writing. Whereas the operas are unperformed and unknown, the songs he wrote at this time are famous. 'Frühlingsglaube' (Faith in Spring), 'Geheimes' (Secrets) and 'Der Jüngling an der Quelle' (The Youth at the Spring) are a few from a long list of favourites. Another beloved work of the period, composed in December 1820, is the single movement for string quartet in C minor (the Quartettsatz), which heralds the chamber music masterpieces of the years between 1820 and 1828.

The Years of Song: Life 1822-26

Once again necessity compelled Schubert to seek his friend Schober's hospitality, and at the beginning of 1822 he took up residence in the Schober family home. He stayed there for a year, paying for his board and lodging as and when publishers' fees became available. Publication of his songs and pianoforte solos had started in 1821 and continued at an increasing rate in the subsequent years; yet without the aid of Schober and other friends he could not have managed financially.

During the early months of 1822 Schubert and Schober grew disillusioned over the possibility of having their opera *Alfonso und Estrella* performed. Hope that eventual success would crown his operatic endeavours was not yet dead in Schubert's thoughts, but it is clear from the work of 1822-23 that he was keeping in mind his other source of income, for they are years rich in songs. Some of them are as greatly loved as any he wrote: 'Wandrers Nachtlied' (Wanderer's Night-Song), 'Auf dem Wasser zu singen' (To be sung on the Water) and 'Du bist die Ruh'' (Thou art Peace). An ambitious composition for pianoforte was finished in November 1822 and published shortly afterwards. It was the Fantasia in C which, since the slow section is based on his song 'Der Wanderer', is called the

'Wanderer' Fantasia. Another work completed at that time, a further indication of the composer's forethought, is a fifth Mass, in A flat major. On its own modest level the Mass is a very likeable composition.

Perhaps the autumn of 1822 is chiefly memorable for the third great masterpiece which Schubert wrote at the time. It is his most celebrated composition, yet a fragment – no less a work than the 'Unfinished' Symphony in B minor. That he left it unfinished is now no longer in dispute and perhaps we make too sentimental a matter of its non-completion when we enquire *why* he left it so. To many musicians the two movements are a perfect whole needing nothing further to be added.

Schubert's social life was that of every other middle-class Viennese. He was an eager member of a circle of like-minded young men, painters, poets and art-loving civil servants, who gathered in this or that favourite coffee-house where they frequently heard 'the chimes at midnight'. He made music, as a pianist, in the regular musical evenings in the homes of the wealthier bourgeois patrons of music. As time went on, and his songs and pianoforte pieces became known and loved, these musical evenings were devoted entirely to his music: they became known as

5

'Schubertiads'. The waltz, inseparably associated with Vienna, was then in its April youth and all Schubert's friends testify to his powers as an improviser of waltzes at the pianoforte while they danced. He frequently wrote down these happy inspirations and his published works contain numerous collections of waltzes. They have not the heady, sensuous tone of the later waltzes by Johann Strauss (nor their expansiveness) but they exemplify the fresh and intimate charm of the period. Schubert is a true child of his time although his supreme genius, far from being cramped by the confining nature of the Biedermeier outlook, transcended it and gave it a voice to which the world listens.

At the end of 1822 Schubert became seriously ill with a venereal infection. He left the Schobers' home and returned to live with his father. The year 1823 was a dismal one in his life; illness and financial stress combined to depress him; yet the astonishing detachment of the artist from his material circumstances is nowhere more strikingly shown than in the existence of a group of songs written during the summer of that year. It is the song-cycle *Die schöne Müllerin* (The Fair Maid of the Mill). The twenty songs are superb examples of Schubert's poetic and lyrical gifts and their range – from the passionate outburst in 'Ungeduld' (Impatience) to the heartbreak of 'Trockne Blumen' (Withered Flowers) – is phenomenal.

The one-act operetta *Die Verschworenen* and the full scale opera *Fierrabras* were composed in 1823, and the incidental music for *Rosamunde* followed at the end of the year. The acceptance of the music for *Rosamunde* brought Schubert much-needed financial help, but his plight was so desperate that once again, and very reluctantly, he agreed to resume the post of music-master to the Esterházy family. In the summer of 1824 he went to Zseliz and stayed, on that occasion, for five months. As in the previous sojourn in Zseliz in 1818, the period is notable for the production of some very fine work for pianoforte duet. The Sonata in C is one of his grandest conceptions. It was published many years after his death under the misleading title 'Grand Duo'. The set of variations on an original theme in A flat

is equally fine, and a third important duet is the 'Divertissement à l'hongroise' in which Schubert is said to have used Hungarian folk-tunes.

Duties at Zseliz in 1818 had been followed by a holiday with Vogl in 1819. The pattern repeated itself. For three idyllic months in 1825, Schubert and Vogl toured Upper Austria, visiting Steyr, Linz, Gmunden and Gastein. The composer told his brother Ferdinand that he found his music wherever they went, and the difference those six years had made in his status is shown by the fact that the music he found was not in manuscript, as in 1818, but published, and purchased by his warm-hearted admirers. Song-recitals and 'Schubertiads' were frequent. The combination of invigorating mountain air and friendly association with other musicians restored Schubert's health and spirits. The year saw the creation of two very fine sonatas in A minor, D.845, and in D major, D.850. A group of well-known songs, to lyrics from Scott's *The Lady of the Lake*, was composed in 1825. The most popular is 'Ave Maria'.

How Schubert subsisted on his return from Upper Austria is a mystery. He lived alone in lodgings near the beautiful baroque church called the Karlskirche, just to the south of the Inner City. For a short period in the late spring and summer of 1826 he stayed at the nearby village of Währing. Here he set to music three of Shakespeare's lyrics, including 'Who is Sylvia?' and 'Hark, hark! the lark'. The third and last of his great string quartets, in G major, was composed in July. Schubert had told his friends that this Third Quartet was to pave the way to his 'grand' symphony. It is a superb work, a masterpiece of the front rank, and although it may have fulfilled its function as a step towards the 'Great' C major Symphony of 1828, it would be idle to look upon it as in any way a mere work of preparation. During October of 1826 he composed the Sonata in G major. This is a more intimate work than the quartet in the same key, but it is full of charming melody and has a most attractive use of dance-rhythms. This sonata was much admired by Spaun, and when it was published, as op. 78, Schubert paid his old friend a warm tribute by dedicating the work to him.

Below:
Schubert at the Biersack Restaurant in Vienna—*a painting by Nowak* (Austrian National Library, Vienna)

Below right:
Nowak's painting of Schubert in the courtyard of his house (Austrian National Library, Vienna)

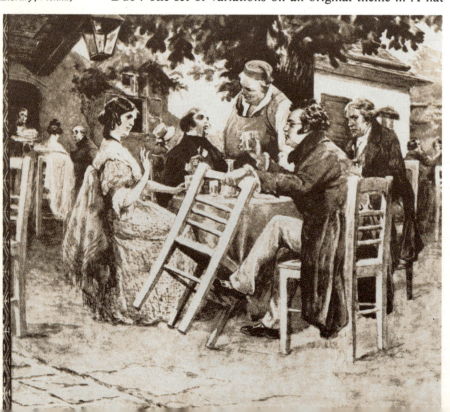

A picture by J. Schmid of Schubert playing in a Viennese salon (City History Museum, Vienna)

Swansong: Life 1827-28

There is little doubt that in spite of the considerable amount of his published work in Vienna, and the frequency of the 'Schubertiad' evenings, Schubert's fame was not general in the city. One has only to read the journals and reminiscences of musicians who visited the capital in the last years of Schubert's life to understand that he was never among Vienna's most notable musical personalities. His life therefore is devoid of that interest which comes from contacts with flamboyant virtuoso figures like Paganini, or from engagements involving travel to other countries, or even from participation in controversial movements in literature, music or politics. Schubert, it is clear, was a humble and insignificant inhabitant of suburban Vienna and the few distinguished people of his acquaintance were chance contacts, members of those private circles so devoted to his music.

On 26th March 1827 Beethoven died. Schubert had never met him. The many anecdotes told in connection with the two composers come from such doubtful sources that probably none of them is true. All that we know for certain is that Schubert was one of thirty-six torch-bearers in Beethoven's funeral procession.

One of Schubert's friends and admirers was the gifted Anna Fröhlich, who taught female choral singing at the Vienna Conservatoire. In order to celebrate the birthday of a distinguished pupil, Louise Gosmar, she persuaded the poet Franz Grillparzer to write a short birthday ode; she gave the poem to Schubert and asked him to set it to music for alto solo and chorus. This he agreed to do and in a short time handed her the composition, called 'Serenade'. Anna looked at it and saw to her astonishment that the composer had written it for *male* chorus! She intended it to be sung by her female singing-class. Schubert amiably rewrote it, making the necessary alterations. The performance was to be a surprise for Louise. A piano was secretly taken into the garden, the ladies of the Vienna Conservatoire assembled, and the 'Serenade' was first performed on a lovely summer night in August 1827.

The following month Schubert spent a fortnight's much needed holiday in Graz. He was the guest of Karl and Marie Pachler, two ardent lovers of music, and Schubert visited them in the company of his friend Jenger. Graz was the home of the brothers Anselm and Josef Hüttenbrenner, active musicians in the town and close friends of Schubert; the fortnight passed in pleasant expeditions into the neighbouring countryside and in much congenial music-making.

But Schubert's health was broken. The severe illness he suffered five years previously still undermined his physique and at this time he was greatly troubled with headaches and nausea. The year 1827 saw the composition of the songs of *Winterreise* (Winter Journey). This song-cycle is among the peaks of all musical achievement. By November 1827, the Piano Trios, in B flat and E flat, were also finished.

The work of his last year gives no hint of its closing tragedy, for the story continues to be one of abundant production. Three magnificent Piano Duets (including the famous Fantasia in F minor), the 'Great' C major Symphony, and the sixth Mass, in E flat, were all completed by the early summer. With his friend Franz Lachner, later to become widely known in Germany as a conductor, he went on a short visit to Baden and Heiligenkreuz, a gem of the Vienna Woods, but that was the only break in the year's routine. The late summer and autumn showed no diminution in his output. The last songs, published after his death as the *Schwanengesang* (Swansong) were finished in August; the settings of six Heine poems at the end of

this collection, including the song 'Der Doppelgänger' (The Spectral Double), point to the possibility of future developments in the *Lied* which he never lived to fulfil. The String Quintet in C major, his greatest piece of chamber music, and the last three Piano Sonatas, in C minor, A major and B flat, were composed by the end of September.

Since living alone in lodgings in his weakened state was out of the question, Schubert took up residence with his brother Ferdinand. The house had been built in a new district where the sanitation left much to be desired. A drink of tainted water infected Schubert with typhoid fever. His last compositions, written during October, include the popular 'Der Hirt auf dem Felsen' (The Shepherd on the Rock), for soprano solo with clarinet obbligato. Extraordinary that this gush of joyous sound, fresh and sparkling as the water of a mountain stream, should come from the pen of a man wasted with disease and near to death. He may have been 'for the dark' but what pure, unflickering light was in him to the very end! Early in November he was confined to bed. In spite of the devoted nursing of his brother the fever proved fatal. He died during the afternoon of Wednesday 19th November 1828, at the early age of thirty-one.

A silhouette by Böhler entitled Schubert in heaven *(Austrian National Library, Vienna)*

An open-air dance – *a drawing by Moritz von Schwind (Albertina Print Collection, Vienna)*

Schubert and the Austrian Note

As with most legendary ideas, the Vienna of gaiety, dancing and glittering society is firmly based on reality, even if that reality falls short of the legend. The Austro-Hungarian Empire of which Vienna was the capital, was a multi-national assemblage, yet there is no question that 'Austrian' can be used to denote certain characteristics shared by these twenty-five million different nationals. Their music and dancing reflected their carefree attitude to life, and their piety expressed itself in the ritual and liturgy of the Catholic Church. These undertones sound when we use the term 'Austrian'.

In a notable passage Schumann once wrote: 'Range in one compact frame the several pictures of the Danube, the cathedral towers and the distant Alpine range and steep all these images in the holy incense of Catholicism and you have an ideal of Vienna itself.' The sacred music of Austria, sung and played in monastic foundations and in the multitude of town and village churches, inspired Mozart, Haydn and Schubert to compose their own; each of these three had, as young choristers, sung in chapel choirs and the Catholic liturgical music was in their blood. Their masses, Schubert's in particular, have that note of piety combined with a relaxed sweetness which is wholly Austrian. It made an instant appeal to visiting musicians, to Carl Loewe for instance, and was to lead eventually to the superb masses of Anton Bruckner.

The sweeter tunefulness of Austrian music stands in marked contrast to the more serious style of northern Germany. We can observe this contrast most clearly in the songs of the two schools. The more melodious type of *Lied* reached its summit in the *Lieder* of Schubert. The influence of his songs in the 19th century, on the work of Schumann, Brahms and Robert Franz, ousted that of the North German schools, and the Austrian note sounded throughout.

The waltz was Austria's passion, and its lilting measures and melodic sweetness penetrated every department of music in the years to come. In Schubert we see its simpler beginnings, but even before he died the two men who were to give it an overwhelming impetus were flourishing. Josef Lanner and Johann Strauss the elder were leaders in a string band which regaled the Viennese in the open air of the Prater. The rivalry between the two men, which led to a split and to the eventual triumph of Strauss, is deeply symbolical. Lanner represented the old school of light music, which was still part of the lyrical tradition of Mozart, Rossini and Schubert. Strauss was typical of the more trivial, popular music of the future. The unbridgeable gap today between light and serious music had its beginnings in the quarrel between the two men. In the music of Strauss's son, Johann Strauss the younger, the Viennese waltz reached its zenith. Its frenzied popularity in Austria, reminiscent of the earlier furore attending the performances of Rossini's operas in Vienna, had a profound effect on music throughout Western Europe. Here most surely we hear the Austrian note. Even Wagner was not unaffected, and in the delightful — though completely anachronistic— 'Dance of the Apprentices' from *Die Meistersinger von Nürnberg* he paid conscious tribute to the Strauss waltz.

The serious-minded Brahms, too, fell under the intoxicating spell of this dance music and in his *Liebeslieder* Waltzes, op. 52, and his *Neue Liebeslieder* Waltzes, op. 65, he dances as gaily, if not quite as lightfootedly, as those to the manner born. The spirit of the waltz still lives spasmodically and with all its old vitality in the symphonic work of Gustav Mahler; even if there the note has elements of parody, it is none the less as fragrant as of old.

After Schubert, Classical sonata-form — especially as exemplified in the symphony — continued to sound the Austrian note which he had so well exploited. The Austrian qualities of easy-going charm, of tuneful and dancing metres, which he had integrated into his symphonies, developed side by side with the more architectural qualities typical of Beethoven. Schumann greatly admired Schubert and his 'Great' C major Symphony, but his own four symphonies show the influence of Beethoven more strongly than that of Schubert. In Mendelssohn and particularly in Brahms the continuance of the Beethovian symphonic tradition is very obvious. It is in the symphonies of Bruckner that we find again the poetic, digressive forms of Schubert's symphonies most surely in evidence, and also in the very individual symphonies of Mahler. Brahms is spiritually Beethoven's heir, but the Austrian note is not absent from his symphonies. He breathed the very air of Vienna, both literally and figuratively, and loved the work of Schubert. When we hear certain melodic phrases, certain dancing rhythms in Brahms, we are again conscious of that Austrian note. Its influence was sometimes obvious, sometimes subtle, but it was unmistakably present in all the music of the 19th century.

Schubert's unique gift, manifested chiefly in his incomparable melody and in the magical changes of key which give freshness and charm to that melody, lies in his direct appeal to the heart of the listener. No composer before him and none since has quite that power of establishing a living communion with the listener, with such an unreserved and frank approach. To some music-lovers this rapport is not wholly congenial, any more than it would be in real life with a friend: to such people Schubert too clearly wears his heart on his sleeve. But to the majority of music-lovers the man who could write songs such as 'Du bist die Ruh'', and movements like the Andante con moto of the 'Unfinished' Symphony is a loved composer – winning from the coming and going generations, as Richard Capell said, 'a tenderness which is more than admiration'.

PROGRAM NOTES FOR THE RECORD

by ROBERT JACOBSON

The Fifth Symphony

Neither Schubert's Fifth nor Eighth Symphony was to receive a public performance during the composer's brief lifetime. After a single private reading by Otto Hatwig at the Schottenhof in Vienna, during the fall of 1816, the Fifth remained unperformed for decades. Following Schubert's death in 1828, the manuscript of the Symphony was lost, and it took some forty years before the orchestral parts were rediscovered in Vienna. Ironically, the work was resurrected by two Englishmen: Sir George Grove, of musical dictionary fame, and Sir Arthur Sullivan, the celebrated composer of light opera. The two had come to Vienna to hunt for lost Schubert manuscripts (a pastime that continues; only a few years ago, for instance, a lost Schubert sonata was found in Graz, Austria). The first public performance anywhere of this Symphony No. 5 took place, fifty-seven years after its composition, in the Crystal Palace of London on 1st February 1873, under the direction of August Manns.

Franz Schubert was a mere nineteen years old when he composed his classically oriented Fifth Symphony in B flat major, sometimes referred to as 'The Symphony without Trumpets and Drums.' He wrote it for an orchestra of chamber proportions, a private ensemble that was an outgrowth of the string quartet which used to meet in his home. At the time he wrote this work, Schubert had passed through an artistic crisis. His preceding Symphony No. 4, given the title 'Tragic,' was written under the influence of Beethoven's stormy later symphonies and chamber music. Yet, intuitively, Schubert knew he could not digest the entire Beethoven heritage as it then existed nor immerse himself completely in it, even though Beethoven was the towering musical figure of the period. In his diary of 1816, there is an illuminating entry in which the disillusioned Schubert characterises Beethoven's manner as 'that eccentricity which joins and confuses the tragic with the comic, the agreeable with the repulsive, heroism with howlings and the holiest with harlequinades, without distinction, so as to goad people to madness instead of dissolving them in love, to incite them to laughter instead of lifting them to God.'

Eventually Schubert was to return to his youthful adoration of Beethoven, but only after having firmly established and affirmed his own strong personality. The Fifth Symphony was his finest effort to date in the idiom. In composing it, instead of looking to Beethoven, he turned to Haydn and Mozart and the Classical symphony. As writer Mosco Carner comments, 'Not only has he here completely mastered the Classical style, but what is more important, he now fuses the traditional idiom with a remarkable individual expression, and the result is a work in which Haydn's wit and Mozart's gracefulness and light touch combine in perfect union with the composer's happy flow of melody and exuberant expression.'

The first movement (*Allegro*) opens with a brief soft introduction, leading directly into the graceful main theme, introduced by the violins. A genial grace permeates both themes of this section in particular, as well as the whole Symphony. Thematic fragments are tossed back and forth between the strings and woodwinds in the development, and the main themes return before the movement ends. The second movement (*Andante con moto*) is Mozartean in feeling. The violins present the first theme, tinged with melancholy, and additional colour is supplied by the winds. Another tender melody is shared by strings and winds, and the two ideas are magically interwoven.

The Minuetto (*Allegro molto*) begins in an assertive mood but turns into an effortless flow of melodic inspiration. Before the main melody returns, there is a contrasting middle section or trio. The opening theme of the Finale (*Allegro vivace*) recalls Haydn's lighthearted rondo finales. The first theme is given out by the violins, as is the second subject. Everything here is graceful and natural, communicating a spontaneous joy that goes far beyond any consideration of Schubert's great technical mastery.

A painting by Nowak of Schubert playing in a string quartet. This type of music-making at home was very popular with Viennese families of the time (Austrian National Library, Vienna)

The 'Unfinished' Symphony

When Schubert's name was proposed for honorary membership in the Styrian Music Society of Graz on 10th April 1823, his qualifications were presented as follows in the nomination papers: 'Although still young, he has already proved by his compositions that he will someday rank high as a composer.' When elected, the twenty-six-year-old composer gratefully accepted and replied thus in writing: 'May it be the reward for my devotion to the art of music that I shall one day be fully worthy of this signal honour. In order that I may also express in musical terms my lively sense of gratitude, I shall take the liberty, at the earliest opportunity, of presenting your honourable Society with one of my symphonies in full score.'

In his *Schubert, A Musical Portrait*, Alfred Einstein surmises that soon afterwards Schubert presented the score and parts of a two-movement Symphony in B minor he had written sometime earlier (probably October 1822) to the director of the Society, his friend Anselm Hüttenbrenner, whose discreet retention of it for over forty years is also a mystery. The Society rehearsed the work but never performed it. Sketches for a third movement—nine measures of a Scherzo—show that the composer planned a full-scale symphony but never completed it. Various guesses have been made as to why the work was left unfinished, and others will continue to be made; unless some new documentary evidence comes to light, these remain guesswork or persuasive hypotheses. Schubert authority Einstein, for example, has declared that the composer never *could* have finished the work, for nothing to approach the originality, power and skill of the first two movements could ever have been made from the material of Schubert's sketch for the Scherzo.

In 1860 Hüttenbrenner's brother Josef wrote to Johann Herbeck, conductor of the 'Gesellschaft der Musikfreunde' concerts in Vienna, that Anselm had in his possession 'a treasure in Schubert's B minor Symphony.' Five years later, in May 1865, Herbeck had occasion to stop in Graz, where he sought out Anselm, telling him he had come to ask permission to play one of the latter's works at a Vienna concert. Flattered, with great enthusiasm Anselm virtually inundated the conductor with manuscript after manuscript of his own uninspired music. Herbeck at long last decided on an overture and then informed Hütten-brenner he intended to give a concert by three 'contemporaries'—namely, Schubert, Hüttenbrenner and Lachner—and that it would be most appropriate to represent Schubert with a new work. Hüttenbrenner, who had many works of Schubert in his possession, proceeded to pull a stack of manuscripts out of an old chest. On the cover of one, Herbeck saw the words 'Sinfonie in H moll' in Schubert's own handwriting. He showed casual interest in the score, and his host promptly obliged by giving it to him for performance, which occurred on 17th December of that year.

This proved to be a work in which the true symphonic voice of Schubert was finally heard, after a series of works in which he had been variously under the spell of Beethoven, Mozart, Haydn or Rossini. As one critic has written: 'Few people have escaped the tragically pungent spell of this music. Its themes, completely individual now as those of the earlier works so often were not, are known even where the work itself is unknown ... Schubert's symphony *is* a classic, although it is the reverse of Classical.' And it remains consistently one of the half-dozen most popular of all symphonies.

The first movement (*Allegro moderato*) opens with a mysterious, almost questioning, introductory phrase for cellos and double basses that seems the epitome of romantic yearning. This theme, the germinal idea of the whole movement, is later re-worked to convey great emotional tension as well. The violins enter with a soft murmuring passage, over which the oboe and clarinet play a poignant melody. This motive grows in intensity as the winds join in, and the mood grows more and more agitated. Suddenly, syncopated chords in the violas and clarinets usher in and accompany one of the most beautiful subjects in all of symphonic literature, a song for the cellos that becomes even more meltingly tender when taken up by the violins. With its gentle, almost waltz-like lilt, it could have been written, as Einstein says, 'by Schubert only in Vienna.' Several abrupt chords then interrupt this lyrical serenity. The agitated mood returns, intermittently relieved by brief recollections of the second theme. The development of the movement is marked by dramatic elements, while the recapitulation of the themes stresses lyricism. It concludes with a return to the opening bars.

The second and final movement (*Andante con moto*) is one of sustained rapture and peace. The violins introduce a melody of other-worldly radiance, played over a quiet, descending accompaniment in the basses. A more forceful subject brought in by trombones and woodwinds is soon dissipated by a return to the opening melody. A second plaintive melody is offered by the clarinets over syncopated strings, after which the full orchestra interjects strong commentary. The magic of this movement continues as the first melody is heard for the final time, softly and sadly, over a descending plucked accompaniment. As Einstein summed it up, 'The whole movement, in its mystery and unfathomable beauty, is like one of those plants whose flowers open only on a night of the full moon.'

A painting by Nowak of Schubert in the country finding inspiration for composition (Austrian National Library, Vienna)

12

Printed in the United States of America

His Life and Times 1873-1943

PROGRAM NOTES FOR PIANO CONCERTO NO. 2 IN C MINOR, SYMPHONIC DANCES OPUS 45, NO. 2 AND 3, AND VOCALISE OPUS 34, NO. 14

By Phillip Ramey

fw

FUNK & WAGNALLS, INC.
NEW YORK, NEW YORK

The Formative Years: 1873-1900

"I reflect the philosophy of old Russia," Sergei Rachmaninoff (1873-1943) was once quoted as saying. "White Russia—with its overtones of suffering and unrest, its pastoral but tragic beauty, its ancient and enduring glory." Indeed, Rachmaninoff, whose aristocratic family of landed gentry traced its lineage back to the 14th century, was White Russian to the core. He was to remain so even during the last 25 years of his life, years spent in self-imposed exile in the West after the "old Russia" he knew had disappeared in the flames of the 1917 Revolution.

Rachmaninoff was born on April 2, 1873 at Oneg, his family's estate near Novgorod. His paternal grandfather, an army officer, had been a highly gifted pianist, a student of the Irish composer John Field, and his father also had pianistic talent. On his mother's side, the family background was somewhat more utilitarian, her father being head of a military college in Novgorod in addition to owning numerous estates there. However Rachmaninoff's father Vassily, although a charming and generous man who had the affection of his several children, held the traditional aristocratic view that music, like the theater, was not to be taken seriously as a career and, so, it was his mother who decided that young Sergei would be a musician. Much later Rachmaninoff recalled: "My memory goes back to my fourth year and it is strange how all my memories of childhood, the good and the bad, the sad as well as the happy ones, are somehow connected with music. My mother began to give me piano lessons when I was four. I must have made pretty good progress for I was made to play to people."

It was not long before a graduate of the St. Petersburg Conservatory named Anna Ornazkaya was engaged to come to Oneg and give Sergei piano lessons. Impressed with the boy's obvious talent she began to urge Madame Rachmaninoff to enroll him in the Conservatory. However because of the family's by now precarious financial condition—caused to some degree by Tsar Alexander II's emancipation of the serfs in 1861 but even more so by the considerable extravagances of Rachmaninoff's father—it was decided that Sergei should instead apply for a scholarship at the Conservatory. This was awarded and in 1882, at the age of 9, he was officially launched on his musical career.

How seriously was another matter. Because of his superiority over his classmates and the gift of absolute pitch, he found it unnecessary to apply himself industriously to his studies and tended to exert minimum effort. The boy spent a good deal of time with his grandmother, rather than with elementary theory, listening to choral music in various St. Petersburg churches and playing piano improvisations on the service at home afterward. His mother, worried by his slow progress, finally turned for advice to her nephew Alexander Siloti, a young pianist who had recently been a pupil of the great Franz Liszt. Siloti suggested that Sergei be sent to his own former teacher in Moscow, Nicholas Zverev, and so, in the autumn of 1885, Rachmaninoff became Zverev's pupil at the Moscow Conservatory.

Authoritarian and demanding, Zverev was exactly what the undisciplined youth needed at that point. A brilliant musician and one of the finest piano teachers in Russia, he was a hard taskmaster. His habit was to allow a few of his most talented pupils to live in his Moscow house with him

A view of the Moscow Kremlin photographed in 1910. (Milan, Italy —USSR Cultural Association)

and his sister. There, they conformed to a rigid discipline that included sharing one room and one piano, wearing uniforms, and rising at six in the morning for supervised lessons and practise. Not only music, but also languages, history and literature were subjects for study, a regimen combined with regular attendance at the theater. This special group of boys was traditionally known as "Zverev's Cubs", and in 1885 the twelve year old Rachmaninoff became one of them.

Zverev's aim was to produce performers of great technical capacity with large repertoires, and under his guidance Rachmaninoff made extraordinary progress. It was not long before the boy was allowed to enter Anton Arensky's classes in composition and advanced harmony at the Conservatory. Subsequently, he had the illustrious pedagogue Sergei Taneyev as his mentor in composition and studied piano with his cousin Siloti. However he was still sometimes lackadaisical where theoretical subjects were concerned and at one point Taneyev actually began sending a messenger to Rachmaninoff's house with the day's homework and instructions to return with it completed. Rachmaninoff remembered that "Once or twice I was caught. But the third time I gave orders to say that I was out, so she was obliged to leave the manuscript paper."

Nonetheless Rachmaninoff was one of the most brilliant students ever to attend the Moscow Conservatory and it was not long before he attracted the attention of Moscow's foremost musical figure, Piotr Ilyich Tchaikovsky. Zverev, a close friend of Tchaikovsky's, showed him a short piano piece by the youngster and introduced them. The precocious Rachmaninoff, then 13, had made a two-piano arrangement of Tchaikovsky's "Manfred" Symphony and this so impressed its composer that he consequently took an interest in the boy, becoming in time his patron and adviser. Tchaikovsky's influence was incalculable, for Rachmaninoff not only adored the music but also the man. Thus, from the very beginning of his career—when Tchaikovsky was the major influence on his composition and Siloti, the Liszt pupil, on his pianism—Rachmaninoff was a decided product of the 19th century romantic tradition.

In 1889 Rachmaninoff left Zverev's house (after a quarrel over his having a separate room and piano) and went to live with his aunt, Varvara Satin. Despite this disruption in his life his progress at the Conservatory continued to be more than satisfactory and by 1891 there was talk of his being awarded the coveted Gold Medal. Along with piano studies, he had been industriously composing, and among his student scores are a scherzo for orchestra, a piano concerto, one movement of a symphony, two unfinished string quartets, a *Russian Rhapsody* for two pianos and a symphonic poem, *Prince Rostislav.*

Even then Rachmaninoff was intent, above all else, upon being a composer. In the book *Rachmaninoff's Re-*

collections Told to Oskar von Riesemann the author remarks that "Rachmaninoff felt he was a composer and nothing else and this was the opinion held by all his circle. If he performed as a pianist he only did so in order to introduce his own compositions, although it must be admitted that on these occasions the audience and the critics invariably expressed their astonishment that a composer should play the piano so surprisingly well."

Indeed, as a composer Rachmaninoff had early and rather easy success. In 1892, at age 19, he produced a *Prelude in C Minor,* a little piece that would soon spread his name around the world, and led to foreign appearances as composer-pianist. Also in 1892, he composed an opera, *Aleko* (based on Pushkin's poem "The Gypsies"), which would subsequently enjoy considerable success. "I cannot describe," Rachmaninoff later recalled, "how thrilled I was at the sound of my own music. I was in the seventh heaven. Tchaikovsky attended the last three rehearsals. We sat together in a corner of the darkened house. The conductor's interpretation of certain parts did not please me. I remember the following dialogue between Tchaikovsky and myself: Tchaikovsky—'Do you like this tempo?' I—'No'. Tchaikovsky could not stand it for long, and during an interval he cleared his throat and said, 'Mr. Rachmaninoff and I think that the tempo here might be taken a little faster.' On this occasion he said to me: 'I have just finished an opera in two acts, *Iolanthe,* which is

Frontispiece of Rachmaninoff's Concerto No. 2 in C Minor for Piano and Orchestra, composed in 1901, possibly the most popular piano concerto ever written. (Paris, Bibliotheque Nationale)

prising that he became overconfident and a bit arrogant. For instance, he played his First Suite for two pianos at a musical gathering in St. Petersburg and Nicholas Rimsky-Korsakov, in a friendly manner, suggested a small change. "I was silly and stuck on myself in those days," said Rachmaninoff, "so I shrugged my shoulders and said, 'And why?'—and never changed a note. Only later did I realize how just Rimsky-Korsakov's criticism had been."

Despite his public self-assurance, Rachmaninoff, now in his early 20s, experienced gnawing doubts. He was out of the small arena of the Conservatory and he may well have wondered whether he would be able to sustain his growing reputation as a composer. More specifically, he was apprehensive about his work-in-progress, the Symphony No. 1 in D Minor (1895), based on chants from the Russian Orthodox Service, his most ambitious orchestral score to date. As was his habit, he took the Symphony to his former teacher Taneyev to get his reaction. Critic Leonid Sabaneyev was present on that occasion and remembered that he himself had liked "the somber originality of its harmonies", but that Taneyev was not pleased. "'These melodies are flabby, colorless—there is nothing that can be done with them,' said Taneyev in his high-pitched, 'tearful' voice, as if he were complaining to the composer." Taneyev then suggested certain revisions which Rachmaninoff, who, as he later admitted, had an "exaggeratedly high opinion" of the work, refused to make.

Almost two years after this incident, on March 15, 1897 in St. Petersburg, Rachmaninoff's First Symphony received its première, an occasion that was one of the most traumatic experiences of its composer's life. "The circumstances attending the performance of my first Symphony affected me very deeply and had a decisive influence on my later development. I imagined that there was nothing I could not do and had great hopes for my future ... I was convinced that here I had discovered and opened up entirely new paths in music ... It is true that the performance [conducted by Alexander Glazunov, a man given to bouts of uncontrollable alcoholism] was beneath contempt and the work in parts unrecognizable, but, apart from this, its deficiencies were revealed to me with a dreadful distinctness ... Something within me snapped. All my self-confidence broke down ...

"There are serious illnesses and deadly blows from fate which entirely change a man's character. This was the effect of my own Symphony on myself. When the indescribable torture of this performance had at last come to an end, I was a different man."

At a rehearsal of the First Symphony Rimsky-Korsakov had said to Rachmaninoff, "Forgive me, but I do not find this music at all agreeable", and now, after the performance, all hell broke loose in the St. Petersburg press, which was delighted to attack this bright light from Mos-

not long enough to fill an evening. Would you object if it was performed together with yours?' This was exactly how he put it: 'Would you object?' He was a famous composer of 53, and I only a beginner of 21." Finally in that auspicious year, Rachmaninoff had been taken on by the important publishing firm of A. Gutheil and had graduated with the Gold Medal of the Conservatory.

Aleko received a glamorous première in Moscow's Grand Theater in 1893 but that year also saw the sudden death of Tchaikovsky. This was a severe blow to Rachmaninoff, who wrote a *Trio élegiaque* in his friend's memory. It was also somewhat of a professional setback, for Tchaikovsky had planned to conduct Rachmaninoff's symphonic poem *The Rock,* in addition to having *Iolanthe* produced in Moscow on the same program with *Aleko.* (Both of the Rachmaninoff works, incidentally, were heavily Tchaikovsky-influenced.)

Nevertheless Rachmaninoff was obviously on the threshold of an important career, both as a composer (his *Prelude* already world-famous, his opera successful in Russia) and as a concert-pianist (he had begun to appear with orchestras in concertos by other composers). He was much admired, especially in Moscow, and it is not sur-

cow. Among the vitriol was a memorable line from Cesar Cui: "If there were a Conservatory in hell, Rachmaninoff would gain the first prize for his Symphony, so devilish are the discords he has dished up for us."

Rachmaninoff's reaction to the fiasco was an intense depression, accompanied by heavy drinking. "Agonizing hours spent in doubt and hard thinking brought me to the conclusion that I ought to give up composing," he said years later. "I was obviously unfitted for it, and therefore it would be better if I made an end to it at once. A paralyzing apathy possessed me. I did nothing at all and found no pleasure in anything. Half my days were spent lying on a couch and sighing over my ruined life. After that Symphony I composed nothing for about 3 years. I felt like a man who had suffered a stroke and for a long time had lost the use of his head and hands." Rachmaninoff never allowed his First Symphony to be played again during his lifetime and it was only after his death that the work was reconstructed from a set of orchestral parts and a two-piano arrangement.

In 1897 Rachmaninoff accepted an offer to become assistant conductor at a Moscow opera house, where he met the great singer Feodor Chaliapin who became a lifelong friend. That same year another friend arranged for the troubled young composer to see Count Leo Tolstoy to talk over his psychological problems. "I then worshipped Tolstoy," reminisced Rachmaninoff. "When I approached him my knees trembled. He made me sit down beside him and stroked my knees. He saw how nervous I was. And then, he said to me: 'You must work. Do you think that I am pleased with myself? Work. I work every day,' and similar stereotyped phrases." Tolstoy was even less helpful when Chaliapin brought Rachmaninoff for a second visit in 1900. As they arrived the apprehensive Rachmaninoff whispered, "My hands are like ice." According to the *basso,* when he sang one of Rachmaninoff's songs Tolstoy asked, "Tell me, does anyone want this type of music? What kind of music do people need, more folk music, or the cerebral, clever scientific offerings?" This was hardly the way to restore the self-confidence of a composer practically undergoing a nervous breakdown.

Meanwhile, Rachmaninoff had been asked to play concerts with orchestra in London during the 1899-1900 season. Feeling that his First Piano Concerto (1891; extensively revised in 1917) was not a strong work, he had been attempting, without success, to write a new one. Members of his family prevailed upon him to visit Dr. Nicholas Dahl, a psychiatrist living in Moscow who was known for his treatment of nervous conditions with hypnotism and suggestion. For three months early in 1900 Rachmaninoff made daily visits to Dr. Dahl, and this is his account: "I heard the same hypnotic formula repeated day after day while I lay half asleep in an armchair in Dahl's study: 'You

will begin to write your Concerto . . . you will work with great facility . . . the Concerto will be of excellent quality . . .' It was always the same, without interruption. Although it may sound incredible, this cure really helped me. At the beginning of the summer I began to compose again. The material grew in bulk and new musical ideas began to stir within me—more than enough for my concerto." By autumn, 1900, Rachmaninoff had composed the second and third movements of his Concerto No. 2 in C Minor, and in the spring of the following year, it was finished. This brilliant and romantic work was to become one of the world's best loved piano concertos, rivaled only by the First Concerto of Rachmaninoff's idol Tchaikovsky.

A view of the concert in the Moscow Conservatory where Rachmaninoff conducted many concerts, as listed in the surrounding programs, (Paris, France—USSR Cultural Association)

Russia and Revolution: 1902-1917

In April, 1902, during a spring rain shower, Rachmaninoff married Natalie Satin in an army chapel outside of Moscow. As she was his first cousin, permission had to be obtained from the Tsar himself. After the ceremony the happy couple left for a long honeymoon in Vienna, Venice, Lucerne and Bayreuth, where Rachmaninoff heard Richard Wagner's operas for the first time. Natalie was to be Rachmaninoff's adoring companion for almost 40 years and would provide him with two daughters, Irina and Tatiana.

Returning to Moscow in October the Rachmaninoffs took an apartment in the same building where years before, in a tiny, furnished room, the now-famous *Prelude in C Minor* had been written. At 29, with his emotional crisis behind him, Rachmaninoff's fortunes had changed. His career was blossoming, as prominent performers and orchestras began to program his music and audiences responded enthusiastically to its melodiousness. He was continually composing now, and performing solo recitals. In 1904, he signed a five-month contract as a conductor at Moscow's Bolshoi Opera House, a highly prestigious post and one in which he excelled.

The Revolution of 1905 brought troubles and unrest, even for the apolitical Rachmaninoff. Discipline broke down at the Bolshoi because of constant arguments over social reforms, and Rachmaninoff became exasperated with the working conditions there. He finally resigned, even though he had been offered the post of music director.

Most of Russia's intelligentsia opposed the Tsarist government and supported the demand for a constitutional monarchy, but Rachmaninoff, having little interest in any subject but music, was unable to take a position. Social gatherings became more and more uncomfortable for him as all Moscow seemed to be in political ferment, so he decided to go abroad for awhile in search of the peace and quiet he needed for composing. Late in 1906 he arrived with his family in Dresden, where he was to live for almost three years.

He worked well there, producing the Second Symphony, the First Piano Sonata and the tone-poem *The Isle of the Dead*. He also found himself in increasing demand in Europe as a pianist and often played in concert, thus contributing to his fame outside Russia.

Rachmaninoff came to the United States for the first time in the autumn of 1909. For his American tour—which comprised twenty concerts in which he was to perform his own works both as pianist and conductor—he had composed a new Concerto, No. 3 in D Minor, a formidable virtuoso vehicle. The Third Concerto had two New York performances under two distinguished conductors, Walter Damrosch and Gustav Mahler, and it was well received. In fact, many critics preferred it to the Second. Rachmaninoff himself conducted the Second Symphony and *The Isle of the Dead* in Chicago and Boston and was by this time being so highly acclaimed that he was offered the position of conductor of the Boston Symphony Orchestra. However, as he did not particularly like America on this first visit nor think that his family would, he refused the post. "In this accursed country," he wrote from New York to a fellow-Russian, "you're surrounded by nothing but Americans and the 'business', 'business', they are forever doing, clutching you from all sides and driving you on. Everyone treats me nicely and kindly, but I am horribly bored with it all."

When Rachmaninoff returned to Russia in February 1910 he was offered an appointment which he gladly accepted—the vice presidency of the Imperial Music Society. This was a signal honor for the 37-year-old composer for it involved control of the conservatories of both Moscow and St. Petersburg, as well as music colleges in smaller towns. He took this position seriously and, among his other achievements during his two years as Vice President (he resigned in 1912 to protest discrimination against a Jewish musician), he established a conservatory in Kiev. He also became conductor of the Moscow Philharmonic, another highly prestigious post.

In 1913 Rachmaninoff went abroad again, this time to Switzerland and Italy. He had had enough of concertising for awhile, particularly conducting, and now wished only to compose. The Rachmaninoffs took an apartment in Rome where Tchaikovsky had once lived and there the composer spent all day "at the piano or the writing table

Rachmaninoff and his cousin Natalie Satin. She became his wife in 1902 and remained an adoring companion for forty years. (Rome, Novosti Press Agency)

and not until the sinking sun gilded the pines of the Monte Pincio did I put away my pen." In this welcome solitude he produced one of his most grandiose works, the choral symphony *The Bells*, based on the poem of Edgar Allan Poe. Soon after *The Bells* was completed the Rachmaninoff family returned to Russia to hear it performed in Moscow and St. Petersburg.

At Ivanovka, near Tambov, Rachmaninoff owned a farm which had once belonged to the Satin family. He loved it dearly and was in the habit of spending his springs and summers there. He was at Ivanovka, eagerly awaiting the arrival of a new tractor, when World War I began in August 1914.

By most accounts a rather reserved and often melancholy personality, Rachmaninoff became even more gloomy during the war. He continued to give concerts, many as benefits in aid of wounded soldiers, but he composed very little from 1914-17. In the summer of 1915 he wrote despondently, "My days were spent in nothing more than reading, walking and sinking further into anguish ... the atmosphere grew heavier and unhappier. Bad news from the front . . . a new draft summons to give me another medical examination, etc.—all this made it absolutely impossible to concentrate on work."

The February Revolution of 1917, which deposed the Tsar and set up a moderate Socialist government in St. Petersburg (now renamed Petrograd) came and went, and the summer found the Rachmaninoffs in the Crimea. Being of an aristocratic family, the composer was worried about his future in Russia. "Almost from the beginning of the Revolution," he said, "I realized that it was mishandled." He wrote Siloti and asked him to arrange for a

passport out of the country through a friend who was an official of the new government but nothing came of it. In September, Rachmaninoff returned to Moscow and began to revise his youthful First Piano Concerto and, when the October Revolution overthrew the provisional government and installed Lenin in power, he was, as he later wrote, "so engrossed with my work that I did not notice what went on around me. Consequently, life during the anarchistic upheaval, which turned the existence of a non-proletarian into hell on earth, was comparatively easy for me. I sat at a writing table or the piano all day without troubling about the rattle of machine guns and rifle shots."

He himself may not have troubled about the gunfire in the streets, but he began to fear for the safety of his family in such uncertain conditions. Above all a practising musician who was relatively uninterested in politics and causes, Rachmaninoff certainly realised, as did his compatriot and fellow-composer Sergei Prokofiev, that an environment of revolution and civil war was—as Prokofiev put it—"hardly the time for concerts". And so, when Rachmaninoff was offered a concert tour of Scandinavia he jumped at it and, by dint of some effort, was able to obtain a passport not only for himself but for his entire family. Supposedly returning to Russia after the tour, the Rachmaninoffs had to leave their money and belongings behind, and when they boarded a train at the Petrograd station on December 23, 1917 Rachmaninoff was carrying only a small suitcase with his sketchbooks and the manuscript of a new opera. In a snowstorm the family crossed the Finnish border by sleigh, never to return. When asked in later years about his homeland Rachmaninoff would say sadly, "There is no Russia."

A nineteenth century palace on the Bolshaya Dmitrovka, which housed an artistic and literary club where Rachmaninoff gave his first concerts. (Rome, Novosti Press Agency)

Exile
1917-1943

If the old Russia that he knew and loved had disappeared, then so had a part of Rachmaninoff. When he emigrated he was 44 years old. For a quarter of a century, Rachmaninoff had played a prominent role in Russian musical life—primarily as a composer, but also as a performer and administrator. It is only a slight exaggeration to say that when Rachmaninoff abandoned his homeland his muse abandoned him, for in the next 25 years few new works of his appeared. As his biographer Victor Seroff put it, "[He] felt very strongly his absence from Russian soil, his separation from his people, his sounding board." Faced with the need to start anew in the West and to support his family, Rachmaninoff would subsequently concentrate on the performance aspect of his art.

It was not long before he had established himself as one of the finest concert-pianists in the world, renowned not only for his virtuosity but also for his scrupulously straightforward approach to most of the classical and romantic repertoire. And his own music continued to be much appreciated and widely performed in Europe and the United States. As the American critic Virgil Thomson wrote, "Rachmaninoff's depressive mentality has come to

Rachmaninoff, not only an established composer, but an astonishing piano virtuoso, revising one of his manuscripts. (Rome, Novosti Press Agency)

represent to the Western world a musical expression both specifically Russian and specifically attractive through the appeal of sadness."

Despite his great public success in all of his endeavors, Rachmaninoff was seldom satisfied with himself. "The more I play " he wrote, "the more I see my shortcomings. Probably I shall never learn; or if I do, then perhaps only on the threshold of death. Years ago when I was composing, I tormented myself because I composed badly; and now I torment myself because I play badly . . . There is no critic in the world who is more doubtful about me than myself." In 1930 he declared in an interview: "Success dominates artistic life . . . the older we get the more we lose that divine self-confidence which is the treasure of youth, and the fewer are those moments when we believe that what we have done is good. Nowadays, it very rarely happens to me to feel sincerely satisfied with myself."

Rachmaninoff came to the United States again in November 1918 and in a few years he had revised his earlier verdict on the country. He now particularly liked its audiences and in 1929 spoke of the great progress made by Americans "both in their power of assimilation and in their musical taste. Their artistic demands have grown to an astonishing extent. The man who exposes his art to public opinion notices this immediately." Although Rachmaninoff would spend much time in Europe (in 1931 he bought a villa on Lake Lucerne in Switzerland), the United States was to be his home from 1918 until his death. Just as he had been in Russia, so now he became a staple of the musical life of America. Rachmaninoff was widely considered the finest concert-pianist of his time and he not only concertised but also made numerous recordings, of which the most important are his performances as pianist in his four concertos and the *Rhapsody on a Theme of Paganini* and as conductor in his Third Symphony and *The Isle of the Dead* (all with the Philadelphia Orchestra, his favourite).

Rachmaninoff seems never to have recovered from his forced departure from Russia, nor to have become resigned to life as an expatriate. He lived for the day when he would be able to return. "Even the air here is not like in Russia," he said. "It smells differently." In his later years he became more reclusive than before, socializing almost exclusively with fellow Russians with whom he was relaxed, charming and friendly. But when of necessity he was restricted to the United States at the beginning of World War II he became increasingly pessimistic and gloomy, causing Igor Stravinsky to characterise him as "a six-foot-two scowl".

The Nazi invasion of the Soviet Union greatly upset Rachmaninoff and made him feel even more homesick. Dolefully he remembered the old days: "In Russia," he told Victor Seroff, "we always had groups of composers and music lovers who used to meet regularly and we would show each other our latest work long before it was published or performed in public. With whom and where could I do this here, please tell me?"

Once, Rachmaninoff's close friend Nicolas Medtner had asked him why he no longer composed and he answered, "The melody has gone . . . If it returns I shall write again." Sadly, it seldom returned during the nearly three decades in which Rachmaninoff lived in the West, for during that time only a half dozen works came from his pen: the Fourth Piano Concerto and *Three Russian Songs* for chorus and orchestra in 1926, the *Variations on a Theme of Corelli* for piano in 1931, the *Rhapsody on a Theme of Paganini* for piano and orchestra in 1934, the Third Symphony in 1936, and the *Symphonic Dances* for orchestra in 1940. "I feel like a ghost wandering in a world grown alien," he wrote in 1939. "I cannot cast out the old way of writing, and I cannot acquire the new. I have made intense effort to feel the musical manner of today, but it will not come to me. Unlike Madame Butterfly with her quick religious conversion, I cannot cast out my musical gods in a moment and bend the knee to new ones."

The Philadelphia Orchestra

LEOPOLD STOKOWSKI • EUGENE ORMANDY
Conductors
EUGENE ORMANDY, Music Director

RACHMANINOFF CYCLE

CARNEGIE HALL

Sunday Evening, November 26, at 8:45

EUGENE ORMANDY *Conducting*
SERGEI RACHMANINOFF, Pianist

First of three consecutive Sunday evenings devoted to the music of Sergei Rachmaninoff

Symphony No. 2 in E minor

    I. Largo—Allegro moderato
    II. Allegro molto
    III. Adagio
    IIII. Allegro vivace

INTERMISSION

Concerto No. 1 in F-sharp minor for Piano and Orchestra

    I. Moderato maestoso
    II. Andante cantabile
    III. Allegro scherzando

Rhapsody on a Theme of Paganini for Piano and Orchestra

Mr. Rachmaninoff uses the STEINWAY Piano

The STEINWAY is the Official Piano of the Philadelphia Orchestra
VICTOR RECORDS

Manager
HARL McDONALD

Assistant Managers
LOUIS A. MATTSON
NORRIS WEST

1910 GIRARD TRUST COMPANY BUILDING, PHILADELPHIA

In 1942 Rachmaninoff bought a small house in Beverly Hills, California—"my last home on earth" as he said prophetically. Now in his 69th year Rachmaninoff was seriously ill, suffering not only from sclerosis and high blood pressure, but also from melanoma, an unsuspected, rare form of cancer. That autumn he began his last concert tour, during which five appearances with orchestras (playing the Beethoven First Concerto and his own *Rhapsody on a Theme of Paganini*) and seventeen solo recitals were scheduled. A few months later, a friend who went backstage at one of his recitals was shocked by his "thin and suffering face" and on February 17, 1943, in Knoxville, Tennessee, Rachmaninoff played for the last time. His condition had so deteriorated that he was forced to cancel the rest of the tour. "The pains in my side seem stronger and I feel terrific weakness," he revealed in a letter. "It's hard for me to play."

After several days of rest in New Orleans Rachmaninoff returned to Los Angeles by train, a torturous three-day journey. At the station was an ambulance and Feodor Chaliapin, son of the great basso. "Farewell my poor hands," sighed the great pianist to his old friend.

During his final days Rachmaninoff was given morphine injections to ease the pain and was often in a semi-conscious state. He sometimes moved his hands as if playing the piano or conducting. Once he asked, "Who is it who keeps playing?" and, when told that no one was playing, said resignedly, "A-a-ah . . . that means it's in my head." He died early in the morning on March 28, 1943.

Rachmaninoff first came to the United States in 1909 and returned several times for concerts prior to settling in 1942 in Beverly Hills. (Lower Left) A program devoted to his music in which he appeared as soloist at Carnegie Hall (upper right).

9

A nineteenth century print of the Moscow Kremlin, which bears comparison to the later view on page 2. (Paris, Polish Library)

ied, folksy nationalism of the Russian "Five" (Balakirev, Cui, Borodin, Mussorgsky and Rimsky-Korsakov), but the cast of his melodies, his orchestration and the acute melancholy—or, if you will, fatalism—which permeates most of his works are nonetheless ineffably Russian.

In 1941, near the end of his long career, Rachmaninoff was interviewed by the magazine *The Etude.* Among his observations were the following:

"Composing is as essential a part of my being as breathing or eating; it is one of the necessary functions of living.

"I have no sympathy with the composer who produces works according to preconceived formulas or preconceived theories. Or with the composer who writes in a certain style because it is the fashion to do so. Great music has never been produced in that way—and I dare say it never will.

"A composer's music should express the country of his birth, his love affairs, his religion, the books which have influenced him, the pictures he loves. It should be the product of the sum total of a composer's experiences.

"In my own compositions, no conscious effort has been made to be original, or Romantic, or Nationalistic, or anything else. I write down on paper the music I hear within me, as naturally as possible. I am a Russian composer, and the land of my birth has influenced my temperament and outlook. My music is the product of my temperament, and so it is Russian music; I never consciously attempted to write Russian music, or any other kind of music. I have been strongly influenced . . . but I have never, to the best of my knowledge, imitated anyone. What I try to do, when writing down my music, is to make it say simply and directly that which is in my heart when I am composing. If there is love there, or bitterness, or sadness, or religion, these moods become a part of my music, and it becomes either beautiful or bitter or sad or religious."

The last survivor of a late-romantic twilight era, Rachmaninoff, despite his sentimentality, often demonstrated in his music a vitality which provides considerable compensation for his outmoded idiom. Scores such as the Second and Third Piano Concertos, *Rhapsody on a Theme of Paganini, Variations on a Theme of Corelli* and *Symphonic Dances* are not only attractive but impressive because of their individual lyricism and ornamentation, their fine structuring and their almost constant sense of momentum. The telling thing is that for all his cliches and his old-fashioned style Rachmaninoff still managed an amazingly personal expression. If he was not the culmination of a musical age as was Bach, or a tireless trailblazer like Stravinsky, he must still be given credit for being one of the more gifted of Romantic composers. Certainly some—or all—of the aforementioned Rachmaninoff compositions will have a place in the repertory for a long time to come.

Rachmaninoff was an extremely conservative and eclectic composer whose forebears were Tchaikovsky, Borodin and Rimsky-Korsakov—in that order. Stemming directly from the 19th century romantic tradition, he was content with that tradition and never attempted to break away from it. In 1939, when Rachmaninoff said that he felt like "a ghost wandering in a world grown alien" it was an accurate assessment of his musical status in the 20th century. Rachmaninoff, an anachronism who belonged in spirit to a preceding generation, was stoically indifferent to the music of his own time. As one critic put it, "He was a 'heart' man who survived into a 'heartless' era." He ignored all of the modern isms (neoclassicism, impressionism, serialism), and only in the 1930s did a contemporary development have even a minimal influence on his work—American jazz in the rhythmic life of one of his finest scores, the *Rhapsody on a Theme of Paganini.* But even there the harmony, melody and piano writing are all too clearly circa 1890. No wonder, then, that Rachmaninoff came to be considered a reactionary and was practically *persona non grata* in progressive circles. "I am very pessimistic about modern music," he would say.

Another aspect of Rachmaninoff that cannot have endeared him to the international modernist camp is the intense Russianness of his music. True, his was not the stud-

PROGRAM NOTES FOR THE RECORD

by PHILLIP RAMEY

Piano Concerto No. 2 in C minor, Op. 18

The unusual circumstances concerning the composition of Rachmaninoff's Second Piano Concerto in 1900-01 have already been related. Suffice it to say here that the initial performance of this music was also a little out of the ordinary, for only two movements, the second and third, were played on that occasion, which was a Prison Charity Concert in Moscow on October 14, 1900. The composer was the soloist and Alexander Siloti conducted. Rachmaninoff finished the remaining movement the following spring and played the first complete performance of the new concerto in October 1901 with the Moscow Philharmonic. The work, a virtuoso display piece *par excellence,* has since become one of the most often heard of all piano concertos, so popular that one of its melodies (the second theme of the Finale) was taken up by Tin Pan Alley and is now known to millions as "Full Moon and Empty Arms".

I. Moderato. The first movement opens with solemn chords tolling in the piano like deep-throated Russian bells. These lead to the first theme, flowing and passionate in its melancholy way, heard in the strings accompanied by piano arpeggios. The lugubrious yet tender second theme, distinctly Slavic in character, is given out by the piano. Both melodies are then manipulated in the development section, although the first receives by far the most attention. There are new, march-like ideas with pounding chords in the piano which rise to a dramatic climax, bringing on the recapitulation of the main materials and a vigorous ending.

II. Adagio sostenuto. This slow movement is pervaded by melancholy and is a veritable Russian nocturne. Muted strings play four preludial bars and lead to the songful principal melody in solo flute and solo clarinet, accompanied by the piano. This theme is then given to the solo instrument. A cadenza passage in the piano serves as a bridge to the livelier middle section, leading to a short cadenza after which the quiet mood of the opening returns with the song-melody in the violins. A ravishing coda in piano, strings, and woodwinds seems to introduce new material but this is in reality based upon the movement's principal theme.

III. Allegro scherzando. A rhythmic orchestral introduction leads to a piano cadenza which in turn leads to the energetic first theme and bravura piano passages. The famous nostalgic second theme is heard in the oboes and violas and is repeated and elaborated by the piano. Both themes are then given a thorough working out in a series of brilliant and often rhythmically exciting episodes. There is a brief, tension-inducing piano cadenza which dramatically sweeps over the entire keyboard, and then a grandiose and quite affecting statement in the piano and full orchestra of the second theme, no longer nostalgic now but, instead, rather triumphant. An effective barnstorming coda brings Rachmaninoff's Second Concerto to a close with a decisive rhythmic flourish.

A nineteenth century print of a convent in Moscow. Rachmaninoff's roots were deep in Russia's past, and most of his creativity was lost in exile. (Paris, Polish Library)

Vocalise, Op. 34, No. 14

Rachmaninoff's *Vocalise* was originally written in 1912 as a wordless song for Mme. Antonina Neshdanov, a famous coloratura soprano of the Moscow Grand Opera. Revised in 1915, it was such a success that Rachmaninoff arranged it for violin, for cello, and for orchestra. This last version, in which the first violins take the vocal melody, was requested by conductor Serge Koussevitzky for his Moscow concerts during the 1915-16 season.

Vocalise, an extended aria, is notable for its graceful and languorous melody.

Symphonic Dances for Orchestra, Op. 45

"My dear Mr. Ormandy," began the letter from Rachmaninoff dated August 21, 1940, "Last week I finished a new symphonic piece, which I naturally want to give first to you and your orchestra. It is called 'Fantastic Dances'. I shall now begin the orchestration." On October 29th he finished the orchestration of his new work—now titled *Symphonic Dances*—and wrote at the end of the score the words "I thank thee, Lord." Rachmaninoff may have suspected that the *Symphonic Dances* might be his swansong, as indeed it turned out to be.

The *Symphonic Dances* were composed at an estate near Huntington, Long Island where Rachmaninoff spent the summer of 1940 resting from a rigorous concert schedule. "I don't know how it happened," he said later, referring to the *Symphonic Dances.* "It must have been my last spark." Happily, his last spark was a bright one, for the subtle and imaginatively scored *Symphonic Dances* is in many ways one of his most successful works.

Intended to be a symphonic treatment of idealised dance patterns, Rachmaninoff first considered giving the movements descriptive titles—"Midday", "Twilight" and "Midnight"—but abandoned the idea because he was afraid that titles might give misleading impressions of the music itself. The three dances in the suite are unrelated and only the second has a clear dance designation, *tempi di valse.* Traditional dance patterns are hinted at only occasionally and that, along with the numerous rhythmic shifts throughout the score, mitigates against viewing the *Symphonic Dances* as choreographic in inspiration or intention. Indeed, Rachmaninoff denied thinking in such terms.

Dedicated to Eugene Ormandy and the Philadelphia Orchestra, Rachmaninoff's *Symphonic Dances* was given its première in Philadelphia on January 4, 1941. Soon after, when the same forces brought the work to New York, most of the critics found it uninteresting, a dim reflection of the Rachmaninoff of the past. "It teems with weird sounds—Mr. Rachmaninoff's orchestra is definitely haunted, especially the wind section, which is a real rendezvous for ghosts," wrote the rather imaginative correspondent of the *New York World Telegram.* Further, "the work is long and derivative . . . and sounds like a rehash of old tricks."

Olin Downes of the *New York Times* was more sympathetic: "The dances are simple in outline, symphonic in texture and proportion [and] bear the unmistakable stamp of Rachmaninoff's creative personality," he said. "They could easily reflect a series of moods, presented in a certain loose sequence—of Nature, and memories, and reveries with some Dead Sèa fruit in them—all unpretentious, melodic, sensuously colored and admirably composed music."

In the present album only the second and third of the *Symphonic Dances* are presented.

Dance No. 2 (*Andante con moto—tempi di valse*) opens with a fanfare played by the muted brass. This motto will recur during the movement, alternating with episodes in waltz-time and creating an ambiguity between motion and repose. Olin Downes rightfully pointed out here the "sensuous melodies, sometimes bitter-sweet, sometimes to a Viennese lilt."

Dance No. 3 (*Lento assai—Allegro vivace*) has a certain *Totentanz* aspect because of the prominence in its pages of the "Dies Irae", the medieval chant for the dead with which Rachmaninoff seemed obsessed (among other works it appears in the First Symphony, *The Isle of the Dead,* Second Piano Sonata and *Rhapsody on a Theme of Paganini*). This last dance is the shortest of the three but it is also the most frenetic, rhythmically complicated and "fantastic" in character.

A manuscript page of Rachmaninoff's Vocalise, Opus 34 No. 14, written in 1912 as a song and then transcribed for violin, for cello and for orchestra. (Paris, France— USSR Cultural Association)

Printed in the United States of America

His Life and Times 1811-1886

**PROGRAM NOTES FOR PIANO CONCERTO NO. 2 IN A MAJOR,
HUNGARIAN RHAPSODY NO. 6, AND
HUNGARIAN FANTASY FOR PIANO AND ORCHESTRA**
By Dorle J. Soria

fw

**FUNK & WAGNALLS, INC.
NEW YORK, NEW YORK**

Childhood and Youth 1811-1833

There is probably no more contradictory, picturesque, complicated figure in the history of music than Franz Liszt. He was the prototype of the romantic hero, and lived like a king but called himself a gypsy. He was the glamour symbol of the world in which he moved, a phenomenon of a time of change and revolt, of rejection of the established and worship of the new, of nature embraced and formalism rejected, of emotional and cultural rebellion. Liszt was the greatest virtuoso of his day, an original and enormously prolific composer who wrote some 700 works, a conductor who championed living composers (above all, Wagner), a teacher responsible for a new generation of keyboard talent, a writer and a critic, a personality whose every action made news—truly, the Renaissance Man of the Romantic Age.

When Franz (Ferencz in Hungarian) Liszt was born on October 22, 1811, Beethoven was almost forty-one, Schubert was fourteen, Berlioz eight, Mendelssohn two and a half, Schumann a little over a year old, and Chopin only a few months older. Wagner, who was to marry Liszt's daughter Cosima, would not be born until May 22, 1813. Liszt was born in a small Hungarian village called Raiding. A comet was visible at the time, and legend has it that on the night he entered the world the comet seemed to light the roof of his house. It was hailed as a good omen.

Raiding was part of the vast Esterházy estates to which Adam Liszt, Franz's father, had been sent in 1810 as a steward. He and his wife, the former Anna Lager, daughter of an Austrian draper, found life in their new home dreary. Adam (and his father before him) had been a retainer in Eisenstadt, a lively and happy post for a man who was a musical amateur of talent and enthusiasm. For

Adam Liszt, who played violin, guitar and piano, it was a personal tragedy to leave the glories of Eisenstadt for the village of Raiding.

As soon as he realised that he had a child of unusual musical talent, Liszt concentrated all his dreams on his son. The boy could not tear himself from the piano and made extraordinary progress. His ear was accurate, his memory remarkable, and his fingers knew no obstacles. He improvised with natural ease; no wonder Adam Liszt began to fancy himself another Papa Mozart.

When he was nine years old, young Liszt gave his first concert at a nearby town, Oedenburg, invited by a young blind pianist, Baron von Braun, to join him in a program. He played with such success that, the same evening, his father was able to organise a second concert with Franz as the solo performer. The next step was to bring him to Eisenstadt to play before Prince Esterházy, who was so impressed that he granted the steward the use of a drawing room of the Esterházy Palace in Pressburg, then an important provincial capital. There Franz gave a concert of Beethoven, and several of his own improvisations, which captivated the aristocratic audience. When it was learned that this prodigy lacked the money for a proper musical education, a group of Counts agreed to help, and settled on the boy the sum of six hundred Austrian gulden for six years. Mission accomplished, Adam Liszt resigned his post and in 1821 the family moved to Vienna.

Vienna was then, without question, the hub of the musical world. Beethoven was there, at the height of his fame. Also in Vienna was Schubert, twenty-four, with only seven more years to live. Over the years Liszt did many transcriptions of Schubert songs and song cycles. The Wan-

Franz Liszt was born in this house at Raiding, part of the Esterházy estates in Hungary.

derer Fantasia, numerous marches, and the nine *Soirées de Vienne* were all based on Schubert themes.

When Adam Liszt first came to Vienna, he asked Hummel to teach his son. But Hummel, despite old Eisenstadt ties, wanted too much money. Instead Franz studied with Salieri and with Carl Czerny, a prolific composer, a brilliant pianist, and a pedagogue whose exercises are still the bane of every struggling young pianist.

In the autumn of 1823, Papa Liszt decided to take the boy to Paris, stopping en route for concerts in Munich, Stuttgart and Strasbourg. Once in Paris, he wasted no time. The morning after his arrival, he set off with Franz to the Conservatory where Luigi Cherubini was Director. But Cherubini refused to allow the lad within the sacred portals, since it was against the rules to admit a foreigner.

Young Franz did study in Paris, with Antonin Reicha, who had been a friend of Beethoven, and with Parma-born Ferdinando Paer, who at that time was the popular successor of Spontini at the Italian Opera. Letters from the high-born of Austria and Hungary to the *haute monde* of Paris opened the doors of the fashionable salons to Franz. He played in the great houses at two thousand francs a concert. He also gave public concerts, and was compared with the young Mozart. Elegant ladies spoiled and petted him, and the phrenologist Gall took a plaster cast of his head.

London was next. Pierre Erard, shrewdly publicising his Erard pianos, brought him there and arranged a concert on June 21, 1824, at the new Argyll Rooms. A concert at Drury Lane followed on June 29. The next season, after a tour of the French provinces, he again visited London and played at the Duke of Devonshire's on May 13, 1825, and at Windsor before George IV. Despite the atmosphere of flattery and acclaim which surrounded him, Franz seems to have remained unspoiled. Charles Salaman, in *Blackwood's Magazine,* reported a family dinner to which he came. "He was a very charmingly natural and unaffected boy, and I have never forgotten his joyful exclamation 'Oh! gooseberry-pie!' when his favorite dish was put on the table."

During the year Franz made his first serious effort at composition. Urged by Paer, he wrote a one-act operetta called *Don Sancho* or *The Castle of Love*. It was produced at the Académie Royale in Paris on October 17, 1825, five days before his fourteenth birthday. Despite great advance expectation the piece was a failure. It was Liszt's first and last opera.

His concert tours continued — Switzerland, France, England. It was an exhausting life and the strain began to take its toll. One day, when his father found him unconscious on the floor, he realised the boy needed rest and change, and took him to Boulogne on the sea. There Franz improved, but his father suddenly became seriously ill and

died. His much-quoted last words were prophetic. "My child, I am going to leave you very much alone, but your talent will protect you against every misfortune. You have a good heart and do not lack intelligence. All the same, I fear for you on account of women. They will trouble and dominate your life."

The youth sent for his mother, who had gone to Austria to visit her sister. He knew he must now provide for himself and for her, and they settled down in a simple apartment in Paris. Franz began to give music lessons and was soon busy from morning to night. One day he was summoned to the home of the Count de Saint-Cricq, Minister of Commerce and Industry to Charles X. His wife, an invalid, received him and asked him to undertake their daughter Caroline's musical education. Franz and Caroline were about the same age, Franz tall, slender, fair; his hair hung long and he had beautiful hands. She was a pretty brunette, they were often alone, and the inevitable happened. They fell in love. The Countess de Saint-Cricq, who died shortly after, was not always present at the lessons, but it was an innocent idyll, sealed with kisses. It came also to its inevitable end when one day the Count showed Franz the door. His daughter was to marry a more suitable match.

The experience was shattering for Franz. He never forgot his first love, and in his will left Caroline a ring. Ill and depressed, he withdrew from the world. He took refuge in religion and books.

The 1830 Revolution shook him out of himself. The air was full of excitement and unrest. The name of Lord Byron, enthusiasm for Greek independence, the Napoleonic legend, and new liberal ideas all fanned the flames of rebellion. When Charles X confronted the people with autocratic ordinances, the people of Paris took up the challenge. In July 1830, Charles X was driven into exile, and the tricolour of the bourgeois revolution flew over the Tuileries. Louis Philippe became the "citizen king". Liszt, inspired by these events, started a symphony in which he planned to use national revolutionary songs; it was never finished.

The new regime was peaceful and dull. The poet Lamartine proclaimed "France is bored." But another revolution was taking place, an aesthetic one. The powerful force known as "romanticism" was at large. The very symbol of the romantic era was Paganini, the violinist who was said to be the reincarnation of the devil. On March 9, 1831, he appeared in Paris for the first time, and made an indelible impression on the nineteen-year-old Liszt. Two other great influences of that Paris period were Berlioz and Chopin. On December 5, 1830, when Berlioz conducted the première of his 'Fantastic' Symphony at the Conservatoire, Franz Liszt was in the audience. He had only met the composer the day before. The work made an enormous impression on him and he begged his new hero to dine in his lodging in the Rue de Provence. Berlioz gave in to his passionate entreaties, they went home together and their friendship began. Berlioz admired Liszt greatly as a pianist, less so as a composer, but there is no question about the influence he had on the younger man. Critic Harold Schonberg has written: "From Berlioz, Liszt discovered the meaning of color, and also the meaning of Thinking Big. Berlioz introduced him to the visionary kind of romanticism, its stirrings and yearnings, its subjectivity and love of the monumental. Liszt tried to do on the piano what Berlioz did with the orchestra, and even transcribed for solo piano several major orchestral works of Berlioz. Among them was the *Symphonie Fantastique* . . . Finally Liszt met Chopin, and realized that there was poetry as

well as bravura to piano playing."

Chopin — a year and a half older than Liszt — was twenty-one when he came to Paris. He immediately became the darling of the salons, the lion of the local nobility and of the aristocratic Polish emigrés. Among the friends he soon made were Berlioz, Paer, Rossini, Bellini, Mendelssohn, Cherubini, Heine — also Liszt. Paris in those days was literally swarming with geniuses — Victor Hugo, Balzac, Merimée, Alfred de Musset, Ingres and Delacroix. When Chopin gave his first concert in Paris on February 26, 1832, two young men in the audience applauded wildly — Liszt and Mendelssohn. Chopin and Liszt were friends, with reservations. Chopin admired Liszt enormously as a pianist, but he was turned away by his showmanship. He once wrote: "I should like to rob him of the way to play my own etudes." It was, however, Liszt who, late in 1836, introduced Chopin to the most famous — or notorious — Frenchwoman of the day, the trousered, cigar-smoking Baroness Aurore Dudevant, better known under her *nom de plume* as George Sand. It was the beginning of one of the great love affairs. It all started at a soirée given by Liszt and the Countess d'Agoult, his mistress, at the Hôtel de France where the composer and Countess, not divorced from her husband, were living together along with their infant daughter Blandine.

The Countess Marie d'Agoult 1833-1839

The *grande passion* between Franz Liszt and the Countess d'Agoult began at the end of 1832, when they met at the house of a mutual friend. She wrote: "I would say an apparition, lacking another word to describe the extraordinary sensation he gave me, altogether the most extraordinary person I had ever seen. A tall figure, thin to excess, a pale face with large sea-green eyes . . . a distracted air, unquiet, and like that of a phantom about to be summoned back to the shades. This is how I saw the young genius before me."

She was twenty-eight when they met, he was twenty-two. She was the daughter of the Vicomte de Flavigny who had fled his country where he had seen his parents go to the guillotine and had settled in Frankfurt. Among his hosts was the head of the great banking house of Bettmann whose young widowed daughter he married. Their daughter, Marie, educated in the Convent of the Sacred Heart, became lady-in-waiting to the daughter of Louis XVI. At twenty-two, she married a man twenty years her senior, Count Charles d'Agoult, and bore him three children.

A contemporary view of the Boulevard Montparnasse in the belle epoque Paris of 1850. (Milan, Bertarelli Print Collection)

Rich and beautiful — it is said even the aged Goethe admired her blond hair — she attracted the social and intellectual leaders of Paris to her salons. She later became a writer under the name of Daniel Stern and wrote a novel, *Nélida,* a thinly disguised and vindictive story of her liaison with Liszt.

She captured Liszt from the first. They burned their bridges behind them. They escaped to Switzerland and, eventually, settled in Geneva. Their first child was born there, Blandine. It was during his travels with Marie in Switzerland that Liszt wrote most of the pieces in the *Album d'un Voyageur* (1835-6), which contains *Le Lac de Wallenstadt* and *La chapelle de Guillaume Tell.*

Liszt started to give lessons at the Conservatory in Geneva. Old friends came to visit, among them the Countess Marie Potocka and the Prince and Princess Belgiojoso, all part of Chopin's circle in Paris. The Princess was a brilliant and original figure in her day — a musician who had studied singing with Pasta, a writer whose subjects ranged from the House of Savoy to Oriental harems, and a revolutionary involved in the Italian *risorgimento.* She was a hostess who attracted everyone from Bellini and Meyerbeer to Mrs. Trollope and the aged Lafayette. Her salon was hung with black velvet, embroidered with silver stars, and she entertained with water lilies pinned in her hair. No wonder Marie d'Agoult kept a watchful eye on her.

And finally George Sand appeared. Liszt had first met the uncrowned queen of Romantics in 1834 when the Baroness Aurore Dudevant, the child of a *mésalliance* between an aristocrat and an ex-milliner, was at the end of her love affair with Alfred de Musset. Liszt might have been tempted to become her lover but he was already involved with Marie, and he might have been uneasy at the thought of betraying a friend. There was, however, a great affinity between them and, unlike the serious Marie, she amused and entertained him. When she came back to Paris from the country in May 1835 (with a new lover) she became part of Liszt's circle.

She had kept promising to come to Geneva and kept postponing her visit. When she finally arrived, she found the Liszt *ménage* had left for Chamonix in the mountains. It was a large, merry and odd-looking party. Marie, in addition to baby Blandine, had with her the two children of her marriage (one had died). George Sand, for travelling, wore an overall type of costume. They spent a week together, walking, picnicking, and talking incessantly.

After eighteen months, Liszt returned to Paris. In his absence a formidable rival had emerged, the Swiss-born pianist Sigismond Thalberg. Liszt was eager to confront him. When he arrived in Paris in December 1836, he found that Thalberg had come, had conquered and had gone. He would have to wait until the spring to meet him. Meanwhile, he appeared in a concert given by Berlioz and had a sensational success. The Thalberg encounter is described by Harold Schonberg: "Thalberg returned to Paris in 1837

A house at Bellagio on Lake Como, where Marie d'Agoult gave birth to Cosima, her child with Liszt.(Bellagio, Bucher Collection)

and appeared on the afternoon of March 12 at the *Conservatoire* playing his *Fantasia on God Save the King* and his *Moses Fantasia.* The following Sunday Liszt took over the opera house, hurling back at Thalberg his (Liszt's) *Niobe Fantasia* and Weber's *Concertstück.* So far it was a standoff, with Liszt showing the greater daring by renting the opera house. When the Princess Belgiojoso invited both pianists to play in her salon on March 31 at a benefit for the Italian refugees, she scored the social coup of the decade. The *Gazette Musicale* announced the greatest interest will be 'the simultaneous appearance of two talents whose rivalry at this time agitates the musical world, and is like the indecisive balance between Rome and Carthage' ... It was decided that Thalberg was the best pianist in the world. And Liszt? He was the *only* one."

The Thalberg duel over, Liszt returned to spend several months with George Sand in the sun at her country house in Nohant. But the relationship between the trio — Marie d'Agoult, George Sand and Liszt — had started to disintegrate. Marie, who was again pregnant, was suspicious, jealous, spiteful. When they left in July, George Sand did not try to hold them.

They went to Italy where they settled in a villa with a flower-filled garden in Bellagio on the shores of Lake Como. There Liszt composed the second book of his *Années de Pèlerinage* with its famous final piece called *Après une lecture du Dante, Fantasia quasi Sonata.* There, on December 24, 1837, another daughter, Cosima, was born. She was destined to marry Liszt's disciple Hans von Bülow, and to desert him to marry Richard Wagner, who was thus to become Liszt's son-in-law.

While Marie was recovering, Liszt invaded Milan, the nearby music capital. He was welcomed by his old friend Rossini and gave three concerts, including one at La Scala. With Marie, still weak and depressed, Liszt went on to Venice, arriving at the end of March 1838. Liszt soon found a reason to leave a "dying city" and a relationship with Marie which was clouded with misunderstandings.

5

In May 1939, their third and last child was born, a son whom they named Daniel. It was a rather unwelcome event to the parents who had outlived their passion and their patience with each other. By autumn they had decided to part. Marie went back to Paris, Franz to Vienna. They would live together, on and off, on summer holidays for some years to come, but the first great love affair of Liszt's life was over. When she sailed in October, Liszt accompanied her to Livorno where he wrote an emotional farewell. "Goodbye, darling Marie. Think sometimes of how much I love you, and let that thought be sweet to you."

Weimar Period 1839-1861

Liszt's greatest triumphs as a piano virtuoso were to begin, taking him across Europe to Germany, Russia, Turkey, Sweden, Spain and Hungary. Everywhere, he was showered with honors and orders. It began with his return in November 1839 to Vienna, where six sold-out recitals awaited him. One of his concerts was a benefit to make possible the erection of a statue to Beethoven in Bonn, his birthplace.

But the greatest event was his return to Hungary which he had left at the age of nine. The first stop was at Pressburg on December 18, the place where he had given his very first public concert. When his carriage crossed the bridge, crowds lined up along the road, shouting "Long live Liszt." He drove on to Budapest with Count Casimir Esterházy as his companion. A troop of twenty thousand people then formed a torchlight procession and accompanied him home. The next day, a deputation handed him the honorary citizenship of the city of Pest.

When he returned to his native village of Raiding, he re-encountered the Tziganes. As a child, Franz had had his introduction to Hungarian gypsy music when the Romanies came to town one day, set up their tents and sang, played, danced, prophecied and told fortunes. Now, twenty years later, he saw and heard them again. The impressions the gypsies made on Liszt led to his involvement in Hungarian popular music, an interest which remained with him the rest of his life. He absorbed the music and melodies he heard and recreated them, transformed, into the Hungarian Rhapsodies, the pieces by which Liszt's name is still best known to the public.

In April 1840, while in Paris, he met Wagner but it was a brief, casual encounter. He then went to England for his first visit since 1827, and played for the young Queen Victoria. He wrote to Marie, asking her to send him from Paris his Hungarian fur cape, his blue Turkish trousers, his medallions and the statuette Dantan had made of him.

A nineteenth century print of La Scala, the famous opera house where Liszt played several concerts throughout his career.

One morning he read in the paper of a disaster in Hungary; floods on the Danube had made thousands homeless. He suddenly was obsessed with the thought of his homeland, the village of his early years, and the language of which he could never speak a word. He left for Vienna and stayed there almost two months. He gave eight concerts, all for the victims of the Hungarian floods. He wrote to Marie: "Without exaggeration no one since Paganini has had such a success. I am the man of the hour." The critic Eduard Hanslick wrote "the ladies lost their hearts and the critics their heads."

When Marie heard that he was returning to Venice, she wrote: "I am at the Piazza San Marco. The message comes that he has arrived at the hotel. I run, I fly. I throw myself into his arms. 'Pray God that I can continue to love you as I have loved you.'" But Venice in the summer was impossible and Franz and Marie went on again, to Lugano, to Genoa, and to Florence. They quarreled. She called him a "Don Juan parvenu." They made up, but things were no longer the same. Early in 1838 they reached Rome, the city where Liszt was eventually to become the Abbé Liszt.

The city appealed to him from the start. At the Villa Medici, he met Ingres who was then head of the French Academy. The painter, a music-mad violinist, made a drawing of Liszt. It shows him as an elegant, well-tailored figure, with hair falling just below his ears. Liszt wrote to Berlioz: "Raphael and Michaelangelo help me to understand Mozart and Beethoven better. Giovanni Pisano, Fra Angelico, Francia, explain to me Allegri, Marcello and Palestrina; Titian and Rossini seem to me like two stars with similar rays."

But this time the spell did not work — the tour was not a great success.

While touring the Rhineland, Liszt discovered a romantic little wooded island called Nonnenwerth. Here, Marie d'Agoult came from Paris to spend three successive summer holidays with him, another futile attempt at understanding and reconciliation. But, during the rest of the year when he was touring alone, he did not lack feminine company. Liszt was a man of great personal magnetism and had an enormous attraction for women. Among his conquests were Charlotte Hagn, a German actress, Marie Duplessis, the courtesan who inspired Dumas' *La Dame aux camelias* and Verdi's *Traviata,* the Irish-Andalusian dancer Lola Montez who afterwards became the mistress of King Ludwig I of Bavaria, and — late in life — Olga Janina, who called herself the "Cossack Countess" and pursued Liszt across Europe.

The endless travels and the endless triumphs continued. In Berlin, during the first ten weeks of 1842 he gave twenty-one public concerts. The Prussian King, Frederick William IV, decorated him with the order *Pour le Mérité* and society women became hysterical, kneeling before him, begging to kiss his fingers. He did little composing during this time. Harold Schonberg states: "Not until 1835 did he start the series of works that were to remain in the repertoire. The four years after 1835 are the years of the Transcendental *Études,* the Paganini *Études,* the first two books of the *Années de Pèlerinage,* the arrangements of Schubert songs, and the series of Bach organ works transcribed for piano. After 1840 came many of the Hungarian Rhapsodies, the large-scale operatic paraphrases and a remarkable series of songs that are seldom sung today but should be."

In November 1841 Liszt visited Weimar, the city of Goethe and Schiller, for the first time. This was to be his residence for thirteen years and there he was to create the centre of a new musical life in Germany. He came to give concerts in 1841 and played on three evenings for the Grand Duchess Marie Paulowna, sister of Tsar Nicholas I. It was through her interest that he went to Russia in April 1842.

He was at the peak of his career and he travelled there in the greatest luxury, accompanied by footman and valet — he needed someone to tie his 360 cravats. His first concert in St. Petersburg was given in the white and gold *Salle de la Noblesse,* before an audience of 3,000 people including the composer Glinka. The critic Vladimir Stassov described the event. Liszt wore a white cravat and over it the Order of the Golden Spur. "But what struck the Russians the most was the great mane of fair hair reaching almost to his shoulders. Outside the priesthood, no Russian would have ventured on such a style of hair-dressing." Stassov was not impressed by "the famous Florentine profile and likeness to Dante" and "affected demeanor" but the concert was another thing. After the concert Stassov and his companion Serov, then a young composer, stayed up all night writing their impressions. "We both vowed to keep this anniversary sacred forever, and never, while life lasted, to forget a single instant of it."

That autumn he returned to Weimar for the marriage of the Grand Duchess's son, Charles Alexander of Saxe-Weimar, with Princess Sophie of the Netherlands. The Grand Duchess, intensely musical, persuaded Liszt of the attractions of the city and, when he was invited to become Kapellmeister to the Grand Ducal Court, he consented. At last he could have a home base, to gain orchestral experience, to compose, to give up his public piano recitals, and to present the music of his own day. However, he did not take up his duties in Weimar until the end of December 1843. In 1848 he accepted the Grand Duke's offer to become director of the court opera and concerts, and from that year to 1861, he settled down permanently in the "city of the Muses".

Meanwhile, he continued his travels as a virtuoso. He gave his final public concerts in 1847 when he toured the Danube countries and southern Russia. In February of that year, he arrived in Kiev. There he met the second woman who was to change his life. The last of a series of recitals in Kiev was a charity benefit and, on the morning of the performance, a letter arrived containing a hundred-rouble note. The following day Liszt, courteous and curious, paid a call to thank his unknown correspondent. He met a dark twenty-eight-year-old Princess, Carolyne Sayn-Wittgenstein. She was the only daughter of a Polish nobleman, a landowner so rich that on his death he left her estates with 30,000 serfs. She was married at seventeen to the penniless Prince Nicholas Wittgenstein, and after the birth of their daughter, they separated. She retired to her Woronince estate in the Ukraine. She was a blue-stocking, who read everything from Hegel, Bossuet and Goethe to Tacitus, Dante and the Talmud. She rode her horses till they dropped, and was a religious fanatic who was later to

A portrait of Liszt by Deveria, done in 1832, shows a romantic image of the young genius. (Vienna, Society of the Friends of Music)

write a twenty-four volume work entitled *Internal Causes of the Church's External Weakness*. But the impact of Liszt's presence seems to have swept all inhibitions away. She invited him to her estate and though he was to leave Russia shortly, he accepted.

Liszt then traveled to Turkey, where he played for the Sultan, and in July, he gave a series of concerts in Odessa. His last concert in September was in Elisabetgrad. In October he was back in Woronince where he stayed until January 1848. The following February, Liszt returned to Weimar, and this time, Carolyne had made up her mind. She would get a divorce from her husband. This would not be easy, since the Prince might not mind losing his wife but would undoubtedly be concerned about losing her money. Besides, even if a civil divorce were obtained in Russia, marriage would not be possible unless she received an annulment from Rome, a process of years. In any case she was determined to cast her lot with Liszt. In April the composer went to the hunting lodge of his friend Prince Felix Lichnowsky to await her arrival. The Princess managed to cross the Russian frontier just in time. With the spread of revolution in Europe, the Tsar had ordered the borders closed. When they returned to Weimar together, they first lived in separate residences. Eventually, however, Liszt moved in openly with the Princess.

During Liszt's residence in Weimar, the city became the capital of a new musical life in Germany. He had at his disposal an opera house, an orchestra, a chorus, even

dancers. With them, he produced some twenty operas by living composers, introduced music of Berlioz, Weber, Schumann, Schubert and Smetana and, most important, had the chance to champion Wagner whose life was to be permanently linked with his.

Liszt never remembered their first meeting in Paris but Wagner did; he had felt repelled by the man who was "the object of general love and admiration at a time when I was being received with universal coldness and lack of sympathy." But the atmosphere changed at their next meetings in Berlin in 1842 and in Dresden in 1844 when Liszt was deeply impressed by a special performance of *Rienzi* which Wagner conducted for him.

In 1848, Wagner visited Liszt in Weimar and even felt free to ask him for money, of which he was always in need. If Wagner's love for Liszt was a selfish one, Liszt's love for Wagner was selfless. He began his campaign for Wagner by staging the four-year-old *Tannhäuser* at the Weimar theatre. In 1850 he mounted the world première of *Lohengrin* which Wagner, then a political refugee in Switzerland, could not attend. Memorable letters were exchanged between them during this period. The ties between the two geniuses lasted a lifetime, surviving many crises including the period when Liszt's daughter, Cosima, left her husband Hans von Bülow to live with Wagner.

Oddly enough, Liszt had met Hans von Bülow through Wagner who had given him a letter of introduction. Von Bülow studied with Liszt for two years, then went back to his native Berlin where he became professor at the Stern Conservatory. About this time Princess Sayn-Wittgenstein decided it was important for Liszt to get closer to his daughters, living a neglected life in Paris with their mother, Marie d'Agoult. The Princess arranged to have them come to Germany and settled them in Berlin with Hans von Bülow's mother as duenna and with the young man in charge of their musical education. The soon enamoured Hans wrote to Liszt of his daughters, "of the admiration, even exaltation to which they have reduced me, especially the younger. As to their musical dispositions, it is not talent but genius that they possess . . . How moved I was to recognize you, *ipsissimum Lisztum*, in the playing of Mademoiselle Cosima." Cosima and he were married in Liszt's presence in 1857. In 1869, Cosima left him for Wagner.

By 1858 Weimar was beginning to lose its charm for Liszt. The old Grand Duke had died. His successor, Karl Alexander, was more interested in theatre than in music. When, on December 15, 1858, Liszt gave the première of the Cornelius opera, *Barber of Bagdad*, it was made the occasion for an anti-Liszt demonstration prepared by partisans of the new theatre director appointed by the young Grand Duke. Liszt resigned.

In March 1860, the Princess had good news. She had received her divorce. Almost immediately, the Bishop of Fulda refused to recognise the validity of the decree. Two months later, Carolyne set off for Rome to ask the intercession of the Vatican, but more than a year was to go by before Liszt left Weimar. Before proceeding to Rome, he visited Paris which, because of Marie, he had not entered for sixteen years. The Weimar period, now over, had been a productive and creative one; the twelve symphonic poems (a musical form invented by Liszt) including *Les Préludes, Orpheus, Mazeppa* and *Hamlet*, the *Faust* and *Dante* Symphonies, works for piano and orchestra, the two concertos, and *Totentanz*. He also wrote considerable organ and religious music, and solo piano music.

In Paris, he saw Marie d'Agoult who had kept herself well-informed over the years of the goings-on at the Villa Altenburg in Weimar. She asked him to call, gave a lunch in his honour and, a week later, received him alone. He talked of himself, of his "egoism and ambition," of "the permanence of that self she had found so 'hateful'" and he left her in tears. "I kissed her on the forehead for the first time in long years and said: 'Come, Marie, let me speak to you in peasant's language. God bless you. Wish me no evil.'"

When Marie died in 1876, Liszt heard of it only through the papers. The news was said to have left him unmoved.

After various stops in Germany, Liszt reached Marseilles on October 12, 1861. On the 17th, he embarked for Italy. He wrote to the Princess: "These are the last lines I shall write to you. My long exile is near its end. In five days I shall find in you country, home and altar."

Rome 1861-1886

Liszt arrived in Rome on October 20, 1861. The wedding was to be on his fiftieth birthday, October 22, at six in the morning. The church was already decorated with flowers. He spent the evening in her apartment in the Piazza di Spagna. There an unexpected caller was announced. It was a messenger from Cardinal Antonelli, Papal Secretary of State, who bore a letter from the Vatican saying the marriage could not take place. The Wittgensteins, the family of Carolyne's husband, claimed the divorce was invalid because she had perjured herself to get it. She had not, as she said, been forced into marriage.

From that time until 1869, Liszt made Rome his headquarters. He lived by himself but every evening went to see the Princess, whose darkened quarters were lit by church candles and adorned with busts of Liszt. She spent her days working on her opus on the church, which was eventually published, at her own expense. She was still addicted to her powerful cigars.

An engraving of a portrait of Liszt by F.J.S. Layraud shows his nearly mystic authority, flowing hair, and refined hands legendary throughout Europe. (Weimar, National Research Center)

As a boy, Franz Liszt had wished to become a priest. Now he was drawn more towards the church. In what he called his "years of seclusion" he turned to the study of church music and devoted himself to the composition of vast sacred works. He completed *The Legend of Saint Elisabeth* in 1862 and *Christus* in 1866; he wrote the Hungarian Coronation Mass for the crowning of Franz Josef as King of Hungary in 1867. One of the last of Liszt's choral works was the *Via Crucia,* finished in 1879; the final symphonic poem, *From the Cradle to the Grave,* was completed four years before his death.

In 1862, Liszt had another personal tragedy. His daughter Blandine, who in 1857 had married a French statesman, Emile Ollivier, died giving birth. Liszt's only son, Daniel, had also died at twenty. Liszt went to live in the little monastery of the Madonna del Rosario on Monte Mario where he was visited by Pope Pius IX from whom Liszt had hoped for an appointment as director of music to the Vatican, a dream never fulfilled. Deciding to take vows, Liszt went for religious instruction and on April 25, 1865, received the tonsure. A few months later, he took three more orders entitling him to be called the Abbé Liszt. He could, however, neither celebrate Mass nor hear confession. He did take a vow of chastity. He moved into apartments in the Vatican opposite the Loggia of Raphael near the Sistine Chapel.

Later Cardinal Hohenlohe, ever his friend, installed him in a luxurious suite in the Villa d'Este at Tivoli, with its beautiful gardens and terraces. Through Hohenlohe, Liszt was made a Canon of Albano in 1879, an honor which entitled him to wear a purple soutane.

In 1869 Liszt emerged from retirement and began to lead what he described as "a trifurcated life," dividing his time between the Villa d'Este, Budapest and Weimar. For a time, however, he had to avoid Rome. He had become involved with Olga Janina, an Ukrainian-born, so-called "Cossack Countess" of nineteen. Liszt enmeshed himself in a love affair with her, then wished himself well out of it and tried to escape. She pursued him. In Budapest, she came to his room armed with poisons and pistols and threatened to kill him and commit suicide. "Fire," Liszt shouted — according to one account — and advanced towards her. "But the unhappy woman dropped her hand, and fell at his feet." The Cossack Countess dropped out of Liszt's life eventually but she wrote a book telling all, or what she thought was all.

Liszt returned often to Villa d'Este after 1873-74. Wherever he went, he was followed by devoted pupils, admirers, and adoring women. In May 1870, he was in Weimar to conduct at the Beethoven Centenary Festival. In 1871, he was appointed Royal Hungarian Counsellor, and in 1875 became President of the newly founded Hungarian National Academy of Music. On March 5, 1876, Countess d'Agoult died. A few months later, another ghost of his amorous past was laid to rest; George Sand died.

Liszt's daughter, Cosima, was married to Wagner in Lucerne on August 25, 1870. On May 22, 1872, Wagner's birthday, the laying of the cornerstone at Bayreuth was celebrated. By intention or not, Liszt received his invitation too late to attend. He went there, however, a half year later, saw the foundations of the Festspielhaus and was overcome with emotion when Wagner read him the first draft of *Parsifal.* He said of Cosima: "Let others judge and condemn her; for me she remains a soul worthy of the *gran perdono* of Saint Francis and admirably my daughter."

When the Festspielhaus opened its doors in August 1876, Liszt travelled to the sacred site for the first performance of the *Ring.* He wrote to Carolyne: "No more doubts, no more obstacles. The immense genius of Wagner has surmounted everything."

Liszt undertook a triumphant "Jubilee Tour" in 1886, in anticipation of his seventy-fifth birthday, and everywhere he was lionized. He had not been to London since 1841, a visit then shadowed by his liaison with Marie d'Agoult. This time he was received like royalty and played for Queen Victoria.

On July 3, he paid a visit to Bayreuth for the marriage of his granddaughter, Daniela, to the art historian, Heinrich von Thode. Then he went on to Luxembourg to visit the painter Mihály von Munkácsy. At a concert of the Luxembourg Music Society, he was persuaded to go to the piano. He played a Chopin *etude* — his last public performance. He returned to Bayreuth and on the train caught a severe cold. Against his doctor's advice, he went on July 24 to hear *Tristan und Isolde;* he was so weak he had to be almost carried from his carriage to the Wagner box. After the *Liebestod* he was taken back to the Villa Wahnfried, as pneumonia had set in. On the night of July 31, he died. The last word he was heard to murmur was "Tristan." He was buried at Bayreuth.

Liszt left behind him music in every style and form, but only one opera, a forgotten juvenile work. But if ever there was an operatic story it is that of Franz Liszt. He lived a life as improbable, as dramatic, as passionate as any opera libretto. As man and as musician he was the epitome of the Romantic Age.

by DORLE J. SORIA

Concerto for Piano and Orchestra in A Major, No. 2

Liszt wrote two piano concerti. No. 1 in E flat was completed from earlier sketches in 1849, and became known as the "triangle concerto", a term of opprobrium in its day. Liszt's use of the frivolous instrument in a respectable, serious work scandalized the conservative press. Liszt himself was at the piano at its first performance on February 17, 1855, in the hall of the palace of the Grand Duke of Weimar. Berlioz was the conductor.

Concerto No. 2 in A major was the second in order of publication but a manuscript in the Liszt Museum at Weimar, dated September 1839, shows its origin as a sketch. This was reworked into a concerto which was scored completely in 1849. It was played from manuscript for the first time in Weimar, in the Grand Ducal Theatre on January 7, 1857, at a concert for the benefit of the Weimar Orchestra's Pension Fund. This time, Liszt was conductor, not soloist. At the keyboard was a pupil to whom it had been dedicated, Hans von Bronsart, a Berlin-born pianist and composer, then still in his twenties. He had not only studied with Liszt, but married another of Liszt's pupils.

The A major Concerto, on its autograph manuscript, bore the title *Concert Symphonique,* and it can be considered a symphonic poem for orchestra with a virtuoso piano part. Like the E flat Concerto it is in one continuous movement with many changes of tempo and mood. After its première it was revised and published in 1863. It is scored for solo piano, two flutes and piccolo, two oboes, two clarinets, two bassoons, horns, two trumpets, three trombones, bass tuba, timpani, cymbals and strings.

William Foster Apthorp, distinguished music critic and early program annotator, once wrote: "Had Liszt seen fit to give the concerto a poetic or dramatic title, it might have been something like *'The Life and Adventures of a Melody.'*"

The Liszt piano concerti, written by one of the greatest piano virtuosi of all time, remain in the repertory as dazzling examples of the romantic era, showpieces to test the hearts and fingers of the pianists of each new generation.

Hungarian Fantasy for Piano and Orchestra

The Hungarian Fantasy has been known under various names: Hungarian Rhapsody for Piano and Orchestra, Magyar Rhapsody, and Hungarian Fantasia. Its original long title was Fantasy on Hungarian Folk Melodies for Piano and Orchestra. No matter what it is called, it is an enormously effective, colourful, perennially popular work. It evolved from the famous Hungarian Rhapsody No. 1 for orchestra, which in turn was derived from the Liszt Hungarian Rhapsody No. 14 in the piano series. With the assistance of his pupil Franz Doppler, Liszt had arranged six of his piano Rhapsodies for orchestra. Later he made a final version of No. 1 for piano and orchestra, a free and brilliant version of the original music.

The Hungarian Fantasy was dedicated to Hans von Bülow who introduced it as soloist on June 1, 1853, at the Hungarian National Theatre in Pest. The conductor was the Music Director of the theatre, Ferenc Erkel, himself a composer identified with the nationalistic music revival in Hungary.

Edward Downes has written of the work (published in 1865) in a program for the New York Philharmonic: "Here in his swashbuckling Hungarian Fantasy, he is first of all Liszt the thunderer, the dazzling virtuoso, the magician of the keyboard who commands our attention. Yet in

back of the thunder, there is the melancholy, world-weary young Romantic who remembers his boyhood in the Hungarian countryside and the gypsy tunes, or rather the Hungarian tunes he heard the gypsies play in their own characteristic fashion ... The Hungarian Fantasy opens, like much Hungarian folk-dance music, with a melancholy introduction and proceeds to a vigorous *allegro,* in this case marked specifically *allegro eroica.* There is a more relaxed middle section, an *allegretto* 'in gypsy style' and a glorious razzle-dazzle finale."

A somewhat idealised group of gypsies, copied from a painting made by Valerio in 1864. (Milan, Bertarelli Print Collection)

Hungarian Rhapsody No. 6 for Orchestra (*Carnival of Pest*)

The Hungarian Rhapsodies were inspired by the composer's experiences of gypsies in his native land. In them he has absorbed and imitated the two-fold character of the Hungarian-Gypsy national dance, the *Czárdás,* with its sad first movement called *lassú* and its fast last one, the hypnotic *friss* when the music rushes on madly to its end, holding the audiences spell-bound.

Liszt wrote to the Countess d'Agoult October 8, 1846: "I have collected a number of fragments, with the help of which one might fairly well recompose the musical epic of this strange country whose *rhapsode* I want to become." About this time, too, he told his friend Count Festetics that he wished to be known as "the first Gypsy in the Kingdom of Hungary."

Walter Starkie, an authority on the life and lore of the gypsies, wrote *(In Sara's Tents):* "The devotees of Bartók and Kodaly accuse Liszt and Brahms of having done great harm to Hungary by their rhapsodies and Hungarian dances, because, though these hybrid works did, it is true, turn the thoughts of Europe towards Hungarian art, it was the art of a foreign race in Hungary. Liszt intended his book on Gypsies to be the prologue to the rhapsodies, which were the separate cantos of a gigantic Gypsy epic in music, but he made the great mistake of calling the Gypsy music Hungarian, as though the wandering Indian race had created all Magyar music. According to his theory, the Gypsies brought their scale as well as their language from the East into Hungary, and the Magyars adapted

A 19th century print of a gypsy encampment. Such scenes were familiar to Liszt from his early childhood. (Milan, Bertarelli Print Collection)

their national dances to the Gypsy airs, and sang melodies of Gypsy origin to Hungarian words. Bartók, Kodaly, and the modern critics have indignantly refuted Liszt. The title of the book of Liszt should have been *'The Gypsies and the manner in which they handle music in Hungary.'*" Explaining the relations between Magyar and Gypsy Starkie states: "The Gypsy fiddler in Hungary, indeed, played the music of the country, whether folk-song or operetta tune, in such a way as to cast a spell upon his listeners, for he employed in his playing the same magnetic powers as his witch of a mother had done out on the Puszta when telling fortunes, and just as she knew intuitively what thoughts were in the mind of the farmer who paid her to tell him what fortune had in store for him, so did the fiddler know what melodies would find true response in his Magyar audience."

If Liszt's music is not authentic it does not really matter. So far as the general public is concerned, his Hungarian Rhapsodies have remained for a century the symbol and sound of the gypsy of romantic legend.

The Hungarian Rhapsodies were first written for piano. Originally there were fifteen, six of which Liszt later arranged for orchestra. The ninth, subtitled *Carnival of Pest* and written in 1848, became the sixth of the rhapsodies in orchestral form. Liszt also arranged this rhapsody for piano duet and for trio: piano, violin and cello. Sacheverell Sitwell calls the *Carnival of Pest* Rhapsody "a delightful example of Liszt in his mood of nationalism."

Printed in the United States of America

His Life and Times 1809-1847

PROGRAM NOTES FOR THE FOURTH SYMPHONY AND MUSIC FROM A MIDSUMMER NIGHT'S DREAM
By Robert Jacobson

FUNK & WAGNALLS, INC.
NEW YORK, NEW YORK

The Gifted Youth: Life 1809-26

Jakob Ludwig Felix Mendelssohn was born on 3rd February 1809 in Hamburg, the second of the four children of Abraham and Leah Mendelssohn. The eldest child, Fanny Cäcilia, was four years older and plays a major part in the story, first as a devoted companion and later as a faithful correspondent. The other two, Rebecca and Paul, are shadowy figures, whose names crop up in the Mendelssohn literature and letters relatively rarely.

As its name suggests, the family was Jewish – something that has, and had, to be reckoned with, given the circumstances of the time. It had a bearing on Felix's background and inheritance, as it also did now and then on the course of his career. Grandfather Moses had been a remarkable man: a philosopher, a humanist, and a protagonist of Jewish emancipation, he was immortalised by Lessing in his play *Nathan the Wise* and known among his intimates as 'the Jewish Socrates'. In the face of Gentile complacency and worse, he made his way from humble beginnings as a scholar – one of the few avenues of advancement open to his race. The other and equally traditional avenue was through finance. Two of Moses' sons, Joseph and Abraham (Mendelssohn's father), went therefore into banking. The latter, who was to describe himself wryly as 'formerly the son of my father and now the father of my son', worked for some years in Paris at the turn of the century, and during one of his journeys called on Goethe at Frankfurt. Welcomed as 'the son of his father', he was instrumental in bringing together the poet (also Minister of State) and the Berlin musician Zelter, who had set some of Goethe's songs· and whom Abraham knew quite well. In due course Zelter was to have Abraham's son as his most brilliant pupil, and was in his turn to take the boy to see Goethe at Weimar.

Abraham's wife, Leah Salomon, came from a more prosperous and settled background, where the arts were cultivated with gusto. She was highly educated, polyglot, read Homer in the original, and was a good pianist into the bargain – a woman of charm and character, and something of a snob. It was on her insistence that Abraham left his post as clerk in Paris, where there was no racial discrimination, in order to return to Germany. There, in Hamburg, he joined his brother Joseph as a partner in his banking firm.

The Mendelssohns' stay in Hamburg was shortlived. The French army of occupation under the command of Marshal Davout was ill-disciplined, and for this and other reasons Abraham came to the conclusion in 1812 that it would be healthier to move to Berlin. Theirs was a happy, hard-working, strictly organised and early-rising household – prosperous, of course, but not showy. The only commodity in short supply was leisure. Abraham ensured a well-rounded education for his children, which included dancing and physical training as well as more bookish activities and, needless to say, the pursuit of music. Instead of going to school, the young Mendelssohns were instructed first by their mother and then by private tutors. General literary subjects were taught by Karl Wilhelm Ludwig Heyse, father of the novelist, piano by Ludwig Berger, a partisan of the Clementi and Field school, violin first by a member of the opera orchestra and later by Eduard Rietz, and harmony, counterpoint and composition by Zelter, by far the strongest personality of all the tutors. This elaborate and systematic education of a master-musician of the 19th century was topped up by Felix's joining the singing classes of the Singakademie when he was ten. Needless to say, his obvious gifts had been recognised at an earlier age, for in 1816 the family paid a visit to Paris, and Felix and Fanny had piano lessons from the celebrated teacher Madame Biget.

Also in 1818, Mendelssohn made his public debut as a pianist in a trio for keyboard and two horns by Woeffler, and parallel with that was his increasing activity as a composer, writing a trio and three piano sonatas. A visit by Weber to Berlin in 1821 sparked off a couple of one-act operettas, followed by a third and later by a three-act opera *Der Onkel aus Boston* (The Uncle from Boston). It was at about this time that Zelter took the twelve-year-old boy to see Goethe.

Meanwhile Mendelssohn advanced in grace and accomplishments, worked very hard and enjoyed the benefits of the musical salon set up by his mother. If in some respects his life was cushioned against the rough and tumble of a more humdrum upbringing, it did not seem to make much difference in the long run, though it may have made him more sensitive than most. Zelter was an excellent teacher and took care that Felix did not let the slightly euphoric home atmosphere of love and encouragement go to his head. Sometimes, indeed, he seems to have gone in the other direction.

New works flowed from Mendelssohn's pen. These included the First Symphony in C minor, op. 11, actually the thirteenth in order of writing, and the Piano Quartet in B minor, op. 3. In addition there were family trips abroad – in 1822 to Switzerland, a country Mendelssohn fell in love with and where he met Spohr and Hiller. Two years later, they went to the Baltic and for the first time Mendelssohn saw the sea. Back in Berlin, the Mendelssohn home had become a natural rendezvous for visiting musicians, among them the outstanding young pianist Moscheles, who gave the awestruck youth and his sister some piano lessons. Subsequently they were to meet frequently in London, and eventually Moscheles was to join the staff at the Leipzig Conservatorium during Mendelssohn's regime.

Meanwhile, it is important to record, the Mendelssohns had decided to abandon their Jewish patrimony and become Protestants. The repercussions of such a step within the family can be imagined, but given the situation at the time, it was a politic move, strongly advocated by Leah and her worldly-wise diplomatist brother. The problem was one that had been faced by many, inside and outside the families immediately concerned. (Indeed, Abraham's sisters had turned Catholic.) That was where the additional name of Bartholdy came in. It had been adopted by Leah's brother Jacob Lewin Salomon, who had taken it from a previous owner of his Berlin property, and then shared it with his brother-in-law. Felix, however, never took kindly to his double-barrelled name and dropped the Bartholdy to all intents and purposes. That was partly a matter of principle and partly, one suspects, of defiance of his uncle. It was no secret that he, Jacob Lewin Bartholdy, was very much against his nephew becoming a professional musician: 'It is no career, no life, no aim.' Unhappily that attitude coincided all too well with Abraham's misgivings about his son's talents. Hence his appeal in 1825 to a higher court – his old acquaintance Cherubini – when father and son were in Paris. Fortunately, the verdict was favourable. As could be expected in so lively a youth as Mendelssohn, his letters from Paris were nothing if not vivid, often scathing, sometimes very funny. He met everybody – Auber, Kalkbrenner, Hummel, Liszt, Onslow, Meyerbeer and Rossini – and he was confirmed in his ingenuous view that charlatanry was rampant, ignorance widespread and frivolity in control. This denunciatory reaction to Paris became something of an obsession with him, and was to be repeated on later visits.

These were happy years for Mendelssohn. The bank flourished, the family moved into an imposing mansion in Leipzigerstrasse, a stream of interesting and amusing people came to the house, and among Felix's closest associates were A. B. Marx (editor of the musical journal the *Berliner Allgemeine Musikalische Zeitung*), Hiller, Zelter, Moscheles, Rietz, and Carl Klingemann, who in due course was to ease Mendelssohn's path in London's musical and social circles. And all the time there was the close companionship of Fanny, who understood him better than anyone else, even if her love for him only just stopped short of the possessive and obsessive. It was during this halcyon period that Mendelssohn wrote two of his most enduring works – the Octet for strings, op. 20 (1825), and his Concert Overture to *A Midsummer Night's Dream*, op. 21 (1826).

Mendelssohn's beloved sister Fanny. The overture to A Midsummer Night's Dream *was originally written as a piano duet for her and the composer when he was seventeen (Mendelssohn Archive, Berlin)*

Far left: *Mendelssohn's father Abraham. He used to describe himself as 'formerly the son of my father, now the father of my son' (Mendelssohn Archive, Berlin)*

Mendelssohn's mother Leah, née Salomon. The Mendelssohn family was already rich: the addition of her family's even greater wealth gave the composer a most unusually comfortable start in life (Mendelssohn Archive, Berlin)

Widened Horizons: Life 1826-33

What could be called a second stage in Mendelssohn's development extends from his matriculation at Berlin University to his acceptance of the conductorship of the Lower Rhine Festival in 1833 – his first professional post. These were years largely taken up with travel, with organising a revival of Bach's *St Matthew Passion* with the Singakademie and, of course, with composition.

It was a happy time on the whole. Grafted on to his happy home life was his ever-widening circle of friends; added to which he was by now to all intents and purposes grown-up. Some setbacks there were. His opera *The Wedding of Camacho*, based on Cervantes, was accepted rather grudgingly by Spontini, director of the Berlin State Opera; and although it did eventually reach the stage on 29th April 1827 and was warmly received by the public, Mendelssohn was hurt by some of the press reviews and was left with a nasty taste in his mouth by the atmosphere of backstage cabal and intrigue. He felt that he had been rejected by his own city – a sentiment that was to remain with him throughout his career, throughout his love-hate relationship with musical and official Berlin. As to his studies at the University, although Felix was clever, well read and polyglot – given his background, how could he fail to be otherwise? – he was no academic, and when at the age of twenty-seven he was given an honorary doctorate by Leipzig University he did not take it very seriously.

On the other hand, the philosopher Hegel, who lectured on aesthetics, left an impression on Mendelssohn's receptive mind, even if the latter affected to despise mere talking about music. Certain Hegelian principles accord closely with those that Mendelssohn expounded in his own scores: 'Like any other art, music must restrain the emotions and their manifestations lest the music plunge into bacchanalian clamour and whirl into a tumult of passion. . . . Music must remain untrammelled and yet in its outpouring serene. . . . The proper domain of music is essentially that of inwardness combined with tone unalloyed. . . . In music, objectivity abates. Being the essentially Romantic art, music withdraws altogether into subjectivity, both as regards inner meaning and outer manifestation.' It looks, then, as though Mendelssohn affected to spurn musical aesthetics, whereas in reality he was not nearly such a pragmatist as he made out.

Musically, 1827 saw the emergence of two by-products of his Bachian enthusiasm, the Fugue in E minor for piano and the motet 'Tu es Petrus', written for Fanny; while his study of late Beethoven was reflected most clearly in his A minor quartet, op. 13. No less important was his meeting on one of his expeditions – and, like other young men of his generation, Mendelssohn made many long trips on foot – with Professor Thibaut, Professor of Law at Heidelberg and a devotee of Palestrina. Of him Mendelssohn was to write: 'One Thibaut is worth six ordinary men – I have learned a great deal from him, and owe him many thanks. For he has revealed to me the merits of old Italian music and warmed me with his enthusiasm for it. . . . When I left him, he said: "Farewell, and we will build our friendship on Luis de Victoria and Sebastian Bach, like two lovers who promise each other to look at the moon and then fancy they are near each other" .'

This encounter had two results: practically, it aroused Mendelssohn's interest in Renaissance music in general and in Palestrina's idiom in particular; in more general terms, Thibaut's concern with the relationship between music and morals blended with analogous views that Felix had heard expounded by philosophers Hegel and Schleiermacher. In the mid-20th century we may raise a sceptical eyebrow at such preoccupations, but at that time they were very much in the air and have to be reckoned with when Mendelssohn's

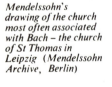

Mendelssohn's drawing of the church most often associated with Bach – the church of St Thomas in Leipzig (Mendelssohn Archive, Berlin)

own attitudes are gauged. These can seem surprisingly priggish from time to time, and seemed so even to some of his contemporaries, but they derived partly from his own seriousness of purpose and partly from indoctrination.

Another important event in 1827 was Mendelssohn's visit to Stettin, where the famous song composer Carl Loewe conducted the first performances of the orchestral version of the Overture to *A Midsummer Night's Dream*, of the Concerto for two pianos in A flat, and, in Northern Europe at any rate, of Beethoven's 'Choral' Symphony.

1828 was a relatively fallow year, though it included in its modest harvest the Goethe-inspired overture *Calm Sea and Prosperous Voyage*, and latterly Mendelssohn began to work on Zelter to let him conduct the Bach *St Matthew Passion* with the Singakademie. In this daring and ambitious enterprise, Mendelssohn was very strongly backed and sometimes goaded by his friend Eduard Devrient, an actor, who was set on singing the part of Jesus. It required the most enormous persistence on the part of the two young men to bring their scheme to fruition. If Zelter, who was, after all, a Bachian zealot, was extremely sceptical of the practicality of the idea, the choir was even more so. Later they were to preen themselves on their achievement: at the time, they were, according to Mendelssohn, as obstructive as possible. At any rate, the performance on 11th May 1829 made a deep impression and was repeated ten days later, though in the face of much opposition from Spontini, who was no friend to Mendelssohn. Shortly afterwards, Zelter himself was to conduct a third performance. Why the fuss? Simply because J. S. Bach and his music had dwindled to a minority cult largely centred on Berlin, though with sundry sturdy outcrops elsewhere. The public at large had forgotten all about him – and did not necessarily want to be reminded. 'Outdated rubbish' was the verdict of some who listened to a performance of the Passion in Königsberg.

Mendelssohn's next move was at the suggestion of Moscheles: a trip to London – the city that was to become a second home to the composer. His object was not so much to take active part in London's music but rather to 'take its temperature', to see what it was like. As things turned out, his expedition was a great success, thanks to the welcome from his friend Klingemann at the Hanoverian legation in London, and from Moscheles and his wife. Through them he had a ready-made entrée into the city's musical and social circles. Soon after his arrival, Mendelssohn wrote to his family in these terms: 'London is the grandest and most complicated monster on the face of the earth. How can I compress into one letter what I have been three days seeing. I hardly remember the chief events and yet I must not keep a diary, for then I would see less of life, and that must not be. On the contrary, I want to catch hold of whatever offers itself to me. Things roll and whirl around me and carry me along as in a vortex.'

That was no exaggeration. He conducted his First Symphony in C minor, op. 11, at a Philharmonic Society concert; he heard the famous Malibran in Rossini's *Otello* and even played for her at a soirée; he appeared as a pianist; he was even asked to write a song for a festival in Ceylon, celebrating the emancipation of the natives. However, as his letters show, he was at this time busier soaking up impressions and meeting people than in writing music – to the extent

A 19th-century print of Edinburgh where Mendelssohn toured and found inspiration for many works, including the 'Scotch' Symphony (Bertarelli Print Collection, Milan)

that his family began to fear that he was becoming a social butterfly. In a sense he was, but it was to pay dividends, for in later years he spent a great deal of time in England and relied very much on the company of his friends in varied strata of society. Came July, and Mendelssohn set off with Klingemann on a tour of Northern England, Scotland and Wales, a hugely enterprising exploit for such a hothouse plant as Mendelssohn was. But he was far tougher than he seemed in the elegant salons of the metropolis. From York and Durham, the travellers came to Edinburgh, a city which Mendelssohn greatly admired, not only for its Mary Stuart/Schiller associations but for its grandeur and its pretty girls.

At Liverpool, Klingemann parted from Mendelssohn, who went on by himself to Wales, where he stayed with the Taylors, kinsfolk of the Horsleys of Kensington whom he came to know so well. Back in London he was knocked over by a cabriolet, injuring his kneecap, and so was not able to return in time to Berlin for the October wedding of his beloved sister Fanny to the painter Hensel. That was one of the few disappointments on an astonishingly fruitful first foray to Britain.

Before leaving London, however, Mendelssohn finished his operetta *Son and Stranger* and on his return to Berlin continued work on his Fifth Symphony, the 'Reformation'. He was now aged twenty, and it gives one some idea of the speed at which he had matured that he was offered the chair of musical history at Berlin University. Judging himself unsuited to the academic life, he declined it and may have been instrumental in getting his friend A. B. Marx appointed to the post in his place. Meanwhile preparations were going forward for a far more elaborate Continental tour which was to take in Italy as well as nearer-lying countries. After various delays, including an outbreak of measles in the family, Felix set off. After Dessau, he went to Weimar to see Goethe. Conversation and music flowed, his portrait was painted, and he played not only Beethoven's Fifth Symphony in C minor to his host but some of his most recent keyboard pieces. A letter from Zelter to Goethe at that particular point is interesting: 'I thank you as much as possible; he [Mendelssohn] can feast on this all during his life. Sometimes

The frontispiece of Bach's St Matthew Passion *which Mendelssohn revived at the Singakademie, Berlin (Mendelssohn Archive, Berlin)*

I am afraid when I look at the boy's rapid rise. Up till now he has hardly met with any opposition.'

The next stop was Munich, where Mendelssohn met all the notabilities, was extremely sociable, fell mildly in love with a gifted and attractive young pianist, Delphine von Schauroth and, in his letters at least, was very rude about the climate of musical taste in the Bavarian capital. Nevertheless from that visit sprang two works, the Rondo Capriccio in E, op. 14, and in due course the first Piano Concerto in G minor. He then travelled on to Salzburg and Vienna, which seemed already to have forgotten the great days of Haydn, Mozart, Beethoven and Schubert, and was given over to frivolity and sentimentalism. Eventually, by way of Pressburg where he saw the coronation of the King of Hungary, Mendelssohn arrived in Venice and wrote: 'Italy at last! What I have been looking forward to all my life as the greatest happiness is now begun, and I am basking in it.' But once again, the standard of music and music-making shocked him. Enthralled as he was by the Titians and Giorgiones on view, he was taken aback by the general and complacent ignorance shown by local pianists.

Arriving in Rome on 1st November 1830, he stayed there till April of the next year. As always he was immediately accepted by society, on the strength of his family name and also because of his own fast-growing international reputation as a composer. As always his letters are a treasure trove of comment and criticism. We read of the receptions he attended, of the boundless hospitality of the Prussian historian/diplomatist Baron von Bunsen and his wealthy English wife, Fanny (Waddington), of life among the cardinals, of the unappetising German colony of painters, of his friendship with Horace Vernet and Thorvaldsen, of the

death of Pope Pius VIII and the celebrations attendant on the election of his successor Gregory XVI, of Berlioz's unstable emotional state, of music in the Sistine Chapel, of Mendelssohn's dislike of plainsong and his contacts with two scholar- and musician-priests, Santini and Baini. From posterity's more selective point of view, Mendelssohn's stay in Rome is particularly important because of the music to which it gave rise. Church music, mostly Protestant, like his Three Sacred Pieces, op. 23, 'Aus tiefer Not', 'Ave Maria' and 'Mitten wir im Leben sind', and also his noble 'Non nobis, Domine' setting, op. 31, can be set alongside his first version of the *Hebrides* overture, his continuation of *Die Erste Walpurgisnacht* and sketches for the 'Scotch' and 'Italian' Symphonies.

After a visit of a few weeks to Naples, Mendelssohn started home, via Rome, Florence, Milan (where the operatic infection nearly caught him and where he met Mozart's son Karl), through Switzerland, mostly on foot, and once more to Munich. There his embryo affair with Delphine von Schauroth showed signs of developing into a *grande passion*, and his First Piano Concerto had its première. He also accepted the invitation to write an opera for the Royal Theatre, though nothing was to come of it. Finally, his route took him to Paris where he stayed from December 1831 till April 1832. It was his third visit and as always he met everybody; but his was not the temperament to make the best of the French capital nor to discover what made it an exciting place to be in during the early 1830s.

A short visit to London came as a relief. He wrote: 'I wish I could only describe how happy I feel to be here again once more; how much I like everything, and how gratified I am by the kindness of old friends.' By 'friends' he meant Klingemann, Moscheles, Sir Thomas Attwood, the Horsley family, Rosen and many others. He felt at ease, loved and praised. For a memento of this recharging of batteries, we need only turn to his Capriccio Brillante for Piano and Orchestra in B minor, op. 22, and his first volume of Songs Without Words, written at the behest of Novello. It was during this second visit to London that Mendelssohn suffered another blow – the death of his mentor, confidant and friend Zelter. This left the directorship of the Berlin Singakademie vacant, which was an appointment Mendelssohn would have welcomed. It would have meant official recognition in his own city, something he craved, though he had no illusions about the snags.

Prodded by his family and his friends, and against his better judgement although he would dearly have loved the job, he allowed himself to become a candidate. The period of waiting was painful, the result even more so. In January 1835 Zelter's former deputy Rungenhagen was chosen by an overwhelming majority of votes, and the Singakademie lived to rue its decision, while Mendelssohn never quite got over it. This was the winter of his discontent. The only consolation, and it was not inconsiderable, was a commission from the London Philharmonic Society for 'a symphony, an overture and a vocal piece' which had come his way in November 1832. First fruit of this request was the 'Italian' Symphony, on which he had been working and which had its première on 13th May 1833. It led to his being invited to become permanent musical director, taking up the appointment on 1st October 1833.

Prolific Productivity: Life 1833-41

Time and again one has to remind oneself how much Mendelssohn packed into his life and how short that life was. He was only thirty-eight when he died in 1847. A span of seven years, like that between 1834 and 1841 in the case of Mendelssohn, would in another musician's life be adequately full of incident, whereas in his career almost every month brought some noteworthy event. The explanation is simple. Mendelssohn was at the heart of musical affairs in Germany, not to mention England, active as a composer, as a conductor, as a performer, even as an administrator, a role he cared least for. When the period begins he is discovered at the age of twenty-four, just about to become Generalmusikdirektor at Düsseldorf. Thereafter he moves to Leipzig where he becomes conductor of the Gewandhaus concerts, makes frequent visits to England (during which he makes his debut at the Birmingham Festival), meets and marries Cecile Jeanrenaud, and at the end of the period, at the ripe old age of thirty-two is appointed director of the music section of the Academy of Arts, Berlin. From the composer's point of view, those years are distinguished by the appearance of such works as the *Rondo brillante* for piano and orchestra op. 29, the oratorio *St Paul*, the D minor Piano Concerto, the E minor String Quartet op. 44 no. 2, the overtures to *Melusine* and *Ruy Blas*, the D minor trio and the *Hymn of Praise*.

Düsseldorf represented Mendelssohn's first official post, and he brought to it energy, enthusiasm and a reforming zeal. Once again, readers must be reminded of his comparative youth and of something else which is often forgotten. Mendelssohn was no stained-glass-window character. With his brilliance and his charm went irritability, impatience and intolerance. At that stage he had had little experience of dealing with others and, as happened at Düsseldorf, he was quite capable of tactlessness, even of irresponsibility. Those defects, especially in one in authority, were marked and commented on by Mendelssohn's father, who from time to time was to send his son a philippic on the subject. The fact was that Mendelssohn had got over-used to having his own way.

Being in the Rhineland, Düsseldorf was Catholic, and so one of Mendelssohn's first tasks was to improve the state of church music. This, in any denomination and at any time, is a notoriously perilous task. As a disciple of Thibaut, Mendelssohn decided that what the locals needed was a diet of Italian Renaissance and Baroque music – Palestrina, Lassus, Lotti, Allegri and Pergolesi. These were the tastes of a purist who looked askance at the colourful masses of Haydn and his contemporaries. Against a good deal of opposition he did manage to persuade the churches to incorporate this older type of sacred music into their services. In his public concerts, there was not the same justification for looking so far back into the past, but he had still to take account of his public's wishes. He could not afford to be too avant-garde, and Beethoven, who had not been dead for long, nearly came into that category.

Childe's watercolour of Mendelssohn painted in 1829 (Mendelssohn Archive, Berlin)

In the theatre Mendelssohn ran into serious trouble. He was an idealist as well as a purist, demanded an exceptional number of rehearsals, fell afoul of the orchestra, and his 'model performance' of *Don Giovanni* caused a commotion. Temperamentally he was ill-suited to the post of intendant of the opera, which formed part of his general duties. He fell out with Immermann and rather abruptly resigned, causing ill-feeling all round. His father, worldly-wise as well as censorious in this affair, observed '. . . you subjected yourself to the imputation of fickleness and unsteadiness and made a decided enemy of a man who, at all events, policy would have taught you not to displease.' The trouble was that although Mendelssohn had a vast number of acquaintances, fundamentally he was a 'loner'. At Düsseldorf his friends tended to be painters, not musicians, and it continued to be his father, Fanny and Klingemann on whom he relied for advice and exhortation. All things considered therefore, the offer of the conductorship of the Gewandhaus concerts in Leipzig could not have come at a more propitious moment. He had also been offered the post of opera director at Munich at a handsome salary, but had the good sense to realise that such a job was not for him. Leipzig was not particularly well paid, but it was a far more important centre than Düsseldorf, had a number of distinguished and historical musical institutions, was closer to Berlin and his parents, and above all was forever associated with J. S. Bach.

One of his first tasks was to finish his oratorio *St Paul*, which had its successful première in Düsseldorf in May 1836. It was a task in which Mendelssohn had been continually encouraged by his father, but Abraham did not live to hear its first performance. He died rather suddenly six months before, a grievous blow, especially to anyone as death-conscious as Mendelssohn. Consolation however came from the daughter of a French Huguenot widow living in Frankfurt, Cecile Jeanrenaud. For the first time, Mendelssohn's emotional security was seriously shaken. 'I can neither compose, nor write letters, nor play the piano,' he wrote. Doubtful of his own sentiments he went off to the Dutch

A painting of Mendelssohn's wife Cecile, who was herself an ardent sketcher and painter (Mendelssohn Archive, Berlin)

watering place Scheveningen to reflect, realised he loved Cecile, proposed, was accepted and in March 1837 was married at the French Walloon Reformed Church in Frankfurt. It seems to have been a very happy marriage.

Cecile was no blue-stocking nor was she particularly musical, but she was intelligent, well-read, attractive, rather shy, and full of wifely virtues. For a pen picture of her, we turn to a letter from Fanny to Klingemann. 'She is amiable, childlike, bright and even-tempered, and I consider Felix most fortunate for, though inexpressibly fond of him, she does not spoil him, but when he is capricious, treats him with an equanimity which will in course of time most probably cure his fits of irritability. Her presence produces the effect of a fresh breeze, so bright and natural is she.' It is hardly surprising if on Felix's next visit to London, a city where normally he was so happy, he was impatient and out of sympathy with the place and its inhabitants and only concerned to return to his bride.

The next few years were devoted to music in Leipzig, interspersed with bouts of travel. Mendelssohn was much in demand as a conductor and had in any case a built-in tendency towards restlessness. Nevertheless his primary task was for the time being the Gewandhaus orchestra, of which his friend David was leader. He increased the size of the orchestra, and revolutionised the programmes. His innate good taste rejected the popular favourites of his predecessors' time, the names of whom would hardly mean anything at all to readers today. In their place, he substituted music by his contemporaries, and near contemporaries – Gade, Schumann, Rossini, Cherubini, Chopin and Spohr – with Beethoven and Mozart strongly represented on the 'classical' side, Haydn, Handel and Bach less so. As a conductor Mendelssohn initiated a new regime altogether, which killed forever the role of the conductor as a mere time-beater. It now included training the orchestra and the conscious interpretation of the music. The result was that the Leipzig Gewandhaus rose from being a competent band of provincial instrumentalists into one of the best orchestras in Europe. He insisted upon discipline and detail for himself and abhorred meaningless gestures. Fast tempi seem to have been features of his performances, but there the evidence is inconclusive, for Wagner is not the most unprejudiced of witnesses. Chorley, visiting Leipzig at that time, commented glowingly that 'never, indeed, did I hear the Symphonies of Beethoven so intensely enjoyed as at Leipzig and never so admirably performed. . . . There was a breadth and freedom in their outlines, a thorough proportion in all their parts, a poetical development of all their choice and picturesque ideas which fully compensated for the occasional want of the hyper-brilliancy and the hyper-delicacy, on the possession of which my friends in Paris pride themselves so vaingloriously.'

In some ways, this was a halcyon period, perhaps the last Mendelssohn was to enjoy. He was famed as a composer, and famed as a conductor (amongst other things he gave the world première of Schubert's 'Great' C major Symphony – in 1839). His home life was secure, and his musical reputation never stood higher. Soon however, the siren call of Berlin was to sound in his ears once again, and the calm sea and prosperous voyage of Mendelssohn's career was to be disrupted.

Work and Worry: Life 1841-47

The last six years of Mendelssohn's life were clouded by overwork and worry largely caused by his acceptance of high office in Berlin at the behest of King Frederick William IV of Prussia. At the same time he was expanding his activities in Leipzig, travelling constantly, conducting and composing. It is sometimes claimed that the calibre of his music deteriorated at this time, almost as if the well of inspiration was running dry. As to that, he was becoming a tired man, and the early fluency and freshness was no longer his to command, but it is exaggerated to assert that 'his right hand had lost his cunning'. Mark some of the works that he produced during those six years: the *Variations sérieuses*, the 'Scotch' Symphony, the incidental music to *A Midsummer Night's Dream*, various Psalm settings, the Cello Sonata, the Violin Concerto, the B flat major Trio and above all *Elijah*. Considering the pace at which he lived and the number of his preoccupations, it was an extraordinarily high-powered output.

Mendelssohn's return to Berlin was perhaps something that he owed to himself. It was a challenge, for professionally

his experiences in that city had been disappointing. Yet for that very reason, he was the more anxious to triumph there, to prove that he could be a prophet with honour in his own land. He had been happy in Leipzig but now was perhaps the moment to strike out anew; furthermore, if he returned to Berlin, he would be near his family. The immediate cause of his decision to go back was a summons from the new King of Prussia, Frederick William IV, a well-intentioned idealist who, quite naturally, was anxious to attract the most famous musician in Germany to his capital. Mendelssohn was offered the post of musical director of the projected Academy of Arts. The post was honourable, the salary higher than he had ever enjoyed before. It soon became clear however that there were snags. Writing to David, Mendelssohn explained the situation. 'You wish to hear some news about the Berlin Conservatory – so do I – but there is none. The affair is on an extensive scale, if it be actually on any scale at all and not merely in the air. The king seems to have a plan for reorganising the Academy of Arts; this will not be easily effected without entirely

9

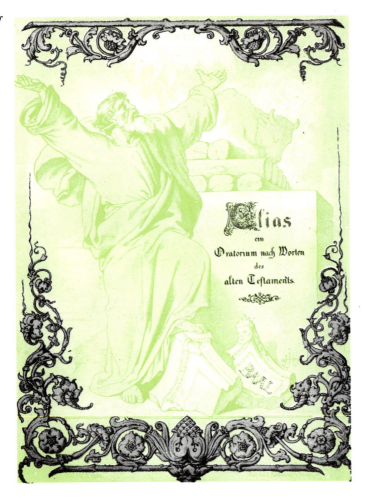

Cover of an edition of Elijah, the oratorio which Mendelssohn wrote in 1846 (Mendelssohn Archive, Berlin)

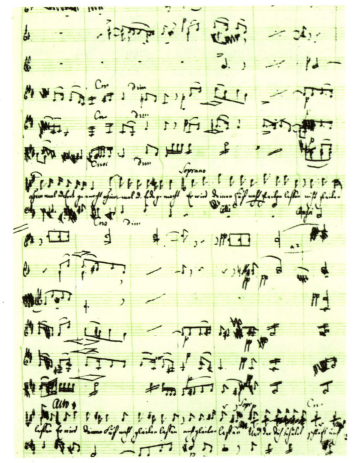

A page of manuscript of Elijah (Mendelssohn Archive, Berlin)

changing its present form into a very different one, which they cannot make up their mind to do; there is little use in my advising it, as I do not expect much profit for music from the Academy, either in its present form or future form. . . . You will ask, then, what in the world do they want with me just now in Berlin? My answer is, on the one side, I really do not know; on the other, I believe that it is intended to give during the winter some great concerts, with the addition of all their best means, and that I am to direct them, some in church and some in the concert-hall, but whether they will ever take place seems to me very doubtful; at all events these are, in my opinion, the only projects which can or will be carried out at this time.' Mendelssohn had no illusions about the future, and he ran into all the difficulties that he expected, not least from the bureaucrats. Part of the problem was the ill-defined nature of his post, added to which he maintained his connection with Leipzig, though most of the conducting was now being done by David. Eventually, the situation became too much for him and he resigned. Quite clearly the king behaved very well and a new arrangement was made, which seemed much more promising. Mendelssohn decided to try again, resigned the Kapellmeistership which the King of Saxony had just offered to him and instead busied himself with setting up a Conservatory in Leipzig. It was at this point that Frederick William IV asked him for a sheaf of new works, incidental music for *A Midsummer Night's Dream*, *Athalie* and *Oedipus at Colonos*, not to mention *The Tempest*.

January 1843 saw the blueprint for the Conservatory made out, with a distinguished staff, including Schumann, Moritz Hauptmann, David and Mendelssohn himself as professors. The next season in Berlin ran more smoothly, though by now his family circle had been diminished by the death of his mother. Later in 1844, the strain began to tell, and he in effect retired from the fray to Frankfurt though he retained his connections both with Berlin and Leipzig. He turned down invitations to travel, declined the directorship of a music festival in New York, and did not even make his usual pilgrimage to England. All was not well, and composition was not easy. This he admitted to his sister Rebecca: 'I myself am as you know me, but what you do not know about me is this: I feel the need for outward repose (not travelling, not conducting, not performing) so strongly that I must yield to it. God willing, I hope to organise my life this way for the whole year.' It did not last of course, and soon Mendelssohn was back in harness, perhaps inspired by the brilliant young singer Jenny Lind whom he regarded as a protegée of his. It was for her that he was to write the soprano part of *Elijah*, and was to think again about opera. But the sands were running out. The strain of completing and giving the première, in Birmingham, of *Elijah* on top of everything else drained his energies. Nevertheless in 1847 he was back again in England with a schedule more crowded than ever, but this time it was to be his last visit. He left on 9th May 1847, heard of his sister Fanny's death in Frankfurt, went for a rest to Switzerland and in September was back in Germany, seemingly in better health. It was illusory. After various ups and downs he died on 4th November 1847. He was thirty-eight.

PROGRAM NOTES FOR THE RECORD

by R O B E R T   J A C O B S O N

The 'Italian' Symphony

'Italy at last!' he cried. 'What I have been looking forward to all my life as the greatest happiness is now begun, and I am basking in it . . . The whole country had such a festival air that I felt as if I were a young prince making his entry.' So Felix Mendelssohn wrote in 1830, at the age of twenty-one, during his first visit to Italy on a holiday. From his native Hamburg he had journeyed south to Weimar, where for two weeks he enjoyed the company of the venerable Goethe; then on to Munich and Vienna, and finally over the mountains to Venice, Rome, Naples, Amalfi, Sorrento and Capri. At the same time as he travelled to these southern places and drank in their beauties, he was also at work — for in a letter from Rome to his sister Fanny he says: 'I have once more begun to compose with fresh vigour, and the Italian Symphony makes rapid progress; it will be the most sportive piece I have yet composed, especially the last movement. I have not yet decided on the *Adagio*, and think I shall reserve it for Naples.'

This sun-filled, extroverted work was to be Mendelssohn's Fourth Symphony, composed just *before* the 'Scotch' Symphony (No. 3) and *after* the 'Reformation' (No. 5), though in actual date of publication it is No. 4. (Mendelssohn published only five symphonies, but actually wrote seventeen. The first twelve — eleven for strings alone and one for full orchestra — were written during his childhood and youth.) Despite the youthful enthusiasm which gripped Mendelssohn in Rome, however, the Fourth Symphony — one of his gaiest, most supercharged works — proved an elusive and worrisome project. Eleven months after the letter quoted above, he wrote to Fanny from Paris, informing her that the Symphony was proving troublesome and that he had put it aside temporarily. Finally, in March of 1833 the score was completed in Berlin, and the following May the Royal Philharmonic Society of London premièred the work, directed by the composer. Still not entirely satisfied with it, Mendelssohn resolved to revise it in 1834. Then years passed without his consigning the score to his publisher. Not until 1849, two years after Mendelssohn's death, was a revised version of the score performed for the first time — and two more years elapsed before it was finally published, in the original version.

George Marek, in his recent biography *Gentle Genius: The Story of Felix Mendelssohn*, writes that the 'Italian' is Mendelssohn's best-loved symphony, and deservedly so. 'More than almost any of his other compositions it brings his excellence to full expression. Exciting in the first movement, stately in the second, elegant in the third, jaunty in the fourth, the "Italian" is a paradigm of Mendelssohn's genius. It, too, is a reminder of vanished glories, of a Rome of the past, a city now half-devoured by a locust swarm of vehicles.'

The first movement (*Allegro vivace*) opens impetuously, with the principal theme stated in the violins over quickly throbbing chords in the winds and horns. There is all the dazzle of brilliant Italian sunshine, and the violins seem to be calling the listener to new adventure. A rocking, gentle secondary theme is stated by clarinets and bassoons, later taken up by the flutes and strings. This movement has the confidence, excitement and optimism of a young man in a land of new beauties. The second section (*Andante con moto*) often bears the subtitle 'Pilgrims' March' since the idea for it had come from a religious procession Mendelssohn saw in the streets of Naples. There is a mock dolefulness about the chanting, almost wailing, woodwinds and the plodding plucking of cellos and basses.

Mendelssohn seems to be looking backwards in time in the third movement of the Symphony (*Con moto moderato*), which recalls the earlier symphonic minuet rather than the scherzo afterwards established by Beethoven. The graceful main theme is contrasted with the delicate woodwind effects of the middle section — very much in the gossamer, enchanted mood of Mendelssohn's *Midsummer Night's Dream* music. The Finale (*Presto*) bears the name of an Italian dance, the saltarello, which derives from the Italian word meaning 'to jump.' This movement reflects the hectic gaiety of the Roman carnival as witnessed by the composer. The main theme first appears in the flutes, and the rest of the orchestra proceeds to build it up in intensity. A quiet second theme is brought in by the violins; then the main melody reappears, followed by a totally new dance motive, a tarantella, which mingles with the other two themes to bring the Symphony to a brilliant, exuberant close.

The frontispiece of the incidental music to Antigone, *which Mendelssohn dedicated to Frederick William IV of Prussia (Mendelssohn Archive, Berlin)*

A Midsummer Night's Dream

Several years before the creation of his 'Italian' Symphony, the seventeen-year-old Felix Mendelssohn had fallen under the spell of William Shakespeare, through the famous German Romantic translations by Tieck and Schlegel. At the height of this enthusiasm he began to dream of composing music for *A Midsummer Night's Dream,* the always popular comedy of romantic confusion between two young Athenian couples in an enchanted wood, with its parallel thread of the fairy rulers Oberon and Titania. During the summer of 1826 Mendelssohn became involved in such a labour of love, namely, writing an Overture to the play. Years later, when the publishers Breitkopf & Härtel asked him to recall the ideas that had suggested the thematic sequence of the Overture and had fired his imagination, the composer wrote: '. . . it is impossible for me to outline for the [concert] program the sequence of ideas that gave rise to the composition, for just this sequence of ideas is my Overture. It follows the play closely, however, so that it may perhaps be very proper to indicate the outstanding situations of the drama in order that the audience may have Shakespeare in mind or form an idea of the piece. I think it should be enough to point out that the fairy rulers, Oberon and Titania, appear throughout the play with all their people . . . At the end, after everything has been satisfactorily settled, and the principal players have joyfully left the stage, the elves follow them, bless the house, and disappear with the dawn. So the play ends, and my Overture too.'

What the composer left behind was a piece of elfin imagination and humour, orchestrated with deftness and delicacy, perfectly prefacing and expressing the spirit of the play. It was first performed on 20th February 1827, at a concert in Stettin, conducted by Carl Loewe.

Towards the end of his life, Mendelssohn challenged his own boyish inspiration when King Frederick William of Prussia invited him to compose incidental music for a Berlin production of *A Midsummer Night's Dream* directed by Ludwig Tieck, the poet and co-translator of Shakespeare's text. Under these conditions, Mendelssohn's youthful passion for the English playwright was rekindled. The first performance of the complete incidental music with the play was heard by an invited audience at the Neues Palais in Potsdam on 14th October 1843. Later the public-at-large flocked to hear it at the Royal Theatre in Berlin. Mendelssohn now went much further than to supply music for Shakespeare's songs; he composed twelve numbers besides the Overture, including substantial entr'actes and long stretches of background music for dialogue, as well as dances, marches, fanfares and atmospheric sounds for this fantasy play of human frailty and magical transformations, of fairies and elves, amorous courtiers and farcical workmen.

The Overture opens with four glistening woodwind chords that summon the other-worldly creatures. After some ethereal fairy music in the violins, we hear certain references to the play such as Bottom's braying after being turned into an ass and a hearty stamping passage associated with the dancing of Bottom and his rustic sidekicks. After some additional fairy music has been developed, the Overture concludes with the four wind chords once more.

The mercurial Scherzo (*Allegro vivace*) is pure orchestral magic, with its shimmering strings, whispering and laughing woodwinds and the punctuation of Bottom's braying. It serves to introduce Act II, presenting a woodland dialogue between Puck and a fairy, and ends with a solo flight by the flute. The famous Wedding March, with its trumpet fanfares, signals and accompanies the wedding celebration of Theseus, Duke of Athens, and Hippolyta, Queen of the Amazons, at the beginning of Act V — after all the lovers' confusion has been untangled. This music of regal splendour is followed by Titania's instructions: 'Hand in hand, with fairy grace, will we sing, and bless this place.' As Shakespeare scholar Henry Hudson wrote of the play, so Mendelssohn mirrored it in his music: 'Great strength of passion or of volition would obviously be out of place in such a performance: it has room but for love, and beauty, and delight — for whatsoever is most poetical in nature and fancy; and therefore for none but such tranquil stirrings of thought and feeling as may flow out in musical expression: any tuggings of mind or heart, that should ruffle and discompose the smoothness of lyrical division, would be quite out of keeping with a dream, especially a midsummer night's dream.'

His Life and Times 1804-1822 (Part 2)

PROGRAM NOTES FOR THE PIANO CONCERTO NO. 5
AND THE CORIOLANUS OVERTURE
By Robert Jacobson

FUNK & WAGNALLS, INC.
NEW YORK, NEW YORK

Between the 'Eroica' and Egmont

The seven years or so between 1803 and 1810 saw the composition of some of the greatest works of Beethoven's so-called 'second period'. This impressive list included the tremendous series of majestic works that flowed from his pen from op. 53 (the 'Waldstein' Sonata) to op. 62 (the *Coriolanus* Overture). Even while he was completing these masterpieces, the Fifth and Sixth Symphonies and *Fidelio* were in his mind and being sketched. The first version of *Fidelio*, Beethoven's only opera, was finished about the middle of 1805 and given its première in November of that year: it was a failure, partly because the performance was far from satisfactory, and partly on account of the French occupation of Vienna, which drove from the capital most of the aristocratic patrons of the theatre. The performance was mostly attended by unappreciative French military personnel.

This original version was in three acts, and had a run of only three performances; a few other isolated productions were no more successful. Beethoven was desolate – for many years he had wished to write a successful opera, and the subject of *Fidelio*, combining the noblest type of womanly devotion with a hymn to human liberty, was one after his own heart. One can hardly begin to imagine Beethoven's feelings at the following incident, related by Schindler: 'On hearing *Fidelio*, Cherubini concluded that the composer was insufficiently schooled in the art of vocal writing. He did not lay the blame on Salieri, Beethoven's teacher of vocal composition, for Cherubini had already heard from him how matters stood with this pupil. The French master, who was at least ten years Beethoven's senior, accordingly took the liberty of recommending that he undertake further study of writing for the voice. To this end, he ordered a copy of the textbook used at the Paris Conservatoire, and presented it to the Viennese composer. The authors of the text are Méhul, Adam, Jadin, Gossec, Catel, Cobert, Eler, and Cherubini.'

This pill must have been the more bitter because Beethoven had on many occasions professed his high regard for Cherubini, who he said was the greatest of living composers, and from whose works he had learned much. This cold-hearted French-naturalised Italian, whose academic mentality was later to conflict with Berlioz's, never had a good word to say about Beethoven, whom he regarded as some sort of madman (he averred that it was impossible to tell what key the *Leonore* Overture no. 2 was in); he could not understand that it was his own objective, Classical mastery that Beethoven so admired – no more than Goethe could he see beyond the turbulent surface of Beethoven's personality into the profound stability beneath. Nevertheless, Beethoven was at length (in 1814) persuaded to reconsider *Fidelio*; its libretto – the cause of much of the trouble – was rewritten by another hand, and cast into two instead of three acts. Some of the revisions constitute wonderful lessons in composition – vocal, instrumental and structural – that would have been utterly beyond the powers of a Cherubini.

Since 1800 Prince Lichnowsky had paid Beethoven a modest annual stipend that gave him some measure of security. By 1809 (no doubt devalued somewhat by monetary inflation) it was still his chief means, supplemented by what income he could get from his compositions and from teaching. Lichnowsky's stipulation had been that the allowance would continue only so long as the composer was without a 'suitable position'. In this year he received an offer of the post of Kapellmeister to Jerome Bonaparte, King of Westphalia. Now Beethoven knew very well (better than anyone else) that his now very serious deafness would make it impossible for him to carry out the duties of a conductor in a regular way. But he did not hesitate to make the offer known in the society of Vienna. The result was that the Archduke Rudolph, Prince Lobkowitz, and Prince Kinsky got together and, with admirable determination to keep Beethoven in Vienna, signed the following declaration: 'The proof that Herr Ludwig van Beethoven gives each day of his extraordinary talent and genius as tone-poet and composer awakens the desire that he may surpass the greatest expectations that his achievements up to this time have justified.

'It is, however, clear that only a person who is as free from worries as possible can devote himself exclusively to his profession, and that such single-minded application, without the intrusion of any other concern, is alone able to produce great and sublime works honouring the name of art.

'The undersigned have accordingly resolved to place Herr Ludwig van Beethoven in such a position that he will not be embarrassed by the necessities of life, and that his powerful genius will have no other distractions. They therefore pledge themselves to pay him an annuity of four thousand gulden according to the following schedule:

His Royal Highness the Archduke Rudolph...		Fl.1500
His Majesty Prince Lobkowitz	...	...	Fl. 700
His Majesty Prince Ferdinand Kinsky	...	Fl.1800

Total Fl.4000

which Herr Ludwig van Beethoven may draw, against receipt, at half-yearly intervals from each of the contributors according to the terms of this agreement.

'The undersigned, moreover, are willing to continue this annuity until Herr Ludwig van Beethoven shall accept an appointment that will assure him the equivalent of the above-named sum. Should such an appointment never be available or should Herr L. van Beethoven be prevented by any misfortune or age from practising his art, the contributors shall continue this annuity as long as he shall live.

'Herr L. van Beethoven shall, for his part, oblige himself to reside in Vienna, the residence of the undersigned, or in another city within His Majesty the Austrian Emperor's patrimonial dominions that may be agreed upon, and shall leave his city of residence only for such periods as may be necessary for errands of business or art, regarding which the high contributors shall be consulted and shall give their consent.'

So Beethoven was secured for Vienna, though he benefited fully for only a couple of years: in 1811 the Austrian currency was devalued to a fifth of its former strength. His patrons did their best to make up the loss, but could not fully do so.

The palace of Schönbrunn at Vienna, painted by B. Bellotto (1724-80). This was one of the Imperial family's residences (Vienna Historical Museum)

A Calmer Air: Life 1809-12

In 1809 Beethoven was in his fortieth year and, as we noted earlier, it was at this time that the Princes Lobkowitz and Kinsky and the Archduke Rudolph together guaranteed him a lifelong annuity, with the sole object of preserving his presence in Vienna and preventing him from being tempted away by Jerome Bonaparte, now king of Westphalia. Beethoven was on a plateau of magnificent confidence as a composer – the year 1809 saw a splendid continuation of the flood that had begun with the 'Eroica' back in 1803. Now, however, the air is generally calmer, less consciously adventurous, more informed by a sense of consolidation than by desire for still further explorations. Beethoven's exploring was by no means done – the astounding last works were still to come – but in this period we find him adding finishing touches to a long central phase of work – the walls and towers of an almost completed city.

It is significant that in 1809 Beethoven seems to have been occupied with two streams of thought, both suggesting a sense of quiet power. He seems to have had a fascination for the key of E flat major (this year saw the completion of three major works in that key – the Fifth Piano Concerto, the majestic String Quartet op. 74 and the Piano Sonata op. 81a, subtitled 'Les Adieux'), and he was also concerned to investigate the possibilities of smaller, more intimate forms – such as the Piano Sonatas, op. 78 and op. 79 (F sharp and G major – the former one of his most exquisite works) and the six charming songs of op. 75. So far as sheer productivity is concerned 1809 shows no falling off; yet the relaxed air is unmistakable, an air in which it is now possible to enjoy for their own sake powers developed earlier with gigantic effort.

There is even a new sense of homogeneity in at least one respect; in the finale of 'Les Adieux' we can find real points of contact with the last movement of the Fifth Piano Concerto, for similar passage-work is used in both. It is unusual to find Beethoven's works overlapping in details like this; normally when he worked on two things simultaneously, they became utterly different in every possible respect. If he found even trivial points of resemblance he would usually make drastic alterations, as he did in the *Namensfeier* Overture when he noticed a resemblance to the scherzo of the Seventh Symphony. In 1809 he was a little more easygoing. We may regard this as Beethoven's E flat year – an E flat more comfortable than that of the 'Eroica'.

Yet Beethoven was by no means serene in himself, which proves that art is unconnected with moods; Romantic subjectivity was as far from his artistic consciousness as ever. His deafness was by now almost total; during the bombardment of Vienna in this very year he was found trying pathetically to save the last shreds of his hearing by burying his head beneath pillows. His emotional life so far as women were concerned was continually unhappy. Physically he was in good health and it may be this fact above all that accounts for the sense of formidable well-being that pervades the music of this time.

The following three years showed an increase of severity in Beethoven's art and, in the F minor Quartet of 1810, a new and violent concentration. In different yet complementary ways the Seventh and Eighth Symphonies (written within a few months of each other in 1812) show a curious self-sufficiency, a certain leathery toughness of consistency, a

3

rough-hewn severity, and a defiant humour possible only to one whose experience had taught him some harsh lessons. They are astringent in a way characteristic of a certain type of maturity, past its central phase of relaxed assurance, with a weather-beaten look. It is also significant, perhaps, that by this time Beethoven's health was not so good; he was ordered to take the waters at Teplitz, and it was here, at the spa, that he met Goethe. If Beethoven's personality had become more wintry by this time (and if Goethe's impressions are anything to go by, this was so) he was by no means always so arrogant as is sometimes supposed. Here is one of the most touching of all his letters, written from Teplitz to a small girl of ten, who had sent him a pocket-book she had embroidered herself:

'My dear, good Emilie, my dear friend,

'The answer to your letter to me is late; a mass of business and constant illness must excuse me. My presence here in search of health proves the truth of my excuse. Do not rob Handel, Mozart, Haydn, of the laurels that are theirs and not yet mine.

'Your pocket-book will be kept together with tokens of respect from many other persons, which I am far from deserving.

'Keep on; do not merely practise art, but penetrate its innermost depths; it is worth it, for only art and science can raise mankind to the divine. If ever you should want anything, my dear Emilie, write to me with confidence. The true artist has no pride; he sees, alas, that art has no limits. He feels dimly how far he is from his goal, and while perhaps he is admired by others, he realises with sorrow that he has not yet reached the place to which the better spirit lights the way before him like a distant sun. Perhaps I would rather come to you and yours than to many a wealthy person who reveals his poverty of soul. If ever I come to H. I will visit you and your family; I know of no good qualities but those that entitle one to be counted among the better men and women; where I find these, there is my home.

'If you would like to write to me, dear Emilie, address your letter to me here, where I shall spend another four weeks, or to Vienna, it does not matter. I am your friend and the friend of your family.

'Ludwig van Beethoven'

A view of the courtyard in the palace of Prince Lobkowitz in Vienna, where the 'Eroica' was first performed

A painting showing Beethoven's friends Schindler, Steiner, Vogler and van Swieten at Beethoven's house (Austrian National Library, Vienna)

Decline in Health: Life 1812-18

We now approach one of the most troubled periods of Beethoven's life. In 1812 his health was worrying him, causing him to make a visit to the spa at Teplitz; his deafness was now very bad. So far as his prestige was concerned, however, the situation had never been so favourable; his work was more than ever appreciated and it was certainly his health rather than lack of encouragement that brought about a certain falling off of output in the following couple of years. The year 1812 itself was highly productive – two symphonies, the Seventh and Eighth, were completed in May and October of that year, and in between them he found time to throw off the orchestral music to *The Ruins of Athens*, not one of his greatest works but still underrated and full of fine things. At the age of forty-two he was artistically at the summit of his powers (we do not often stop to realise that Beethoven had written all but one of his symphonies at this age). In 1813 he was persuaded to go to yet another spa, Baden; the Archduke Rudolph was staying there at this time. On hearing that the composer had arrived, he wrote:

'Dear Beethoven!

It was with great pleasure that I read in your letter of the 27th of last month, which I did not receive until the night before last, of your arrival in my beloved Baden. I hope to see you here tomorrow morning if you have the time, for the few days of my stay here have been so beneficial to my health that, without fearing any ill effects, I may again listen to and even play some music. If your stay in this healthful and beautiful place has the same good effect on your condition, my intentions in taking care of your lodgings will be completely fulfilled.

Your friend,

Baden, 7th July 1813   Rudolph'

This gives some idea of the personal affection in which Beethoven was held by his pupil and patron. The composer at this time was beset by financial as well as health worries; his work demanded enormous effort, with consequent neglect of proper food, and he was trying to help his brother Karl with money as well as vehement advice against his sister-in-law, whom he despised and detested, regarding her as a bad influence on her son Karl, Beethoven's nephew. Schindler remarks: 'According to the information communicated by Frau Streicher, who also spent the summer of 1813 in Baden, our composer's general physical condition was in a state of neglect. He lacked good clothing, especially linen. It cannot be said whether this neglect was caused by his total absorption in his work or by brother Karl, for whom he felt a constant responsibility. Perhaps both are to blame.' In a footnote Schindler quotes a *cri de coeur* from Beethoven's diary of 15th May 1813: 'It would be a great deed to stop altogether. O how different that would be from the slothful life I so often appear to be leading. O dreadful circumstances that do not impair my desire to be frugal but my ability to practise frugality. O God, O God, look down on unhappy B. and do not let it continue thus any more.' The very incoherence of this is revealing, even though it is hard to descry Beethoven's meaning.

The year 1814 saw the painful revision of *Fidelio*, a task that was one of the most arduous Beethoven ever undertook and which he himself described as far more difficult than composing a new work. On 27th February Beethoven conducted another of those huge concerts in which from time to time he plunged his energies. This time the programme was as follows:

Seventh Symphony in A major
Tremate empi: Trio for soprano, tenor and bass

5

Eighth Symphony in F major
The Battle of Vittoria

The Seventh Symphony and the *Battle of Vittoria* had been performed before, in the previous December, with great success; the other two works were receiving their first performances. Indeed the success of the December concert had prompted a repeat in January, for which occasion (as in February, too) the great Redoutensaal in Vienna was made available. The Battle Symphony (not a symphony in the normal sense) was Beethoven's one pot-boiler, and it created a furore, having been at first composed for a mechanical instrument devised by Maelzel (the inventor of the metronome), then subsequently orchestrated. Schindler, who was present at all these performances, says of the Redoutensaal: 'This hall afforded an opportunity to put into execution for the first time the many subtleties written into the Battle Symphony. From the long corridors and opposed rooms one could hear the enemy armies advance towards each other, creating a stunning illusion of the battle. I was present and can testify that the enthusiasm of the audience, heightened by patriotic emotions because of the victory just won, reached overwhelming proportions.' Not long after this Beethoven was involved in a bitter and costly legal dispute with Maelzel over the proprietorship of the *Battle of Vittoria*. This, together with various costs connected with the concerts, and family problems, aggravated his monetary circumstances still further. And by this time the Austrian currency had only a fifth of its former value – so his annuity was nothing like what it had been before. Kinsky had been

killed in a riding accident in 1812, and it was not until 1815 that his share of the annuity was restored to Beethoven; neither of the other two (Prince Lobkowitz and the Archduke Rudolph) could afford to increase their contributions. It is not surprising that as a composer Beethoven was less productive than he had been for a long time.

In November 1815 Beethoven's brother Karl died, appointing in his will Ludwig as guardian to his son Karl, then about nine years old. This shows that the composer's brother must have had little confidence in his wife. Either that – or he must have been very stupid to suppose that Ludwig and the woman would see eye to eye about anything whatever. They did not, and Beethoven's first action was to remove the boy from his mother's influence. She contested this in court. It was a savagely fought action; judgment was given to Beethoven, but this was only the beginning of a long, running fight, costly in terms of money, enmity, and heartache. It was not until 1820 that the matter was finally disposed of, Beethoven agreeing that the mother should have joint guardianship, with limited access to the boy. In the meantime the composer had paid for the child's schooling, as well as many of the legal costs. One can feel pity for all three protagonists in this dismal drama – the mother who, whatever her personal character (and there is no doubt that Beethoven's judgment of her was substantially accurate), must have suffered deeply; the composer himself, sinking inextricably into legal and emotional quicksands, obstinately ignoring the advice of more worldly-wise friends; and the pathetic object of all this uproar, the helpless boy.

The Roman Emperor Hotel in Vienna, which Beethoven used to frequent in 1816 (City History Museum, Vienna)

Carriages setting out for the Prater, a park beside the Danube which, in Beethoven's time, was a fashionable promenade (Albertina Print Collection, Vienna)

Tribulations: Life 1818-22

The last ten years of Beethoven's life were beset with trouble and ill-health. By 1816 his deafness was complete; nearly everything had to be written down for him, and he could no longer hear himself play. Yet it would be wrong to suppose him to have been the ill-natured bear some have suggested. The English composer Cipriani Potter visited him in 1818 and, like many other musicians, was received with much kindness. He wrote, 'Many persons have imbibed the notion that Beethoven was by nature a morose and ill-tempered man. This opinion is perfectly erroneous. He *was* irritable, passionate, and of a melancholy turn of mind – all of which affections arose from the deafness which, in his latter days, increased to an alarming extent. Opposed to these peculiarities in his temperament, he possessed a kind heart, and most acute feelings. Any disagreeable occurrence, resulting from his betrayal of irritability, he manifested the utmost anxiety to remove, by every possible acknowledgement of his indiscretion. The least interruption of his studies, particularly when availing himself of a happy vein of ideas, would cause him to expose the peculiarities of his temper; a capriciousness not at variance with, and perfectly excusable in, professors of other arts and sciences, when placed in a similar situation.'

Beethoven had long resigned himself to loneliness; his deafness and uncertain temper had made marriage a lost cause. His brothers were disappointing to him, and their wives worse. Both these women seem to have been of easy virtue and they aroused Beethoven's most vehement detestation. The death of Kaspar Karl, the brother next to him in age, precipitated one of the greatest and most prolonged crises in the composer's life. Kaspar Karl's wife evoked the fiercest antipathy in Beethoven, who called her, among other

things, the Queen of Night; there is no doubt that this castigation of her on moral grounds was justified, and her own husband in his will had indicated his lack of confidence in her by making Ludwig co-guardian with her of their young son Karl.

It may well be imagined what storms ensued, and their effect on the unfortunate boy caught in them. The result was a long-drawn lawsuit, lasting from 1816 to 1820, which drained Beethoven emotionally, physically, and financially. Eventually he won complete custody of Karl, on whom he showered tyrannical affection and erratic care. The boy has sometimes been represented as something of a ne'er-do-well, but this is unfair; considering his unfortunate experience as a child, his uncertainty as to where his loyalties (if any) were due, the confusion that must constantly have been visited on him during the lawsuit, and his terrifying uncle's domineering solicitude, it is surprising that he was, in fact, a decent lad, not of strong character or great ability, but musical, and affectionate by nature. It is not, however, surprising that the cumulative effects of all this eventually drove Karl to an attempted suicide (or possibly a dramatic demonstration in which he intended only to injure himself); it was probably the shock of this that finally broke Beethoven's health. Karl at length became a respectable and unremarkable civil servant; this was after the composer's death – he seemed able to find his own level only after Beethoven's fierce care was removed from him, when too much was not expected of him.

A vivid picture of Beethoven in 1819 is given by the publisher Schlesinger, who subsequently acquired several of the late works, including the C minor Sonata, op. 111. From the following account it is possible to sense that Beethoven, though undoubtedly deeply unhappy at this time, was nevertheless capable of simple human pleasure:

'I cannot refrain from telling how, in the year 1819, I made Beethoven's acquaintance, and owing to what chance I was lucky enough to have him become fond of me. I was in Steiner and Company's vault when Haslinger, their partner, said: "There's Beethoven – would you like to make his acquaintance?" When I said I would, he continued: "He's deaf. If you want to say something to him write it down at once. He doesn't like to reveal his disability to people." Then he introduced me and Beethoven suggested I might visit him in Baden. I did so a few days later. Stepping from my carriage I went into the inn, and found Beethoven stalking out of the door in a rage, slamming it after him. When I had got rid of some of my travel-stains, I went to the house they told me was his. His housekeeper said that I would probably be unable to see him, as he had come home in a rage. I gave her my card, which she took to him and, to my great surprise, returned a few minutes later, telling me to go in. The great man was sitting at his writing desk. Immediately I wrote down how happy I was to meet him. This seemed to make a favourable impression. At once he vented his feelings and said he was the most wretched fellow in the world; he had just got back from the tavern, where he had asked for some veal which he fancied – they had none! All this was said seriously and gloomily. I consoled him, and we discussed other things (I writing all the time); so he kept me for nearly two hours, and although I got up several times, being afraid to impose on him or bore him, he prevented me every time from going. Eventually when I left, I hurried back to Vienna in my carriage, and straight away asked my innkeeper's son if he had any roast veal. He said he had, and I made him put it in a dish, carefully cover it, and send it (without a word of explanation) by the same carriage back to Baden, to be presented to Beethoven with my compliments. I was still in bed the following morning when Beethoven came in, kissed and hugged me, and said I was the most kind-hearted person he had ever met – never had anything given him so much pleasure as the roast veal, just when he so much wished for some.'

Three years later, in 1822, the writer Johann Rochlitz, whom Beethoven would have liked to write his first biography, described how he met the composer in the summer of that year.

'Having never seen Beethoven, I wanted all the more to meet him as soon as possible. No later than the third day after arriving I mentioned it to N.N., his close friend. "He's out in the country", he said. "Then let's drive out there!" "We can, but unfortunately his deafness has gradually made him quite unsociable. He knows you want to see him, and he'd like to meet you – all the same, we can't be sure that when he sees us he won't run away, because although he's often spontaneous and gay, he's just as often seized by the deepest gloom. It strikes him out of the blue, with no apparent cause, and he can't throw it off. But at least once a week he comes into town, and always sees us, because we attend to his letters and other things. Then, usually, he's in good spirits, and we've got him where he can't get away. So if you're willing to humour the poor tormented man by letting us tell you on the spur of the moment so that you can come in as if just by chance . . . it's only a few steps. . . ."

'Of course I was only too pleased to agree. The messenger came the next Saturday morning; I went in, and there was Beethoven in lively conversation with N.N. Beethoven is used to him and seems to understand him fairly well, following his words from the movements of his face and lips. Beethoven seemed pleased, but also in a way disturbed. And if I had not been prepared for it, his appearance would have disturbed me, too. It was not that outwardly he seemed neglected, almost uncivilised, nor that his thick black hair bristled about his head. It was his appearance as a whole. Imagine a man of about fifty, small rather than medium-sized, but with a very strong, stocky figure, compact, and with a notable bone structure, rather like that of Fichte, but fleshier, and especially, with a rounder, fuller face; a ruddy, healthy complexion; the eyes restless, glowing, even piercing when fixing his gaze; not given much to movement, but when moving, moving hastily; the facial expression, especially the eyes, intelligent and full of life, shyness and

hearty friendliness mingled or momentarily alternated; in his whole attitude that uneasy, worried striving to hear peculiar to the deaf who are keenly sensitive; now a cheerfully, freely spoken word, then at once a relapse into melancholy quiet – such is the man who has given joy to millions, a joy of the spirit.

'His phrases fragmentary, he made friendly remarks to me. I spoke as loudly as I could, and slowly, with clear accentuation, and with a full heart conveyed to him my gratefulness for all his works, what they meant to me and would continue to mean while life remained. I mentioned some of my favourites and dwelt on them; I told him how finely his symphonies were played in Leipzig, how they were all played every winter, and how enthusiastically they were always received. He stood near me, sometimes concentrating hard on my face, sometimes dropping his head. Then he would smile to himself, or nod amiably, all without a word. Had he understood? Had he not? Eventually I had to finish, and he gripped my hand powerfully, saying curtly to N.N.: "I've still got some errands to do." As he left, he said to me: "Won't we see each other again?" N.N. came back. "Did he understand what I said?" I asked. I was deeply moved and disturbed. N.N. shrugged. "Not a word!" For a long time neither of us said anything and I cannot say how affected I was. At length I asked him: "Why didn't you at least repeat this or that to him, since he understands you quite well?" "I didn't want to interrupt you, and anyway he easily gets very sensitive. I was hoping he'd grasp a lot of what you said, but the street noises, your speech, which he's unfamiliar with and, maybe, his own anxiety to follow you because it was obvious to him you were telling him pleasant things . . . he was very unhappy." I left filled with indescribable sensations. The man who solaced the whole world with the voice of his music could hear no human voice, not even one that thanked him – it became even an instrument of torture for him.'

(Part 3 of Beethoven continued in Album 20)

A 19th-century print showing Archduke Rudolph's residence at Olmütz (Austrian National Library, Vienna)

The title page of the 'Eroica' Symphony, whose dedication to Napoleon was angrily withdrawn when Beethoven heard that he had crowned himself Emperor (Society of the Friends of Music, Vienna)

A medallion of Napoleon Bonaparte (Museum of Fine Arts, Angers)

PROGRAM NOTES FOR THE RECORD

by ROBERT JACOBSON

The 'Emperor' Concerto

'It is without doubt one of the most original, imaginative, most effective but also one of the most difficult of all existing concertos,' wrote the *Allgemeine Musik Zeitung* in January of 1812. The event being reviewed was the first performance of Beethoven's Fifth Piano Concerto, which had taken place the previous November in Leipzig. The work had been finished in 1809, the year of the Austrian defeat at Wagram, which led to Napoleon's siege and occupation of Vienna in May of that year. It is reported that when the bombardment of the city grew too loud, Beethoven took refuge in the cellar of his brother Karl's house and covered his head with pillows. This was no display of cowardice, but a way of protecting his ears and the little hearing he still had left in his fortieth year. This state of affairs accounts for the fact that the Fifth Concerto was the only one Beethoven himself did not play at its première performance. In Leipzig that November (1811), Friedrich Schneider was the soloist, and Johann Philipp Christian Schulz was the conductor.

The success of that occasion was not matched by the Concerto's première in Vienna on 12th February 1812, when Beethoven's pupil Carl Czerny was soloist. The periodical *Thalia* spoke of the refusal of the 'proud and overconfident' Beethoven to write down to his audience. 'He can be understood and appreciated only by connoisseurs.' The 'Emperor' Concerto did, in fact, remain neglected for a long period. The full score did not appear until 1857, and the feeling prevailed, as expressed by one critic, that 'the immense length of the composition robs it of the impact that this product of gigantic intellect would otherwise exert upon its hearers.' The work, which was heard in public only three times during the composer's lifetime, was passed over for the more easily accessible salon concertos of Hummel, Moscheles, Czerny and others.

One thing is definite, however: Beethoven did not name his final piano concerto (dedicated, in reality, to his patron Archduke Rudolph) after the all-conquering Emperor Napoleon. In 1803 Beethoven had dedicated his 'Eroica' Symphony to Napoleon and then angrily withdrew it when unrestrained personal ambition led the French ruler to proclaim himself emperor. One story concerning the naming of the Concerto is that a French army officer in that first Vienna audience was so carried away by the music that he proclaimed it 'an emperor among concertos.' No-one really knows whether a publisher or a pianist tacked on this majestic sub-title; but it undoubtedly remains the emperor among Beethoven's five piano concertos—a fitting climax to Beethoven's concerto style, which had evolved from Mozart and Haydn and which sowed the seeds for Liszt and Brahms—and is consistently his most popular.

The key of E flat major was one Beethoven used often during 1809. His 'Emperor' Concerto, the Sonata No. 26 ('Les Adieux') and the String Quartet Opus 74 (the 'Harp') all share this key, which conveys a heroic optimism and a bold, positive character.

The music opens nobly with a decisive E flat major chord in the orchestra, launching the *Allegro* section. The piano—always on equal terms with the orchestra in this work—enters unconventionally with a sweeping solo passage, or cadenza, which until this point in history had been used only for the closing moments of a movement. Two more orchestral chords are heard, followed by similar rhapsodic outbursts from the piano. After this impulsive opening, the orchestra announces the grandiose principal theme of the movement in traditional style. This branches out into a rich variety of other musical thoughts, the main one being a gently rocking figure presented first by softly plucked strings and then by two horns. Both themes are presented by the orchestra and developed at some length before the piano returns with its own version of these materials. There is an epic, stormy development and a dialogue between piano and orchestra before the themes

The cover of the edition of the 'Emperor' Concerto published by Breitkopf & Härtel (Austrian National Library, Vienna)

Grand

CONCERTO

Pour le Pianoforte

avec Accompagnement

de l'Orchestre

composé et dedié

à Son Altesse Imperiale

RODOLPHE

Archi Duc d'Autriche etc.

par

L. v. Beethoven

Propriété des Editeurs

à Leipsic

Chez Breitkopf & Härtel

M.S.31043

are re-stated in more or less their original form. At the point where the traditional solo cadenza is expected, Beethoven has noted in the score for the pianist thus: 'Do not play a cadenza but attack immediately the following.' This refers to material he based on the two main ideas that prevail in the movement. Finally, the orchestra joins in for a triumphant close.

The central slow movement (*Adagio un poco mosso*) is a stately romantic piece of mystery and calm. Its simple, hymn-like melody is sung chiefly by the orchestra, while the piano weaves strands of variations, with a freedom that is seemingly improvisational. Eventually the piano takes up the melody, while the violins are plucked in accompaniment. Towards the end, there is a sustained, hushed atmosphere that unfolds into one of the most magical moments in all of music.

The piano then begins to muse over the principal theme of the third movement and, without a break, the orchestra moves from its mood of lingering hushed expectancy and launches majestically into the joyful Finale (*Rondo: Allegro*). The main theme bounds upwards in excited, powerful syncopation—a refrain that continually appears in many forms in this Finale. The tone is one of dynamism and exhilaration, spontaneity and impulsiveness, though Beethoven's manipulation of form is always masterful and original. The piano writing is brilliant and mesmerizing,

as momentum builds to the climax. Critic Donald Francis Tovey justly noted 'the sublime depths from which all these outbursts of hilarity spring,' for in this lies one of Beethoven's greatest strengths.

Beethoven, although subject to Napoleon's power during the occupation of Vienna, exulted in the power of the free individual; and his works constantly speak of super-human strength in all kinds of adversity, against all odds. But human strength—man's spirit—is triumphant in all the composer's symphonies and chamber works, just as it is most magnificently displayed in *Fidelio* and the 'Ode to Joy' finale of the Ninth Symphony. Biographer Romain Rolland once stated: 'Beethoven belongs to the first generation of those young German Goethes . . . those Columbuses who, launched in the night on the stormy sea of the Revolution, discovered their own Ego and eagerly subdued it. Conquerors abuse their power; they are hungry for possession; each of these free Egos wishes to command. If he cannot do this in the world of facts, he wills it in the world of art; everything becomes for him a field on which to deploy the battalions of his thoughts, his desires, his regrets, his furies, his melancholies. He imposes them on the world. After the Revolution comes the Empire. Beethoven hears them both within himself, and the course they run in his veins is the circulation of the blood of history itself . . .'

Coriolanus Overture

In 1807, two years before the creation of the 'Emperor' Concerto, Beethoven dedicated an Overture to *Coriolanus*—or *Coriolan*—to its author, Heinrich von Collin (not, as might be expected, to William Shakespeare and his mighty drama on the same subject). The Collin tragedy had been successful in Vienna since its première in 1802, and Beethoven obviously had seen the work. He came away impressed by the defiant character and ultimate fate of its hero, who must go against his people and thereby brings about his own downfall.

Drawn from Plutarch's writings, the drama deals with the struggle between the plebeians and patricians of ancient Rome. Coriolanus has been reared as a proud warrior, belonging to an elite caste accustomed to despising the plebeians. This pride, however, is his tragic failing. After he has saved his country and earned every honour, he seeks the consulship through election by the plebeians —but he behaves with such haughty pride that he defeats his own aims and ends up at the mercy of the rabble. Cruelly and unjustly, Coriolanus is banished from Rome; in revenge he joins the hostile Volscians and uses his military prowess against his native land. Eventually he is persuaded to renounce his vengeful campaign and spare Rome, thereby surrendering himself to death at the hands of the Volscians, whom he has betrayed. It is a tale of

patriotism, faithfulness to principle, defeat and tragic self-destruction.

The Overture to the play was written not on commission but on impulse. It is similar to Beethoven's *Leonore* and *Egmont* Overtures, in that none of them relates directly to the drama which follows, but rather each is a symphonic tone poem based on various general themes contained within the play. 1807 was also the year of Beethoven's 'Waldstein' and 'Appassionata' Sonatas, the Violin Concerto and the Fifth Symphony. Like the Symphony No. 5, the *Coriolanus* Overture is in the 'tragic' key of C minor. It begins abruptly, followed by a defiant, agitated motive of gloomy harmonies and quick syncopations. There is a dramatic silence, which is characteristic of the Overture and gives it an air of bitterness and power. An intense climax is reached, after which comes the second theme, of great beauty and with a suggestion of pleading. This can be said to represent the women who try to dissuade Coriolanus from his headstrong pride and fatal course. But his pride and combativeness break out again in restless syncopation. The various themes are worked over until the finale brings the Overture to a powerful, tragic peak as the hero relentlessly dooms himself. It then ends in a hushed tone of sorrow and desolation.

Printed in the United States of America

His Life and Times 1825-1899

**PROGRAM NOTES FOR TRITSCH-TRATSCH POLKA,
EMPEROR WALTZ, VOICES OF SPRING WALTZ,
THE BLUE DANUBE WALTZ, "ARTIST'S LIFE" WALTZ,
AND "VIENNA BLOOD" WALTZ**

By George R. Marek

fw

Funk & Wagnalls, Inc.
NEW YORK, NEW YORK

Vienna

If truth is stranger than fiction, music is stronger than truth. Or it can be.

Vienna! What springs to your mind when you hear that name? It is a curious name, a single long syllable in its native German — "Wien" — a tri-syllable in English, two in French, "Vienne". By whatever name, we all recognise what it is, the city nestled on the shores of the blue Danube, the motto of which is gaiety, the spirit of which is carefreeness. Music sounds from open windows, linden trees stand guard on the Ringstrasse, the giant ferris wheel shines in the Prater like a fallen moon, and every night a dance is going on somewhere. The dance is a waltz, and the dancing couples are beautiful people, he the Herr Lieutenant in shining tunic with an arrogant monocle clamped in his eye, she a gorgeous creature dressed in a decolleté evening dress showing off her marmoreal shoulders. After the dance, they go and munch pastry topped with a double portion of whipped cream.

In Vienna — wrote the poet Schiller — every day is Sunday. The Viennese do not walk, they amble, they saunter — or they whirl in a *ronde* of amorous and abandoning pleasure. The city pulses with a three-quarter rhythm.

But none of this is strictly true. It is the Vienna of our imagination we have been describing. The Vienna of reality is very different: it contains as many poor as any metropolis, men struggling for existence, a whole family living in two rooms which smell of sour cabbage, women hard skinned and old before their time, young girls dream-

A view of Vienna from the Grinzing Forest. Watercolor by B. Wegand (Vienna, Albertina Museum, Print Collection)

ing of a future less dull. The Viennese temperament is not by nature gay: rather, it is inclined to pensiveness, self-doubt, gnawing dissatisfaction, a veiled looking inward which at its best has produced a Freud or a poet like Rilke and at its worst has lamed the faculty of action. The Danube, which touches the city only on the outskirts, can be green or silvery or muddy; it is never, *never,* blue, and by the time the river reaches Vienna it is not particularly beautiful.

The Vienna we think of, gay Vienna, glittering Vienna, waltzing Vienna, does exist — or did exist before World War I — but it was largely a creation of artifice. If only subconsciously, the Viennese like to escape from an existence of bad economics, invasion by foes from the East (the Turks), from the West (Napoleon and Bismarck and Hitler) and their own "Oh-what's-the-use?" disposition, by means of makebelieve. To them, fiction is more real than truth, legend stronger than fact. It has always been a town in which the theater flourished and it has always been a town in which music was beloved — provided that the music wasn't too cerebral. Music provided the antidote to melancholy. The composers who furnished it were a little like the English authors who wrote eloquently about food, English food being nothing to write home about. Aren't Lamb's essay on roast pig, Gissing's thoughts on the baked potato, and Dickens's wonderful descriptions of Christmas feasts "escape literature"?

In Vienna, the road which led to escape was built by

many musicians. It is easy to trace the development of the Viennese waltz from its ancestor the Ländler, an Austrian peasant dance, and one may draw a continuous line from Mozart to Schubert to Josef Lanner to Johann Strauss, Sr., to his son. If we wish, we can continue this line to all those who are in debt to Strauss Jr.: Suppé, Lehar, Romberg, Friml, Oscar Straus, etc. Yet when we think of a "waltz" we think first of the composer of the "Tales from the Vienna Woods", and when we think of "Vienna" we think of a pleasure dome which he decreed, and of which he was the chief architect. Indeed, he built a Vienna of invention which seems indestructible and belongs to everybody everywhere, even to those who have never been within in sight of the *Stephanskirche*.

A portrait by Kniehuber of Johann Strauss, Sr., a "bold and passionate man" who fathered eleven children including Johann Jr. (Vienna, Austrian National Library)

The Father

A whirling dance in 3/4 time, in which the partners occasionally held each other in a decorous but reasonably close embrace, had become so popular that by the end of the eighteenth century, one Jakob Wolf published a pamphlet entitled, "Proof that Waltzing Constitutes a Major Source of the Weakness of Body and Mind of Our Generation". However, Wolf cried in vain when he pleaded for the restoration of the old Minuets, Polonaises, and "Allemandes". There was something in the turn and movement, the dip and swing, and what another moralist called the "Bacchanalian orgy" of this swifter tempo that appealed to the mood of a Europe torn by the Napoleonic wars. As nations met to discuss peace once more, as diplomats at the Congress of Vienna in 1814-15 gathered to decide the new frontiers, dancing offered them diversion and relief. The Prince de Ligne scoffed, "The Congress dances, but it does not progress". (*Le congrès danse, mais il ne marche pas.*) That wasn't quite true, but all diplomats returned home enthusiastic about the new rage, spreading a tale of delight. The Viennese waltz was *it*! It had already been described by a traveler, Ernst Moritz Arndt:

> The men held the long dress of their partners, so that it would not drag or be stepped on ... They lifted the dress to form a covering under which both bodies were brought as closely together as possible. In this way the whirling continued in the most indecent positions, the male hand pressed firmly against her breast, performing little lustful caresses. The girls were ecstatic and ready to swoon. When waltzing at the dark side of the hall, bolder embraces and kisses were attempted.

This sounds as if Arndt were reporting more of what was in his mind than what he actually saw. We are on safer factual ground when we examine the music played: the tunes were simple, the numbers short, the accompaniment an artlessly steady oom-pa-pa with the accent on the "oom".

In 1804, the year Arndt wrote his diatribe, a male child was born to a tavern-keeper named Strauss in one of Vienna's poorest suburbs, the Leopoldstadt. They christened the baby Johann. The boy lost his parents when he was only seven, and was apprenticed to a bookbinder at thirteen. He detested the steamy smell of glue, escaped, and was befriended by a kindly musician. Strauss showed immediate talent, was taught the violin, and eventually got a job in one of the innumerable little dance bands which played the night through in Vienna's many halls, such as the "Apollo Hall", which had room for 4,000 dancers. They catered to high and low, united only in the desire to forget the day's burden under the glitter of chandeliers. Sitting next to Strauss was another young violinist, Josef Lanner, only three years his senior. The two lived together to save expenses.

Eventually, Lanner managed to get his own dance band together and he was the first to expand the waltz to compositions more ambitious than the often naive and casual concoctions which up to then had served their purpose well enough. He wove several tunes into a garland, and set it forth beribboned with an introduction and a formal ending. From him, the elder Strauss learned his craft — but the talent of Strauss Sr. grew above that of Lanner as much as Strauss Jr.'s genius was to surpass his father's. The senior Strauss soon became wildly popular in his own right — he had sex appeal as well as virtuosity — and Vienna was divided in a Guelph-Ghibelline dispute as to who was better, Lanner or Strauss. One critic issued a Solomonic judgment: "With Lanner, it's 'Please, dance, I beg you!', with Strauss, it's 'You must dance, I command you!'"

Here is Heinrich Laube, one of the outstanding journal-

A drawing of Johann Strauss, Jr., by L. Horowitz (1838-1917). His resplendent mustache was familiar to all Vienna's waltzing enthusiasts. (Austrian National Library)

ists of his time, writing about Johann Sr.:

You will be asked, I said to myself, the generations of the future will ask, what does he look like, this Johann Strauss? If Napoleon's appearance was classically Roman and calmly antique, if Paganini's was as romantic and arresting as moonlight, that of Maestro Strauss is African and hot-blooded, crazy from the sun, modern, bold, fidgety, restless, unbeautiful, passionate ... The man is black as a Moor, his hair is curly; his mouth is melodious, energetic; his lip curls; his nose is snub; if his face were not white, he would be the complete king of the Moors from Ethiopia, the complete Balthazar.

This "bold and passionate" man, this celebrity who could have had his choice among Vienna's most fascinating women, married a prosaic, unfascinating one, Anna. She bore him six children, of whom Johann Jr., born in 1825, was the eldest. She made a good home for him, well-ordered and of sufficient luxury. But Strauss Sr. was untrue to her in several casual affairs. In addition — and incomprehensibly — he involved himself with a steady mistress, as unattractive a woman as could be imagined, a boor and a bore, a rude milliner, whose name was as unmelodious as she: Emilie Trampusch. She bore him five children. Finally Strauss left his wife and his legitimate children for Emilie. In his forty-sixth year he was found dead in Emilie's apartment, a victim of scarlet fever. Emilie had fled, taking with her the children and whatever possessions she could find, including Strauss's nightshirt, the bedding, his clothes. Naked he had tumbled to the floor, where a delivery boy found him. Anna was sent for. Emilie reappeared but once, years later: the police arrested her trying to steal a bronze lantern from her lover's grave.

Such then were the circumstances under which Johann Strauss, Jr., grew up, and such was his inheritance. He carried a double legacy: talent and turbulence.

The Son

Restlessly, almost crazily, the father rushed from country to country, from concert to concert. He seemed to be mesmerized by the clicking wheels of a train. In a fever of fretting, nothing was ever enough. During one tour his nerves gave out and for four days he lay unconscious in a hotel room in Strasbourg. He was brought back to Vienna, only to start out again, driven by he knew not what. He paid little attention to his family. But he did want to save his first-born from the virtuoso vagabondage, the hectic chase. Johann the younger was not to become a musician. He was to go to the *Gymnasium* (high school), learn languages, get a good education, become a merchant or a teacher — anything, but not a performer.

The boy wanted to learn the piano. He begged for lessons. Well, all right. Respectable people played the piano. However, no further!

Then one day Strauss Sr. heard the sound of a violin being played in the room where the boys slept. There was fifteen-year-old Johann playing with great verve, fiddling before a mirror and swaying like a dancer in obvious imitation of his father. It didn't strike Papa as funny. He grabbed the boy's violin out of his hand. "Where did you get the money for violin lessons?" — "I paid for them myself. I am earning money. I give lessons." ... "Lessons, what kind of lessons?" ... "I teach piano to the tailor next door. He pays me sixty Kreuzer a lesson." Father Johann confiscated the violin. The next day, the mother secretly bought her son a new violin.

Talent can be helped or hindered. Genius cannot be hindered or suppressed. No obstacle will stop it. It breaks forth with the force of the wave which, stirred from the depths, punches against the rock. His father could object all he wanted, it did not stop the son. Indubitably the father's ukase was not issued only to "save" the son: early, Strauss Sr. sensed that his son's ability was to outrank his own. The older man feared the competition, if only half consciously at first. Later the fissure between the two widened into a visible gulf of dislike — no, worse, into open hatred and warfare. It was a sorry conflict, which went so far that young Strauss secretly commissioned a series of articles attacking his father (the articles appeared in the *Pester Spiegel*, a Hungarian newspaper), while the elder's business manager was sent to talk to the owners of the leading ballrooms of Vienna, intimating — over a cup of coffee and in ever so dulcet a voice — that if young Johann was to be permitted to appear there, they might no longer be able to count on Strauss Sr. to play for their customers.

Anna supported her son, surreptitiously provided two good teachers for him. One was a renowned organist, Joseph Drexler, who introduced him to the more learned form of music, and was astonished one day to hear in the quiet of his church some impudent waltz-tune springing from the organ. "I meant to play a fugue", the boy was supposed to have said, "but it came out a waltz".

When the time came for Johann to make his debut, it was Anna who gave him the money to hire the musicians and the hall. Was she prompted only by mother-love, or by a wish to revenge herself on the husband who had left her?

The establishment of Vienna being closed to him, Johann went to the suburbs to perform. In Hietzing, near the palace of Schönbrunn, stood a large cafe surrounded by a spacious garden. Dommayer's Casino was four miles from the center of the city, a goal for excursions on a summer Sunday. But now it was no longer summer, it was October, the leaves were falling, and it was turning cold. All the same, Johann, nineteen years old, decided to make his debut there. The round kiosks which in Vienna serve to announce artistic events proclaimed:

Invitation to a Soirée-Dansant

On Tuesday, the fifteenth of October 1844, at Dommayer's Casino in Hietzing, Johann Strauss (the son) will have the honor of leading, for the first time, his own orchestra in a program of overtures and opera pieces as well as in a number of original compositions of his own.
Commending himself to the favor of his public,
Johann Strauss, Junior.
Tickets available in advance for 30 Kreuzer, at the box office for 50 Kreuzer.
Beginning 6 o'clock.

"His public" — he had none. But the Viennese realised that this was likely to be what they call a *"Hetz"*, a spree, an occasion for disputes, for taking sides, and for making noise. The young man had his nerve: how dared he compete against so beloved a musician? How dared he challenge his father? Others said, "Serves Papa right". Either way, one had to be there. By good luck, the day turned out to be warm and sunny. Hours before six, a stream of curious poured from the city.

Cover for "The Rape of the Sabines, a Characteristic Tone-Poem for Piano." (Vienna, Austrian National Library)

Most of them hadn't bought a ticket. Why should they? Who would want to pay in advance for a concert given by an uncertain youngster? When they got there, they found the box office closed. Everything was sold out, even though at the last hour, extra tickets had been put on sale by making standing room available on the dance floor. The whole square outside of Dommayer's was blocked with people. Those who had tickets tried to reach the café. Any moment there was going to be a riot. The police came, firmly sealed off the place, got rid of the extra crowd, and the concert could begin. It was so crowded that the waiters could not get through to serve either food or wine. Surely such lack of refreshment would displease the Viennese, who have to have their buffet even during the interval of a short play. Besides, there was a clump of adherents of Johann Strauss, Sr., present, eying the scene with black looks. In short, the atmosphere was tense.

Fifteen minutes after six, young Strauss appeared. He was dressed in the height of fashion, in clothes which had not yet been paid for. His blue coat with silver buttons was parted at the waist and trailed off in two tails, his silk waistcoat was embroidered with flowers, and he wore tight grey trousers, their bottoms fastened under the buckles of his pumps. White lace cuffs dangled from his sleeves.

His hair was jet black and curled, and he had tried without much success to grow a moustache to make himself look older. He was, as he confessed later, frightened to

death; yet he gave no sign of that as he jumped on the podium and began. His first number was the then popular overture to a French opera by Auber, *The Mute of Portici*. Nothing much happened. Next came a waltz of his own composition. He had entitled it somewhat fatuously "The Favor Seekers". Even this early waltz, hardly a masterpiece, showed some of the characteristics of his later works: he endowed it with a sensuous rhythm of such freedom and plasticity as to sound fresh and daring. The audience was impressed and demanded a repeat. That was all he needed; nervousness vanished, belief in his own talent swept over him. He played the next number, again a waltz of his own, with a brio, a swing, a passion which forced his orchestra to play better than they thought possible. This mesmerized the audience into a shouting ovation. Again and again he had to repeat the waltz — its title was "Poems of the Senses" — until he had played it nineteen times. Yes — nineteen times!

When the concert ended, very late that starlit night, Johann Strauss the Son had established himself as a new force in Viennese music. The year was 1844, a year planted in the flowering thicket of the romantic movement, the year in which Dumas published both *The Three Musketeers* and *The Count of Monte Cristo*, and the year in which Verdi fashioned a revolutionary opera from Victor Hugo's play *Ernani*.

A 19th century print of the Chinese Pavilion at Laxenberg. "Chinoiserie" was highly fashionable among the European aristocracy as far south as Sicily. (Vienna, Albertina Museum, Print Collection)

The Voice of Vienna

The clothes bought on credit were quickly paid for. The brain shadowed by the black hair worked incessantly. From it poured one inspiration after another, sometimes hastily sketched on note paper, laundry list or menu. But, more often, his works were carefully considered, studied over and several times revised, giving the impression that even in his early compositions, he was conscious of a higher function for his music than a night's dance. He wrote polkas, quadrilles, marches, mazurkas, variations interspersed with waltzes. But it was the waltzes that sprang from the center of his talent which so warmed and delighted a world that was growing colder. Europe was swept by the revolution of 1848. Nationalism threatened to tear apart the old Austro-Hungarian Empire, and in Vienna, students marched, and people mounted the barricades. Shots were fired. Metternich was forced to resign, and the Minister of War, Latour, was strung up on a lantern and brutally killed. Quickly the Habsburgs called a new Emperor to the throne; a young man who promised reform and stood as a symbol of progress took the oath: he was eighteen-year-old Franz Josef.

Strauss Sr. sided with the loyal-to-Habsburg side. He composed a March in honor of Jellacic, a debased general who led the army against the rebelling Hungarians. He composed "The Radetzky March" — his most famous composition — in honor of the General who was trying to battle the insurgent Italians. It was then natural that the son should side with the revolutionaries: a "Liberty Waltz" and a "Revolution March" belong to his early compositions. In due course he was summoned to the Police. Why, they wanted to know, had he played the *Marseillaise*? "Because", he answered, "the *Marseillaise* is good music and good music is what I'm concerned with".

As the revolution fizzled and as the Viennese, longing for peace, returned to their accustomed coffee-sipping, tomorrow-will-take-care-of-itself, let's-live-for-the-day ways, Johann Strauss, Jr., became the voice of Vienna. His waltzes became more elaborate, more symphonic, richer in melodic and harmonic ideas, until they grew into tone-poems rather than dance compositions. Not that he forgot dancing: standing triumphant on the podium, he would play his violin or lay it down from time to time and lead the orchestra with his bow, while his audience turned and gyrated ecstatically. At carnival time the various guilds and professions held dance festivals and all of them tried to get Johann to furnish special music. He would oblige, composing "The Due Process Polka" or "The Torts Dance" for the lawyers, the "Electronic Polka" for the engineers, the "Telegraph Waltz" for the postmen, the "Heightened Pulses Waltz" for the physicians. But other waltzes — they tempted you more to listen than to dance, so intricate did they sound, so colorfully were they orchestrated. And with all the insouciance which floated on top

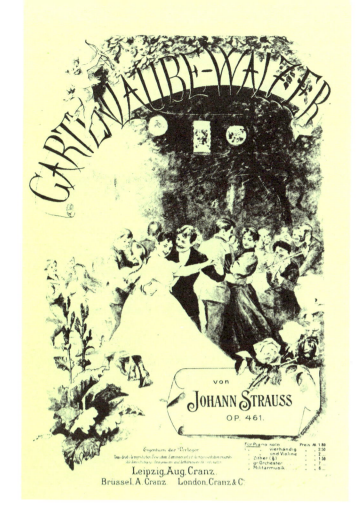

Cover for "The Garden Bower Waltz." (Vienna, City Library)

like sweet cream, they contained an undertone of melancholy and of longing. They were both carefree and sad. They were sighs wrapped in smiles. In short, they were Vienna.

The Waltz King

Strauss Jr. was vain, superstitious, kind-hearted, extravagant with money. With all his success, with all the adulation, in spite of the fact that he became the reason that tourists made their way to Vienna and took back such memories as the "Tales from the Vienna Woods" or "Vienna Blood", he was prone to deep depressions. He was deathly afraid of trains: "going on a train is for me like going to be hanged", he said. He drew down the blinds of the train-window and spent most of the trip cowering under the seat, which he considered the safest place. He always had champagne with him to deaden his fright. Yet he undertook long journeys: the Tsar invited him to St. Petersburg and the Russian Court learned the Viennese waltz. Later he appeared as Austria's good-will ambassador at the Paris World Exhibition of 1867. His most frantic foreign success was scored in America, five years later. Boston held its Independence Celebration, and for it, what greater attraction could they offer than the man who had come to be known as "The Waltz King"? He was paid an enormous fee — a cool $100,000 plus travel expenses for himself, his wife, and two servants — before he would brave the peril of an ocean voyage. Boston was blanketed with posters showing a crowned figure standing on top of

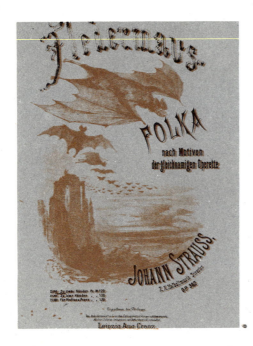

Strauss Music Covers. Upper left: "The Cat Waltz" from The Gypsy Baron. Upper right: "The Devil's Polka." Lower left: "The Fledermaus Polka." Lower right: "Quadrille from a Night in Venice." (Vienna, City Library)

the globe and wielding a baton in the form of a scepter. A special shed had been built to hold an audience of more than a hundred thousand. When the "King" appeared, pandemonium broke loose in the city. Strauss had difficulty reaching the hall, and policemen had to clear away the clamouring mob. On a platform sat the musicians, some thousands of singers, and a multitude of assistant conductors. There he stood, raised high, petrified with the enormity of it all. Let him tell the story:

> Suddenly, a cannon shot rang out, a gentle hint for us twenty thousand to begin the 'Blue Danube'. I gave the signal. My hundred assistant conductors followed me as quickly and as well as they could. And then there broke out an unholy row such as I shall never forget. As we had begun more or less together, I concentrated all my attention on seeing that we should all finish together. Thank Heaven, I managed even that.

It was all that was humanly possible. The hundred thousand mouths in the audience roared applause, and I breathed a sigh of relief when I found myself in fresh air again and felt the firm ground beneath my feet.

After Boston, he conducted a series of concerts in New York. "He speaks only German", the New York *World* reported, "but he smiles in all languages". Of course he was lionized in New York as in Boston.

The inevitable autograph and souvenir hunters pursued him wherever he went. Women bribed his valet to obtain just a tiny snippet of his luxurious hair. The valet, no fool, clipped Strauss's black-maned Newfoundland dog, sprayed the curls with perfume, and did a good business.

Women — he was as attracted to them as his father had been. At the home of a rich and cultured Jewish industrialist, Baron Moritz Todesco, whose palace was one of the

show-places of Vienna, he met Jetty. She was the beautiful common-law wife of Todesco — they could not marry, Austria not recognising unions between members of different religions — but in fact she acted as wife and brilliant hostess, until Strauss came along. She left Todesco, who treated her magnanimously and, though he loved her, let her go, and she married Strauss. As a girl Jetty had been on the stage, and it was she who first guided Strauss's interest toward operetta. Older than Strauss, Jetty mothered him, and they had some happy years together until they drifted apart, he toward other women, she toward an aging coldness. One day a young man appeared at the Strauss house, called Jetty "mother", and claimed to be her illegitimate son. Strauss threw him out, with Jetty's approval. But he returned while Johann was away and began to blackmail Jetty. When Johann came back, he stumbled over something lying in the entrance of the house. It was Jetty's corpse. Nobody knows whether her death was traceable to shame over the extortionist son or a weariness of life or a sheer physical cause. Whatever the cause, Strauss was overcome by a paroxysm of grief. He rushed away as if unable to face mortality, went to Italy, and left his brother Eduard to arrange the funeral. Johann did not return for many months.

He was fifty-three when he married his second wife, twenty-six-year-old Angelika. She was anything but angelic, a bored and capricious girl who soon enough deceived her husband and eventually ran off with a younger man. Strauss accepted his fate philosophically, or so he made believe.

He found contentment and understanding with his third wife, Adele. The very opposite of Angelica, Adele was soft-spoken, gentle, delicate in manner, and self-effacing. She gave him renewed youth and the peace of a home. From a philanderer he changed to a doting husband. Completely in love, he wanted always to be with her. Before going to the theater to conduct, he would write her a note: "Adele! I shall change the tempo from *maestoso* to *allegro,* so I can come back to you sooner and kiss you a few minutes earlier". He would work at his desk at night standing — he composed standing as Verdi did — and between melodic inspirations he would send love notes up to

The Leopold Theater in Vienna painted by F. Scheyerer (1790-1839). Many of Strauss's operettas were performed here. (Vienna, Historical Museum)

Cover for "Viennese Tivoli Music," showing the amusement park in the woods. (Vienna, City Library)

her room. He was in his sixties now and she was years younger; he dyed his hair, but in most other respects he seemed no older than she. Though other people were longing to make the acquaintance of the celebrated couple, they led an intimate life, restricting themselves to only a few friends. One of these was Brahms, who, bear-like and gruff on the outside, had a soft heart, loved Johann and Adele and much admired Strauss as a composer. Once, during a ball in Vienna, when a pretty young girl approached Brahms to ask him for his autograph, he wrote on her fan the first few bars of the "Blue Danube" Waltz and underneath, "Unfortunately not by Johannes Brahms". Brahms, who was a pianist, often played variations on that waltz, which according to contemporary testimony, were marvels of charm. Unfortunately no notation was made of them.

On May 22, 1899, a high holiday in Austria, a special performance of *Die Fledermaus* was given, and Strauss himself conducted the overture. He led it with all the enthusiasm of a twenty-year-old. He decided to walk home from the opera through the balmy spring air filled with the fragrance of Vienna's linden trees. He caught a chill, which developed into pneumonia. On the morning of June 3, he took his wife's hand and kissed it twice. That afternoon, he died.

With him died much of the spirit of that unique Viennese romanticism — a dance performed on a polished floor, the wood of which broke all too easily. It was a dance performed under the light of a hundred candles which could be snuffed all too quickly.

Yet a heritage remains. Johann Strauss published no fewer than 479 orchestral compositions and more than a dozen operettas. Of that vast and occasionally casual output, only a small fraction belongs to the living repertoire of the world. But what does belong is likely to enchant us as long as melody is an ingredient of the music we hold dear. Strauss's monument, a good one, is gaped at by the tourists to Vienna. His grave in Vienna's Central Cemetery lies near the graves of Beethoven, Schubert and Brahms. It, too, is visited by many music lovers. Yet there is no need of material signposts, no need of a marble monument, to make him immortal.

PROGRAM NOTES FOR THE RECORD

by GEORGE R. MAREK

Tritsch-Tratsch Polka

A fast dance, the title meaning "tittle-tattle", or gossip. Strauss used to play it as a change of pace between the waltzes, and as such it is presented here.

Emperor Waltz

The young revolutionary turns into the middle-aged conservative. Johann Strauss was no exception. Anti-Habsburg in the Revolution of 1848, he soon became a more or less loyal adherent of the Emperor Franz Josef. He even tried to become official "Court Conductor". Even though he played at Franz Josef's wedding to the beautiful Elisabeth, the Emperor never quite forgave him and Strauss never achieved that coveted post. When Franz Josef celebrated the fortieth anniversary of his ascension in 1888, forty years after the revolution, Strauss was sixty-three and composed this celebrated waltz. The Habsburgs have not endured; the waltz, indeed a royal tribute, has.

Voices of Spring Waltz

A 19th century print of the Ring Theater, in the heart of Vienna. (Milan, Bertarelli Print Collection)

Unlike many of Strauss's waltzes which begin in a rather hesitant way, as if the couple about to dance weren't sure they could manage it, unlike those waltzes which seem to float into our presence after a far-off nebulous introduction (like the *sfumato* in Italian painting), "Voices of Spring" plunges right into a fast tempo, a joy which reflects the reappearing sunshine and the flowers which suddenly pop from the earth. Johann Strauss dedicated the waltz to Alfred Grünfeld, one of Vienna's renowned pianists. Grünfeld played it from manuscript, and Strauss, with a modesty rare for a composer, said to him, "I think this waltz is not as beautiful as the way you played it". It quickly became one of the Waltz King's most popular compositions, surpassed only by the "Blue Danube".

"Vienna Blood" Waltz

This is one of Strauss's later waltzes (Opus 354) and it shows the slight tinge of melancholy typical of Vienna. H. E. Jacob, one of Strauss's biographers, points to its "dreamy, heavy-lidded sensuality." The title by which it is known in English is, I think, misleading: It would be better translated as "Viennese Heart" or "The Spirit of Vienna." It must have inspired Richard Strauss (no relative) to compose the famous *Rosenkavalier* Waltz.

The Blue Danube Waltz

His most famous composition was perhaps his most signal failure. It was composed in Vienna in 1866, immediately after Austria had been defeated by the Prussians. At the first performance, it was performed with a chorus which sang a political poem, a wretched poem, to the effect that in spite of the defeat things would get better, Austria would rise again. The audience, gloomy and ashamed, remained unconvinced. Strauss shrugged his shoulders — what was one waltz more or less to him? The following year he appeared at the Paris World Exhibition. He was asked to compose something new, to play something special, for the dandies of the Second Empire. He remembered the 'Blue Danube' and he now performed it as a purely orchestral composition, without the words. It proved an immediate sensation. Paris went mad over it. He had to perform it every night. The Prince of Wales heard it and, returning to London, whistled it to his mother, Queen Victoria. It made its triumphant way through Europe and America, and though it has been maltreated in a hundred versions, and though it is over-familiar to all of us, it still delights and enchants — if it is played well. Here it is played in its original version, as Strauss played it in Paris.

A cut-out by Otto Böhlen of The Waltz King surrounded by musical angels. (Milan, Bertarelli Print Collection)

A caricature by J. Pierre Dantan (1800-1869) of Johann Strauss, Sr. (Milan, Bertarelli Print Collection)

"Artist's Life" Waltz

After a slow symphonic opening — extraordinarily poetic even for Strauss — the waltz charges ahead into gaiety, glitter, carefreeness. It is in a way a romantic comment on a romantic period. People believed that the artist lived a carefree life, untroubled by the demands of the day, his head in the sky, his heart forever in love. Songs and symphonies, poems and plays, they thought, were created by the inspiration of the moment. Common mortals struggled, the artist soared. One envied him and gazed at him in wonder. This famous waltz pays tribute to that belief, and it is not surprising that many artists, and not musicians only, accepted the tribute. At any rate, we know that Verdi, Wagner, Delibes, Gounod, and Delacroix were among the artists who, whatever their lives really were, admired Strauss and his idea of an artist's life.

O. Tschaïkovsky

His Life and Times 1877-1893 (Part 2)

PROGRAM NOTES FOR THE PIANO CONCERTO NO. 1 AND NUTCRACKER SUITE SELECTIONS
By Robert Jacobson

fw

FUNK & WAGNALLS, INC.
NEW YORK, NEW YORK

Tchaikovsky's Life 1877-84

A new period began in Tchaikovsky's life, though he certainly did not realise it at the time, in December 1876, when he received his first commission from Nadezhda von Meck, a recently widowed mother of eleven children and one of the richest women in Moscow. Her marriage had left her emotionally unsatisfied, and Tchaikovsky's music had come to her as a revelation of that hunger. For the next fourteen years the two were to conduct a correspondence (which fills three large volumes in the Russian edition) without ever meeting – an agreement reached by mutual consent and allowing Mme von Meck to identify Tchaikovsky the man with the composer of his works and Tchaikovsky himself to enjoy the solicitude, boundless admiration and financial generosity of a woman without being obliged to enter into a close personal relationship with her.

His work on the Fourth Symphony, which he eventually dedicated to Mme von Meck, was interrupted in the spring of 1877 by a sudden decision to use Pushkin's *Eugene Onegin* as the subject of his next opera and by the emotional crisis that this immersion in the poem caused in his own life. 'I am in love with the image of Tatyana,' he wrote, '. . . compelled to compose the music as if by irresistible attraction. I am lost in the composition of the opera.' By a most unhappy coincidence he received in the middle of May, when he was most deeply identifying himself with the story of Onegin's cold-hearted rejection of Tatyana's love, a fan-letter from one of his pupils at the Conservatoire. Antonina Ivanovna Milyukov was twenty-eight years old and reasonably good-looking, but unintelligent and afflicted with the delusion that she was irresistibly attractive to men.

Tchaikovsky was a natural victim for such a woman, as he believed that marriage would be good for his reputation, would silence his own feelings of guilt and perhaps even bring about a lasting change in his sexual habits. In addition to this Antonina Milyukov became confused in his imagination with Pushkin's Tatyana, and he saw any refusal of her love as laying him open to the same charge of heartlessness as Onegin. After a number of half-warnings and self-deprecations, which the young woman certainly did not understand, he announced to Mme von Meck his forthcoming wedding in a letter, adding: 'My conscience is clear. I am marrying without love, but I do it because circumstances have left me no alternative . . . I have not lied or pretended to her. I have told her what she can expect from me, and on what she cannot count. Please tell no one what led to my marriage.'

He only told his brother and confidant Modest – who was also homosexual – of the marriage after it had taken place. This was on 18th July 1877 at the church of St George on the Malaya Nikitskaya in Moscow. Between that date and 6th October, when the marriage finally collapsed, Tchaikovsky found every possible excuse to spend as little time as he could with his wife. He spent more than a month with his married sister Sasha Davidov in the country and even managed to work on his symphony and the new opera. When he returned to Moscow and his wife on 23rd September the old terrors soon got the better of him. He attempted suicide by standing up to the waist in the icy autumnal water

of the River Moskva; and when he finally fled to St Petersburg on 6th October he was at such a pitch of hysteria that he seems to have collapsed into two days of unconsciousness after a crisis which only his brother Anatol witnessed.

His wife agreed to a divorce with surprisingly little complaint, and Tchaikovsky escaped abroad, where Mme von Meck's money enabled him to rent a villa at Clarens, on the Lake of Geneva. From now on she gave him an annual allowance of 18,000 francs. He never saw his wife again.

During November he started orchestrating *Eugene Onegin*, and during the next six months – while he travelled restlessly with Anatol to Paris, to Vienna, to Venice, to San Remo, back to Switzerland, back to Vienna and so eventually at the end of May 1878 to Sasha's home at Kamenka – he finished the work. In his absence the Fourth Symphony had its first performance, under Nikolai Rubinstein, in Moscow on 22nd February. During these months he exchanged long letters with Mme von Meck on the subjects of music (especially his new symphony, about which he showed himself remarkably clear-sighted), religion (Mme von Meck professed herself a believer only in her own religion of music, while Tchaikovsky admitted to at least a sentimental attachment to Orthodoxy) and love, on which subject Tchaikovsky was guarded but strictly speaking truthful as far as he went. At Clarens his young violinist friend Joseph Kotek had arrived as a guest and was able to advise him on the writing of the solo part in the violin concerto which he had started. Back in Russia, he spent part of the summer at Brailov, an unoccupied country estate belonging to Mme von Meck. *Eugene Onegin* was finished in August and at the end of September Tchaikovsky returned to his lecturing at the Moscow Conservatoire. But only for a short time: in October he resigned and before the end of 1878 he was abroad again, staying in Florence, where Mme von Meck had taken rooms for him. She herself was staying at the Villa Oppenheim, and despite careful arrangements they did in fact once set eyes on each other in the street; but they passed on without speaking, and the original agreement was never altered. Tchaikovsky now started his opera based on Schiller's *Maid of Orleans*, which he completed the following March in Paris, only a few days before returning to Moscow for the first night of *Eugene Onegin*, which took place on 29th March. The work was far from achieving at once the success that it was later to win, and the composer left for St Petersburg the next day.

The rest of the year was spent moving from one place to another inside Russia until in November Tchaikovsky went abroad again, first to Berlin and then to Paris, where he heard of the attempted assassination of Alexander II and wrote to Mme von Meck: 'So long as all of us – the citizens of Russia – are not called upon to take part in our country's government, there is no hope for a better future.'

After completing the first draft of his Second Piano Concerto in G major on 15th December, Tchaikovsky left Paris for Rome, but he was back by March 1880 and went from there to Russia, where the same nomad life continued between the two capitals and the country estate of his sister, or, in the owner's absence, that of Mme von Meck. The attack on Alexander II and the death of Nikolai Rubinstein, both occurring in March 1881 when Tchaikovsky was in Italy, disturbed him deeply and momentarily stopped the flow of his musical ideas.

Back in Russia again, Tchaikovsky heard that his Violin Concerto, dedicated to Leopold Auer but then rejected by him as unplayable, had been taken up by Adolf Brodsky. The first performance was on 4th December 1881 in Vienna, where Brodsky was the soloist and Hans Richter the conductor. At Rome a few months later he announced the completion of the Piano Trio in memory of Nikolai Rubinstein, which had its first performance in Moscow that October, five months after the Second Piano Concerto. By September he had finished the first draft of his next opera, *Mazeppa*, which he continued during the months of January to June 1883, spent mostly in Paris. This had its first performance in February 1884 at the Bolshoi Theatre in Moscow and was not a great success. A month later he was received and decorated by Alexander III and the Tsarina Marya Fyodorovna. The summer of 1884 he spent at Kamenka where he played piano duets with 'my darling, incomparable, wonderful, ideal Bobyk' (his favourite nephew Vladimir Davidov), read English and worked on his Third Suite.

Tchaikovsky's Life 1885-93

The year 1885 opened happily for Tchaikovsky with the success of his Third Suite, first performed in St Petersburg in January and conducted by Hans von Bülow, whose enthusiasm for this music greatly cheered the composer. For his next opera he turned, unfortunately, to Shpazhinsky's *Sorceress*, a play about princes and princesses, drinking and roistering, wizardry and 'illicit passion' in an old Slavonic setting, of the sort in which Tchaikovsky must by now have known that he could never hope to succeed. It is possible that in the character of Nastasia (the Sorceress herself) he saw the possibility of creating a kind of Russian Carmen.

He was now looking for a country property, some house that he could hope to make a home. At Maidanovo, within easy reach of Moscow and well placed for St Petersburg, he found a furnished house that seemed to suit him. Here he spent much of the spring and summer reworking his opera *Vakula the Smith* and starting his 'Manfred' Symphony, which he finished in October and heard at its first performance in Moscow the following March. 'Half successful,' he noted in his diary; but to Madame von Meck: 'I think that this is my finest composition.' There had been, exceptionally, no excursion abroad in 1885, but in April 1886 Tchaikovsky interrupted his work on *The Sorceress* to visit his naval brother Ippolit at Taganrog, on the Sea of Azov, and to see the Caucasus and Armenia. A concert of his works was well received in Tiflis; and he then continued his journey to France, regaled on his sea voyage from Batum to Marseilles by a minor eruption of Mount Etna. In Paris itself he was flattered by the reception which he enjoyed from French musicians, including Pauline Viardot, Lalo, Delibes, Fauré (one of whose piano quartets he heard and admired) and Ambroise Thomas. Back in Maidanovo he spent all August working at his *Sorceress*, disturbed only by two letters from his wife, who had taken a lover and had a child – a circumstance that reassured Tchaikovsky. From this autumn dates a diary-entry in which he confides his musical tastes – his adoration of Mozart and his inability to love Beethoven ('In general I hate the last period, particularly the last quartets. There are glimmers here and nothing more. The rest is chaos over which, surrounded by impenetrable mists, hovers the spirit of this musical Jehovah'). In the same way he expressed admiration for the music of Wagner's *Parsifal* but bewildered incomprehension of the drama.

Early in 1887 the new version of *Vakula the Smith*, now called *Cherevichky* (The Little Shoes) had its first performance on 31st January and at the beginning of June Tchaikovsky left Maidanovo for a ten days' journey which took him first by river-steamer down the Volga and ultimately to Tiflis and the spa of Borzhom, where he took the waters and worked on *Mozartiana* – his Fourth Orchestral Suite, consisting of arrangements of music by his hero Mozart – and the String Sextet. At the end of July he travelled – via Batum, Odessa, and Vienna – to Aachen, where he spent six weeks at the deathbed of his friend Kondratiev and finished *Mozartiana*. An entry in his diary (3rd August) is characteristic and endearing: 'Sitting at home repenting of something.... Life is passing, nearing its end, yet I have come to no conclusions.... Take, for example, this moment. Here I am, everyone is admiring my self-sacrifice. But there is no sacrifice. I sit here placidly, stuffing myself at the table d'hôte, do nothing, spend my money on trifles when others lack the bare necessities. Am I not a pure egoist? Even with those close to me I am not what I should be.' *The Sorceress* had its first performance, under the composer, at St Petersburg on 1st November and was followed by a Moscow concert at which Tchaikovsky again conducted a programme of his own music, including the new *Mozartiana*.

At the end of 1887 Tchaikovsky set off on his first international tour as composer-conductor. In Germany he met his old flame Désirée Artôt at a performance of Berlioz's *Grande Messe des Morts*, and Brahms and Grieg at Brodsky's in Leipzig, where Brahms's new Double Concerto bored him. He thought Brahms looked like a Russian priest ('we are ill at ease because we do not really like each other') but found Grieg immediately sympathetic. The Leipzig critics were polite about the concert of his own works which he conducted, but in Hamburg, where he was welcomed by Hans von Bülow, he was sternly rebuked for having been, as his music showed, 'born and bred in a country so unenlightened and so inferior to Germany'. In Berlin his reception was warmer still, and in Prague he was serenaded by students and altogether treated as a cultural ambassador of 'the greatest of Slav nations'. In Paris, the Russian Embassy gave a party for him, though the French press had begun to find his works too German compared with the newly familiar music of the nationalist 'Mighty Handful'. After a very rough Channel crossing he arrived exhausted in London, where his concert was well received but he felt personally neglected. Immediately afterwards, at the end of March, he returned to Tiflis, from where he wrote to Modest announcing plans for a fifth symphony and an interest in Pushkin's *Queen of Spades* for a new opera.

In May Tchaikovsky returned to Russia and the new house at Frolovskoye, which he had taken in succession to Maidanovo. There he finished the Fifth Symphony and incidental music to *Hamlet*, promised to Lucien Guitry, whom he had met on his travels. The Symphony had its first performance at St Petersburg in November of this year (1888), when although it was generally well received it also suffered some heavy criticism. Tchaikovsky conducted a much less happy performance of the same work in Prague a few weeks later. In December he wrote to Madame von Meck from Vienna that he had come to the conclusion that the Symphony was not successful: 'It contains something repellent, an excess of colour and some insincerity, something laboured that audiences instinctively recognise.' He escaped from his depression by throwing himself wholeheartedly into the composition of his new ballet *The Sleeping Beauty*, finishing the first four scenes at Frolovskoye during January 1889 before setting off for his next foreign tour. This took him to Cologne, Frankfurt, Dresden, Berlin and Hamburg, where he found himself staying in the same hotel as Brahms, who shared the orchestral players' dislike of the Fifth Symphony's finale. In Paris during March Tchaikovsky saw a lot of Massenet and heard Lalo's *Roi d'Ys*, Gounod's *Romeo and Juliet*, and Berlioz's *Damnation of Faust* ('How I love this composition!').

After only three days in London, where he found the orchestra cold and unsympathetic, he set off for Tiflis, travelling by sea from Marseilles to Batum. The contrast between a London fog and April days in a rich spring atmosphere with the far-away snow peaks of the Caucasus rounding off the picture, delighted him; but in May he returned to Russia and eventually to Frolovskoye, where he worked hard at *The Sleeping Beauty*. By the end of August

the score was completed. Tchaikovsky was in St Petersburg for rehearsals and the first performance of *The Sleeping Beauty*, which took place in January 1890. He spent the whole of February and March 1890 in Florence, working on *The Queen of Spades*, and after an April stay in Rome was back in Russia at the beginning of May. The score of the opera was finished at the beginning of June, at Frolovskoye, and work began at once on the Sextet. Late in August he paid a visit to Kamenka and arrived in Tiflis in September. While he was there he received a strange, cold note from Madame von Meck, saying that she could not continue his pension, and ending, 'Do not forget, and think of me sometimes.' The loss of the pension was no longer important, but the final phrase, suggesting the termination of a cool and conventional relationship, hurt Tchaikovsky bitterly. In fact Madame von Meck was seriously ill and more than usually neurotic at the time, and one of her sons was dying of a particularly distressing disease.

Back in St Petersburg Tchaikovsky attended the enormously successful first performance of *The Queen of Spades* under Napravnik in December, leaving soon afterwards to spend the New Year of 1891 at Kamenka. The first three months of the year were taken up mostly with work on a new ballet, *The Nutcracker*, and a new opera based on a fashionable play called *King René's Daughter*; but in mid-March he left for a much more ambitious tour than any he had undertaken before. On 18th April he sailed from Le Havre on his first visit to the United States.

After a rough crossing, during which he preferred the second-class passengers to his companions in the first, he arrived in New York a week later. He was entertained and fêted unceasingly throughout his visit, especially by the conductor Walter Damrosch and his wife and Andrew Carnegie, whose 'Music Hall' was opened on 5th May. Baltimore, Philadelphia and Washington repeated the festivities and Tchaikovsky, though flattered, was glad to sail for home on 20th May. He was back in St Petersburg by 1st

Décor by Alexander Benois for Tchaikovsky's opera, The Queen of Spades. *When the opera was performed at the Maryinsky Theatre in St Petersburg a special telephone link with the Imperial Palace was installed so that the Tsarevich (later Nicholas II, last Tsar of Russia) could hear the performance relayed direct from the stage (Collection of Anna Tcherkessoff, Paris)*

June. While he was away his manservant and factotum, Alexey Sofronov, had moved the household back from Frolovskoye to Maidanovo, and it was there that Tchaikovsky completed the score of *The Nutcracker* and, in September, his new opera, which was to be called *Yolanta*. Late this year, after a visit to his brother Anatol in Estonia, he heard a performance of Mascagni's opera *Cavalleria Rusticana* in Warsaw and wrote to a friend: 'This opera is truly remarkable, particularly in its happy choice of subject. Let Modya [his brother Modest] smell out a subject of this type.'

In January 1892 Tchaikovsky visited Hamburg for a performance of *Eugene Onegin* under Gustav Mahler, which he characterised as 'positively superb'. After ten days in Paris he returned to Maidanovo and polished the details of *The Nutcracker*, from which he extracted an orchestral suite that was to prove most popular. In April he conducted performances of *Faust* and Rubinstein's *Demon* in Moscow and received an ovation; and in the following month he moved to Klin, the last of his houses and now the Tchaikovsky Museum. Installed here, he began work on a new symphony (which was never completed but used, in parts, as material for the Third Piano Concerto) and then took his favourite nephew, Bob Davidov, to Berlin, Paris and Vichy. This, and a visit to Vienna in September, probably reflected his intense dissatisfaction with his work and the feeling of having written himself out. In December both *Yolanta* and *The Nutcracker* had their premières in St Petersburg. 'The opera was evidently very well liked, the ballet not,' he wrote. 'And truth to tell, it was a little boring despite the magnificence of the sets.'

Immediately after attending these performances Tchaikovsky went abroad again and spent New Year's Day calling on his old governess, Fanny Durbach, at Montbeillard. Paris, Brussels, Odessa and Kamenka exhausted him, but back in Klin in mid-February he started furious work on a new symphony, the idea for which had occurred to him during his travels. At the end of May he went to England to receive his Doctorate at Cambridge (with Saint-Saëns, Bruch, Boito and Grieg), and was entertained in London ('one of the worst of cities' but possessing 'incredible chic and sumptuousness'). In July and August he finished both the Third Piano Concerto and the Sixth Symphony ('I love it as I have never loved a single one of my offspring'). The Sixth Symphony had its first performance at the end of October and seems to have left both players and public indifferent. On 2nd November Tchaikovsky was not well – he had not been able to sleep and suffered from indigestion. At lunch with Bob and Modest he drank a glass of water, disregarding their protests that there was much cholera in St Petersburg at the time. The disease declared itself within a matter of hours and ran its normal course despite expert medical attention.

By the evening of 5th November, when the priest was summoned and read the prayers for the dying, Tchaikovsky was unconscious and the following day he died. Four days later he was buried in the cemetery of the Alexander Nevsky Church.

Nadezhda von Meck, Tchaikovsky's patroness. Mme von Meck first became interested in Tchaikovsky after hearing his incidental music for The Tempest —*she later wrote to the composer: 'I cannot tell you the impression it made on me. For several days I was half demented'* (W. Speiser, Basle)

Tchaikovsky's house at Klin, where he spent the last years of his life, and which is now a Tchaikovsky museum (France-U.S.S.R., Paris)

Tchaikovsky's Inheritance and Legacy

The two men who most influenced Tchaikovsky in his student days had strong views about music. Anton Rubinstein, founder of the St Petersburg Conservatoire, had studied in Paris and Berlin; and Zaremba, Tchaikovsky's chief teacher, was a staunch conservative who taught from German textbooks.

As Western-trained professionals they despised Glinka and his successors – the 'Mighty Handful' of St Petersburg – as amateurs who had never bothered to learn their craft. But, as stern traditionalists, they forbade their pupils to take for models any composers later than Mendelssohn and Schumann.

However, Tchaikovsky's experience of music was less circumscribed than the prejudices of his mentors might suggest. Although he kept his distance from them, he was not blind to the merits of the Nationalists who had learned composition by composing. Secondly, though Rubinstein forbade his pupils to study Liszt, Berlioz and Wagner, he conducted performances of their latest works at the Russian Musical Society, where Tchaikovsky certainly heard them. So in practice Tchaikovsky, living and studying in St Petersburg, enjoyed very much the same contacts with the 'advanced' music of his day as he would have as a student in Berlin, Vienna, or Paris – though he may have heard the Viennese classics less often and less well played than he would have done in Western Europe; and certainly he must have heard less Bach and less Handel than he would have at the same period in England.

Among the chief formative elements in Tchaikovsky's musical experience was opera. His first favourites were Glinka (inevitably) and Mozart's *Don Giovanni*. Meyerbeer – and his Russian disciple Serov – had a strong, probably unconscious influence on his ideals and methods of dramatic presentation, and he could not resist the Italian eloquence and dramatic lyricism of Verdi. It was not until later, in France itself, that he came to know the new, intimate operas of Massenet and Bizet, but Gounod's *Faust* was an early favourite. His notorious preference for Delibes to Brahms – foreshadowing Stravinsky's seemingly paradoxical musical judgments — was merely the reflection of a temperamental affinity.

About Wagner Tchaikovsky had mixed feelings. *Lohengrin* was his favourite among Wagner's works, but he could not help being aware of the greatness and significance of *The Ring:* 'I feel respectful admiration for the enormous talent of the composer and the richness of a technique such as has never been known before . . . Even if the *Ring* bores one at times, if much of it is at first incomprehensible and vague and Wagner's harmonies may be objected to as over-complicated and manufactured, if his theories are false – even if the results of his vast labour should at last be forgotten and the Bayreuth Festspielhaus fall into eternal decay, yet *Der Ring des Nibelungen* is an occurrence of the greatest importance to the world and an epoch-making work of art.'

Wagner certainly exercised a practical influence on Tchaikovsky in the matter of instrumentation and harmony; though in both fields he owed more to Liszt, whose music was more temperamentally akin to him. In his keyboard writing, and overwhelmingly in the three piano concertos, Tchaikovsky inherited and developed the virtuoso style of the day. Liszt had perfected this style by combining the traditional virtuosity of Kalkbrenner, Moscheles and Thalberg with Paganini's new 'transcendental' style. Although Tchaikovsky expressed a great admiration for Berlioz, both as a person ('the personification of selfless work and burning love of art' and a 'noble and energetic fighter against ignorance, stupidity, vulgarity and routine') and as a composer (particularly of the *Damnation of Faust* and *Grande Messe des Morts*), it is only in his 'Manfred' that we can trace unambiguously the influence of Berlioz's 'Fantastic' Symphony. Like all Russian composers (except Scriabin in the next generation), Tchaikovsky felt himself instinctively closer to the Liszt-Berlioz stream of modernism, which was indeed to prove one of the chief lines of advance in the development of the art, than to Wagner, whose 'music of the future' proved to be the crowning point of the Classical-Romantic tradition rather than a new departure.

Tchaikovsky's influence on the music of other composers has been far stronger in his own country than elsewhere. This fact confirms Stravinsky's assertion that it is Tchaikovsky's music rather than that of the 'Mighty Handful' that is truly and representatively Russian. There is, for example, no instance of Tchaikovsky's influence on a Western European composer in any way comparable to that of Mussorgsky, who played a crucial part in Debussy's development, or even of Rimsky-Korsakov, whose orchestral palette was imitated by a whole generation of composers both in France and Italy.

In Russia, however, and more generally in the Slav world, Tchaikovsky has exercised a deep and long-continuing fascination. The first and most marked of Tchaikovsky's disciples during the composer's lifetime was Arensky, a weak

personality but technically accomplished. Far more remarkable and individual, Sergei Rachmaninoff received his whole education from masters who were either Tchaikovsky's personal friends or members of his circle – Zverev, Siloti, Taneyev and Arensky. After Tchaikovsky's death in 1893 and Anton Rubinstein's in 1894 it was Rachmaninoff who both carried on the tradition of Russian pianistic virtuosity in Western Europe, and also explored the symphonic field in Tchaikovsky's spirit, if not always in Tchaikovsky's own language. Rachmaninoff had presented his set of Five Piano Pieces (including the popular C sharp minor Prelude) to the older composer a few months before his death, and a few weeks later, in May 1893, Tchaikovsky had attended the first performance of Rachmaninoff's opera *Aleko* at the Bolshoi and described it as 'a charming work that I very much like'.

Many of Rachmaninoff's early songs are settings of poets also set by Tchaikovsky – Alexis Tolstoy, Apukhtin, Pleshcheev, Shevchenko, Tyuchev – and his First Piano Concerto was dedicated to Tchaikovsky's pupil and friend Siloti. It is impossible not to recognise in many of the songs, in the Second and Third Piano Concertos, the E minor Symphony and the tone-poem *The Isle of the Dead* a note of that elegiac world-weariness – or *toska*, as the Russians call it – and that despair that sometimes verges on the hysterical, both of which we find in Tchaikovsky's music, and especially in the Sixth Symphony. Like him, too, Rachmaninoff had received a thorough academic training and shared the cosmopolitan background and interests of the Russian gentry of his day. Tchaikovsky had found an unmistakably Russian musical language for this cosmopolitanism, and Rachmaninoff did not need to embody any further foreign elements in his style. Instead, he gave his piano writing a greater elegance and variety, and a more refined virtuosity. He expanded but at the same time smoothed out Tchaikovsky's very personal, often abrupt harmonic progressions; and muted, made more conventionally 'tasteful', the brilliant colours of Tchaikovsky's orchestration.

Later Tchaikovsky's spirit, and much of his practise, continued to exercise a strong influence on Russian composers even after the Revolution. It is significant that, in the directive issued to them in November 1946 by Commissar A.A. Zhdanov, Tchaikovsky's music was held out as a model and as an antidote to the bourgeois intellectualism of new Western European music.

In Britain, Tchaikovsky's music has never ceased to be popular since it was first introduced during the 1880s; but that popularity reached a new and altogether unprecedented height during the years of the Second World War. These coincided with the new popularisation of music in general, and many people who had never given much attention to classical music before found there – and particularly in Tchaikovsky's highly coloured, intensely emotional music – both a release for their own emotional tensions, and a reflection of their own anxieties and moments of self-pity. The popular demand for Tchaikovsky's music during those years and the years immediately after the war was mercilessly exploited by those whose interests in music were primarily commercial. The result was that for a time Tchaikovsky's stock sank among musicians and people of taste. But this was only a momentary setback; twenty years later Tchaikovsky's symphonies and concertos may figure less frequently in concert programmes, but his operatic production is becoming increasingly well known and such once despised works as the sextet *Souvenir de Florence* and the string quartets are winning new admirers.

Two Russian composers who, in different ways, were influenced by Tchaikovsky: (opposite) Stravinsky, and (left) Rachmaninoff (Keystone Press; French Association for Cultural Relations with the Soviet Union, Paris)

Tchaikovsky's Operas, Songs and Ballets

The stage played an important part in Tchaikovsky's life, and from the age of twenty-seven onwards he was hardly ever without an opera or a ballet, or both, on his hands. Of his ten operas only two, *Eugene Onegin* and *The Queen of Spades*, have survived in the general repertory outside Russia. The early *Voyevoda* and *Oprichnik* and the middle period *Maid of Orleans* and *Mazeppa* are not likely to enjoy anything but an occasional revival. But his fourth opera, which started life as *Vakula the Smith* and was rewritten as *Cherevichky* (it is also known as *Oxana's Caprices*), and *The Sorceress* both contain enough good music to justify their revival outside Russia; and his last opera, *Iolanthe*, has recently enjoyed some success in a London revival.

Like most opera composers, Tchaikovsky suffered from the difficulty of finding a suitable libretto; and in his case this meant one in which there were features or even characters with which he could identify himself. *Eugene Onegin* gave him the country-house setting which he knew so well from summers at Kamenka and, in Tatyana, a character naïve and passionate like himself and cruelly punished, as he felt himself to be, because her love made her transgress the accepted code of society. In *The Queen of Spades* Hermann is a fated, mysterious, Byronic figure, whose existence is dominated by a fearful secret, and love brings him to nothing but disaster and remorse.

Tchaikovsky was well aware that this new, intimate, intensely personal kind of opera, which Gounod and Massenet had initiated in France, was the field in which he could hope to succeed, rather than cardboard historical dramas or impossible, highly coloured stories of murder and witchcraft. The scenes of social life in *Eugene Onegin* and *The Queen of Spades* – peasants in the garden of the big house, an old nurse talking of the past to a growing girl, the French tutor with his birthday verses, the ballroom scenes with their mixture of brilliance and petty gossip, the gambling club and the urban scenery of St Petersburg – all bring out the best in Tchaikovsky; his sense of atmosphere sums them up in a melodic phrase, a rhythm or an orchestral colouring.

In both these works he was himself part-author of the libretto, sharing the task with Konstantin Shilovsky in the one case and with his brother Modest in the other. Neither does justice to Pushkin's original poems; but if *The Queen of Spades* contains a good deal of rank sentimentalising, *Eugene Onegin* is a fair picture of at least part of the story. Prince Gremin's aria in the last act is a rare example of a minor character perfectly summed up in a single musical number; Lensky's arias after the quarrel with Onegin and before the duel combine penetrating lyrical sweetness and nostalgia with an excellent sense of youthful character, and the opening scene in the public gardens, the scene in the old Countess's bedroom and the barracks and gambling-club ambiance in *The Queen of Spades* are perfectly designed both musically and dramatically.

To the ballet Tchaikovsky was instinctively drawn, not only by his very characteristic decorative sense but also by his strong feeling for children and for the fairy world in which their imaginations move naturally. His first essay, *Swan Lake*, had its first, wholly unworthy performance in 1877, but was begun in 1875. The accepted story of Delibes's influence is difficult to accept, in view of the fact that in January 1878 Tchaikovsky did not know *Coppélia* and had only heard the music of *Sylvia* played in Vienna in 1877. What is certainly true, however, is that Tchaikovsky's ballet music was completely revolutionary in Russia, where the dancing was excellent but where the music for the ballet had hitherto been entrusted to hacks and nonentities.

His next ballet, *The Sleeping Beauty*, was written in 1889 and performed on New Year's Day 1890, and his last, *The Nutcracker*, just two years later. In each of these works Tchaikovsky showed his quite uncanny gift for summing up, or evoking, a personality in musical terms. Among many other examples which will leap to any ballet-lover's mind are the rhythm and orchestration of the Dance of the Cygnets and Odette's Adagio in *Swan Lake;* the arrival of Carabosse, the Lilac Fairy's music and that accompanying the Prince's journey to the enchanted castle, Puss-in-Boots, the Blue Birds and Little Red Riding-Hood in *Sleeping Beauty;* and the exquisite miniatures of the divertissements in *Nutcracker*.

In his ballet music Tchaikovsky could forget the problems of symphonic architecture which gave him (and indeed almost all Russian composers) such trouble, for the very good reason that Russian composers have been painters and not architects, and mostly miniature or genre painters, decorators or illustrators. The very scale of ballet movements, short and finely etched, suited Tchaikovsky, and his marvellous sense of orchestral colour and melodic shape found uninhibited expression in the creation of the vignettes and their fantastic, dreamlike background. In the music of *The Sleeping Beauty* Stravinsky finds the perfect combination of simplicity, poverty (by which he seems to mean naïveté) and spontaneity, as well as that power of melody which he describes as 'the centre of gravity in every symphony, opera or ballet composed by him'. Many people today would probably agree with Stravinsky in rating Tchaikovsky's ballet music higher than his symphonies, where he was for the most part struggling with an ideal that was fundamentally alien to him.

Swan Lake,
danced by the Bolshoi Ballet, Moscow (Scala Theatre Museum, Milan and Glinka Museum, Moscow)

TATJANA

I.

ländliches Hauskleid

ONEGIN

1

Costume designs for
Tchaikovsky's opera
Eugene Onegin
by H. Lefler
(1863-1919): Tatyana
(left) and Onegin
(right). The choice of
singers for the opera
worried Tchaikovsky
enormously—he wrote
to Mme von Meck
'Composing music for
instruments alone is
far more satisfactory,
has fewer
disappointments'
(Austrian National
Library, Vienna)

Song-writing was an entirely secondary part of Tchaikovsky's creative activity, and he often fell back on this when unable to progress with more important work. Yet although none of his songs have the stark dramatic power of Mussorgsky's or the harmonic originality of Borodin's and Balakirev's best, their melodic appeal and dramatic personality often make them striking enough. Any comparison with the masters of the German Lied or the French 'mélodie' is irrelevant, because it ignores the specific character of the Russian 'romans' as inherited from Glinka and Dargomyzhsky.

Outside Russia Tchaikóvsky is not known by his most forceful or original songs, but by his more conventional 'None but the weary heart' (Nur wer die Sehnsucht kennt), 'Mid the din of the ball' or 'Don Juan's Serenade'. In fact, however, there are interesting examples of dramatic ballads ('The Corals' and 'If I'd only Known', or the extraordinary 'New Greek Song') or such mood-songs as 'Night' from the year of the composer's death. A. K. Tolstoy, Maikov, Mey and the composer's friend Apukhtin were typical late 19th-century poets whose verses Tchaikovsky instinctively chose for their ability to echo his own feelings. He was not always scrupulous in his setting of words, though his prosody could on occasion be unusually telling as well as correct. The emotional 'message' of the poem was probably always more important to Tchaikovsky – as to many other composers – than the actual language.

Sketches by Alexander Benois for décor and costumes of the Nutcracker *ballet (La Scala Milano; collection of Anna Tcherkessoff Paris)*

by ROBERT JACOBSON

Piano Concerto in B flat minor

Tchaikovsky's thunderous First Piano Concerto remains the most popular and most melodic work of its kind ever written, as well as a dazzling virtuoso showpiece. The thirty-five-year-old composer began work on it in December 1874 and finished it during the following month. The fact that it would eventually become such a favourite work both of the public and concert pianists was not evident when Tchaikovsky asked a professional performer's opinion of his new work about that time. Not a professional pianist himself but always extremely self-critical, he asked the advice of his friend Nikolai Rubinstein, brother of the famous musician Anton Rubinstein (who was head of the Moscow Conservatoire where Tchaikovsky was a faculty member), then the virtual arbiter of Russian musical life. Rubinstein suggested that Tchaikovsky play over his new work in one of the Conservatoire classrooms, after which they would adjourn to a Christmas Eve party to which both men had been invited. Later, in a letter to his patroness Mme von Meck, the composer described the humiliating rebuff he and his concerto then received. When Tchaikovsky had finished playing the mighty first movement, Rubinstein said nothing whatsoever. In the composer's own account:

' If you knew how uncomfortably foolish you feel if you invite a friend to share a dish you have prepared with your own hands, and he eats and is silent. At least say something! If you like, find fault, in a friendly way, but for heaven's sake speak — say something, no matter what! But Rubinstein said nothing. He was preparing his thunder . . . As a matter of fact, I did not require any opinion on the artistic form of my work; it was purely the technical side which was in question . . . I took patience and played the concerto to the end. Again silence.

'"Well," I asked, and rose from the piano. Then a torrent broke from Rubinstein's lips . . . My concerto was worthless, absolutely unplayable; the passages so broken, so disconnected, so unskilfully written, that they could not even be improved; the work itself was bad, trivial, common; here and there I had stolen from other people; only one or two pages were worth anything; all the rest had better be destroyed, or entirely rewritten.

'I was not only astounded, but deeply mortified by the whole scene. I require friendly counsel and criticism; I shall always be glad of it, but there was no trace of friendliness in the whole proceedings. It was a censure delivered in such a form that it cut me to the quick. I left the room without a word and went upstairs . . . Presently Rubinstein came to me and, seeing how upset I was, called me into another room. There he repeated that my concerto was impossible, pointed out many places where it needed to be completely revised,

and said if I would suit the concerto to his requirements, he would bring it out at his concert. "I shall not alter a single note," I replied, "I shall publish the work precisely as it stands." This intention I actually carried out.'

But the angry Tchaikovsky did even more than that. He erased the intended dedication to Rubinstein and inscribed it instead to the famous German pianist Hans von Bülow, who he had been told was a great admirer of his works. The pianist was flattered by the dedication and thrilled with the new concerto. He wrote Tchaikovsky a warm letter, in which he praised the originality, nobility and power of the work: 'The ideas are so original, so noble, so powerful; the details are so interesting, and though there are many of them, they do not impair the clearness and unity of the work. The form is so mature, ripe, distinguished in style, for intention and labour are everywhere concealed. I should weary you if I were to enumerate all the characteristics of your work — char-

Frontispiece of The Snow Maiden, *the incidental music to Alexander Ostrovsky's play of the same name, which Tchaikovsky composed in 1873 (Bibliothèque Nationale, Paris)*

acteristics which compel me to congratulate equally the composer as well as all those who enjoy actively or passively the composition.'

Von Bülow was just about to leave on a tour of North America, with the result that the Concerto had a phenomenally successful première in Boston on 25th October 1875. The pianist sent the composer the press clippings, and Tchaikovsky was delighted. 'Think what healthy appetites these Americans must have,' the composer wrote when he learned of the work's rapturous reception. And he was amazed by the audience's taste for encores: 'Each time Bülow was obliged to repeat the whole finale of my concerto! Nothing like that happens in our country.' Soon the work was taken up by most of the leading pianists of the day, including Rubinstein himself, who played it frequently from 1878 on.

The first movement of the B flat minor Concerto (*Allegro non troppo e molto maestoso*) begins with one of the longest introductions in the annals of the concerto. The strings play the now-famous, noble, arching melody under the crashing, rising chords of the piano. This theme is repeated twice before the main melody of the movement is introduced by the piano. This is a jerky, vivacious, surging figure, based on a Russian folk-song Tchaikovsky had heard sung at Kamenka by a blind beggar. ('It is curious,' he wrote to Mme von Meck, 'that in Little Russia every blind beggar sings exactly the same tune with the same refrain. I have used part of this refrain in my pianoforte concerto.') Eventually the clarinet, with bassoon and horns, brings in the tender second theme. These two ideas are developed and then recapitulated, ending brilliantly for pianist and orchestra.

Plucked strings announce the poetic *Andante semplice*, followed by the main elegiac theme in the flute and then the piano accompanied by the strings. A new idea is heard in the oboe, with a running accompaniment of clarinets and bassoons. The scherzo-like middle section is introduced by the piano, and the main waltz theme is provided by the violas and cellos. This is said to be the melody of a French popular song Tchaikovsky loved as a boy. The first part of the movement is then repeated to close this quiet interlude.

The final movement (*Allegro con fuoco*) has its principal theme stated by the piano. This is a wildly energetic Russian dance soon taken up by the full orchestra. The violins then offer a contrasting lyrical theme, echoed by the piano and orchestra. These themes are repeated, combined and developed until orchestra and soloist build to a grand climax. The majestic Concerto ends dramatically with the main theme restated in its full glory.

The Nutcracker Suite

If Tchaikovsky created one of the landmarks in concerto history with his First Piano Concerto, he did much the same in ballet. With *Swan Lake* (1876) and *The Sleeping Beauty* (1879) behind him, he was commissioned by the director of St Petersburg's Imperial Theatre to write a new ballet to a book by Marius Petipa, who completely outlined the moods and dances the musical score was to fit. Tchaikovsky's Opus 71, *The Nutcracker*, premièred by the composer himself as an orchestral suite on 19th March 1892, is based on Alexandre Dumas's version of a story by E. T. A. Hoffmann. It was then choreographed by Lev Ivanov for a first performance at St Petersburg's Maryinsky Theatre on 18th December 1892. The first night was not the triumph *The Sleeping Beauty* had been. Russian audiences of the day did not know what to make of a first act dominated by children, and they did not exactly favour the German story on which it was based either. Today, however, there is hardly a major world dance company or regional ballet that does not mount an elaborate Christmastime production of *The Nutcracker* — the most noted version in the United States being George Balanchine's staging for the New York City Ballet. At the same time, the orchestral suite arranged from the full score has become a staple in the symphonic repertory.

The story begins with a Christmas party in the Silberhaus home, where, after exchanging various toys, Councillor Drosselmeyer gives the girl Clara an old-fashioned German nutcracker in the shape of an old man (its movable jaw cracks nuts). Her brother Fritz manages to break it in a squabble, and during the night Clara sneaks back to the livingroom to nurse her broken toy under the darkened Christmas tree. At the stroke of midnight, the room is invaded by mice, led by the Mouse King. His forces are defeated by toy soldiers led by the Nutcracker, who is afterwards transformed into a handsome prince. He then takes Clara through a wintry pine forest to the Kingdom of Sweets, ruled over by the Sugarplum Fairy. There they are entertained at festivities with characteristic dances from Spain, Arabia, China and elsewhere, all culminating in the extravagant 'Waltz of the Flowers.'

This suite from *The Nutcracker* opens with a 'Miniature Overture' scored for woodwinds and high strings, a prelude to the ballet having thematic material from the March as well as a lively middle section. From Act I we hear first the March to which the children enter the party scene. After Clara and the Prince tell their story in Act II, we hear the 'Dance of the Sugarplum Fairy,' a delicate melody played on the celesta. Then follow a dynamic Russian trepak, an exotic Arab dance and the Chinese dance. The suite concludes with the 'Dance of the Mirlitons' (flutes, with contrasting trumpets) and the well-known 'Waltz of the Flowers,' introduced by the horns. Throughout this richly melodic music, Tchaikovsky gave free rein to the various colouristic effects that typify the best of his scores and to the pulsating dance rhythms which are the essence of his music — whether he wrote for the ballet or otherwise.

Printed in the United States of America

G. F. Handel

His Life and Times 1685-1759

PROGRAM NOTES FOR HIGHLIGHTS FROM THE MESSIAH,
MUSIC FOR THE ROYAL FIREWORKS,
AND HIGHLIGHTS FROM THE WATER MUSIC
By Robert Jacobson

fw

FUNK & WAGNALLS, INC.
NEW YORK, NEW YORK

The Barber's Son

Georg Friederich Händel, or as he is more usually known nowadays to English-speaking music-lovers, George Frederic Handel, was born at Halle in Saxony in the year 1685. His actual birthday was probably about 23rd February, as he was baptised on 24th February. His father was an elderly barber-surgeon, a member of a respectable profession which combined the tonsorial with the surgical – barbers, being handy fellows with razors, seem to have been gradually employed to perform the then common operation of bleeding sick patients.

Handel senior was rather a severe man, and when his small son began to show an interest in music he discouraged him, preferring that the boy devote himself to more serious pursuits, such as the law, rather than follow the precarious career of a musician. It is said that the boy managed to smuggle a small clavichord up into an attic room, where he practised secretly at night, after the rest of the family were abed, until he was eventually discovered. Whilst young George was still only a little boy, his father set off by coach for Saxe-Weissenfels, where a son by his first wife was in service with the Duke. He had no intention of taking little George with him, but the boy ran after the coach until he managed to catch it up, and pleaded with his father to be

A print of Handel's father, Georg Händel (1622-97), who was a barber-surgeon of some repute (Handel's House, Halle)

allowed to go with him to see his step-brother. Father at last assented and so the boy got to Saxe-Weissenfels. It was whilst they were there that the Duke overheard the boy Handel playing the organ in the ducal chapel, and was amazed to discover that the performer was a mere child. The Duke enquired of Handel's father as to what he meant to do with his son, and was disappointed to hear that he intended him for the law. However, Handel's father did at least consent to have the boy taught music properly. A master was found for him in the person of F.W. Zachau, organist of St Mary's Church at Halle. Zachau was a competent composer, a good all-round musician, and an excellent teacher, and the little Handel learned a great deal from him; for one thing, he had quite an extensive musical library, which contained French and Italian music, as well as German, so that the boy was able to learn something of music in the various national styles.

Before he was ten years old, the youthful Handel was composing music for use in the church. But he naturally longed for more opportunities than Halle could supply and somewhere about the year 1695 he went to Berlin, where the King of Prussia maintained quite a flourishing musical establishment, with resident composers as eminent as Bononcini and Attilio Ariosti, both men whom Handel was to meet again in more adult years. But Handel did not stay long in Berlin, for his father died in 1697, and a few years later, in 1702, the seventeen-year-old boy entered the newly founded University of Halle, ostensibly to study law, in deference to his dead father's wish. But music obviously had a stronger appeal for him, and soon he was appointed organist of the Cathedral. However he did not stay there very long either, but went off to the free city of Hamburg, which was then a flourishing musical centre with a famous opera house 'on the Goosemarket', where the musical director was the gifted composer Reinhard Keiser. At Hamburg he met a clever young man named Johann Mattheson, who later became a well-known critic and writer on music, but who at the time of Handel's residence in Hamburg was busy as a composer, singer and harpsichordist in the opera house. Mattheson, being a little older than Handel, seems to have taken the younger man under his wing, rather as a slightly older student might help a freshman. In August 1703 they went off together on a jaunt to Lübeck, to meet the aged composer and organist Diderik (or Dietrich) Buxtehude, who was contemplating retirement. But any thoughts the young men might have had of succeeding him evaporated when they learnt that Buxtehude's successor was expected to marry his presumably no-longer-quite-so-young daughter. They beat a hasty retreat, as J.S. Bach did in his turn from the same city and tricky situation.

Soon after this Handel was engaged as a performer in the Hamburg opera orchestra, first as a violinist, then as harpsichordist, whilst his friend Mattheson sometimes sang, and, in his own operas, directed from the keyboard.

An 18th-century print of the Piazza di Spagna in Rome. Handel went to Rome in 1707 where he met Corelli and the two Scarlattis (Bertarelli Print Collection, Milan)

Handel himself took to composing grand operas, his first being *Almira,* which was produced with great success on 8th January 1705. Six weeks later he produced a second opera, *Nerone,* but this was much less successful, probably owing to a poor libretto; as the music is lost it is hard to say one way or the other.

Handel now decided to make a journey to Italy, then the Mecca of all operatic musicians. By the summer of 1706 he seems to have been in Florence, perhaps at the invitation of one of the Medici family, who were still the rulers of Tuscany. He seems to have been well received in Florence, and is supposed to have written his opera *Rodrigo* for performance there. From Florence he went to Rome, where he was welcomed by the great Cardinal Ottoboni, a notable patron of the arts in general and music in particular. Among the musicians in the Cardinal's service was the eminent violinist Arcangelo Corelli, then reckoned to be the greatest violinist and the finest composer of music for stringed instruments in the whole of Italy, perhaps Europe. It is evident that Handel had a great admiration for Corelli and his music, an admiration which is still displayed in many a Handel concerto, written in his later years.

Other outstanding composers whom he may have met at Cardinal Ottoboni's were the Neapolitans Alessandro and Domenico Scarlatti, father and son, two members of a musical dynasty almost as gifted as that of the Bachs. Alessandro was the leading opera composer not only in Italy but in the whole of Europe; Domenico was a fine harpsichordist, and a composer who was to write some of the most brilliant of all harpsichord pieces.

In Rome, Handel found himself in considerable demand as a composer. His own passionate temperament responded warmly to the Italian style, and from the time of his Italian visit his music became much more Italian than German. During the spring and summer of 1707 he composed some magnificent sacred music to Latin words – a Dixit Dominus, a Laudate Pueri and a Gloria Patri, although he kept tenaciously to his own firm Protestant faith. He also composed, either in 1707 or 1708, a sacred *serenata*, *Il trionfo del tempo e del disinganno*. Much of this music was used again later in England – Handel was never a man to waste anything. Meanwhile, back in Hamburg they were still performing his operas, and he was anything but forgotten in the Fatherland. But Handel had his mind not on Germany, but on Italy. He paid a visit to Venice, probably in the autumn of 1707, then returned again to Rome, where he composed a splendid oratorio, *La Resurrezione*, which was performed at the palace of Prince Ruspoli in Rome on Easter Sunday 1708 with Corelli leading an orchestra of about forty musicians – twenty violins, four violas, five cellos, five double-basses, four oboes, two trumpets and one trombone. Handel actually lived in the Ruspoli palace whilst he was composing and preparing the work. From Rome, Handel went on to Naples in the summer of 1708, where he composed and performed the Italian *serenata*, *Aci, Galatea e Polifemo*, which must undoubtedly have suggested the later English version, the serenade or masque *Acis and Galatea*.

He was back in Rome again by the spring of 1709, where he may have met the famous composer-diplomat Agostino Steffani, who had been music-director to the Elector of Hanover but had moved to a similar position with the Elector Palatine at Düsseldorf in the Rhineland. It was probably through Steffani that Handel received an invitation to visit Düsseldorf. Meanwhile, he had received a commission to write an opera for Venice, and there he produced his *Agrippina*, on 26th December 1709. In Venice he encountered

An 18th-century
print of Cardinal
Grimani, who wrote
the libretto for
Handel's opera
Agrippina (*Handel's House,
Halle*)

Prince Ernst of Hanover, the Elector's younger brother, and was invited to Hanover. So, after some four years, Handel left Italy and returned to Germany, where he was appointed music-director to the Elector of Hanover. Some time during the summer or autumn of that momentous year of 1710 he visited his mother at Halle; she was approaching sixty, which was quite elderly in the early 18th century. He no doubt also visited his sister Dorothea, now married to the lawyer Michaelson; the younger sister, Johanna, had died whilst Handel was away in Italy. Another old friend was Zachau, who no doubt listened eagerly to his former· pupil's account of music in Italy. But Handel did not stay long in Germany. He had received an invitation to visit London, so after obtaining leave of absence from his new employer, the Elector, he set off for England via Düsseldorf.

He arrived in London either late in November or early in December 1710 – a memorable year indeed for British music. For some years, since the premature death of Henry Purcell in 1695, English music had lacked a leader. There were several talented English composers: men like John Eccles, William Croft, William Turner and John Weldon – poor Jeremiah Clarke had killed himself in 1707. Music was flourishing, but there was no one great man of genius to lead it. Concerts, both public and private, abounded, perhaps more than anywhere else in Europe except in Italy. The opera was in a strange condition. With Purcell's death the English form of semi-opera had fallen somewhat in abeyance, and as far as is known no one had attemped another through-composed opera like that little miracle, Purcell's *Dido and Aeneas*. Instead, a kind of polyglot opera had grown up, part-English, part-Italian.

Handel soon began to make himself at home in London. He was presented to Queen Anne and, as Mainwaring says,

'many of the nobility were impatient for an opera of his composing'. The manager of the Opera House in the Haymarket was John Jacob Heidegger, a Swiss, reputed to be the ugliest man in London. Heidegger soon commissioned the librettist Giacomo Rossi to write an Italian opera-script on a subject proposed by Aaron Hill, but taken from Tasso's famous epic poem *Jerusalem Delivered* (*Gerusalemme Liberata*), from which most of the 'Armida' operas were derived. But Hill and Rossi called their opera *Rinaldo*, and it was under this title that Handel's first London opera was mounted at the Haymarket on 24th February 1711, with the famous castrato Nicolini in the title role. Handel had written his opera at top speed, like the librettist, who claimed that it had taken him only a few evenings; Handel took a little longer – under a fortnight – to compose the entire opera. True, he fell back to some extent on old material: for example, the one really famous aria in *Rinaldo* – 'Lascia ch'io pianga' – was originally a saraband in Handel's first opera, *Almira*. But even so, it was a remarkable feat. For all its haste, it proved a masterpiece, and a tremendous success with the British public. In June 1711 he had perforce to return to Germany – having been feted everywhere in England. But back to Hanover he had to go, by way of Düsseldorf once more, where the Elector Palatine delayed him long enough to have to give him letters of apology for his real master and mistress in Hanover.

England was still in his mind, however: in July 1711 he wrote back to a friend in London that he was making progress with his English. In the autumn of 1712, he was back in London again, on condition that he returned to his duties in Hanover 'within a reasonable time' – a phrase which Handel interpreted in a somewhat elastic way, to say the least. His immediate reason for this second visit was no doubt to compose and produce another opera, *Il pastor fido*, which was performed at the Haymarket on 22nd November 1712. Less than a month later he finished another opera, *Teseo*, which was performed on 10th January 1713. Unfortunately neither opera was an outstanding success, and the new manager, one 'Mac' Swiney, foreseeing bankruptcy, absconded, leaving everyone unpaid. However, Handel's old friend Heidegger came to the rescue, and took over the management.

Meanwhile Handel was getting more and more practise at setting English words to music, and for the birthday of Queen Anne on 6th February 1713 he composed a charming birthday ode which was sung by a cast of mainly English singers. For this the Queen awarded Handel a pension of £200 per annum. A few months later, on 7th July, his grand setting of the English Te Deum was sung at St Paul's Cathedral, by some of the same singers who had performed in the *Ode for the Birthday of Queen Anne*. Handel stayed on in England, apparently paying little or no heed to the fact that his promise to return to Hanover 'within a reasonable time' was very much in default.

But on 1st August 1714 his royal patroness Queen Anne

died, and her Protestant relation the Elector of Hanover succeeded as King George I of England, landing a few weeks later (on 18th September) in Britain. Whether Handel had then to make peace with his master, or whether he had been acting as a kind of secret agent for him in England, we shall never know. What we do know is that by 28th September they were probably reconciled, as on that day the new king went to a service at his Royal Chapel at St James's, where Handel's Te Deum was sung.

He had other patrons, such as the Earl of Burlington, at whose house Handel lived for a time during his early years in England. At Burlington House Handel met many of the famous artists, poets and other notable men of the period. Even more important to Handel was an equally resplendent figure, that of James Brydges, Earl of Carnarvon, later Duke of Chandos.

The first mention we have of him in connection with Handel is when he had commissioned some anthems from the composer, for use in his chapel at Cannons. For Cannons Handel composed not only the 'Chandos Anthems', but also some secular works with English words, including the 'masques' of *Haman and Mordecai* (later transformed into the English oratorio, *Esther*) and *Acis and Galatea*, one of the most enchanting of all his works, as well as one of the most enduring.

At Cannons, Handel worked with old friends and new, some of whom he had already met, probably at Burlington House – Alexander Pope and John Gay, among others, who both seem to have helped with the libretti of *Esther* and *Acis*. In the latter case, Handel seems to have been somewhat unaware that he had created one of the undying masterpieces of music – he tossed off *Acis and Galatea* for his noble employer and was then much more concerned with starting a new Italian opera company, to be called The Royal Academy of Music – not to be confused with the present institution of the same name, which flourishes in the Marylebone Road. Handel's Royal Academy was obviously named after the Paris Opéra, founded in the 17th century as the 'Académie Royale de Musique'.

Handel must have left Cannons by the early months of 1719, for on 21st February of that year the newspaper *The Original Weekly Journal* reported: 'Mr Hendle, a famous Master of Musick, is gone beyond Sea, by Order of His Majesty, to collect a Company of the choicest Singers in Europe, for the Opera in the Haymarket.' He wrote home from Dresden in July 1719, to the Earl of Burlington, that he was hoping to persuade the great castrato Senesino to come to London. By the end of the year Handel was back in London, and early in the spring of 1720 the Academy opened its first season with an opera by Porta, *Il numitore*. At the end of April Handel produced his own first work for the new company, *Radamisto*, dedicating it to King George I: it was a great success, although Senesino was not in the cast – he arrived at last in

September. By then England had undergone a major economic crisis – the bursting of the notorious South Sea Bubble, a speculation which ruined many hundreds and must have occasioned great hardship to thousands more. It was scarcely the best financial atmosphere for a new opera project. However, after the initial crash, things began to right themselves again – Britain was in an aspirant mood, and in November 1720 Handel felt himself justified in publishing his first collection of harpsichord lessons – the *Suites de Pièces pour le Clavecin*, which included, among other things, the air and variations later famous as 'The Harmonious Blacksmith' – a title which, it seems, was quite unknown to Handel himself. The opera project was now flourishing, and a new work, *Muzio Scevola*, was produced on 15th April 1721, in which three composers were concerned, one composing each of the three acts; Filippo Amadei (nicknamed Pippo or Mattei) wrote the first act, Bononcini the second and Handel the third – a state of affairs which inevitably led to more odious comparisons, but which was no doubt also good for the box office receipts.

At the end of the year Handel produced his own new opera *Floridante*, with Senesino in the title-role. Another new member of the cast was the famous prima donna, Cuzzoni. Now the operatic war really got under way, with rival factions supporting Handel or Bononcini, Senesino or Cuzzoni. Handel produced score after score, some of them

An 18th-century print showing the German composer Telemann, whom Handel first met in Halle. The two composers remained lifelong friends (Bibliothèque Nationale, Paris)

of great merit. *Flavio* came on 14th May 1723, and less than a year later one of his greatest masterpieces, *Giulio Cesare* (Julius Caesar), on 20th February 1724. Six months on, and he produced his *Tamerlano*, on 31st October 1724, and his *Rodelinda* early the next year, on 13th February 1725. 1726 saw *Scipione* and *Alessandro*, and in January 1727 came a new opera, *Admeto*, and a new idol – another celebrated soprano, Faustina Bordoni, as beautiful as Cuzzoni was ugly. In this year, 1727, Handel applied successfully for naturalisation as a British subject; he had obviously decided that he would rather live in England than anywhere else. But within a few months King George I, who had granted him his naturalisation, died, and Handel was busily composing anthems for the coronation of King George II. Four magnificent anthems were the outcome, which still serve their original purpose as some of the grandest royal music ever written: *Zadok the Priest* is the Coronation Anthem *par excellence*, the prime example of Handel's astonishing gift of obtaining the utmost effect with the least complicated means. The new King was crowned on 11th October 1727.

Towards the end of the year, Handel produced his latest opera, *Riccardo Primo*, on an English theme. A rival sprang up in a rather unexpected quarter: Handel's old acquaintance John Gay produced his immortal *Beggar's Opera* on 29th January 1728 at John Rich's Theatre in Lincoln's Inn Fields – an event so successful that it drew from one wit the telling epigram that 'it made Gay rich and Rich gay'. The music consisted of old ballads, dance-tunes, and borrowings from here, there and everywhere else, not excepting Purcell and even Handel himself. Nothing daunted, however, Handel struggled on, producing two new operas, *Siroe* on 17th February and *Tolomeo* on 30th April 1728. But that was the end of Italian opera in London, for the time being, at any rate. Cuzzoni, Faustina and Senesino departed for their native Italy, a good deal richer than when they arrived

in England, and London was without Italian opera for a year.

Italian opera did not perish with the end of the first Royal Academy of Music. A new subscription was proposed and Handel set off once again for Italy to collect singers, returning to London via Germany on 29th June 1729. Among his new stars was the prima donna Strada del Po, who was to become one of his staunchest supporters for many years, singing in his English as well as his Italian productions. Handel wrote a new opera, *Lotario*, to open the season on 2nd December 1729, but it failed to please, and the composer turned to his earlier successes, such as *Giulio Cesare*, to help fill the theatre. But he composed a new opera, *Partenope*, produced on 24th February 1730, and a little later entered into fresh negotiations with Senesino, to try to persuade him to return to London – which he did – to sing in the season of 1730–31. Early the next year Handel finished yet another opera, *Poro*, produced on 2nd February 1731. During that winter, he heard that his aged mother had died, in Germany. And in March 1731 an event took place which was to have important consequences; his English pastoral *Acis and Galatea* was publicly performed in the theatre in Lincoln's Inn Fields. Handelian revivals were obviously in the air, for on 6th April his twenty-year-old *Rinaldo* was revived at the Haymarket, as was *Rodelinda* on 4th May. But he had not relinquished new composition, bringing out two new operas, *Ezio* and *Sosarme*, in the early months of 1732. *Sosarme*, according to Viscount Percival, 'took with the town, and that justly, for it is one of the best I ever heard'.

But on 22nd February 1732 another event occurred which was to influence Handel in future years. A colleague, Bernard Gates, Master of the Children of the Chapel Royal, revived Handel's old Chandos piece, *Haman and Mordecai*, rechristening it *Esther*, and performing it at the Crown and Anchor tavern in the Strand for the 'Philharmonic Society of Gentleman Performers of Musick'. Handel himself may have gone to this performance of his earlier work, done now as an 'oratorio' or religious opera, and he himself revived it a few months later, in May 1732, 'with several additions'. A note in the advertisement adds: 'There will be no Action on the Stage . . .', for the Bishop of London had stepped in with his veto to forbid a Biblical story being actually acted on the public stage. Another significant revival was that of *Acis and Galatea*, brought out as 'an English opera' by the Arne family at the Little Theatre in the Haymarket. Handel countered this with his own revival of the work at the Opera House on 10th June 1732, presenting it in an odd form, the English version being mixed up with excerpts from his earlier Italian *Aci, Galatea e Polifemo*. However, for the most part, Handel was still much more set on Italian opera than English oratorio. He finished one of his most fascinating dramatic works, *Orlando*, on 20th November 1732 and presented it on 27th January 1733.

A ticket for a charity performance of John Gay's Beggar's Opera *at Covent Garden. This work, which was first produced in January 1728, was so successful that it temporarily destroyed the interest in the Italian operas which Handel was writing*

FOR THE BENEFIT OF M.ᵣ WALKER.

THEATRE ROYAL

COVENT GARDEN.

But he was having difficulty with his audiences – ever fickle, the aristocratic London public had taken against him.

But for the moment Handel's mind was turning in another direction. He had composed, or rather compiled, another English oratorio, *Deborah*, which he performed on 13th March 1733, and which can be thought of as the germ of these Lenten oratorio seasons which were to become so characteristic of his later years. About a month later he revived *Esther* again, and with it began the practise of playing organ concertos 'between the acts', to serve as an added attraction. In the early summer of 1733 he finished another oratorio, the magnificent *Athalia*, which he took with him to Oxford in July of that year, to assist at the 'Act' ceremonies. He seized the opportunity to turn the academic occasion into a kind of Handel festival (much to the disgust of the more conservative-minded dons, who objected strongly to Handel and 'his lowsy crew of foreign fiddlers'). Handel is said to have toyed with the idea of accepting a D. Mus., but withdrew sharply when he discovered how much it was likely to cost him; proceeding to a doctorate, especially a musical one, was an extremely expensive business in the 18th century. He certainly gave the academics a rare treat, producing not only *Deborah*, *Athalia*, and *Esther*, but also the 'Utrecht Te Deum and Jubilate' and *Acis and Galatea*, for the delectation of his Oxford audiences. He is also said to have cleared something like £2,000 by his trip to Oxford, a sum which must have come in very handy towards recouping some of his operatic losses.

Back in London, there was talk of a royal wedding in November 1733, between the Princess Royal (Anne, a favourite pupil of Handel's) and the Prince of Orange; but the latter fell ill, and the event was postponed. John Rich having moved to Covent Garden, his old Theatre in Lincoln's Inn Fields was taken over by the new Opera of the Nobility, with Porpora as composer, who wrote and produced an *Ariadne in Naxos* just about the same time as Handel was working on his *Ariadne in Crete* – a piece always more famous for the minuet in its overture than for anything else.

Ariadne in Crete was produced at the Haymarket on 26th January 1734 with a good cast including Strada, Durastanti and Carestini – the latter a new castrato from Italy. The royal wedding now really was about to take place, and for it Handel prepared an Italian *serenata* called *Parnasso in festa* (or as an English sub-title had it, 'Apollo and the Muses celebrating the Nuptials of Thetis and Peleus'). The music was taken largely from *Athalia*, with superimposed Italian words; that work had so far been heard only in Oxford and was therefore novel to most of Handel's London public. For the first night of *Parnasso in festa* (13th March 1734) the Court appeared in full force, it being the eve of the royal wedding. The ceremony itself took place in the French Chapel in St James's Palace, with

Handel directing the wedding anthem 'This is the day' which he had rehashed from earlier music.

At the end of the season Heidegger suddenly let the King's Theatre to the Opera of the Nobility – they had succeeded in persuading the greatest of all the castrati, Farinelli (whose real name was Carlo Broschi) to join them. Handel, at a loss for a theatre, entered into an arrangement with John Rich to perform operas at Covent Garden, which normally staged only English works.

Then, early in 1735 he produced his *Ariodante*, and three months later, on 16th April, one of his greatest masterpieces, *Alcina*. By the end of 1735 Carestini and Sallé had returned to the Continent and Handel, casting about for some surer road to fortune, took up Dryden's *Ode for St Cecilia's Day*, first set by Jeremiah Clarke in 1697. The resultant work, *Alexander's Feast*, proved one of Handel's most enduring successes. He first performed it on 19th February 1736. 'Never was upon the like occasion so numerous and splendid an Audience,' commented the *London Daily Post*. He also revived his old favourite *Acis and Galatea*, in its original Cannons version, apparently, without the Italian interpolations. Then once again he found himself providing music for a royal wedding, this time that of the Prince of Wales to the Princess of Saxe-Gotha, in the Chapel Royal at St James's Palace. He also composed and produced an 'occasional' opera, *Atalanta*, 'In honour of the Royal Nuptials'.

But even royal weddings could not counterbalance public indifference, and both opera companies were now in serious difficulties. Handel struggled on, loath to give up his old love, Italian opera. He composed two new works, *Giustino* and *Arminio*, and started a new season by reviving *Alcina* – without the ballet. In December he began composing *Berenice*, one of the best of all his Italian operas, and famous for the ever-popular minuet in its overture. He produced these latest works early in the New Year, between January and May 1737, as well as a new version of his old Italian oratorio, *Il trionfo del tempo e del disinganno*.

In the autumn, Handel went to Aix-la-Chapelle, 'to take the waters'; on 7th November the newspapers reported that he was back in London, 'greatly recovered in his Health'. Soon he was busy composing again – an Italian opera, *Faramondo*, and an English funeral anthem, 'The ways of Zion do mourn', for his late patroness Queen Charlotte, wife of George II. It was performed in Westminster Abbey on 17th December and was much approved. It was strange that although the London theatre-going public could act in so cool a way with regard to his operas, no one seemed to have the slightest doubt that he was England's musical poet laureate, to be called in for duty on any important state occasion.

He produced *Faramondo* in January 1738 at his old house, the King's Theatre in the Haymarket, now vacated by the defunct rival company. This he followed with a *pasticcio* (i.e. an opera with music selected from works by various composers) called *Alessandro Severo*; then came his one and only comic opera, *Serse* (Xerxes), which opens with his most famous single melody, 'Ombra mai fu' – more generally known as 'Handel's Largo'.

In the summer of 1738 Handel began to compose one of the greatest of all his English oratorios, *Saul*, to a text by Charles Jennens. In October Walsh published Six Organ Concertos, op.4, which were a tremendous success 'with performers on keyed instruments' as Dr Burney recorded. By November he had finished not only *Saul*, but another large-scale oratorio, *Israel in Egypt*. He produced these two works in January and April 1739, only to be disappointed with the public lack of appreciation for *Israel in Egypt* — which, being made up largely of choral numbers (mostly 'borrowed' from a work by Stradella), was little to the taste of the general 18th-century public, which preferred solo arias. A *pasticcio*, *Jupiter in Argos*, followed in May, but in September 1739 Handel set another Dryden *Ode for St Cecilia's Day*, and then went straight on to compose his twelve concertos for string orchestra, published the next year as Twelve Grand Concertos, op.6. He seems to have written these deliberately as a set of twelve, with publication very much in mind, for Walsh was advertising a subscription for the set before the last concerto was even finished. Handel performed the new *Ode for St Cecilia's Day* on that day itself, 22nd November 1739, along with *Alexander's Feast*, two of the new concertos and an organ concerto – he was obviously right on the top of his form, composing, directing, and playing the organ as if he had never had that 'paraletick Disorder' a year or so before.

A drawing, dated 1785, depicting a dance at an aristocratic party (Windsor Castle – reproduced by gracious permission of Her Majesty Queen Elizabeth II)

The End of an Era

The beginning of the year 1740 saw Handel busy at work on one of his greatest choral masterpieces – the setting of Milton's English poem with an Italian title *L'Allegro ed il Penseroso*, in Handel's arrangement modified to *L'Allegro, il Penseroso ed il Moderato*, the faithful Jennens having added a gratuitous albeit somewhat feeble third part called typically *Il Moderato*. It was a bitter winter and a proposed performance of *Acis* at Handel's new venue, the Theatre Royal in Lincoln's Inn Fields, had to be continually postponed owing to the severe cold and consequent indisposition of the singers. However, on 27th February the new work *L'Allegro* (as it is usually affectionately known) was performed there, 'with two new Concertos for several Instruments, and a new Concerto on the Organ' – the 'new concertos' probably being part of the still unpublished Opus 6. Handel played some more of his new concertos at subsequent performances, with revivals of *Saul*, *Esther* and *Israel in Egypt*. He also performed some of his works for the benefit of the 'Fund for the support of decayed Musicians and their Families', a charity of which he was a founder-member, and which still exists as the Musicians' Benevolent Society. On 21st April he published his Twelve Grand Concertos – the work which we know as his Opus 6. In the autumn he composed his last two Italian operas, *Imeneo* and *Deidamia*, and Walsh published 'A Second Set of Six Concertos for the Harpsichord or Organ, compos'd by Mr Handel' – they were in fact less composed than arranged, for they consisted largely of organ arrangements of some of the Grand Concertos op. 6. He revived *Parnasso in festa* and produced *Imeneo* before Christmas 1740, and in the following January, he produced *Deidamia*, but it reached only three performances, and with its last showing Handel quitted forever Italian opera, to which he had devoted the major part of his efforts for some thirty years or more. He obviously loved Italian opera, and only gave it up with marked reluctance. But by the 1740s his own operatic style was becoming very old-fashioned by the newer Neapolitan standards of Hasse, Leo, Vinci, Pergolesi and so on. He must at last have realised this, and in the end, came to laugh at the absurdities of that 'exotic and irrational entertainment' to which he had formerly devoted so many precious hours.

But Handel was not only a great composer; he was also a hard-headed businessman, who had a great deal of mental and financial capital invested in the genius of G. F. Handel, Esq. Sooner or later, he was bound to decide to cut his operatic losses and follow what now promised to be a much safer and less costly venture – English oratorio. For the next dozen years or so, his life began to take on a regular pattern, with the composition of a couple of oratorios in the late autumn of each year, followed by their production

on the stage, but without costumes or acting, of Covent Garden Theatre the following Lent. In general, *Messiah* was the only oratorio he produced in church or chapel, and that he obviously always thought of particularly as his 'sacred' oratorio. It was in the late August and early September of 1741 that he composed this immortal work, to a text selected by Jennens (or, as some say, his chaplain) from the Bible. Handel was in a state of high exaltation when he wrote it: he was a sincerely religious man, in spite of his habit of cursing and swearing in several languages at once when his 'Great Bear' of a temper was aroused. His inspiration was running high – scarcely had he finished *Messiah* when he was busy on another superb work, *Samson*, to a text 'altered' by his friend Newburgh Hamilton from Milton's *Samson Agonistes*. But Handel did not produce *Messiah* in London; he had received an invitation to go to Dublin, to direct his music there.

Dublin was the seat of a viceregal court, and was second only to London, in the British Isles, for the number and variety of its entertainments, music included. An old acquaintance of Handel's, the violinist Matthew Dubourg, was 'Master of the Musick of the King's State in Ireland' and it was probably through him that Handel received his invitation to Dublin.

Handel arrived in Ireland on 18th December and was soon busy directing *L'Allegro* at the 'New Musick Hall' in Fishamble Street and following it with the *Ode for St Cecilia's Day*, *Esther*, *Alexander's Feast* and other works. Georgian Dublin was a handsome city, full of cultured middle-class citizens who were more than ready to support the concerts of their highly distinguished visitor. Then on Tuesday 13th April 1742 came the crowning success of his visit to Ireland, with the production of his new oratorio, 'the *Messiah*, in which the Gentlemen of the Choirs of both Cathedrals will assist, with some Concertos on the Organ by Mr Handel.' But Dublin had already had a pre-hearing of the music at a public rehearsal on 9th April and had deemed that 'in the opinion of the best Judges, it far surpasses anything of that Nature which has been performed in this or any other Kingdom.' At the actual performance, a great crowd was expected and came, so that the stewards of the Charitable Musical Society (for whose benefit it was given) had to 'request the Favour of the Ladies not to come with Hoops' to their dresses, whilst the gentlemen were 'desired to come without their Swords'. The Dublin public was full of enthusiasm for this 'sublime Oratorio'.

One way and another Handel's trip to Ireland was an immense success, and he stayed on until mid-August 1742, arriving back in London after some ten months' absence. The next year Handel was busy running his Lenten oratorio season, producing *Samson* at Covent Garden in February. Horace Walpole, in a typical letter to Horace Mann, was somewhat rude about Handel and his singers, but *Samson* succeeded well, and was thought by the Londoners to be 'the finest piece of music he ever composed' – London had yet to hear *Messiah*, and when it did, on 19th March, it failed to appreciate this work at its true worth. Later *Messiah* grew in public esteem so as to outweigh all Handel's other oratorios, even before his death. But Handel, who had been so well in Ireland, was ill again in London: Walpole, writing to his friend Mann in May, reported that 'Handel has had a palsy and can't compose. . . . .' If so it could not have been very serious, for between 3rd June and 4th July Handel wrote one of his finest works, the secular 'oratorio' or rather drama, *Semele*, to a libretto written long before by Congreve. Soon afterwards he was hard at work writing a Te Deum to celebrate the victory of Dettingen, the last battle in which a British monarch led an army on the field of battle. Meanwhile he composed another oratorio, *Joseph and his Brethren*, and an opera ostensibly by Handel was produced at the Haymarket on 8th November. Entitled *Rossane* (Roxana), it was apparently a revival of his old *Alessandro* of 1726, produced under a different name.

In the following January Handel advertised that he proposed to perform at Covent Garden Theatre, during the following Lent, twelve subscription concerts, to include two new oratorios. The first of these was *Semele*, the second being *Joseph and his Brethren*.

A couple of months further on, and Handel was reading a new Jennens libretto, *Belshazzar*, with which he was much taken. In thanking his correspondent, he wrote: 'Be pleased to point out those passages in the *Messiah* which you think require altering. . . .' Jennens was never completely satisfied with Handel's setting of what he no doubt considered *his*

A painting by Richard Wilson (1713-82) of the Foundling Hospital. For the last ten years of his life Handel gave generous donations to the Hospital and was appointed one of the Governors (Foundling Hospital Offices, London)

Messiah! On 20th August Handel finished setting another 'secular oratorio', *Hercules*, and three days later started on Jennens's *Belshazzar*, although he still had only part of it.

He opened a subscription at the Haymarket for twenty-four concerts, beginning in November, and continuing through until Lent, starting with a revival of *Deborah*, plus of course the now inevitable organ concerto. The new oratorios followed with *Hercules* and *Belshazzar* but the season lacked support, and Handel actually made a public appeal for more response in the newspapers, but without much success.

It was an anxious time, for everyone who supported the monarchy; for the Young Pretender, Bonnie Prince Charlie, had landed in Scotland and was eventually to lead his troops as far south as Derby, only to be forced to retreat and to lose his cause at Culloden Moor, defeated by the Duke of Cumberland. With the end of the Jacobite Rebellion, England breathed a sigh of relief and proceeded to make a hero of the Duke of Cumberland. Handel, always a strong supporter of the Hanoverians, hastily threw together an 'Occasional Oratorio' in praise of the victors, which he produced at Covent Garden on 14th February 1746. It was largely a *pasticcio* of his earlier music.

It was about this time that Christoph Gluck was in England to direct some of his 'Pre-Reform' Italian operas at the Opera House, and is reputed to have met Handel and to have discussed with him the vagaries of English musical taste, about which at this particular moment Handel was understandably bitter. However, he was soon to produce one of his greatest successes; this was *Judas Maccabaeus*, to a libretto by the Rev. Thomas Morell, a parson who was to write several libretti for Handel. For Lent 1747 Handel opened with the 'Occasional Oratorio' and had intended to follow it with *Joseph*, but the trial of the Jacobite peer Lord Lovat interrupted everything – the public could think of nothing but trials and executions for the time being. Once the excitement had died down, Handel resumed his interrupted season, eventually producing *Judas Maccabaeus*, which was an instant triumph, as everyone saw it as a compliment to the Duke of Cumberland 'upon his returning victorious from Scotland'. It also attracted a new kind of audience, the wealthy London Jews, who came to hear the Gentiles praise one of their own great national heroes and, having come, remained to support Handel. In the summer he composed two more oratorios, *Alexander Balus* and *Joshua*, and during the autumn the management at the Haymarket mounted a *pasticcio*, *Lucio Vero*, selected from various Handelian operas; and a little later *Rossane* was revived again for the singer Galli's benefit. The next night she sang in the first performance of one of the new oratorios, *Joshua*, and again in *Alexander Balus*. The summer saw him busy with two of his finest masterpieces, *Solomon* (which is a kind of oratorial *festa teatrale*, with very little plot, but a great deal of pomp and splendour), and *Susanna* (which is the nearest thing to a comic oratorio that Handel ever wrote, and is indeed much more amusing than his one so-called comic opera, *Serse*).

In the autumn of 1748 the Peace of Aix-la-Chapelle was signed, bringing to an end the long-drawn-out War of the Austrian Succession. This peace treaty was to have a notable musical consequence in due course, but meanwhile Handel was busy with his usual Lenten oratorios, producing *Susanna* in February and *Solomon* in March 1749. He also revived *Messiah*, which he had not performed since 1743 – which shows how little it had been in demand in London up to that time. But during this oratorio season, his mind must also have been preoccupied with another project. Handel was by now the musical poet laureate of Britain – uncrowned, it is true, but more truly remembered than any of the now forgotten poets who held that office during the reigns of the first two Georges. In celebration of the Peace of Aix-la-Chapelle, it had been agreed to have a grand fireworks display, in the Green Park, to take place in April 1749. Someone or other (not the King, apparently) commissioned Handel to provide 'a martial overture' to accompany the fireworks, and from this came the grandest of all Georgian occasional pieces, the *Musick for the Royal Fireworks*. In addition to this, that summer he composed *Theodora*, which was his favourite among his oratorios; he also wrote incidental music for a play on the subject of Alcestis, by the novelist Smollett, but it was never mounted. Handel used the music later in an English work called *The Choice of Hercules*.

He was in good health now, and seemed to be reaching the golden autumn of his life. He was accepted as the greatest of composers by all and was secure in his financial position. The great burly Handel of the memoirs, with the look of 'his sire the sun', who could be seen in the park, taking his walk from his house in Brook Street, and sometimes 'talking to himself, so loud, that it was not very difficult for those not near him, to hear what he had to say.' Contemporary reports describe Handel at this time of his life, in his great white wig, which nodded quite happily when things went well at rehearsal, but which lost its 'certain nod or vibration' when things went wrong, at which its owner 'began to call names'. Financially he was well enough off to present the Foundling Hospital with an organ for its Chapel. On 1st June 1750 he made his will; he was now 65, which was quite elderly by 18th-century standards, but he lived long enough to make several codicils to it. He felt well enough, too, to travel to Germany; unfortunately on the way home, in Holland, his carriage was overturned and he was 'terribly hurt' but quickly recovered. Back in England, he started to compose his last oratorio, *Jephtha*, but became much troubled with his sight – especially that of his left eye. On 13th February he had to stop composing, but by 23rd February managed

A painting by Canaletto showing a procession of Knights of the Order of the Bath outside Westminster Abbey (Dean and Chapter of Westminster Abbey, London)

to write some more – meanwhile he had to carry on with his new oratorio season, and produced *The Choice of Hercules* in March. He was still playing the organ, apparently, and six weeks later directed *Messiah* at the Foundling, and 'himself play'd a Voluntary on the organ'. By the end of August he had managed to finish *Jephtha*, but with great difficulty. Later, in 1752, he was operated on for cataract, but the operation was only temporarily successful. There was a tantalising return of sight for a few days, but by the end of January he was almost completely blind.

Fresh composition was now difficult for him, but he did manage to adapt some of his earlier works to new words, including an English version of his Italian oratorio *Il trionfo del tempo e del disinganno* as *The Triumph of Time and Truth*, with words by Morell, 'altered from the Italian, with several new Additions'. And each time he revived one of his older oratorios he advertised 'Additions' and 'Alterations'. To what extent Handel himself played the organ in these later years is not exactly known, although Burney spoke of seeing him 'led to the organ . . . at upwards of seventy years of age, and then conducted towards the audience to make his accustomed obeisance . . . a sight so truly afflicting and deplorable to persons of sensibility, as greatly diminished their pleasure in seeing him perform.' The inevitable parallels were drawn between him and his own great hero Samson from Milton's work, who cries, 'O loss of sight, of thee I most complain' and 'Total eclipse, no sun, no moon. All dark within the blaze of noon!' On 6th April, after his last performance of *Messiah*, he had to go to bed. He died on Saturday 14th April, the day after Good Friday, at his house in Brook Street.

PROGRAM NOTES FOR THE RECORD

by ROBERT JACOBSON

Messiah highlights, *Royal Fireworks Music,* *Water Music* highlights

One of Handel's biographers, Sir Newman Flower, rightly noted: 'It is questionable whether any music, composed in England or imported into it, has reached the heart of the people so truly as Handel's.' If he were to be remembered for only a single work it would be his oratorio *Messiah,* which has made Handel a household name. As Paul Henry Lang writes in his exhaustive study of the composer: '*Messiah* is perhaps the only major work about which public sentiment is unanimous. Its freshness, its warmth, its beautifully rounded forms and sculptured melodies offer universal experience to men of all walks of life and all shades of faith. Handel achieved with this work the most widespread critical recognition ever accorded a composer, for among his acclaimers are not only every English-speaking church congregation, small or large, but also Mozart, Haydn, Beethoven, Brahms and every musician who ever tried his hand at choral writing.'

Yet Handel was a prolific composer of music in almost every form known in his day: operas, oratorios, concerti grossi, orchestral suites, masques, church works, anthems, organ concertos, harpsichord music, etc.—a mass of music almost equal to all we know of Bach plus all of Beethoven. Only in this twentieth century has the music world come to know the full range of these works, as musicologists have explored this wealth and prepared editions of many of Handel's compositions to be performed in the manner in which they were originally written. For the public at large, however, Handel is *Messiah,* and it remains an epic creation of its kind. The première and subsequent performances for the benefit of the Foundling Hospital are fully described in the preceding pages.

Messiah's great popularity in London began in 1749 when the composer himself led a benefit performance for the Foundling Hospital, and for the next nine years he conducted the oratorio annually. Since that time, its universal popularity has hardly wavered, for it is music of strength, sincerity, religious passion and meaning, set down with the greatest skill for chorus and soloists. Handel cast it in three parts, the first telling of the prophecy of the Messiah's coming, the second relating the suffering and death of Christ, and the third describing the resurrection of the son of God. Jennens, the compiler of the libretto, sent a text to be printed at the head of the oratorio, summing up its spirit: 'And without controversy, great is the mystery of Godliness; God was manifested in the Flesh, justified by the Spirit, seen of Angels, preached among the Gentiles, gave man belief in the world, and was received up in Glory. In whom are hid all the treasures of wisdom and knowledge.'

London was the setting for the *Water Music* in 1717, when the royal family and members of nobility took part in a royal water-party on barges floating on the River Thames. For this event, Handel created music for a large orchestra of over fifty musicians including horns, oboes, bassoons, flute, trumpets and strings. Music historians question exactly how many pieces Handel wrote for the event, since twenty-two exist in three suites: No. 1 in F major, No. 2 in D major and No. 3 in G major. It was very possible that he composed perhaps two-thirds of them for this royal evening, adding others later for similar occasions. After all, in those days such music was written and used for special events as needed. The *Allegro* is a lively dance, the Air a melodious English-type folksong, the Bourrée and Hornpipe two more jaunty dances that typify the many sections that make up the *Water Music.*

The *Royal Fireworks Music* came much later, in 1749. The occasion was the peace treaty signed at Aix-la-Chapelle, in 1748, to end the conflict between France and England. The celebration was set for Green Park, London, on April 27, 1749. These festivities—marred when the fireworks set off a blaze which completely destroyed the structure especially built for the event—were launched by an Overture which, in Handel's original orchestration, required 24 oboes, 12 bassoons, 9 trumpets, 9 horns, one contrabassoon, three pairs of timpani and a kind of cornet known as a 'serpent horn.' There followed a royal salute from 101 brass cannon and various pieces by Handel, all originally scored for winds and a large force of strings, bringing the number of original players to well over 100. Fortunately, the magnificent ceremonial music was completed before the fire caused complete pandemonium. The *Royal Fireworks Music* was next heard on May 27, 1749, played by a much smaller band in the chapel of the Foundling Hospital during a benefit attended by the Prince of Wales. Again, an introductory Overture is followed by a series of dance rhythms, including a bourrée, a Siciliana called 'La Paix' (The Peace), a brilliant 'Le Réjouissance' and ends with two minuets—all conveying a spirit of celebration and rejoicing. As biographer Herbert Weinstock has said of Handel, his is 'one of the most majestic, tender and human voices ever lifted in praise of life, of love, of beauty and of the art of music.'

Printed in the United States of America

His Life and Times 1872-1897 (Part 2)

PROGRAM NOTES FOR THE VIOLIN CONCERTO IN D MAJOR AND HUNGARIAN DANCES
By Robert Jacobson

FUNK & WAGNALLS, INC.
NEW YORK, NEW YORK

A Spate of Composition: Life 1872-81

The death of his father in February 1872 broke another big link between Brahms and his native city of Hamburg. He loved his stepmother dearly, and continued to send her affectionate letters and generous gifts of money for the rest of his life. But Brahms could never quite forget his disappointment ten years earlier when the conductorship of the Hamburg Philharmonic had been offered to someone else. And now, without his father, he felt no further constraint about fixing his roots in Viennese soil – forever.

When offered the conductorship of Vienna's famous Gesellschaft der Musikfreunde as from the autumn of 1872, characteristically he worried a bit about possible loss of freedom, but it did not take him long to accept. The salary was generous, and he was allowed a free hand in programme-building and the selection of artists. His first step was to strengthen the orchestra, bringing it up to a hundred players and replacing all amateurs by professionals. For the choir of three hundred he insisted on more rehearsal time, since the works he chose were frequently more demanding than anything previously attempted. He is known to have included Beethoven's Mass in D and Bach's *St Matthew Passion*, besides exploring still further back into the 17th century. His own carefully marked scores revealed the thoroughness with which he considered every point of interpretation, and he won respect among scholars for his concern for period style – such as in spurning popular re-orchestrations and insisting on the use of a keyboard instrument for the continuo in the accompaniment of recitative. But after three seasons he resigned. A conductor's job, however congenial, kept him away from composition, and prevented him from packing his bags and disappearing into the country whenever the impulse to escape from the public eye became overpowering. When a few years later he was approached in turn by Düsseldorf and Leipzig to take charge of municipal music – as well as the Lower Rhine Festival for the former and to become Music Director of the Thomasschule in the latter – he was adamant in his refusal in spite of the fact that these posts had once been occupied by his idols Schumann and Bach respectively.

But right as he was to discard the Vienna job when he did, his three years at close quarters with the instruments of an orchestra were far more valuable to him than he ever realised at the time. Having previously felt more at ease in practically every other genre, it was from about 1873, having just turned forty, that he plunged headlong into a great spate of orchestral composition. The Haydn Variations came first. Still more significantly, by 1875 he was deep in a C minor symphony, a work he had conceived in his early twenties but never previously felt assured enough to bring to fruition. After the Symphony's successful première in Carlsruhe under Dessoff on 4th November 1876 (and never had any composer's first symphony been awaited more impatiently by critical wolves ready to pounce), he quickly followed it up with the Second Symphony in D major

(1877), then the Violin Concerto introduced by Joachim (1878), followed by the *Academic Festival Overture* and the *Tragic Overture* (1880) written for Breslau in acknowledgement of his honorary degree, and the second and last Piano Concerto in B flat (1881), whose solo part he was still able to play himself at the première in spite of a keyboard technique growing a bit rusty for want of practise time. All these works reached the world almost as soon as the ink was dry, for Brahms, in spite of the opposition of the avant-garde, had by now a very large following of his own. Thanks, moreover, to the splendid business acumen of his publisher, Simrock, he was also beginning to grow prosperous as well as famous.

His working life gradually settled into its own routine. Every year brought its quota of professional tours, sometimes as conductor, sometimes as pianist – either alone or with Joachim, such as when in the early months of 1879 they went off to Hungary and in 1880 to Poland. In Switzerland and Holland Brahms was always assured of a particularly warm welcome, and interest in his activities was also developing from as far afield as England. In 1876 he was offered an honorary degree by Cambridge University and invited to come in person to receive it, but at the last moment he took fright at so extended a journey into the unknown, and in fact never did cross the Channel – not even when London's revered Philharmonic Society offered him its Gold Medal the following year – in spite of the fact that Clara Schumann, Joachim and several other of his friends and associates were frequent visitors to England.

Increasingly, in fact, Brahms had begun to count on those periods when he could turn his back on public life and escape to the country to compose, his whereabouts known only to his closest friends. As soon as the fine weather came he would leave Vienna for some chosen hideout, where ideas that had come to him during the winter could be worked out in simple, harmonious, rural surroundings. He was not given to wearing his heart on his sleeve, or sharing his innermost experiences with the outside world, but it is clear that the greater part of his spiritual nourishment came from these periods of communion with mountains, lakes, valleys and villages. He took a lot of trouble in finding the right spot. In 1873 it was Tutzing, near Munich, on the Starnbergersee, where he could enthuse about the colour of the lake – even when black in a 'gorgeous thunderstorm' – against the background of snow-covered mountains. In 1874 it was Rüschlikon, by the lake of Zurich, where his pleasure also embraced the freshwater fish and the lakeside wines. In 1875 Clara Schumann found him uncommonly happy at Ziegelhausen, near Heidelberg, and in 1876, just for once, he tried the sea – at Sassnitz, on the island of Rügen, in the Baltic. In 1877 he discovered Pörtschach, on the Wörthersee, in Carinthia, and found it sympathetic enough to return for three consecutive years – the Second Symphony in D and the Violin Concerto are outstandingly eloquent tributes to its assuaging, lyrical beauty. In 1880 he changed to Ischl, which had the advantage of being a little nearer Vienna, and where he found several congenial friends in residence, including Johann Strauss, the waltz king. He was a frequent visitor at Strauss's villa, for Brahms admired Strauss as much as Strauss admired him. A new window on the world had also opened for him in 1878 when he went for the first time on a tour of Italy. Delighting in its architecture and art as much as its natural scenery, he wrote enthusiastically to Clara Schumann, begging her to make herself free in the spring of the following year so that they could share all these new discoveries.

Clara was still the person to whom he felt nearest, and with whom he remained most closely in touch – even if only by letter, for both were constantly on the move. But no opportunity was ever lost to spend time together, sometimes at Clara's house near Baden-Baden, or wherever their paths could most easily be made to cross. On one of her birthdays, for instance, they managed to meet at Berchtesgaden, where in spite of appallingly wet weather they spent the happiest day playing through all his latest scores. Her criticism was always invited on practically every note he ever wrote. But there were still difficult passages in the friendship, as ever, for Brahms lacked suavity and tact, just as Clara lacked humour. A misunderstanding over programme-building for a small festival in Bonn in 1872 to raise funds for a monument over Schumann's tomb prompted a heart-felt cry from Clara in her diary: 'What a splendid conductor Joachim proved himself! Johannes Brahms was there too, but not in the best of tempers, which distressed me as he was so much to my Robert.' In May 1880, at the unveiling of the monument, Brahms was in a better mood, and won warm praise from Clara for his conducting of Schumann's E flat Symphony and *Requiem for Mignon*. But this time his piano playing no longer satisfied her: 'Unfortunately the end, with the E flat major quartet, was disappointing. Brahms was not at his best . . . so that I felt as if I were sitting on thorns and so did Joachim, who kept on casting despairing glances at me . . . I was deeply distressed that I had not undertaken the quartet myself.'

Other feminine friendships, because less involved, were smoother. Besides keeping up with several of the attractive ladies for whom he had written songs, particularly Luise Dustmann, he made the acquaintance of a vigorous young hunting, riding and fishing composition student from England called Ethel Smyth, later to become a noted composer and a passionate champion of women's rights. He was still more interested in the talent of a young violinist called Marie Soldat, with whom he even went so far as to give a concert in Pörtschach besides celebrating on the roundabouts and swings of Vienna's Prater with her after a superb performance of his Violin Concerto.

The most important of his new friendships was nevertheless with a former pupil, Elisabeth von Herzogenberg. Before her marriage to Heinrich von Herzogenberg, then a respected Leipzig composer and conductor, Brahms had fought shy of her charms – even to the extent of declining to give her any more lessons. But once danger was past, both she and her husband became part of his personal

inner circle. The good-looking Elisabeth, with her radiant light-heartedness as well as deep musical intelligence, perhaps succeeded better than anyone in dealing with Brahms's moods. Never with her – any more than with children, who invariably adored him – could he for long hide the warm, susceptible nature which since 1878 he had attempted to conceal from the rest of the world under a large, bushy beard.

The only serious cloud on the horizon, at this time of rich fulfilment, was his estrangement from Joachim at the end of the decade. Their friendship, close as it was, had not been without its strains over the past twenty-seven or so years. Brahms was often bothered by Joachim's Hungarian emotional excitability, his hypersensitivity and 'scenes evoked by imaginary causes' – to such an extent that he had always avoided living in the same town. And now, when the great violinist's marriage was on the point of collapse as a result of totally unprovoked jealousy, Brahms openly sided with Joachim's wife, the singer Amalie Weiss, for whom he had written his Alto Rhapsody, op.53. When Brahms's spontaneous letter of sympathy to Amalie, referring to those specific aspects of Joachim's character he deplored, was produced in the divorce court (to Brahms's chagrin), Joachim felt betrayed. Immediately he ended all contact between them. The breach was not repaired until Brahms composed his Double Concerto for Joachim and the cellist of the Joachim Quartet. But that was in 1887, and the full story must wait.

Brahms photographed at Gmunden with the daughters of one of his friends, Miller Aichholz (Austrian National Library)

3

Reconciliation with Joachim: Life 1882-92

The great violinist, Joachim, was bitterly hurt when Brahms openly sided with his wife at the time of their divorce, hurt enough to break off a close friendship which had lasted, in spite of temporary strains, since their first meeting in 1853. Brahms, by no means happy about the course of events either, managed to find quite a lot of consolation in the professional co-operation and company of Hans von Bülow, himself smarting after his wife, Cosima, had deserted him for Wagner. Once a passionate champion of the music of Wagner and all the New German School (for Cosima was a daughter of Liszt), Bülow was now very ready to transfer his allegiance to Brahms, and quickly put the resources of his Meiningen Orchestra at Brahms's disposal for trying out any new work. Standards there were exceptionally high owing to Bülow's then revolutionary insistence on sectional rehearsal. He also liked to take the orchestra on tour – a procedure far less common in those days than now. Brahms's B flat Piano Concerto was the first of his works to reach a wider public more quickly than before in the course of one of Bülow's tours (his Third and Fourth Symphonies were shortly to benefit in the same way), though Clara, amongst others, raised a critical eyebrow at Brahms's personal participation in these travels as pianist or conductor. 'Not worthy of his high position as a creative artist' she confided to her diary, though she subsequently expressed pleasure in the triumphs he enjoyed as a result. His association with the orchestra brought him into contact with Duke Georg II of Meiningen

Brahms's house on the lake of Thun in Switzerland,where the composer went in the years 1886-88 (Society of the Friends of Music, Vienna)

and his wife, both discriminating music lovers, who not only quickly put him at his ease as guest at their Residenz, but knowing of his love of lakes and mountains and Italy, also lent him their villa by Lake Como on one occasion. Brahms in his turn dedicated his *Gesang der Parzen* for chorus and orchestra (1882) to the Duke.

As always his new works invariably came to full fruition during his periods of escape from Vienna into the country, and the selection of each year's hide-out was one of his annual major decisions. Ischl had become a great favourite: it was not too far away, and many good friends were to be found there, including the waltz king, Johann Strauss, with whom Brahms was on the most cordial terms. But to the dismay of half the population, Ischl was abandoned in 1883 for Wiesbaden. The explanation was not only that he had got tired of Ischl's rain: more significantly, he had recently met a delightful young contralto called Hermine Spies, and wanted her company. As usual, nothing came of the affair save another outpouring of wonderful song, but the friendship generated a lot of happiness on both sides without going deep enough to cause any heartbreak, or embarrassment, when she eventually announced her engagement to someone else. It was at Wiesbaden that Brahms completed his Third Symphony (the première took place under Hans Richter in Vienna on 2nd December 1883), but the following two summers he was back again in the Austrian mountains, this time at Mürzuschlag, in Styria, busily occupied with a Fourth Symphony in E minor. The première of this went to Bülow at Meiningen in October 1885, who then took the symphony – with its composer as conductor – on a tour extending as far as Holland. Trouble blew up en route, for with characteristic thoughtlessness Brahms accepted an invitation to conduct the symphony with the Frankfurt orchestra just a few days before the Meiningen orchestra was due to play it in that city. But Brahms himself eventually poured balm on Bülow's wound by making it quite clear how much he valued their friendship.

From 1886 to 1888, Brahms chose a spot near Thun, on the Swiss lake of that name, as his summer hide-out. His rooms permitted him magnificent views of the Eiger, Jungfrau and neighbouring peaks of the Bernese Oberland; he had many congenial friends, including the Swiss poet, Joseph V. Widmann, within easy reach, his delightful Hermine paid him a holiday visit, and his content overflowed in a spate of new compositions – significantly including two more Sonatas for violin and piano and the Double Concerto for violin and cello. Of all the eulogies which his Fourth Symphony had inspired, none gave him greater pleasure than those of his old friend, Joachim. At this moment he was overwhelmed with a desire for reconciliation — and realised that the best possible way of bringing it about was by writing music for Joachim to play. By September 1887, both Joachim and the cellist of his quartet, Robert Hausmann, were involved in rehearsals of the Double Concerto, prompting Clara's diary observation:

'This concerto is a work of reconciliation – Joachim and Brahms have spoken to each other again for the first time for years.' Its première in Cologne in October 1887 sealed their friendship anew – never, perhaps, quite as spontaneous as of old, but nevertheless without major disturbances in the years that remained.

No-one rejoiced in the reconciliation more than Clara, still devoted to her Johannes in spite of intermittent laments in her diary that this or that of their sporadic meetings seemed difficult or superficial. Now only a year or so off seventy, she naturally felt a few pangs when Brahms was engrossed with some new singer or other – it was not long before Hermine Spies was followed by Alice Barbi – or when the gay, intelligent and beautiful Elisabeth von Herzogenberg appeared to be a closer confidant, or a more eagerly sought after critic of his new works than she was. In her diminishing energy it was not even always easy to take comfort in some of his uninhibited Italian effusions – and no year was complete for Brahms without his spring-time recourse to Italy's sunshine, wine and architectural and natural splendour in the company of one or two congenial male friends – such as 'All the time I have been in this glorious Italy I have been thinking of and longing for no-one so much as you. How I wished that you still had strength enough to enjoy this, as you have to enjoy your art. I know no-one else who would appreciate it all so much so unreservedly – if your physical strength did not prevent it.' In 1888 he tried to show his affection more practically by sending her a gift of money to ease the financial responsibilities she was facing through the frequent ill-health of her children – and grandchildren – a gift only accepted at his second attempt. The next few years brought a few professional misunderstandings which for a while threatened a total breakdown of their relations. Clara was incensed by Brahms's publication of the first version of her husband's First Symphony even though he had written to tell her why he thought it preferable to the more thickly scored revised version. He in his turn was bitterly hurt when Breitkopf published a complete edition of Schumann, edited by Clara, without the manuscripts he himself had salvaged as worthy of inclusion, such as five variations which Schumann had discarded from the Symphonic Studies. However, this was put right when Clara decided on a supplementary volume. And whatever their personal difficulties, her belief in his genius was rock-like. 'I once more thanked heaven for sending so strong and healthy a genius into the world in the midst of the Wagner mania, one who counteracts it for the moment and who must soon conquer it entirely. Mankind must in the long run regain its health through the true and great works which Brahms produces as he advances along the path marked out by his predecessors,' was her affirmation in her diary in January 1889.

1889 was also memorable for certain official marks of recognition which not even Brahms, much as he disliked official pomp and ceremony, could wholly discount. He was awarded the Order of Leopold by the Austrian Emperor. More significant still, he was awarded the Honorary Freedom of his native city of Hamburg. Ever since 1862 he had harboured a secret resentment against Hamburg for not making him conductor of its Philharmonic Orchestra. And even though he now liked to pretend that the gesture had

come too late, he was pleased all the same – enough to go to Hamburg that September for its Industrial and Commercial Exhibition, to dedicate a new choral work, *Fest und Gedenksprüche*, to the Burgomaster, and allow Hamburg's Cecilia Society to give its première.

In Vienna, a splendid new housekeeper called Frau Truxa (the widow of a writer) had solved all his domestic problems. He grew very attached to her two children, and at Christmas, a time of special celebration, always insisted on a tree for them in his library. His main meals he nevertheless liked to take in a restaurant called 'The Red Hedgehog', where they were only too pleased to humour him (for his patronage was by now a first class recommendation) by cooking his favourite dishes and laying in a large stock of his favourite wine. As President of the Wiener Tonkünstlerverein (since the end of 1886) he came into contact with all the city's up and coming younger musicians, and particularly enjoyed walking with them in the Wienerwald – if they could keep up with his own vigorous gait. When he needed erotic pleasure, well, the city had plenty of that to offer him too – for a price, to the occasional embarrassment of his more respectable friends.

For composing, however, he still needed the country. There was much rejoicing in Ischl when in 1889 he decided to return there: though no-one could know it at the time, it was to remain his choice for all the summers left to him. By now only a few years off sixty, he no longer felt driven to plunge anew into turbulent symphonic waters. Miniatures for the keyboard and intimate chamber works seemed more in tune with his growing autumnal nostalgia. 1890 saw the completion of a second String Quintet – in G. In 1891, after a spring visit to Meiningen, his imagination was suddenly fired anew by the playing of the orchestra's first clarinettist,

5

Richard Mühlfeld, for whom he wrote a Clarinet Trio and Clarinet Quintet in quick succession. Elisabeth von Herzogenberg, by now showing serious symptoms of a heart disease, probably rejoiced more than anyone at this turn of events, for as early as 1882 she had sung Mühlfeld's praises in a letter to Brahms. Could the aching nostalgia of the Clarinet Quintet have been inspired by a strange kind of premonition? For by January 1892, Elisabeth was dead. Not easily given to outward expressions of verbal emotion, Brahms was sufficiently moved to write to Heinrich von Herzogenberg 'You know how unutterably I myself suffer by the loss of your beloved wife, and can gauge accordingly my emotions in thinking of you, who were associated with her by the closest possible human ties. As soon as you feel at all inclined to think of yourself and others, let me know how you are, and how and where you intend to carry on your own life. It would do me so much good just to sit beside you quietly, press your hand, and share your thoughts of the dear marvellous woman.'

Shortly afterwards Brahms's sister died – and some other close friends were soon to follow. The shadows had begun to fall. . . .

A photograph of Brahms with a friend at Gmunden (Society of the Friends of Music, Vienna)

The new Burgtheater, Vienna, photographed in 1895 (Austrian National Library, Vienna)

The Last Years: Life 1893-97

On 7th May 1893 Brahms was sixty. Fearing official ceremonies in Vienna, he designed his eighth spring tour of Italy to last a little longer than usual so as to include Genoa, Pisa, Rome and Naples before he crossed to Sicily for Palermo, Girgenti, Catania, Syracuse, Taormina and Messina. Had he realized that he was destined never to return to this southern sunshine he loved so well, no doubt the journey would have been extended further still As he invariably outdid all his friends – and he had a select group of stalwarts at his side – in zest for exploring, he was sufficiently roused to indignant amusement on receiving a *seventieth* birthday congratulatory telegram from the Vienna Conservatoire to send it back marked 'Not accepted: I protest!'

After returning at leisure via Switzerland, Brahms moved on to Ischl for the summer, taking life easily by restricting composition to arrangements of German folksongs and yet more miniatures for the piano, i.e. the Six Pieces op. 118 and four Pieces op. 119 in succession to the Fantasias op. 116 and Three Intermezzi op. 117 of the previous summer. Part of his reason for reverting to the piano was to bring solace to Clara Schumann in her declining health. She was now well into her seventies, and suffering much physical and mental discomfort, with a strange droning in her ears. But as she confided to her diary, 'How grateful I am to him [Brahms] for the comfort which he gives me in the midst of my sorrow! How fortified I always feel when I have been able to forget myself for a short half-hour! . . . It really is marvellous how things pour from him, and how each new thought is full of grandeur,

depth and imagination. It is wonderful how he combines passion and tenderness in the smallest of spaces.' Many of these miniatures, in their tender, autumnal nostalgia, reflect Brahms's own state of mind at the time, and his ever-increasing awareness of life's transience. Clara was ageing: others close to him were dying. Elisabeth von Herzogenberg, his sister Elise, his singer friend Hermine Spies all died between 1892-93. 1894 was to rob him of staunch masculine associates like the historian Spitta, the surgeon Billroth, and the conductor Hans von Bülow.

But Richard Mühlfeld, the great Meiningen clarinettist, was still in his prime, and while at Ischl in 1894 Brahms wrote two more works for him, the Sonatas in F minor and E flat major (op. 120 nos. 1 and 2), which they played a lot together, especially in 1895, when several places honoured Brahms with small festivals of his music, starting with Leipzig in January. At Meiningen he shared the programmes with Bach and Beethoven as proof of where he stood in this town's estimation, while at Zurich there were similar testimonies to his place amongst the immortals. Although Brahms had always doggedly refused to visit England, he was gratified to learn that there, too, his music had taken root. A rich English admirer even left him £1,000 in his will as an expression of gratitude, a sum which Brahms, with characteristic generosity, immediately put to charitable musical use. He also received an offer of the conductorship of the Philharmonic Orchestra in his own home town of Hamburg – the recognition he had so ardently desired as a youth of twenty-nine. Now, his reply could only be a bittersweet 'too late'.

7

A photograph taken
on 15th June 1896 on
the occasion of the
silver wedding
anniversary of
Brahms's friend
Maria Fellinger
(Society of the
Friends of Music,
Vienna)

On his way home from Meiningen in October 1895 Brahms paid a brief visit to Frankfurt to call on Clara Schumann, and was shocked to find her so patently weakening. When in March 1896 she had a stroke, it became clear to all her friends – as also to Clara herself – that the end could not be far off. In his profound sorrow, Brahms turned to music, and by his birthday on 7th May he had completed the *Vier ernste Gesänge*, with words (drawn from both Old and New Testaments) veering from deep pessimism (nos. 1 and 2) towards the blessedness of death's release (no.3) and the all-conquering power of love (no.4). 'Who would not hope to pass away to the sound of such rich, bittersweet, yearning harmonies' wrote Heinrich von Herzogenberg of the third song in a letter to Brahms. But Clara was not granted that last solace: by 20th May she was dead. Brahms, informed by telegram at Ischl, set off for the funeral service at Frankfurt but, inadvertently getting on the wrong train in his distress, arrived too late. Immediately he went on to Bonn, where Clara's body was to rest alongside that of her husband, and arrived just in time to scatter earth on the coffin of his oldest, closest and dearest friend. But the forty hours of travelling, coupled with his mental anguish, took their toll. Back in Ischl his strained appearance caused many a raised eyebrow as he again turned to composition as an outlet for his grief, this time a set of eleven intimate Chorale Preludes for organ – of which the closing one had the significant title 'O Welt, ich muss dich lassen' (Oh world, I must leave you).

It was the last music he was ever to write. Soon realising that things other than weariness and sorrow were respons-

ible for how he looked, friends pressed him to summon the Ischl doctor, and this time, notwithstanding a life-long contempt of everything connected with illness, Brahms allowed himself to be persuaded. Jaundice was the immediate verdict, and he was sent off to Carlsbad for a course of its remedial salts and waters. When a Viennese specialist was called in, the diagnosis was much more serious, though naturally Brahms himself was not told the worst – that, like his father before him, he was suffering from cancer.

He was back in Vienna by early October, and surrounded by kind friends who did everything in their power to make life easy for him, he stoically tried to pretend that little was wrong. On 2nd January 1897 he attended a performance of his G major String Quintet by Joachim's team, and on 7th March heard his Fourth Symphony conducted by Richter – on both occasions enjoying a rapturous reception from the audience. On 13th March he struggled out for the première of a new operetta by his old friend, Johann Strauss, and even a few days after that listened to chamber music in a friend's house. But on 24th March he confessed to Joachim 'I am going downhill; every word spoken or written is a strain', and by 26th March, with no more strength left to fight, he was driven to bed. In another week, he was dead. With his hatred of official ceremony, and his lack of belief in a world beyond this one, he himself might well have chosen Mozart's fate – to sink, unsung, into a pauper's grave. But he was given a memorable funeral, he was mourned not only in Vienna, but by the entire musical world, and through the order and beauty of his music has now entered into unchallengeable and indestructible immortality.

Brahms and the Schumanns

When, in the course of his wanderings in 1853, Brahms was pressed by Joachim and others to go and call on the Schumanns in Düsseldorf, he was extremely reluctant. He could not forget that three years before, when Schumann and Clara were visiting Hamburg, he (then only seventeen) had dared to send them a parcel of his manuscripts which they had returned unopened.

But in 1853 he did eventually pluck up courage to knock at their door, and a visit that might have ended after a few hours in fact lasted just over a month. Recognising Brahms as a musician after his own heart, whose Romanticism had not killed respect for Classical principles, Robert Schumann could not keep silent. After nearly ten years of absence from the pages of the *Neue Zeitschrift für Musik* he took up his pen again to proclaim Brahms's genius to the world in the article he called 'New Paths'. Not content with that, he sent him to Leipzig armed with introduction to Breitkopf & Härtel and other leading publishers. Brahms, shy and diffident, was keenly aware that such enthusiasm would win him as many enemies as friends. All the same, he was profoundly grateful, and not least for what he had experienced in the Schumanns' own home – simple family life with the children, like-minded friends, long evenings of music-making. When, after only one further brief meeting in Hanover early in 1854, Brahms heard of Schumann's mental breakdown and attempted suicide in the Rhine, he was totally shattered. His only wish was to return to Düsseldorf just as quickly as possible to see how he could help.

Almost immediately after he arrived, Schumann was taken to the private asylum of Endenich, where Brahms was one of the very few people allowed to visit him. Clara herself was not permitted and, to support her children, was accepting as many concert engagements as possible – at this time she gave a great number of sonata recitals with Joachim. But for comfort in her heartbreak, it was always to Brahms that she turned. Young and impressionable, he was soon deeply in love with her, in spite of the fourteen years' difference in their ages.

Yet, absolutely loyal to the absent Schumann, Brahms wrestled continuously with his feelings. He tried to express his devotion only through acts of kindness to Clara, to Robert, and not least to their children – taking infinite care over choosing Christmas presents for them and hoping against hope that they might share his own child-like pleasure in tin soldiers. The full impact of the tragedy – Robert's, Clara's and his own – can only be fully appreciated through the music he sketched at this time, although much of it did not immediately reach the world. The C minor Piano Quartet, conceived at this time, drew some revealing observations from him when it was eventually prepared for publication after twenty years. To Simrock he wrote, 'You might put a portrait on the title-page! A head with a pistol in front of it. Now you'll have some idea of the music. I will send you my photograph for that purpose! Can you also have a blue dress-coat, yellow pantaloons and topboots, as

The frontispiece of Brahms's Sonata in F sharp minor for piano, op.2, dedicated to Clara Schumann (Verdi Conservatoire Library, Milan)

Clara Schumann in 1838 (Schumannhaus, Zwickau)

you seem to like colour printing?' The reference is to Goethe's *Werther:* Brahms saw himself in the title role, with Clara playing the part of Charlotte.

On 29th July 1856 Robert Schumann died. Brahms (now twenty-three), his sister Elise, Clara (almost thirty-seven) and two of her sons set out on their Swiss tour. What questions were faced on that journey will never be known. By the time they returned an understanding had been reached; they subsequently went their several ways.

But, in her lifelong devotion to Robert's memory, Clara never had a closer friend than Brahms. He, in his turn, though constantly attracted by other women, never married. In the summer of 1858, spent at Göttingen, all his friends expected him to announce his engagement to the young Agathe von Siebold, who would have gone to the end of the world with him. Clara, also in the party, was human enough to be hurt by his behaviour. The following year Brahms renounced Agathe. His explanation was complex: he valued his freedom, he did not want her pity at a moment when Leipzig was hissing his D minor Piano Concerto. But could there have been some strange, secret loyalty to Clara that at the eleventh hour, at this moment as throughout his life, always prevented him from taking the final step that would have severed a precious link?

As the years passed, Clara's own attitude grew more understanding. By the autumn of 1869, when she was fifty,

The printed frontispiece of a set of Variations on a theme by Schumann, op.23, for piano duet, with a dedication to Schumann's daughter Julie (Verdi Conservatoire Library, Milan)

she could make compassionate comments in her diary about Brahms's affection for her daughter, Julie – and his obvious distress when Julie announced her engagement to another. It was at this time that Brahms wrote his Alto Rhapsody.

From such happenings and many other specific references in Clara's diary to occasions when Brahms had been notably genial and easy, it is plain that, superficially at any rate, Brahms was not the easiest of friends as he grew older. Having been deeply seared by life at an early age, he all too frequently hid his heart – longing both to give and receive love – under a facade of cynical brusqueness. Clara, on the other hand, lacked the lightheartedness and humour with which several other women succeeded in dispelling his storm clouds. Yet, however much they remonstrated with each other – and perhaps not least over the matter of counting their blessings – their destinies were irrevocably linked. Clara's opinion was sought on practically every new composition. Sometimes (but not often) her comments were not to his liking, prompting a rejoinder to which she in her turn would retort: 'You are a regular good-for-nothing: first one is to say all that one thinks, then if one does, one gets a rap over the knuckles.' She, of course, was no less tetchy if the trials of her life, particularly on the platform, drew less than the expected sympathy from him: she was indignant when in 1868 he suggested she should give up her public career. But, characteristically, tension was quickly relaxed. 'Life is a wild polyphony, but a good woman like you, can often bring some exquisite resolution of its discords,' was Brahms's final riposte.

In 1888, as Clara approached her seventieth birthday, Brahms sent her practical help in the form of a considerable sum of money, a commodity he felt he had too much of, in view of her responsibilities towards her children, in their frequent ill-health, and grandchildren. Only at the second attempt did she accept, reluctantly, for fear of hurting him. Far closer to her heart lay a sentence he had written to her at a time of deep trouble exactly twenty years after Robert's breakdown: 'Let this deep love of mine be a comfort to you; for I love you more than myself, more than anybody or anything on earth.'

On 26th March 1896 Clara Schumann had a slight stroke, from which she recovered only to have a second more severe one on the night of 16th May. By 20th May she was dead. At once Brahms set off on the lengthy overnight journey to Frankfurt but, missing his connection, arrived too late for the funeral service. On he went to Bonn, and after thirty-six hours of continuous travel arrived just in time to pay homage as the coffin was laid into the earth alongside Robert Schumann. The strain took its toll on his own precarious state of health: in less than a year he too was dead.

His own words, written to Joachim shortly before Clara's death, can serve as epitaph to a legendary friendship: 'We can no longer be horrified at the thought of losing her – not even I, lonely as I am, with all too few ties to bind me to the world. And after she has left us, will not our faces light up with joy whenever we think of her? The wonderful woman in whom we have delighted throughout a long life, with ever-increasing love and admiration. That is the only way we should mourn her.'

PROGRAM NOTES FOR THE RECORD

by ROBERT JACOBSON

The Violin Concerto

Like Ludwig van Beethoven, Johannes Brahms composed only one violin concerto. Commentator Hubert Foss finds that of all the large-scale works by Brahms this is the one which shows the 'reconciling of the two opposite sides of his creative mind—the lyrical and the constructive: Brahms the song-writer and Brahms the symphonist. For this Concerto is a song for the violin on a symphonic scale—a lyrical outpouring which nevertheless exercises to the full his great powers of inventive development. The substance of it is, throughout, the growth of the themes; they blossom before us like opening flowers in a richly stocked garden.'

Most Romantic violin concertos offered a strong element of pure virtuoso show. Brahms, like his friends Robert and Clara Schumann, looked down on such self-centred display and shallowness, though he never hesitated to write music that was difficult to play, either for the violin or the piano; yet it was never a case of fireworks for their own sake. Despite the undeniable technical hurdles posed in his Violin Concerto, Brahms did consult with his friend the famed violinist Joseph Joachim in writing it. In August 1878 he sent Joachim a copy of the violin part for his criticism. With his characteristic humility, the composer wrote: 'It was my intention, of course, that you should correct it, not sparing the quality of the composition, and that if you thought it not worth-while scoring, you should say so. I shall be satisfied if you mark those parts which are difficult, awkward or impossible to play.' Joachim then took great pains to go over the solo part, pointing out any technical details he felt should be changed. Brahms listened solemnly and then, despite his typical humility, changed almost nothing but bow markings and fingering. Still, we know from Joachim's preface to his edition of the Concerto that he thought very highly of it. The work was dedicated to Joachim, who was soloist for the first performance at a Gewandhaus concert in Leipzig on New Year's Day of 1879, with Brahms himself conducting.

One critic wrote of the première: 'As to the reception, the first movement was too new to be distinctly appreciated by the audience, the second made considerable way, the last aroused enthusiasm.' This pattern of audience reaction is entirely comprehensible, for the first movement is by far the longest and most complex, while the third is an exciting gypsy melody that impresses with its breathtaking virtuosity—and no doubt in the hands of the Hungarian Joachim it was all the more striking.

Because of the inordinate difficulties it posed for the soloist, the Concerto was initially regarded with some disdain. Conductor Hans von Bülow summed up this attitude most graphically by remarking that Max Bruch, a contemporary of Brahms, had written concertos *for* the violin and Brahms instead had written one *against* the violin. The violinist Bronislaw Huberman later modified this claim by stating that it is 'a concerto *for* violin *against* orchestra—and the violin wins!'

Brahms originally conceived his Violin Concerto in four movements, as he did his Second Piano Concerto. But a scherzo movement was discarded, and Max Kalbeck, an early biographer of Brahms, believed that this section probably found its way into the Piano Concerto No. 2. The composer also revised the original slow movement. 'The middle movements have gone,' he wrote, 'and of course they were the best! But I have written a poor adagio for it.' With this self-deprecation, Brahms was describing one of his warmest, most profound slow movements. Warmth, expansiveness and robustness characterise the harmonies, melodies and rhythms of this work—perhaps the result of the idyllic surroundings in which it was created, at Pörtschach on the Wörthersee, in the southern Austrian Alps, where Brahms spent the summer of 1878. Commentators often link the Concerto with the Second Symphony of the same period, both in D major. Both are also sunny works abounding in melodic simplicity and charm, qualities balanced in the Concerto by a rugged grandeur and violinistic virtuosity.

The programme for a concert by Brahms in 1896 (Gmunden Museum)

The Concerto in D major opens with a traditional introduction by the orchestra, announcing the warm yet sober first movement (*Allegro non troppo*). The first theme, begun with bassoons, horns and lower strings, is extended by the oboe with string accompaniment. Next this is taken up by full orchestra, after which the second theme appears in the oboe, followed by a figure in the flute, clarinet and bassoon. Finally, with a flourish and great bravura, the solo violin makes its entry in a dizzying preamble. It then takes up the opening theme with fierceness that eventually diminishes to a point at which this motive takes on a serenity as it soars high over the orchestra. In the development of this material, the violin brings in a new theme, which then passes to the orchestra while the soloist takes up a delicate counter-subject. The violin returns to its entrance melody and then proceeds to an extended solo cadenza, and the movement ends in a sudden burst of energy. Critic Lawrence Gilman writes: 'The caressing and delicate weaving of the solo instrument about the melodic outlines of the song themes in the orchestra is unforgettable.'

The second movement (*Adagio*) opens with a serene main theme by the oboe, said to be based on a Bohemian folk-song. It is prolonged and confined at first entirely to the woodwinds. Then the violin enters with an extensive variation on this theme, plus a contrasting episode that is briefly expanded, leading to a varied restatement of the first part of this section. The solo violin is given a profusion of delicate tracery and imaginative ornamentation of the main melodic material. Gilman notes: 'Perhaps not since Chopin have the possibilities of decorative figuration developed so rich a yield of poetic loveliness as in this Concerto. Brahms is here ornamental without ornateness, florid without excess; these arabesques have the dignity and fervour of pure lyric speech.'

The violin states the Hungarian-tinged principal theme at the outset of the Finale (*Allegro giocoso ma non troppo vivace*). This is repeated by the orchestra and then embellished by soloist and orchestra. The violin—with double stops and other brilliant effects—has two episodic themes that are then treated by the orchestra. These ideas are repeated and developed until the violinist breaks out in an accompanied cadenza. The main theme is quickened, leading to a breathless virtuoso conclusion.

Hungarian Dances

Nos. 17, 19 and 21 for orchestra

The spirited Finale of the Violin Concerto and Brahms's sets of Hungarian Dances are close kin, since both draw upon the then fashionable gypsy music of Central Europe. Brahms heard these tunes in his youth when he was accompanist to the Hungarian violinist Eduard Reményi, who ended his concerts with a brilliant gypsy medley of his own devising. These melodies and syncopated rhythms are felt in much of Brahms's work throughout his lifetime, apart from these specifically 'Hungarian' Dances.

The title 'Hungarian' has a very special significance. For the nineteenth-century composer, the adjective Hungarian as applied to music meant, quite simply, gypsy music. True Hungarian music—that of the Hungarian peasants—was unknown until the twentieth-century research of Kodaly and Bartók. All other 'Hungarian' music by earlier composers elsewhere invariably drew its inspiration from gypsy airs, not from authentic Hungarian folk music.

In 1852, before he turned twenty, Brahms began to put together 21 Hungarian Dances for Piano Duet, based on existing melodies revitalised in fresh and imaginative treatments by the composer. This first collection was completed in 1869 when Brahms decided to publish the first ten in two sets. Their overwhelming success, which put Brahms on the musical map of Europe as a composer for the first time, persuaded the publisher Simrock and their author to put out two more sets in 1880. Described as 'arrangements' rather than original compositions, the Dances were published without opus numbers. Later the Czech composer Dvořák orchestrated Nos. 7 through 21 with a brilliant and effervescent spirit, adding his own Slavonic character to their music. Since this last set seems to have been completely of Brahms's own invention, in that no models for their tunes have been found, these melodies inhabit a stylistic area common to both Brahms and Dvořák, and to both types of national folk music, gypsy and Slavonic. As to authenticity, Brahms himself stated he was presenting these dances to the world 'as genuine gypsy children which I did not beget but merely brought up with bread and milk.' According to Walter Niemann, these gypsy airs 'are pure nature music, full of unfettered, vagrant roving spirit, and a chaotic ferment, drawn straight from the deepest well-springs of music by children of Nature.'

Printed in the United States of America

Richard Wagner

His Life and Times 1813-1883

**PROGRAM NOTES FOR OVERTURE TO TANNHÄUSER;
PRELUDE TO LOHENGRIN (ACT 1), PRELUDE AND
WEDDING CHORUS (ACT 3); PRELUDE TO DIE
MEISTERSINGER; SIEGFRIED'S RHINE JOURNEY AND
FUNERAL MARCH**
By Harvey E. Phillips

fw

**FUNK & WAGNALLS, INC.
NEW YORK, NEW YORK**

An Uncertain Start

Richard Wagner was born in Leipzig on 22nd May 1813. Probably no one will ever know for certain whether he was really the child of Karl Friedrich Wilhelm Wagner, the Leipzig police-actuary, or whether his father was a family friend, the actor-playwright-painter Ludwig Geyer. Karl Friedrich died in the typhoid epidemic which followed the Battle of Leipzig when Richard, his ninth child, was six months old, and as soon after his death as possible, his widow moved to Dresden and married Geyer. Late in the 1870s, when he had seen the letters of his mother and step-father, Wagner seems to have come to the conclusion for a time that Geyer was his father, and to have made this sug-gestion to a number of his friends; later still, he seems to have changed his mind.

Music only slowly revealed itself to be Wagner's destiny. He was a violent, sensitive, intelligent, almost ungovernable boy given to wild if not long-lived enthusiasm. For a time, ancient Greece and its mythology absorbed him; in his early teens he wrote a huge tragedy, based on Shakespeare, Goethe, Schiller and Lessing; so many of its characters were killed – he remembered in his autobiography – that he had to resurrect most of them as ghosts to have enough left to finish the play. As a member of a theatrical family (his brother Albert became an operatic tenor, two of his sisters and another brother entered the straight theatre) he was familiar with opera from his earliest childhood and when the Wagners moved from Dresden, where Geyer had been a member of the court theatre, back to Leipzig the Gewand-haus Concerts brought him to orchestral music and the

great revelation of Beethoven's symphonies – and it was Beethoven who made him a composer.

To all intents and purposes he was self-taught. He lacked the patience to master an instrument and remained a hap-hazard pianist throughout his life. His first teacher of harmony, a violinist in the Leipzig theatre orchestra, left him believing that nothing in the text books had any rele-vance to music as he heard it in the concert hall and as he imagined it. A second teacher, Weinlig, the Cantor at St Thomas's Church, left him free to write as he wished, simply discussing what he had done and suggesting other ways of achieving the same result. His real teachers were the scores he studied to such good effect that when he was seventeen he offered the publishers of Beethoven's Ninth Symphony a piano transcription of the work which they did not accept because they feared that such wild, obscure and difficult music had too limited an appeal to make publication worth-while; it says much for the youth's ability to educate himself that he could see his way clearly through a work which many musicians believed to be eccentric to the point of lunacy.

By the time he left Leipzig University, where he had sown a plentiful crop of wild oats (he drank heavily and gambled passionately, always ready to borrow money to attempt to make good his losses), he had composed two piano sonatas, one of which had been published; a symphony, which had been well received at a Gewandhaus Concert; several con-cert overtures, piano pieces and a string quartet. He had done nothing, however, to train himself for a routine position in the German musical world and would have been quite con-tent to go on for the rest of his life composing what he wished to compose and paying no attention to the financial facts of life. The Wagners, however, were anything but rich and Albert, feeling that the youngest of the family should now make some effort to become independent, found him a post

A 19th-century print showing a view of Leipzig (By permission of Kalenderverlag Brönners Druckerei, Frankfurt am Main)

as a chorus master of the tiny opera house at Würzburg, in Bavaria.

The end of his first engagement did not worry him, but his success in it did not prompt him to look for another. In Würzburg he had finished his first opera, *Die Feen* (The Fairies), and he spent six months at home in Leipzig trying to arrange a production of the work and, at the same time, being converted to Italian opera (which he had previously disliked on national rather than musical grounds). It was the authorities of the Leipzig Opera who found him a new post, apparently only to get rid of an obviously gifted but importunate young man whose determination to get *Die Feen* on to the stage irritated them. He was offered the musical directorship of the theatre at Magdeburg and accepted it because, for neither the first time nor the last time, he fell in love.

Magdeburg had a fifth-rate company teetering on the verge of bankruptcy, and the salary Wagner was offered, like that of any comparable post in provincial Germany, was pitifully low, but the drama company there included an actress, Minna Planer, several years older than Richard and quite unlike any other actress he had known; she was quiet, reserved, good-looking and naturally graceful. She had chosen the stage as her career because she had an illegitimate child, born when she was sixteen, to bring up. Good looks and charm had won her some success; she was thrifty, domesticated, simple in tastes; she had nothing in common with the brilliant, erratic, flamboyant young conductor who refused to give her a moment's peace until she agreed to marry him. She never understood his complete failure to master the practicalities of life or his devotion to a musical ideal for which he was ready to sacrifice everybody and everything, including his own comfort and safety. As far as she was concerned, the theatre was simply a way of making enough money to live a decent, middle-class life, and her husband's improvidence was something she regarded as outrageous.

At Magdeburg, Wagner proved himself to be a first rate conductor, able not only to penetrate to the heart of whatever music he played but also able, as only the greatest can, to infect orchestras and singers with his own confidence and conviction. When the company broke up at the end of the season, the orchestra and singers were willing to stay on to perform their conductor's second opera, *Das Liebesverbot* (The Ban on Love), for his benefit. Unfortunately, a quarrel that had been smouldering among some of the singers throughout the season burst out into violence during the overture, and the benefit performance had to be cancelled.

This disaster would have been less serious had Wagner been content, like any other theatre-music director, to live the sort of life his salary allowed him. But his sense of everyday reality was never strong and what others regard as luxuries were necessities to him. He was deeply in debt and his

Otterstedt's 1836 painting of Minna Planer, Wagner's first wife. It was mainly because of his love for Minna that the composer accepted the post of musical director of the theatre at Magdeburg (Wagner Museum, Bayreuth)

creditors expected some relief from his benefit performance; as it produced nothing for them, the unfortunate Wagner left Magdeburg as secretly as he could after spending several days in hiding.

Because he thought of his future only in terms of the works he would compose, he worked harder to secure a performance of *Das Liebesverbot* in Berlin than to secure a better conductorship; and having failed, followed Minna to Königsberg, where she had found an engagement. A few months' conducting in Königsberg added new debts to those left from Magdeburg, and the entirely respectable Minna left him, running away from him twice and returning only when she found that he had been appointed musical director of the theatre in Riga, where events repeated themselves exactly – a new mountain of debts was added to his already Alpine obligations and, in 1839, he had to smuggle himself out of Riga, in Russian territory, and out of Germany, to avoid his creditors.

His goal was Paris, where he felt certain that his new opera, *Rienzi*, would win him immediate success and wealth. The Paris Opéra was almost alone in paying a royalty to the composer for every performance of his work, and *Rienzi* was grand opera in the style of Meyerbeer or Spontini, full of huge crowd scenes and sensationalism; Paris would accept it at once and his struggles would be over.

A 19th-century print of the Court Theatre in Dresden where Rienzi, The Flying Dutchman *and* Tannhäuser *were first performed* (*Staatliche Kunstsammlungen, Dresden*)

For three years, the optimistic young German whose name was unknown even in his own country did all he could to conquer Paris. Meyerbeer, whom Wagner came to hate, did all he could to help the young man to establish himself, but the authorities of the Opera were not interested. Wagner did the dreariest musical chores – piano scores of Italian operas, arrangements for cornet and voice and even a cornet teaching book, for a pittance.

In addition, he wrote music criticism, but also for a pittance. He impressed himself not only on Meyerbeer, but on the far greater Berlioz and Liszt. But it was only his confidence in himself that kept him going. He knew that he would be great and was convinced that any sensible man of means would finance him until his greatness was recognised and all would be well. His fantastic success as a borrower indicates something of the enormous charm he exerted on everyone he met, just as his refusal to be crushed indicates his extraordinary courage. In 1842, *Rienzi* rescued him; it was accepted, partly on Meyerbeer's recommendation, for production in Dresden; forgetting all the difficulties of the past, Wagner returned to Germany believing that the struggle was over and that his success was assured.

Rienzi, produced in Dresden on 20th October 1842, was a great success in spite of its length, the five hundred costumes it required and the elaborate effects and scenic devices it demanded. The later *Flying Dutchman* was produced in Berlin in the following January; the Berlin Opera was not only a theatre of much greater prestige than that of Dresden, it was also the only opera house in Germany which allowed the composer a royalty on every performance of a work – similar to the Opéra in Paris. The deaths of the Dresden Kapellmeister and his assistant shortly after the triumph of *Rienzi* led to Wagner's ap-

pointment in the senior position after he had refused the junior. He was appointed for life at a salary of 1500 thaler – about £225 in English money of the period – a sum which seems derisory to us but which was as much as any other opera director in a similar position might expect. It seemed that all his troubles were over and that his musical integrity had finally triumphed.

Wagner, however, was born to troubles. Those which arose from his determination to improve the standards of performance (Berlioz gave a concert in Dresden shortly after Wagner's appointment and claimed that one of the double-bass players was so enfeebled by age that he could not even hold his instrument) were settled by his combination of efficiency, determination and charm. But he was still pursued by creditors from every city in which he had lived, and he was not prepared to settle into a situation which he knew to be less than satisfactory, particularly when he considered that his new position gave him the duty of paying off his debts.

The creditors were silenced for a time because Wagner's boyhood heroine, Wilhelmina Schröder-Devrient, a member of the Dresden company, believed in him sufficiently to lend him enough money to keep them quiet; this encouraged him to live from the start beyond his income and to buy, among other things, an extensive and expensive library.

The annual concert for the pension fund at Easter 1846 gave Wagner the opportunity, again in spite of opposition, to conduct a historic performance of Beethoven's still barely understood Ninth Symphony, thus adding weight to the memoranda he was preparing to submit to the authorities. One deals with the complete reorganisation of the Dresden court music (not only in the opera house but also in the King's chapel), offers a scheme for regular orchestral concerts and shows how greater efficiency could be obtained from the orchestra by using its members for fewer performances at very little extra cost. The other, more doctrinaire but equally practical, suggests a reform of the theatre. Both were rejected, and Wagner found his interest in his official work killed by the rejection. He concentrated on the composition of *Lohengrin*, gave himself up to the reading which eventually led to the composition of the *Ring* and plunged, with the extremist Röckel and the exiled Russian anarchist Bakhunin, into revolutionary politics.

The wave of liberal revolutions which spread across Europe from Paris after 1848 reached Dresden in the spring of 1849. Among its most active leaders there was Kapellmeister Wagner, whose politics were some distance away from those of his associates but who was convinced that his mission to save Germany through art had been baulked by obscurantist courtiers. When the rising failed, he escaped from the country. Röckel and Bakhunin, less far-sighted, were imprisoned for life, while Wagner, in his absence, was exiled from the whole of Germany. For the rest of his life he did his best to persuade the world that he had never really joined in the rebellion but had simply found it an interesting spectacle to observe.

Until 1864 he was left to live as best he could. He was utterly convinced that he was in the world to compose and that any other activity was a betrayal of his mission. Making his home in Zurich, he became a popular figure there as a concert conductor, but the refusal of his plan to reorganise the city's music through a municipal subsidy killed his interest in Zurich's musical life. The first half of 1855 he spent in London, as conductor of the Philharmonic Society's concerts, but he was annoyed by the lack of proper rehearsal time and by the attacks of senior London critics. Nevertheless, though he made little money out of his engagement, he won the adherence of the orchestra and the approval of audiences.

The basis of his financial plans was his certainty that sooner or later his music would be extremely popular and would earn vast sums of money. This belief had already persuaded him to print the scores of *The Flying Dutchman*, *Tannhäuser* and *Lohengrin* at his own expense, so that he and not a mere publisher might reap the eventual profit. By the middle of the 1850 s, *Tannhäuser* and *Lohengrin* were extremely popular works, but they brought Wagner no advantage because he had already sold all his rights in them for ready cash. A variety of friends loaned him money – which he saw as a demonstration of their faith in his mission and their right-minded readiness to share his sufferings. Such was the generosity of his friends that he was never actually in want until 1862 and 1863, and even then he spent whatever money came into his hands with a blind refusal to face reality. Twice, in the first years of exile, he returned to Paris, hoping to solve all his problems with a success at the Paris Opéra, but Paris paid little attention to him. After his second visit, he planned to run away with Jessie Laussot, a French wine merchant's English wife with whom he had fallen in love. But Minna, now an invalid soured by the misery of life with an impossible husband who had thrown away his secure and

A watercolour by Echter of the sets for Act III of Lohengrin *at its first performance*

A 19th-century print of Zurich. The Wagners lived in a house in Zurich provided by the Wesendoncks until Minna's jealousy forced them to leave and go to Venice (Bertarelli Print Collection, Milan)

socially enviable post in Dresden but who would no longer write profitable operas like *Rienzi* and *Tannhäuser*, took him back to Zurich.

The impossibility of any understanding with Minna, who had no conception of his greatness, his aims or the tortuosities of his character, threw him into love with Mathilde Wesendonck, the pretty wife of a German business man who lived in Zurich and who was one of his most generous supporters. To Mathilde he poured out all his hopes, ambitions and miseries as well as his complex dreams and beliefs. It seems unlikely that she understood much of what he said to her, but she was flattered and delighted to be the inspiration of a great composer, to be portrayed in the Sieglinde of *Die Walküre* and to be the propulsive power behind the composition of *Tristan und Isolde*. Minna's jealousy put an end to a curious love affair which was as much talk as action and made Zurich, because they lived in a house provided by the Wesendoncks, an impossible place for him.

He fled to Venice, where he finished *Tristan und Isolde* and thus worked out of his system his devotion to Mathilde, and then, with Minna, moved again to Paris to make a last effort to conquer the French capital. This time, after three concerts which won him a great acclaim, he succeeded in persuading the Opéra to accept *Tannhäuser*, which he remodelled partly to strengthen the opening scene in the Venusberg and partly to satisfy French taste with a lengthy ballet-scene. The aristocratic French audience, however, attended the opera after a lengthy dinner to be in time for a ballet in the second act. *Tannhäuser* was hooted off the stage through three performances, and Wagner withdrew it.

He had literally nothing left. All his earlier rights, even those in his published works, had been sold. Supporters like Madame Ritter, a friend of his disciple Hans von Bülow, who for years had allowed him 2,400 marks per annum, had lost patience with him. Even Liszt, the most generous of great virtuosi, had grown distant, for the Princess Sayn-Wittgenstein, his second aristocratic mistress, cared nothing for Wagner. The only possible source of money was *Tristan*, and fruitless efforts to arrange a production of the latest work took him, eternally hopeful, to Vienna. Concerts there won him his usual success as a conductor and as a composer, for his concerts included excerpts from his own operas. But the delaying tactics, common in any opera house trying to find the courage to stage a difficult new work, eventually ended in *Tristan's* rejection.

It was in March 1864, as Wagner drifted aimlessly across Europe, with every note he had so far written of *Die Meistersinger* sold and the money spent, borrowing what he could but writing nothing, that King Maximilian II of Bavaria died. The new King of Bavaria was Ludwig II, a boy of eighteen who had fallen in love with *Lohengrin* when he had heard the work five years before. Ludwig's great mission in life, he had already decided, was to save from a life of poverty and suffering the composer whose work he idolised. Almost his first act as king was to send for Wagner.

The Royal Saviour

Ludwig II of Bavaria, Wagner's saviour, was a tall, brilliantly handsome young man. He had seen *Lohengrin* and *Tannhäuser*, had read the composer's prose and the libretto of the *Ring* and fervently believed all Wagner's doctrines. Although he was later to lose contact with reality even more disastrously than Wagner – being deposed as insane – at eighteen he had a strong sense of political reality, though little interest in the life expected of a monarch.They planned Bavaria's musical future: Wagner's debts were to be paid and he was to be provided with a house and an income. His only duties were to finish the works which he had planned – *Die Meistersinger*, the *Ring*, *Parsifal* and the Buddhist opera *Die Sieger* (The Conquerors), which had been vaguely in his mind for several years. He was to undertake to arrange worthy productions of all these works. The 4,000 florins per annum which he was to receive from the King gave Ludwig all rights in his future works; both of them regarded this as a wise investment which would, in the course of time, repay the King whatever he lavished on the composer.

To create the necessary Wagner singers (only one tenor in the Europe of 1864 was capable of singing Tristan – Ludwig Schnorr von Carolsfeld) a new conservatory was to be established on Wagnerian principles, and because there was no theatre capable of housing an adequate production of any of Wagner's later works, a new one was to be built to the composer's specifications. These schemes required not only the presence of Wagner but also that of many convinced Wagnerians, for whom the King found well-paid posts. Chief of the Wagnerian phalanx to reach Munich was the pianist-conductor Hans von Bülow, whose fervent devotion to Wagner was balanced by neurotic, arrogant contempt for almost everyone else. Bülow was appointed pianist to the King.

The Bavarians were not happy to see their national resources squandered by Wagner; they knew that he was a great composer, but they knew too that his extravagance and unscrupulousness were notorious. They disliked the crowd of foreign hangers-on and the plans to create a new conservatory and a new theatre, as though nothing in their city was good enough for the Wagnerians.

Tristan und Isolde was produced in 1865. Schnorr von Carolsfeld and his wife sang the principal roles and Bülow conducted an exemplary performance. The converted, including King Ludwig, were ecstatic, but the idiom of the work was far beyond the uninitiated. Three weeks after its final performance, Schnorr died of typhoid.

By this time, Wagner had added a scandal to the other reasons the Bavarians had discovered for disliking him. In 1857, when he was twenty years old, Bülow had married Cosima, the younger daughter of Liszt and his mistress the Countess d'Agoult. The marriage was a disaster from the start and by 1863 Cosima and Wagner, thrown together by Bülow's work, had recognised that they were in love. Bülow brought Cosima with him to Munich and from then on the three lived a peculiar *ménage à trois*. In 1865, their daughter, Isolde, was born, but Bülow accepted her as his own chiefly, it seems, because he was not willing to injure the Wagnerian cause by creating a public scandal.

Nevertheless, by the end of 1865, Wagner had made Munich too hot to hold him. He had boasted of his power over the King but had disdained to make influential friends at court, so that Ludwig, on 7th December, had to ask him to leave Munich for a time to prevent public disorder. Wagner left, taking Cosima with him and never returned to the city except as a casual visitor.

The two settled at Triebschen, on the shores of Lake Lucerne. Wagner's income from Ludwig continued; he finished *Die Meistersinger* in 1867. It was produced in Munich (again Bülow conducted a model performance) in 1868 and Wagner's presence in the royal box caused trouble among the people. *Siegfried* was completed in 1871 and *Götterdämmerung* in 1874. Relations with the king were strained because Ludwig was eager to see the productions which were legally his right, while Wagner was unwilling

A print of King Ludwig II of Bavaria, who was Wagner's leading disciple and who financed him from the year 1864 onwards (Bertarelli Print Collection, Milan)

7

to allow the works on to the stage unless he supervised the production, and he refused to go to Munich. What he needed was the new theatre for which his architect friend Gottfried Semper had drawn up plans when there had been hopes of building it in Munich.

The birth of a son, Siegfried, to Cosima in the summer of 1869 made it impossible to continue the pretence that she was merely Wagner's devoted secretary lent by an equally devoted husband. Bülow obtained a divorce and the lovers were married. Ludwig, by this time reconciled to the fallibility of his idol, continued his support. Cosima, however, was the perfect wife for Wagner; she was convinced that her mission in life was to serve him and she accepted all his doctrines and prejudices as gospel – even his German racialism, although she herself was half-Hungarian and half-French.

In 1871, Wagner settled on Bayreuth as the home of his theatre and found that local notables were ready to support his plan by presenting him with the site he needed. He moved there, renting a house until the house which King Ludwig had promised him was ready. This last and most splendid of Wagner's homes was to give him the luxury and the pompous grandeur which made him happiest. He began to collect singers to train for the first complete cycle of the *Ring; Siegfried* and *Götterdämmerung* had never been produced. He mobilised his wealthy supporters and encouraged the members of Wagner societies to pay contributions towards the 300-thaler shares, a thousand of which had to be bought to finance the theatre.

Though the new copyright law of 1870 added to his income, though he made a concert tour in 1873 to add to the theatre fund and though disciples like the philosopher Nietzsche drummed up support wherever they could, by 1874 only the shell of a temporary wooden theatre had been built and there was no money for further progress. At this point Ludwig again came to the rescue, lending the Theatre Fund 100,000 thaler on condition that everything bought with his money remained his property until the theatre committee could repay him. Wagner could now plan his first festival, to include the complete *Ring*, for 1876. He engaged hand-picked artists from all over Germany, and such was his prestige that they agreed to come and learn his enormously difficult music for no more than expenses.

The opposition to Wagner, which had picked on Brahms as its leader though Brahms was not totally opposed to Wagner's music, failed to prevent the theatre from being built and the public from taking Wagner seriously; they were compelled to sit and watch the enemy's victory. Ludwig attended a general rehearsal of the *Ring* early in August, thus being reunited with Wagner after eight years. The Emperor attended the performances on 13th and 14th August and the three complete cycles were an artistic triumph. Through its composer's determination and Ludwig's dedicated generosity, the *Ring* had been brought to the stage more than twenty-five years after Wagner had begun to write it.

A watercolour of the library at Wahnfried, the house in which Wagner and Cosima finally settled (Wagner Memorial Centre, Bayreuth)

A God on the Decline

The first Bayreuth Festival established Wagner as the great international celebrity he had always felt himself to be. Its excitements over, the fee he had earned by writing a march commissioned to celebrate the centenary of the American Declaration of Independence paid for a family holiday in Italy. He was treated as an honoured visitor, given a civic banquet in Bologna and introduced to the great, including Count Gobineau, whose theories about race provided Wagner with a new, and to his self-educated mind, philosophical, way of rationalising his prejudices. Gobineau's teachings cast a baleful influence on the essays and articles his new disciple continued to produce. In Italy, too, Wagner met the greatest of his disciples, the philosopher Friedrich Nietzsche, for the last time.

Of all the young men who fell in behind Wagner's banner, Nietzsche was the most original and creative. He was thirty-two at the time of the first Bayreuth Festival, for which he had worked valiantly, a professor of philology, a poet, an amateur composer and a powerful prose writer. The events of 1876 and his feeling that the Festival was more a great religious ceremony at which strange, irrational gods were worshipped than a performance of great music, had already made him question his discipleship to Wagner. Their conversations in Italy, with Wagner's mind already full of the strange amalgam of Christianity and other ideas from which *Parsifal* grew, seemed to Nietzsche both foolish and intellectually unhealthy. The disciple was near enough in temperament to his master for their parting to be bitter and acrimonious. Nietzsche refused to accept Wagner's conviction that 'great art is intrinsically religious, began to demand lightness and grace rather than power and grandeur from the music he heard, and did not endure Wagner's attacks in silence; he pointed out that Wagner's possible descent from an actor named Geyer (commonly a Jewish name) might well mean that the greatest of anti-Semites was himself half-Jewish. Wagner was dead before Nietzsche became insane, but his insanity left the Wagnerians convinced that there was an obvious reason for Nietzsche's departure from their ranks.

Despite his celebrity and the artistic success of Bayreuth, Wagner could not relax; his theatre had to be made secure. Though he disliked London, in 1877 he accepted an invitation to conduct twenty concerts there on the understanding that he could expect a profit of £10,000 by filling the then new Albert Hall with its seven thousand seats.

However the London promoters had forgotten that about one-third of the seats in the hall were privately owned, so that the hall was not full and the £10,000 profit turned into a loss of £1,200 which Wagner himself had to bear; and in the end only eight concerts were given. There was violent criticism from some of the critics and from senior academic figures in English music, but the audiences were receptive and enthusiastic. The composer was invited to lunch with Queen Victoria and feted by the intelligentsia, especially the circle round the novelist George Eliot, where a seriousness of mind sympathetic to a serious-minded German was taken for granted.

A photograph taken in 1873 of Wagner with his second wife Cosima and their son Siegfried (Wagner Memorial Centre, Bayreuth)

In 1877 Wagner experienced the last of his great love affairs. At sixty-four, he was still obviously capable of fascinating women in their twenties, and away from Bayreuth and Cosima, in a mood of excitement and stress, he was thrown together with Judith Gautier, the wife of his friend and propagandist Catulle-Mendès, the most ardent champion of his cause in France. The affair was brief, and Wagner's letters to Judith mix passionate avowals of love and regrets that she had not been available to give him her love when he was young, with more mundane shopping-lists demanding perfumes, bath salts and cosmetics. Quite soon a letter in a different tone, friendly and paternal, explained that Cosima was in a position to do his shopping, and all was over between them.

His life-long self-confidence was justified by the popularity of his works, despite their difficulty and expense, but fame elsewhere did nothing to lighten the financial burden on Bayreuth, with its vast deficit from the first Festival and its mountain of debts to King Ludwig. A second Festival, to produce the still-unwritten but deeply pondered *Parsifal*, was suggested, but finances made it impossible until Ludwig made the last of the splendid gestures of faith in Wagner which had made the composer's later life possible in spite of the difficulties he had put in the King's way. The popularity of Wagner's operas in Munich, according to the King's plan, was slowly to wipe out the Festival Theatre's indebtedness to him; a royalty of ten per cent of the takings of all Wagner performances should be paid to the Bavarian state, which had taken over the Bayreuth debt, so that the theatre was freed. *Parsifal* could be produced at the second Festival with the orchestra, singers and staff of the Munich Opera, after which Munich would have the right to produce the work. In 1880 Ludwig personally cancelled this provision out of respect for Wagner's wish to reserve *Parsifal* for Bayreuth.

Parsifal had been in the composer's mind since 1857. He had written his prose sketch of the libretto in 1865, but he did not start on the detailed work until 1877, and it was completed in 1882. Failing health (though he was still capable of wild outbursts of high spirits) made the work slow, and he found that he could not settle to it except in a perfumed room after a lavish use of bath salts and cold cream and wearing silk.

But his health worried others more than it worried him. His refusal to live as quietly as his ill health demanded meant that he often overstrained himself. It was for this reason that, in 1881, when four cycles of the *Ring* in Berlin (the city's first production of the work) were attended by the Prussian Royal Family and by Bismarck, Wagner's speech

A view of the park of the Hermitage, a rococo castle near Bayreuth

of thanks after the last *Götterdämmerung* was interrupted by a heart attack.

Parsifal was produced in July 1882. Again the artists were hand-picked and the rehearsals as thorough as Wagner could make them. At the end of the Festival, he announced to the subscribers to the Wagner Associations, for whom all tickets were reserved, that in future the theatre would be open to the general public.

This done, he left Bayreuth to winter in Venice, musing over rather than planning a symphony he hoped to write. Friends, Liszt among them, visited him; he talked as wildly and indefatigably as ever. He planned a festival for the following summer, convinced that he would live to arrange standard performances of all his operas. The manuscript of the Symphony in C which he had written in 1832 – Mendelssohn seems to have mislaid the score long before – turned up in time to be performed in the Fenice Theatre on Christmas Eve 1882, to celebrate Cosima's birthday on Christmas Day. At the rehearsal, Wagner was taken ill, but he recovered to conduct the performance.

On 13th February 1883 he died. For more than twenty-four hours, Cosima refused to leave his body. He was taken to Munich, where, to the sounds of Siegfried's Funeral March, the King's representatives and state officials boarded the funeral train. At his graveside, in the grounds of his 'Wahnfried', the Funeral March was played again and the chorus he had written for Weber's reburial in Dresden was sung. Forty-seven years later Cosima, a blind old woman of ninety, was laid beside him.

PROGRAM NOTES FOR THE RECORD

by HARVEY E. PHILLIPS

Tannhäuser

New York first heard *Tannhäuser* in 1859—the first Wagner performance in the United States—and a revised version was prepared for Paris in 1861. This Paris *Tannhäuser,* the *Tannhäuser* most commonly heard in the opera house today, is thus, like some Verdi reworkings of youthful scores (*Macbeth* and *Simon Boccanegra*), a curious amalgam of styles. It incorporates post-*Walküre, Tristan* and *Meistersinger* thinking into what was in 1842 a milestone very much on the way to Wagner's maturity.

The changes for Paris were originally meant to put the work into acceptable shape for the grand-opera-nurtured public of the French capital. The primary objective was to add the customary ballet, and while Wagner did this — untraditionally, for Paris, placing it in the first act instead of the second — his efforts and an extraordinarily lavish and extensively rehearsed production were for nought. Paris was even more hostile than Dresden nineteen years earlier. *This* local judgment was not to be reversed for another thirty years.

Certainly time has proved the Overture among Wagner's most enduringly popular pages. In it he skillfully sets out the essential conflict that motivates this medieval tale of the minstrel knight Tannhäuser and of his dalliance with Venus, the classical goddess of love, his return to the chivalric circle he promptly scandalizes with a song in praise of sensuality, his banishment and pilgrimage to Rome, and final redemption through the love-death of the noble Elisabeth. It begins with a subdued statement of the famous Pilgrim's Chorus for Clarinets, bassoons, and horns, a combination joined by strings and eventually the rest of the orchestra until the theme blazes forth powerfully in the trombones. These pious measures subside and are supplanted by the glowing accents associated with Venus and the revelry in the Venusberg. A yearning, insistent violin figure climbs to Tannhäuser's song itself. His stirringly ardent theme alternates with the siren sounds of Venus, which gradually dissolve into an uneasy, descending repeated two-note pattern for the strings, a murmur over which is superimposed a return of the Pilgrim's Chorus, steadily growing in force toward the fortissimo conclusion.

Lohengrin

Wagner's champion and future father-in-law, Franz Liszt, gave *Lohengrin* its first production in Weimar in 1850. Like *Tannhäuser,* it was written to the composer's own libretto, the story based on a German legend from the Middle Ages. But, unlike *Tannhäuser,* in its wholehearted embrace of motivic devices to underscore the drama, it serves as the real point of departure of the so-called Wagnerian style. In every subsequent opera can be seen the formula of organic construction — the development and interaction of *leitmotifs* — as it was given its first real exercise in *Lohengrin.*

Liszt made sure that some of the most influential intellectuals of Europe were present for the première, and although the critics again proved predictably harsh, that *Lohengrin* performance succeeded in spreading the cult of Wagner far beyond his German adherents. With *Lohengrin* Wagner truly became a musical pioneer to be reckoned with.

It is interesting to note that the composer introduces this 'romantic drama,' as he dubbed it, with a Prelude, a piece of music that reproduces the aura of the work, rather than an 'Overture' made up of a summary of principal tunes, although he himself had always treated the overture form with great sophistication and individuality. The Prelude to Act I, the scene in which Elsa of Brabant, unjustly accused of sorcery, is saved by and consequently betrothed to the mysterious knight Lohengrin, begins with a theme of quiet, ethereal radiance played by the flutes and violins. This immediately evokes the hero and his sacred heritage as the son of Parsifal, defender of the Holy Grail. It is developed in an immense crescendo, slowly taking on other instruments, first oboes and clarinets, then lower winds and brass. When stated by the full orchestra — brass over a string tremolo — the theme becomes a revelation on earth of the Grail's supernatural power. A climactic crash of cymbals signals a decrescendo, a withdrawal to the initial timbre of the Prelude. The luminous measures disappear as does, later, the grace of the knight's presence as Elsa's rescuer when, prompted by the drama's villains, Telramund and Ortrude, she contravenes the conditions of her marriage and asks her husband to reveal his identity.

If the Prelude to Act III stems from more tangible stuff, it is still a brilliant depiction of splendid celebration, a tone poem of the events of the wedding festival. It opens with a wild fanfare for violins, winds, and brass (on the repeat, trombones and tubas are added) in combination with quasi-barbaric horn and bassoon calls over a pulsing string, woodwind, and trumpet ostinato. A decorous march-like middle section of ritual propriety follows. The fanfares return, and then there occurs a striking modulation from G Major to B flat denoting the end of the public ceremonies and the beginning of the Wedding March. This melody, perhaps the best known Wagner ever penned, is an invocation sung by the couple's attendants, a blessing and intimate prayer for the future happiness of the bride and groom.

11

Die Meistersinger

The final pages of *Die Meistersinger* took form during Wagner's discreet exile from Munich at Triebschen on Lake Lucerne. The date was October 1867, a full twenty-two years after he began the first sketches. For *Meistersinger* and *Tristan* before it the composer had interrupted work on the gigantic *Ring des Nibelungen* project, leaving it in 1857 in the middle of *Siegfried* and not returning to that hero's side until some ten years later.

If anything, *Die Meistersinger,* even more than *Tristan,* marks a departure for Wagner from the symbolic world of Nordic gods and goddesses, for this comedy, his first since the youthful *Liebesverbot* (a setting of Shakespeare's *Measure for Measure*), springs from the specific milieu of Nuremberg in the late sixteenth century. One of the characters, the poet-cobbler Hans Sachs, existed in history; and the events of the story, which is built around the courtship and winning of Eva, daughter of the goldsmith Pogner, by the young aristocrat Walther von Stolzing, are filled with a rich, lifelike detail worthy of the best Nurem-berg artists during that city's great Renaissance.

The real subject of *Meistersinger,* however, is not young love or even the humanistic wisdom of the warmhearted Sachs. Rather, Wagner intended the opera as a plea for new forms in art, and as an argument that the voice of the people would lend its instinctive support to what is best, purest, and most natural in German culture. Fortunately, this most nationalistic of polemics, this defense of himself and attack on his enemies is wrapped in a masterpiece, a festival opera that never fails to delight no matter on what level it is understood. "Such a wonder, and a treasure of everything lovely and happy in music," is the way George Bernard Shaw described *Meistersinger,* and so it has been received since its first, meticulous performance under Hans von Bulow in Munich in 1868.

The Prelude, already known to German audiences from concert performances as much as six years before that première, synthesizes both the style and the conflict of the opera.

Götterdämmerung

The last opera of the *Ring* tetralogy brings the destruction of Valhalla, fire, flood, the death of the world the gods have made. Yet, in its very final moments, *Götterdämmerung* also extends a hopeful promise, Wagner concluding all with the redemption-through-love theme first sung by Sieglinde when told of the coming birth of Siegfried (*Die Walküre,* Act III).

Siegfried, as *Götterdämmerung* shows, is not the instrument of the world's salvation. His drama, once he has come to maturity as the husband of Brünnhilde, is in his precipitate fall.

Siegfried is then a central figure who, without knowing it, carries forth the enormously convoluted action and all it symbolizes to its inevitable dénouement. That the life of this hero as seen by Wagner in *Siegfried* and *Götterdämmerung* first came to be known to the rest of the world within two days at the inaugural Bayreuth sea-son places the dates of August 16 and 17, 1876, among the most historic in the annals of music.

Siegfried's Rhine Journey is the orchestral bridge between his leavetaking of Brünnhilde and his arrival at the hall of the Gibichungs.

The Funeral March, the music that accompanies the body of Siegfried back from the hunt where Hagen has killed him to the waiting Brünnhilde, is a summation of the hero's life. In it, Wagner brings together the motifs associated with Siegfried, all linked by the chords thundered out when he is struck down. Siegfried's own music, his heroic, identifying motifs, appear next and finally Brünnhilde's love is remembered and worked into the Siegfried themes. But the two-chord death motif, now muted and somber and drained of its original, terrifying power, ends the interlude.

Printed in the United States of America

His Life and Times 1841-1904

PROGRAM NOTES FOR THE NINTH SYMPHONY
By Robert Jacobson

FUNK & WAGNALLS, INC.
NEW YORK, NEW YORK

Entertainer at the Inn: Life 1841-75

It was a tradition in Dvořák's family that all the sons should be innkeepers. The composer's great-grandfather was a farmer as well, but from his grandfather's time it was customary to combine innkeeping with a butcher's business. Dvořák's mother does not appear to have been particularly musical, but his father played the zither and even composed a little, and his uncles played the violin and in one case the trumpet.

Antonín Dvořák was born on 8th September 1841 in the quiet hamlet of Nelahozeves on the banks of the river Vltava, close to the Lobkowitz castle and a dozen miles north of Prague. Frántišek Dvořák, the composer's father, naturally assumed that his eldest son Antonín would follow the traditional trades, and so when the lad was barely twelve years of age he left school and became his father's apprentice. A year later he was sent to stay with his uncle Antonín Zdeněk at Zlonice so that he could continue his apprenticeship there.

It is probable that the young boy first began to have violin and singing lessons from the local schoolmaster, Spitz, soon after he entered the primary school at the age of six. Before very long he joined the local band, and played his violin at the inn to entertain his father's customers. Once he reached Zlonice there were greater musical opportunities, for the schoolmaster, Toman, was a baritone singer and church organist, and able to play several other instruments; and Antonín Liehmann, the German teacher, was a prolific composer and an all-round musician. During his stay there Dvořák studied harmony and made such excellent progress on the viola, organ and piano that Liehmann and Zdeněk urged František to allow his son to take up music professionally. However, František was determined that his son should follow in his footsteps, so after Antonín had gained his journeyman's certificate on 1st November 1856 he packed him off to Česká Kamenice (Böhmisch-Kamnitz) to attend school there for a year. The reason for this was that Antonín needed a better knowledge of German if he was to be a successful innkeeper. While he was there Antonín had lessons in theory and organ-playing from a musician called Hancke, and was also given opportunities to conduct the church choir.

In the meantime František had moved to 'The Big Inn' at Zlonice to improve his prospects, but was having difficulty in making it pay. Probably this change of fortune helped him to see his son's future in a new light, for when Zdeněk generously offered to bear the cost of Antonín's musical education in Prague, František accepted with gratitude. So the sixteen-year-old boy was able to go to the Organ School for two years.

Before long Zdeněk found he could no longer pay for his nephew's education, so Dvořák was obliged to earn what he could by taking pupils. Karel Bendl, a fellow student, kindly lént him various scores and allowed him to use his piano. Dvořák supplemented his modest income by playing in concerts of the St Cecilia Society. The Organ School was run on very strict and orthodox lines, whereas the St Cecilia's orchestra was much more radical and brought him in touch with the work of modern composers. His enthusiasm was aroused by concerts given by Liszt, Clara Schumann and Hans von Bülow, and he attended opera performances whenever possible.

When Dvořák left the Organ School in 1859 his report stated that he was a good practical musician but weak on theory. If he had refrained from annoying his professors by deliberately writing incorrect progressions and had been more fluent in the German language, it is probable that he would have been placed first among the twelve students who graduated that year, instead of second.

He joined the Komzák band as a viola player, and three years later when the Provisional Theatre was opened these players became the nucleus of the opera orchestra with J. N. Mayr as their conductor. These were lean years for Dvořák. His salary for the orchestral work was only eighteen gulden a month, so he was forced to supplement his income with whatever teaching he could pick up. He wrote his first string quintet (1861) and a string quartet (1862), and in 1865 composed two symphonies, a cello concerto and a song cycle entitled *Cypresses*. These songs were inspired by his pupil Josefina Čermáková, a pretty young actress with whom he fell deeply in love, but who failed to respond to his attentions.

Over this period Dvořák's musical horizons continued to expand. Early in 1863 he had the unique experience of playing in a programme of Wagner's music with the great man himself conducting. He took part in Berlioz's *Romeo and Juliet* when Smetana conducted this during the Shakespeare tercentenary celebrations, and also played in the highly successful première of Smetana's first opera, *The Brandenburgers in Bohemia* on 5th January 1866. For the next five years, during Smetana's conductorship at the Provisional Theatre, Dvořák played in many other interesting works, including the first performances of Smetana's next two operas, *The Bartered Bride* (1866) and *Dalibor* (1868), the latter being performed on the great day when the foundation stone was laid for the nation's permanent National Theatre.

Having already composed symphonies, chamber music and songs, it was a natural step for an ambitious young composer, who spent a good deal of his time in the orchestra pit, to attempt to write an opera himself. In the greatest secrecy, without any of his friends being aware of it, he composed his first stage work, *Alfred*, in 1870. Being an enthusiastic admirer of Wagner he tried rather unsuccessfully to apply Wagnerian principles. The Saxons' struggle to repel their Danish invaders appealed to him, because it had similarities with episodes in his own country's history, but it is curious that he used a German libretto. Writing this opera gave him some experience, but he made no attempt to have it performed. At this time, even his string quartets were strongly influenced by Wagner.

A year later he composed a comic opera, *King and Charcoal Burner*, which was rehearsed at the Provisional Theatre after a delay of two years, but proved to be too difficult for the singers and was withdrawn. However, he had the pleasure of hearing the overture to this work conducted by Smetana at a Philharmonic concert on 14th April 1872.

Dvořák was slow to mature as a composer, and so had to wait a long time for recognition. It is unwise to place too much importance on the success he achieved when his patriotic cantata, *The Heirs of the White Mountain*, was performed in Prague on 9th March 1873, because this was a provincial success and the work is not particularly distinguished. Yet the composer was greatly encouraged, and was soon at work on the Symphony in E flat, his finest work up to that time. On 17th November that year he married Anna Čermáková, the sister of his former love Josefina.

During 1874 Dvořák was busily engaged on a fourth symphony, a rhapsody for orchestra, another setting of *King and Charcoal Burner* that was new from beginning to end and a one-act comic opera. Further performances of his compositions took place, including his E flat Symphony,

which Smetana conducted at a Philharmonic concert on 30th March, and the scherzo of the new symphony. In February he was appointed organist and choirmaster at St Adalbert's Church at an annual salary of 126 gulden.

He was greatly interested to learn that the Austrian Ministry of Education was offering a prize of 400 gulden to a young, poor and talented poet, artist or musician. Having obtained a certificate from the Town Clerk confirming that he was poor, he submitted three of his compositions, very probably his two most recent symphonies and his String Quartet in B flat, op. 9. After waiting for more than seven months he heard in February 1875 that he was the prize-winner. The handsome windfall was most welcome, but official recognition by the Austrian government was of even greater importance to him. It really seemed as if he was at last set on the road towards success.

The Years of Travel: Life 1875-93

The excellent news of the award of the Austrian State Prize was a great stimulus to Dvořák, and compositions began to stream from his pen. His most ambitious works of 1875 were his Fifth Symphony in F major and *Vanda*, a grand opera on a Polish subject which failed miserably when it was mounted in the following year. These works were followed by a piano concerto (1876), the Stabat Mater (1876-77), the *Symphonic Variations* and the comic opera *The Cunning Peasant* (both 1877), together with several smaller compositions, including two piano trios, a piano quartet, the String Quartets in E major and D minor, a Theme and Variations for piano and three sets of Moravian Duets.

Dvořák continued to enter annually for the State Prize. Hanslick was still one of the judges, but Johann Herbeck, the Director of the Court Opera, had been replaced on the commission by Brahms, who therefore became familiar with Dvořák's works. For three years Brahms and Hanslick recommended Dvořák for the stipend. Brahms's interest in the future of the 36-year-old composer was so keenly aroused that he advised Simrock to publish his music. Once Simrock had issued the Moravian Duets and Slavonic Dances, and Ehlert had written so enthusiastically about them in the Berlin *Nationalzeitung* of 15th November 1878, Dvořák's future seemed assured.

August Manns performed three of the dances at the Crystal Palace on 15th February 1879, just three months after Ehlert's review, and during the same year Dvořák's Sextet was given in Vienna and Berlin, his String Quartet in E flat was played in Vienna, and his third Slavonic Rhapsody was heard in Berlin, Vienna, Budapest, Dresden and other German cities. From that time onwards his music was frequently heard abroad, and an ever-growing number of people became convinced of Dvořák's exceptional musical talent. The most significant pointers to the future were Manns's performance of the new Sixth Symphony in D major at the Crystal Palace on 22nd April 1882 and Richter's repetition of the same work at St James's Hall,

London, three weeks later; the performances of the Stabat Mater, which Bellowits conducted in Budapest in April 1882 and which Barnby gave at the Royal Albert Hall on 10th March 1883; and the production of *The Cunning Peasant* at Dresden on 24th October 1882 and at Hamburg on 3rd January 1883.

In the meantime Dvořák had completed the Violin Concerto, the song cycle *Gypsy Melodies,* a String Quartet in C major, ten *Legends* for piano duet and for orchestra, and a four-act grand opera, *Dimitrij*, which occupied him from 8th May to 23rd September 1882 and was successfully performed on 8th October.

In a still unpublished letter from Hanslick of 11th June 1882, the Viennese critic suggested that Dvořák should make settings of fine German poetry for the large German-speaking musical public, rather than fob them off with poor translations of Czech verse. He also advised him to leave Prague for a year or two and move to a more important musical centre, such as Vienna. Jauner, who was Herbeck's successor as Director of the Vienna Court Opera, had previously requested Dvořák to write an opera on a German libretto, and in May 1884 the offer was repeated. Another invitation, dated 3rd August 1883, came from the Philharmonic Society in London begging him to conduct some of his compositions at one of their concerts in the coming season.

He responded readily to the offer from London, but Hanslick's advice and Jauner's request posed far graver problems. Hanslick did not believe that a stay in Vienna would make Dvořák into a renegade, but the composer was far less sure of this. He was afraid that if he compromised himself by seeking fresh laurels on the operatic stage of Vienna, he would be betraying his nationalist principles and letting down his compatriots. The pressures were strong and the temptation great, so that the quandary in which he found himself remained unresolved for a long time.

GREAT SYMPHONY.

"From the New World" Heard for the First Time at the Philharmonic Rehearsal.

ABOUT THE SALIENT BEAUTIES.

First Movement the Most Tragic, Second the Most Beautiful, Third the Most Sprightly.

INSPIRED BY INDIAN MUSIC

The Director of the National Conservatory Adds a Masterpiece to Musical Literature

MR. SEIDL LEADING THE NEW DVORAK SYMPHONY.

An article in the New York Herald *of 26th December 1893, giving an enthusiastic review of Dvořák's 'New World' Symphony at its first performance (Artia, Prague)*

Spectre's Bride for Birmingham, then he composed the great D minor Symphony, and finally he turned his attention to *St Ludmila* for Leeds. Dvořák composed *The Spectre's Bride* in the tranquillity of his brother-in-law's estate at Vysoká, forty miles south of Prague. Thanks to his new-found affluence, he was able to buy some land and a small house there to which he could escape when it was necessary for him to work without distractions.

The D minor Symphony was the last composition to bear the unmistakable imprint of Dvořák's great dilemma over composing a German opera for Vienna. As he told his friend Judge Rus, he was determined to make the symphony a work 'capable of stirring the world'. It is possible that his secret hope of conquering the German stage may have been partly sublimated by the exceptionally enthusiastic welcome he was given in England. But in view of his sensitivity to the patronising attitude of Germans and Austrians towards Czechs, and the bitter complaint he made to Simrock about his first name being invariably printed in the German form 'Anton' on his compositions, it seems impossible that he could have yielded to Jauner's demands.

Having completed his three works for England, Dvořák felt able to relax. Six years earlier Simrock had requested him to write a second set of those lucrative Slavonic Dances, and now at last, during the summer of 1886, he felt in the right mood to comply. It is very strange that he had allowed his *Symphonic Variations* to lie forgotten for nine years. He brought them out in 1887 and offered them to Hans Richter, who was delighted with them. After conducting them in London on 16th May, the German conductor declared: 'At the several hundred concerts which I have conducted during my life, no *new work* has ever had such a success as yours.'

Having made five visits to England in three years,

We can learn something of Dvořák's state of mind from the defiant spirit of two works he wrote in 1883. The Piano Trio in F minor foreshadows in a remarkable way the epic spirit of the D minor Symphony of two years later. The 'Hussite' Overture, on the other hand, is founded upon two celebrated melodies, the 'St Wenceslas' plainsong and 'Ye who are God's Warriors'. This hymn of the militant Hussites has powerful associations in the minds of Czechs with their struggle against the Germans for political independence and for greater tolerance from Rome.

1884 was a most eventful year for Dvořák. During his visit to London in March he conducted his Stabat Mater at the Royal Albert Hall, his 'Hussite' Overture, the second Slavonic Rhapsody and the Sixth Symphony at a Philharmonic concert and his recently composed *Scherzo Capriccioso* at the Crystal Palace. He was also invited to conduct his own compositions at the next Three Choirs Festival, and was commissioned to write large choral works for the Birmingham and Leeds Musical Festivals, with a fee of £2,000 for the second of these. Two months later he was elected an Honorary Member of the Philharmonic Society and asked to compose a symphony for them. Dvořák therefore had enough work to keep him fully occupied for a long period. First of all he wrote *The*

The small hut on the grounds of Dvořák's house at Vysoká to which he went in order to compose in peace

4

Two sketches for costumes to be used in a production of Armida, *the last opera which Dvořák wrote* (*National Museum, Prague*)

Dvořák found himself in demand in other foreign cities. He conducted his Violin Concerto in Vienna during May 1887; his Stabat Mater in Budapest in March 1888; and the revised version of his F major Symphony (No. 5) and his second Slavonic Rhapsody at Dresden in March 1889. These concerts were followed by a performance of the 'Hussite' Overture and Eighth Symphony at Frankfurt-am-Main in November 1890. Following an invitation from Tchaikovsky to visit Russia, he went there in March 1890 to conduct concerts in Moscow and St Petersburg. The Moscow concert was devoted entirely to Dvořák's music, which was far more than the audience and critics could stand, but the German and Czech communities of Moscow rallied round the composer. Dvořák was decorated with the Austrian Order of the Iron Crown in June 1889, made an honorary Doctor of Philosophy of the Charles University, Prague, in March 1891 and three months later became an honorary Doctor of Music of Cambridge University. In January of that year he became Professor of Composition at Prague Conservatory.

During these years Dvořák composed the perennially fresh Piano Quintet, the opera *The Jacobin* (performed in Prague on 12th February 1889), the Piano Quartet in E flat major, the Eighth Symphony in G major referred to above, a Requiem Mass, commissioned by Birmingham and conducted there by the composer on 9th October 1891, the 'Dumky' Trio, and three overtures—*In Nature's Realm*,

Carnival and *Othello*. When Dvořák's fiftieth birthday was being celebrated in Prague the composer preferred to remain at his beloved Vysoká, and he did not trouble to travel to Vienna when *Dimitrij* was performed there in June 1892.

An enticing offer of the Directorship of the National Conservatory of Music of America, in New York, reached him in the summer of 1891 and gave him a great deal to think about. At first he felt inclined merely to agree to a concert tour, but by Christmas he had amended the contract to his liking and accepted the post for two years at an annual salary of 15,000 dollars. In the first five months of 1892 he made a concert tour of Bohemia and Moravia with the violinist Ferdinand Lachner and the cellist Hanuš Wihan, playing the 'Dumky' Trio wherever they went.

Leaving the rest of his family with his mother-in-law, Dvořák departed for New York with his wife and two eldest children on 10th September 1892. The National Conservatory gave him an official welcome on 1st October, and during the Columbus Fourth Centennial celebrations he conducted the Te Deum he had composed before leaving home. He did not find it easy to settle down in the strange environment, but by 19th December he had begun to sketch themes for future compositions. On 24th May in the following year he completed the first of his American compositions, the Ninth Symphony in E minor, 'From the New World'.

The Homecoming: Life 1893-1904

During Dvořák's first winter in America, he was told about a settlement of Czechs at Spillville in north-east Iowa. By mid-February he had decided he would send for the rest of his family so that they could all enjoy the summer together at Spillville. On the day he finished the 'New World' Symphony he heard that his four youngest children had reached Southampton, and was so overjoyed that he forgot to add the trombone parts in the final bars, and did not discover the omission until the work was rehearsed several months later. Dvořák was happier at Spillville than at any other time during his stay in the United States. He settled down immediately, played the organ at seven o'clock Mass on his first morning, much to the surprise of the congregation, and two days later, in the best of humours, began composing his String Quartet in F major. He finished the sketch on the third day, and wrote on the last page: 'Thanks be to God. I am satisfied. It went quickly.' The score was completed in less than a fortnight, and three days later he started on his String Quintet in E flat major. Dvořák made friends with some Indians who visited Spillville and invited them to the inn, where they entertained his family on two or three occasions with singing and dancing.

On 12th August Dvořák conducted his Eighth Symphony, three Slavonic Dances and *My Home* Overture at the World's Fair, Chicago. This was Czech Day at the Fair, and in the parade 30,000 Czechs from all corners of the United States took part. At the beginning of September he travelled to Omaha and St Paul, Minnesota, and at both places he was honoured with sumptuous banquets. From St Paul he went to see the Minnehaha Falls, and on his return journey to New York he stopped at Buffalo to see Niagara, which impressed him so much that he exclaimed: 'Damn it! That will be a symphony in B minor!'

He thought it appropriate to make his opus 100 a Sonatina for violin and piano for Otilie and Antonín, his eldest children, and in the slow movement used a melody he had jotted down on his shirt cuff when he visited the Minnehaha Falls. The first performance of his 'New World' Symphony, conducted by Anton Seidl on 16th December 1893, was a tremendous occasion. In a letter to Simrock, Dvořák said: 'The papers state that no composer has ever had such a success. I was in a box. The hall was filled with the best New York audience, and they applauded so much that I had to thank them from the box like a king *à la* Mascagni in Vienna (don't laugh!).' His new quartet was played at Boston on 1st January and the Quintet in New York on the 12th.

Mrs Thurber, the President of the National Conservatory of Music, wanted to make certain that Dvořák would continue as Director for another two years, but he was in no hurry to make up his mind. He was rather worried about his salary, which was seriously in arrears because Mrs Thurber's millionaire husband had become a victim of the panic of 1893 and was on the verge of bankruptcy. However, Dvořák finally agreed to continue and signed the contract on 28th April 1894. A month later he was on his way home for the summer.

Dvořák composed the Humoresques at Vysoká and presented an organ to the neighbouring village of Třebsko on his birthday in gratitude for his safe return, but otherwise the months passed uneventfully. After conducting the 'New World' Symphony in Prague on 13th October he set off once again for America, taking with him only his wife and his second son Otakar. He was far more homesick than before, and his six months in New York dragged on interminably. With his thoughts turning homewards he composed his great Cello Concerto between November and February. He sailed for home on 16th April 1895. During the summer he made contact with Simrock and Hanslick and looked up close friends. He finally decided that various family reasons made it impossible for him to return to New York for eight months in the winter of 1895-96, as had been agreed. In any case Mrs Thurber had not been in a position to keep to her side of the bargain.

Once he knew he was home for good, Dvořák returned to a more normal routine. He resumed teaching at the Prague Conservatory, wrote the String Quartets in G major and A flat major during November and December, and composed two symphonic poems and sketched a third early in 1896 in only seven and a half weeks. He paid several visits to Vienna, where he saw Brahms, Richter and Bruckner, and went to London for the last time to conduct the first performance of his Cello Concerto. Towards the end of that year he wrote a fourth symphonic poem. Dvořák went to see Brahms once more during his last illness and returned for his funeral on 6th April 1897. During June and July he was busy revising his opera *The Jacobin*, and after that he composed yet another symphonic poem. Dvořák must have been pleased by his appointment as one of the judges for the Austrian State Prize, the award which twenty-two years earlier had been so important a factor in his own life. His silver wedding

A letter, dated 5th March 1894, from Dvořák to the publisher Simrock, confirming the title of the Ninth Symphony as 'From the New World'

One of the main bridges over the Vltava in Prague seen from the island of Kampa

on 17th November 1898 was a particularly happy occasion because on that day his daughter Otilie married his pupil Josef Suk.

From May 1898 up to the end of his life Dvořák devoted all his energies to the composition of operas. He had become famous as a composer of orchestral, choral and chamber music, but in opera international fame had eluded him, and up to that time he had not even written a work for the stage to win the hearts of his own people, as *The Bartered Bride* had done. He chose a Czech fairy tale, *Kate and the Devil*, for his new opera, and worked on it from May until the following February. It was performed on 23rd November 1899 and was warmly acclaimed.

Now that the opera fever was upon him, Dvořák immediately started looking for another libretto. After some time he discovered that Kvapil had written one on the old legend of the water nymph who falls in love with a prince. He immediately pounced upon this and set about composing *Rusalka*. He worked at this ambitious project with such enthusiasm that the whole three-act opera was written in only seven months, and was complete by 27th November 1900. When it was first presented on 31st March 1901 it was hailed as a great triumph – the greatest he ever experienced in the theatre. At last he had succeeded in composing the work he had dreamed about, an opera that would be treasured by his fellow Czechs. Mahler was most anxious to mount it in Vienna and rehearsals began, but for some unexplained reason Dvořák never signed the contract and no performance took place.

Towards the end of his life Dvořák received several more honours and distinctions. The Emperor Franz Josef I awarded him the rare Medal of Honour for Arts and Sciences, which the composer called his 'big golden platter'. He was also elected a life member of the Austrian House of Lords, but he appeared there only once. In recognition of his commanding position in Czech music he was appointed Director of the Prague Conservatory in the summer of 1901, but he was simply a figurehead. It was well known that he had no flair for administration, so that was left entirely to Professor Knittl.

It was no easy task to find a libretto for another opera, but eventually Dvořák decided upon *Armida*, the Italian subject that Lully, Handel, Gluck and many others had set. Possibly the success of *Rusalka* made him hanker once more after international acclaim. It took a year and a half to complete *Armida*. The rehearsals at the National Theatre did not go smoothly, and when the work was performed on 25th March 1904 it was considered a failure. This was a bitter blow to Dvořák. At this very moment his health began to give cause for alarm; he was obliged to leave the theatre early owing to a pain in his side. A few days later he caught a chill and received further medical attention, but on May Day his doctor declared him well enough to join the family for lunch. He enjoyed his soup, but then collapsed, and before the doctor arrived he was dead.

He was honoured with a national funeral, during which part of his own Requiem was sung. His burial took place at the Vyšehrad, in the cemetery high above the river Vltava where the most illustrious men and women of the Czech nation are laid to rest.

Slav Nationalism

The reasons for the remarkably rapid rise of national awareness in so many countries during the 19th century must be sought in the political, social and economic conditions of those times, as well as in the spheres of philosophy and culture. The wind of change was already manifest in the previous century in the writings of men like Rousseau and Voltaire, but only the French Revolution was able to shake the people as a whole out of their unthinking acceptance of the *status quo*. Once Napoleon Bonaparte succeeded in making himself the dominating figure in Europe, further tensions were created. Some of these remained pent up until they finally exploded in the numerous revolutions of 1830 and 1848.

The Italian revolutionary Mazzini strove to destroy the corrupt Kingdom of Naples and unite the whole of Italy, from Piedmont, Lombardy and Venetia in the north to Sicily and Sardinia in the south. He had visions of an ideal republic. Little did he realise that his dream of a united Italian-speaking nation would only materialise in the form of a monarchy under Victor Emmanuel. Nevertheless the *risorgimento* movement succeeded in its primary aim.

Similar ferment occurred in many other areas. Belgium became a nation in its own right. Poland, after revolting valiantly against the might of Russia, was brought to its knees. Hungarians and Czechs pressed their claims before the Austrian Emperor, but met with mixed success. The Norwegians resented the privileged position of the Danish aristocracy in their country, while making the best they could of their union with Sweden.

Glinka (1804-57), the father of Russian music, was undoubtedly influenced by the stirrings of liberal nationalism in Italy when he was in Milan, Naples, Rome and Bologna in the years 1830-33. It was at that time that he became fully aware that there was a great deal wrong with music in his own country. Italian opera had been the basic musical fare in St Petersburg for several decades. It is true that French *opéra comique* made its appearance later and in 1824 Weber's *Der Freischütz* was performed there, but up till that time no Russian composers came forward who were capable of competing with all this imported music from countries with a long musical history. Neither did they make very much use of the Russian language. Glinka was convinced that he had to write music that was 'Russian', and hoped that his example would be followed by others. He was unable to shake off foreign influences, but made an important start towards establishing a Russian style in opera. Apart from the obvious cosmopolitanism of *Ruslan and Lyudmila* (1842), he tried to introduce the spirit of the age-old Russian *bilini* in the wedding scene.

How is it possible for a composer to infuse his music with a national spirit? For the most part Glinka's solution was crude and unsatisfactory. In his earlier opera *A Life for the Tsar* he used mazurka rhythms in the Polish scenes, and in *Ruslan* a Persian melody adds a pseudo-oriental touch and a Caucasian *lezginka* provides an astonishing element of barbaric modernity. But he made no attempt to use his exotic material consistently. In contrast, Borodin made a determined effort to provide the Polovtsy with genuine Polovtsian music in *Prince Igor* (1869-87).

Russian composers had no difficulty in suggesting orientalism with pseudo-eastern arabesques, as we may see in Balakirev's *Islamey* and *Tamara* and Rimsky-Korsakov's *Scheherazade*. They could invoke a Spanish atmosphere by means of Spanish dance rhythms, as in Glinka's *Summer Night in Madrid* and Rimsky-Korsakov's *Spanish Capriccio*. It was much more difficult for them to convey a Russian spirit. Sometimes the composers of the second half of the century attempted this by using Russian or Ukrainian folk melodies as themes. At other times their 'Russianness' consisted of no more than recollections of the music of Glinka. They placed considerable reliance on what they found valuable in the music of other nations. The experience and example of Weber, Berlioz and Liszt were invaluable to men who had so little of their own music to turn to, but this factor raised its own problems. When Tchaikovsky's music proclaims his love for Mozart and French opera, can it still be regarded as wholly Russian?

All the composers in Balakirev's little group are to a greater or lesser degree nationalists, but one of them entered far more deeply into the Russian soul than was possible for the others. It was Mussorgsky who possessed this remarkable understanding of the many facets of the Russian character. Thanks to this he could vividly depict a peasant in a few bars of a song, and portray the tragic

The cover of an edition of Dvořák's opera Rusalka. *(National Museum, Prague)*

RUSALKA

growth of a tsar's madness in *Boris Godunov* (1868-69).

In Bohemia Smetana (1824-84) was forced to learn what he could from composers of other countries, just as the Russians were. He particularly admired Berlioz, Schumann and Liszt, and in addition Liszt was a most valuable friend to him. Smetana believed that if national music drew its themes from folk-songs it would not be possible to create a unified artistic work, and something like a quodlibet would result. He therefore endeavoured to write music that embodied the spirit of his nation without relying on direct borrowings from folklore. This was a bold and wise step, for folk-songs are usually too simple and primitive to be suitable for symphonic treatment. Dvořák was also keenly aware of all this. On the few occasions when he turned to a folk source he either borrowed only a fragment from it, or transformed the folk melody with considerable skill and artistry.

Smetana's remarkable achievement in creating a Czech musical style was of the utmost importance to Dvořák, for this meant he was far better placed than the Russian composers who followed Glinka. Besides, the Russians were on the peripheries of European culture, whereas Dvořák lived close to that great hub of musical activity and development – Vienna. He was a deep admirer of the great Classical composers and found Wagner's music thrilling.

At first no clear national tendencies were apparent in his music. In the late 1870s, however, his national consciousness became fully awakened. He seized upon the dance rhythms of Bohemia, Moravia and Slovakia, making them serve as a foundation for movements of his symphonies, chamber music and Violin Concerto, as well as in his **Slavonic Dances**.

When Smetana used folk melodies, he did so quite deliberately. He wrote piano fantasias on a few of them in his Czech Dances, borrowed a lullaby for his opera *The Kiss* and introduced a *furiant* into *The Bartered Bride*. Dvořák, on the other hand, absorbed the spirit of the folklore of his country to such an extent that characteristic traits of that music emerge from time to time in his compositions. Dvořák's musical nationalism therefore is manifest in his use of numerous dance rhythms and small elements taken from folk sources and his assimilations from Smetana, which are all amalgamated with his own highly individual and personal style.

Between them Smetana and Dvořák gave their country a rich heritage of music, a heritage that shows clearly that Czech music had reached maturity, that it possessed a distinction and individuality of its own, and had earned for itself a vital and important place in the music of the 19th century.

A dancer performing the kolecko, *depicted in a drawing by Maly in 1890 (National Museum, Prague)*

Dvořák in America

When Dvořák arrived in New York in 1892 the National Conservatory of Music of America had been in existence for seven years. Mrs Jeannette Thurber, the President of the Conservatory, felt that it was time for the United States to provide an institution where such excellent musical education would be available that Americans would not need to go to such places as Paris or Leipzig for their training. She was also a firm believer in opera in English, and hoped to make it unnecessary for America to import so much foreign talent. Her millionaire husband was prepared to support her in these ventures, but the opera project was shipwrecked quite early with losses of more than 100,000 dollars. The curriculum of the National Conservatory was modelled on that of the Paris Conservatoire, and free tuition was given to talented and needy students, which meant that it was very largely a philanthropic institution.

With her eye on the forthcoming Columbus Fourth Centennial celebrations she decided she must have at the head of her large staff a composer of world renown. There seemed to be two possible candidates, Dvořák and Sibelius, and she chose the former. She cherished the idea of founding an American school of composition and was confident that Dvořák, so distinguished an exponent of nationalism in music, was the right person to provide the necessary training and leadership for talented young Americans. She envisaged an art stemming from the folk music of her country, the spirituals, the plantation songs and Indian music. It is curious that she did not include the songs of white settlers, but perhaps a partial explanation for this lies in her sympathy for the underdog, a viewpoint shared by Dvořák. The Negro students at the Conservatory did not pay fees. It was natural for her to hope that the music that Dvořák would write in the United States, including the opera based on *Hiawatha* which she wanted from him, would breathe the spirit of America and set an example to the students of his composition class.

Mrs Thurber had no intention of giving Dvořák the responsibility of organising and administering her National Conservatory. He had no direct say in policy or finance, which were fully controlled by her. He undertook to teach composition and orchestration only to the most talented students, to conduct the rehearsals and concerts of the Conservatory orchestra and choir, to take a leading part in the institution's examinations, and to conduct not more than six public concerts in New York and other cities in each year if required. His teaching, rehearsing and examining occupied him for three hours on six mornings a week during term time, and he was free in the afternoons and evenings to compose or spend the time as he wished. He was not tied in any way during the four summer months.

The public concerts were not particularly successful, especially as so many people were hard up because of the panic of 1893, so these were discontinued altogether after a while. Since there were to be no concerts in Dvořák's third year and he was only required to act as Director for six months that winter, his salary was reduced to 8,000 dollars, but if he had returned for eight months in the winter of 1895-96 as he had agreed, his salary would have risen to 10,000 dollars. But that was not to be.

Dvořák allowed a number of misleading statements to be reported regarding his views on Negro and Indian melodies, possibly because he, or more probably Mrs Thurber, fancied that when his 'New World' Symphony was about to be played, this was the kind of thing the public would like to be told. We may be sure, however, that when writing his Symphony he was keenly interested in Negro spirituals but knew very little about Indian song. It is possible that he deliberately wrote more pentatonic melodies in his American works than was usual for him, knowing that these gapped scales serve as the basis of many Negro melodies. Occasionally he wrote a relatively primitive theme. Dvořák explained that he did not use actual American folk melodies but tried to reproduce their spirit.

When Dvořák went to America, Edward Macdowell, at the age of thirty, had already made a name for himself as composer, pianist and teacher at Boston, Mass., but he was the only musician of that time to achieve such distinction. Apart from him the best known composers were Sousa and Stephen Foster. Dvořák did not have any really outstanding pupils in New York, but undoubtedly the most significant was Rubin Goldmark, who composed *Hiawatha*, *Negro Rhapsody* and *The Call of the Plains*, in addition to the successful opera *The Queen of Sheba*. He became director of composition at the Juilliard Graduate School of Music in 1924, and hence the teacher of Aaron Copland and George Gershwin. These three composers in their respective ways incorporated indigenous musical material into their compositions. But it can hardly be claimed that either Copland or Gershwin bears any conspicuous Dvořákin imprint. Even if Dvořák did not succeed in bringing into being an American school of composition, he drew attention to some of the possibilities that lay open to American composers, and by living in their midst for a while, brought them into closer contact with the mainstream of European music. In this way he contributed something of importance towards the development of American music of the present century.

PROGRAM NOTES FOR THE RECORD

by R O B E R T   J A C O B S O N

The 'New World' Symphony

Dvořák was just past fifty years old—and had already composed the bulk of his work—when he came to America for the first time, in 1892, to assume the post of director of the National Conservatory in New York as well as to conduct six concerts of his own music. He was encouraged by his patroness Mrs Thurber to air his views on founding an American school of composition, just as he and Smetana had by then established a recognisable Czech national style. This was one of Mrs Thurber's main purposes in inviting the Bohemian-born composer to her country, for his reputation was already international.

During his American stay Dvořák finished his *Te Deum* for chorus and orchestra and *The American Flag*, scored for chorus, orchestra and soloists and set to a poem by J. R. Drake. At the same time he began work on his Ninth Symphony in E minor, which was completed on 24th May 1893. Though he may have intended to return home to Europe for his summer vacation, he was instead persuaded to go to the little Czech farm community of Spillville, Iowa, where he produced his Quartet in F (the 'American') and the String Quintet in D flat. His first year in the United States had indeed been a profitable period for his composing career. Later, after an idyllic summer holiday among countrymen and a festive appearance at Czech Day at the Chicago World Exhibition, he returned to New York for the second year of his contract at the Conservatory. This second season was highlighted by the world première of his new symphony in Carnegie Hall on 16th December 1893, with Anton Seidl conducting the New York Philharmonic Society. This first work which Dvořák had written completely on American soil represented a new stage in his creative development, in which he began to make use of American themes. Nostalgia for his Bohemian homeland left him undecided about whether to accept a third-year contract in America, but he did return for six months the next year. This was to be his last visit to North America.

In that busy year of 1893, while sketching the second movement of his last symphony, Dvořák wrote: 'It seems to me that American soil will influence my thought beneficially, and I could almost say that something of that kind is already heard in the new symphony.' Later he wrote: 'I have just finished a new symphony in E minor. It pleases me very much and will differ very substantially from my earlier compositions. Well, the influence of America can be felt by anyone who has "a nose".' The 'influence' encompasses his new-found interest in Negro spirituals, the plantation songs of Stephen Foster and songs of the North American Indians. On this subject he commented: 'The music of the people is like a rare and

A drawing of peasants from the northeast of Bohemia (National Museum, Prague)

lovely flower growing amidst encroaching weeds. Thousands pass it, while others trample it underfoot, and thus the chances are that it will perish before it is seen by the one discriminating spirit who will prize it above all else. The fact that no one has yet arisen to make the most of it does not prove that nothing is there.'

While at the National Conservatory, Dvořák asked a black student, Harry T. Burleigh, to sing spirituals for him. These and Stephen Foster's songs impressed him greatly. Regarding Indian music, he offered: 'Here and there another spirit, other thoughts, another colouring flashes—in short, Indian music, something "à la Bret Harte".' He absorbed all these elements, declaring: 'It is this spirit which I have tried to reproduce in my new symphony. I have not actually used any of the melodies. I have simply written original themes embodying the peculiarities of the Indian music, and using these themes as subjects, have developed them with all the resources of modern rhythms, harmony, counterpoint and orchestral colour.' Dvořák employed the general characteristics of the American Indian scale in what is basically Czech music, but Negro melodies are more in evidence than anything else in his works of this period. What he created from these disparate elements was a paean to the folk spirit of two countries—the United States and his native Czechoslovakia.

Dvořák began to sketch his themes in mid-December of 1892, and the work was completed by late May of 1893. The descriptive title 'From the New World' was added just before the finished score was delivered to Seidl for the first performance. Dvořák explained that all this phrase meant was 'Impressions and greetings from the New World.' Most of its themes are found in initial forms in one of the composer's American sketchbooks, but only those for the slow movement were written down in the same key as they appear in the symphony. Throughout, Dvořák shows a preference for themes in flat keys.

A dark-hued Adagio introduction moves dramatically from a melancholy and hesitant statement to passionate outcries, sung first by the cellos, then by flutes and oboes, with answers from the drums and winds. The main theme, introduced by violas, cellos, and two horns (over violin tremolos), eventually becomes *Allegro molto*. The whole orchestra takes up this rising, pulsating music and proceeds to the second subject: this has two themes, one in minor key played by the horns with strings, and the other in major, first heard in the flutes and then in the violins. (This latter is reminiscent of 'Swing Low, Sweet Chariot.') Rhythmically, too, this last motif resembles the opening theme. These thematic materials are then developed, leading to the return of the principal idea, but in a distant key. Finally the original E minor is restored in a furious climax to the movement.

The famous Largo in D flat opens with wonderful orchestral chords, their harmonies ushering in the beautiful Negro melody that was later turned into 'Goin' Home.' Introduced by the English horn, there is a helpless quality about this theme, in contrast to a vivacious but ghostly variation that appears in the flutes and oboes and is then taken up by the rest of the orchestra. Dvořák indicated that this skipping oboe variant was intended to suggest the gradual awakening of animal life on the prairie. He was inspired by the scene of the woodland funeral of Minnehaha in Longfellow's epic poem *The Song of Hiawatha*, which he considered as a subject for an opera. The main theme of the first movement bursts out again, then the dying Largo motif of this movement returns, only to fade away.

The vigorous Scherzo (*Molto vivace*) is marked by reiterated notes, contrasted with two interludes of enthusiasm and sentiment. The lively tune for flute and oboe (answered by the clarinet) sounds like American Indian music, rather than being of Negro inspiration. A fragment of the first movement again returns. Here Dvořák said he was inspired by the scene in *Hiawatha* where the Indians dance at the feast.

The Finale (*Allegro con fuoco*) has a powerful theme announced by horns and trombones, which is impressive in its nobility and breadth. A more animated repetitive theme follows (similar to 'Three Blind Mice'), after which the solo clarinet takes up a beautiful second melody. Once again, themes from the earlier movements begin to pass in review—from the Largo, the Scherzo and the first movement. In the Coda the main theme of the first movement angrily shouts through and the introduction to the Largo is stridently reiterated. Fragmentary echoes of all four sections then fade off, interrupted by a brief storm. The last chord, violently struck, dies away into silence.

In a way, the Symphony in E minor was Dvořák's testament to what he believed about national music. During an interview given while in New York, he said: 'I am convinced that the future music of this country must be founded on what are called Negro melodies. These can be the foundation of a serious and original school of composition to be developed in the United States. . . . These beautiful and varied themes are a product of the soil. They are American. They are the folk-songs of America, and your composers must turn to them. . . . Only in this way can a musician express the true sentiment of a people. . . . In the Negro melodies of America, I discovered all that is needed for a great and noble school of music. They are pathetic, tender, passionate, melancholy, solemn, religious, bold, merry, gay, gracious, or what you will. . . . There is nothing in the whole range of composition that cannot find a thematic source here.'

Printed in the United States of America

Wolfgang Mozart

His Life and Times 1782-1791 (Part 2)

PROGRAM NOTES FOR THE SYMPHONY NO. 40 IN G MINOR AND THE JUPITER SYMPHONY NO. 41 IN C MAJOR
By Robert Jacobson

fw

FUNK & WAGNALLS, INC.
NEW YORK, NEW YORK

Poverty despite Success: 1782-90

'When he is in no pressing need, he is quite content and becomes indolent and inactive. Once set going he is all on fire and thinks he is going to make his fortune all at once. Nothing is allowed to stand in his way, and unfortunately it is just the cleverest people, the exceptional men of genius, who find continual obstacles in their path.' So wrote Leopold of his son's character, in the light of the composer's fortunes in Vienna, and the last part of his statement was to become tragically true.

The newlyweds settled down to a life which, if fairly stable emotionally, was always to be precarious financially. Little money was to be earned through publishing, which was a cut-throat racket at the time, of little benefit to the composer – in today's conditions, with his vast output and his popularity, Mozart would have been a millionaire. Only six months after his marriage, Mozart had to appeal for funds to meet a debt for which he was about to be sued. Public appearances as pianist, concerts, private lessons, the occasional commission . . . these were the means with which he eked out an existence, all the while in the hope of a permanent court post being offered to him.

However, there was spiritual and musical comfort to be drawn from friends. None more so than from Baron van Swieten to whose house Mozart went for regular Sunday morning music making, from the beginning of 1782 onwards. Van Swieten's musical interests were severe – mainly the baroque contrapuntists, Bach and Handel, who were a revelation to Mozart. He copied and studied many of their works. At the time he wrote a baroque-type suite for piano (K.399) and some fugues but the influence was to be less localised than that, as his mastery of counterpoint in the later symphonies – or in any of his mature scores – shows.

A son, who tragically died a few months later, was born to the couple and Leopold was named godfather as Mozart was very anxious to smooth over Leopold's resentment and displeasure. It still remained for Constanze to meet her in-laws and accordingly at the end of July 1783 they set out for Salzburg. It seems that the visit was not a great success, for neither father nor sister particularly liked Constanze, which disappointed the young couple, especially the fact that Leopold did not offer her some family knick-knacks to prove his fatherly acceptance of the girl.

In this atmosphere they stayed in Salzburg for three months, a time which was not exactly inactive musically for the composer. He brought with him, and had performed on 26th October, the Mass in C minor (K.427) which he had promised to write for Constanze before their marriage. Constanze herself sang the taxing soprano part. Likewise he worked for a while on an abortive opera, *L'oca del Cairo* (The Goose of Cairo) (K.422), with Varesco, the librettist of *Idomeneo*. In addition he wrote two Duets for Violin and Viola (K.423/4) for Konzertmeister Michael Haydn who was unable to write them owing to illness. They were presented to the Archbishop under Haydn's name!

On their way back to Vienna in October, the couple stopped off at Linz at the invitation of Count Thun. Mozart was asked to provide a symphony for a concert which was to take place within a few days. He did not have one with him and had to write a new one. On 31st October he wrote to his father: 'On Tuesday 4th November I shall give a concert in the theatre here, and as I have not a single symphony with me I am writing one for dear life to be ready in time.' The result was the 'Linz' Symphony, No. 36 in C (K.425), a work which shows no signs of the haste in which it was written.

Back in Vienna he set hard to work, composing a Fantasy for Piano, two works using horn (a Quintet and a Concerto) and the very striking String Quartet in E flat, K.428 (the third of the set he dedicated to Haydn) and some concert arias for his former love Aloysia Lange (née Weber).

Some of the latter were performed with great success during the Lent concert season of 1783. Mozart wrote to his father with pride: 'Gluck had the box next to the Langes, in which was also my wife. He could not praise enough either the symphony or the song and he invited us all to dinner next Sunday.' Equally successful was Mozart's concert on 22nd March: 'What pleased me most was the sight of the Emperor, and how pleased he was and how he applauded me.'

It was at the end of 1783 that Mozart wrote a work of no particular musical significance, but which was one of the first to manifest his interest in Freemasonry – the Masonic cantata 'Dir, Seele des Weltfalls' (To Thee, Soul of the Universe), K.429. Mozart became a full-fledged Freemason in 1785 when he entered the Crowned Hope Lodge (Zur gekrönten Hoffnung).

1784 shows Mozart at work on various things – one of which again shows his capacity to work under great pressure with, seemingly, little injury to his music. A violin sonata (K.454) written for a young Italian violinist Regina Strinasacchi was finished only on the morning of the concert and Mozart played a visually non-existent part from memory, his only aid being a few hastily jotted-down notes.

Meeting other famous composers at the time may have been the occasion for an exchange of ideas. Late in 1784 he met both Sarti and Paisiello and showed his respect for them by writing sets of variations on tunes written by them. Paisiello had written a very famous opera *The Barber of Seville* and, as has been pointed out, this may have suggested the idea of basing an opera on Beaumarchais' sequel, *The Marriage of Figaro*.

Leopold visited his son and daughter-in-law in 1785 some six months after another child, Karl, had been born. The old man was very pleased and proud of his son as performer and composer. After a concert where Mozart performed the concerto he had written for the blind pianist Maria Therese Paradies (he often wrote works for his more talented pupils) Leopold wrote: 'I had a very good box and could hear every gradation of the instruments so perfectly that the tears came to my eyes for very joy.' He was truly astonished by the staggering romantic D minor concerto (K.466) which he heard at another concert. This D minor concerto – the finest of his concertos so far – was to be followed over the next few years by an extraordinary sequence of concertos: E flat, K.482; C, K.467; and early in 1786 the two probably most well known: A, K.488 and C minor, K.491.

The day after his arrival in Vienna, Leopold met Haydn at a quartet party at Mozart's house. It was on this occasion that the older composer said: 'I assure you before God and as an honest man that I consider your son to be the greatest composer I know or of whom I have ever heard; he has taste and what is more, he possesses a thorough knowledge of composition.' Mozart and Haydn had renewed their earlier acquaintance and had become great and mutually respecting friends. Haydn often came to Mozart's house to play quartets, with two other composers, Dittersdorf and Vanhal, and Mozart in deepest respect dedicated six quartets to him.

He also played quartets at the lodgings of his new pupil Stephen Storace, then aged twenty-two. In fact Mozart became friendly with quite a little British colony in Vienna – Storace's sister, another young English composer by the name of Thomas Attwood, and the Irish singer Michael Kelly. Indeed Kelly has given us one of the best contemporary pen-portraits of Mozart:

'He was a remarkably small man, very thin and pale, with a profusion of fine fair hair, of which he was rather vain. He gave me a cordial invitation to his house, of which I availed myself, and passed a great part of my time there. He always received me with kindness and hospitality. He was remarkably fond of punch, of which beverage I have seen him take copious draughts. He was also fond of billiards, and had an excellent billiard table in his house. Many and many a game have I played with him, but always came off second best. He gave Sunday concerts, at which I was never missing. He was kind-hearted, and always ready to oblige; but so very particular, when he played, that if the slightest noise were made, he instantly left off.'[1]

But Mozart was not happy merely to write instrumental works and to be known as a soloist in brilliant piano concertos of his own composition. He was still an opera composer whose last opera, *Die Entführung,* had been produced as long ago as 1782. And it was at this time that he met the man, a Venetian Jew, who was to provide him with the libretti for the operas for which he is revered: *The Marriage of Figaro, Don Giovanni,* and *Cosi fan tutte.* The librettist was Lorenzo da Ponte, born Emmanuele Conegliano.

Although da Ponte's name first appears in Mozart's correspondence as early as 1783 it seems that the two men met only in 1785. Mozart persuaded da Ponte to furnish him with a libretto from Beaumarchais' *The Marriage of Figaro* by underlining the fact that this play's attack on the present social order would give them a chance to get their own back on the society whose tyranny they had both experienced. The National Theatre was badly in need of a good opera and

da Ponte, recognising their opportunity, agreed to the plan and wasted no time in producing his contribution. He boasted that his libretto was completed in six weeks but this needs to be taken with a pinch of salt, although it certainly indicates that he was able to work at extreme speed without prejudice to quality. He was, however, careful to take some of the sting out of Beaumarchais' work in order not to anger the Emperor, Joseph II.

As the Emperor had expressed doubts about Mozart's ability as an operatic composer, da Ponte also made it clear that he was prepared to stake his own reputation on Mozart's gifts in this particular field. This tactical move on da Ponte's part induced the Emperor to send for Mozart and ask to hear some of the music from the new work. Mozart obliged, the music was approved and the order was given for the National Theatre to start plans for the production.

For the next months, Mozart worked under pressure. He was obliged to fulfil all his normal concert-giving duties at the same time as composing the opera and we find various references in his father's letters complaining that he received only the most infrequent news of his son.

However, in spite of all the difficulties and much intrigue by the factions of Mozart's rivals, Salieri and Dittersdorf, plans for the production went ahead and, on 1st May 1786, *The Marriage of Figaro* was at last given its first performance. The opera was a resounding success. Leopold recounts in a letter that 'at the second performance . . . five pieces were repeated, and at the third performance seven, among which a little duet had to be sung three times.' The audiences were so appreciative that an order had to be given banning encores, but, after a token honouring of this legislation, excitement overcame their restraint and they once again clamoured for repeats. The success of *The Marriage of Figaro* continued until November when Martín y Soler's *Una cosa rara* was given its first performance. The fickle musical public of Vienna seemed to forget their love of Mozart's work and *The Marriage of Figaro* went out of the repertory for the best part of two years.

On 18th October a third child, baptised Johann Thomas Leopold, was born to the Mozarts – a cause for joy that must have distracted Mozart from the imminent closure of his opera. When this did finally occur, Mozart turned once again to the idea of going off to some other city to try his luck, particularly as Dittersdorf was once again enjoying great success in the capital. In 1782 Mozart had told his father of his plan to go to Paris and had been sharply reprimanded for such a reckless proposition. In spite of this parental warning he had soon after started to consider going to Italy. In actual fact, neither of these expeditions took place but now, in 1786, the possibility of going to England was put to Mozart by Thomas Attwood, one of his pupils who also happened to be the protégé of the Prince of Wales. Mozart once again wrote to his father, this time asking if he would be prepared to look after the children in the event of this journey taking place, but, on 17th November, Leopold wrote back refusing emphatically. However by the time this letter reached Vienna from Salzburg the baby had died. Once again the plans for travelling were shelved and instead Mozart made arrangements for a series of concerts for his fourth winter in Vienna.

[1] *Mozart* by Eric Blom, Master Musicians series, Dent 1966.

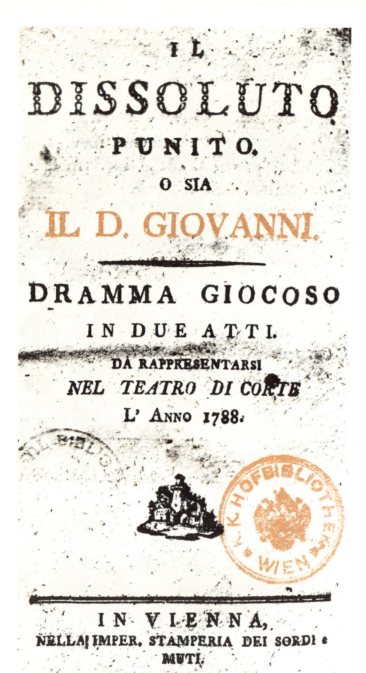

IL
DISSOLUTO
PUNITO.
O SIA
IL D. GIOVANNI.

DRAMMA GIOCOSO
IN DUE ATTI.

DA RAPPRESENTARSI
NEL TEATRO DI CORTE
L' ANNO 1788.

IN VIENNA,
NELLA IMPER. STAMPERIA DEI SORDI e
MUTI.

Cover of the libretto of Don Giovanni (*Austrian National Library, Vienna*)

A letter from Mozart to his friend Gottfried von Jacquin details the type of life that he and Constanze led in Prague. From one sumptuous meal on to a session of private music-making to another meal followed by a ball, they led a life of carefree gaiety. Mozart attended *The Marriage of Figaro* on 17th January and conducted a second performance on 20th January, being regaled by the enthusiastic audience on both occasions. But perhaps the highlight of the weeks in Prague was his concert at the theatre the day before the second of these performances of the opera. At this concert Mozart intended to introduce himself to Prague as a pianist. There are various descriptions of the concert which Mozart ended by improvising for an hour and a half to thunderous applause.

Another great success was the presentation of the D major Symphony, K.504, now known as the 'Prague' Symphony, a somewhat misleading name as it had actually been written in Vienna some time before.

But the pleasant life in Prague could not last forever and in the middle of February 1787 Mozart and his wife returned to Vienna. Back in the capital he approached da Ponte again for a new libretto. In fact, at the same time da Ponte was also asked for libretti by both Salieri and Martín y Soler. Da Ponte wrote: 'I loved and esteemed all three of them, and hoped to find in each compensation for past failures and some increment to my glory in opera. I wondered whether it might not be possible to satisfy them all and write three operas at one spurt.' And this is exactly what he did, writing all three simultaneously! For Salieri, he produced an Italian adaptation of *Tarare*; for Martín y Soler *L'arbore di Diana*; and for Mozart, *Don Giovanni*, which was based on the then very popular Don Juan theme. The libretto of *Don Giovanni* was completed by the end of May 1787 and during the next months Mozart composed little besides the music for this opera.

In April, the young Beethoven came to see Mozart but the latter was so taken up with *Don Giovanni* that he was able to devote little time to his visitor. The situation was not helped by the news that Leopold's health was failing. It had begun to decline at the beginning of the year and although there had been a temporary improvement he was still not well. By the middle of March he was suffering badly from what now seems to have been dropsy. Mozart wrote to his father expressing his concern for his health and this letter must have patched up the differences that there had been between them over the past few years. Although Leopold's condition had changed little at the beginning of May, on 28th May he quite suddenly died.

In April, Mozart himself had fallen ill and although he soon recovered, the expense incurred by the medical attention obliged him to give up the rather extravagant apartment in the Schulerstrasse and to move to the Landstrasse. This new home was outside the city walls and the composition of *Don Giovanni* must have been completed in surroundings which were relatively rustic.

On 6th October 1787 Mozart was once again in Prague. The Prague newspaper, *Oberpostamtszeitung*, announced that he had arrived and that the new opera – at that stage referred to as *The Stone Banquet* – was to be performed in the near future. The plan was that it should be produced for the visit of Prince Anton of Saxony and his wife, the Arch-

Mozart's friends in Prague had, however, been busy championing his cause and – probably with the aid of the Freemasons in the city – had persuaded the manager of the Prague National Theatre, Pasquale Bondini, to stage *The Marriage of Figaro*. In December 1786, it was given its first performance there and was received with great acclaim — 'No work . . . had ever created so much of a sensation as the Italian opera *The Marriage of Figaro,* which has already been given here several times by Bondini's company of operatic virtuosos and has received the greatest applause.' With this sort of reception from Prague following soon after the sad events in Vienna and the collapse of his planned journey to England, it was natural that Mozart should now see Prague as a possible place in which to settle.

A few weeks later, early in the bitter January of 1787, Mozart set out for Prague with Constanze and Franz Hofer, his future brother-in-law, at the invitation of Count Thun. The Thun family were also Freemasons and Mozart consequently saw a great deal of such prominent Masonic figures in Prague as Count Canal, Dr Ungar – both founders of the Masonic lodge Veracity (Zur Wahrheit) – and General Count Johann Pachta, who were all amateur musicians.

duchess Maria Theresa but Mozart reported that the artists were 'not as skilled as in Vienna and could not learn the opera in so short a time'. Instead the royal visit was celebrated by a production of *The Marriage of Figaro*. Da Ponte arrived on 8th October and put up at a hotel opposite the Mozarts who were lodged at an inn called 'Zu den drei Löwen' (The Three Lions). He set to work to train the singers and the première was fixed for 24th October.

The story of the composition of the overture for *Don Giovanni*, as the opera was now called, is one of the best known legends about Mozart. Two days before the first night it was still unwritten. Niemetschek, Mozart's biographer, relates: 'The anxiety of his friends which waxed with every passing hour seemed to amuse him. The more frantic they were the more nonchalant Mozart pretended to be. Finally, the evening before the performance, after he had had his fill of pleasantries he went to his room around midnight, began to write and within a few hours completed the remarkable masterpiece.'

As it happened, the première was postponed because one of the singers was ill but it was rescheduled for 29th October. Mozart then began to get cold feet about his new work, fearing that it would not be up to the standard which he had set himself with *The Marriage of Figaro*. He set about the rehearsals with great zeal and when the opera was finally produced it was another triumph.

For a few weeks more, Mozart and Constanze stayed on in Prague but at the news of the imminent death of Christoph Gluck they hurried back to Vienna. Mozart must have wanted to be present at the funeral of this famous composer but there is also no doubt that he harboured hopes of improving his position on Gluck's death. For once his hopes were justified. Gluck died on 15th November and on 7th December Mozart was appointed 'Imperial and Royal Court Composer' at a salary of 800 gulden. This was the position which his father Leopold had always wanted for him and it is ironic that, after waiting for seven years, Mozart should have obtained it only six months too late for his father to witness his success. To add to this new achievement, in the last days of the old year, Constanze gave birth to their first daughter, Therese.

The first performance of *Don Giovanni* in Vienna took place at the beginning of May 1788 but it was received by the Viennese without any great show of enthusiasm. From this time on, Mozart was again in financial difficulties. Vienna, always on the lookout for something new, seemed once again to have forgotten her old favourite. Through the summer things continued to go badly and, pressed by debtors, Mozart moved to the suburb of Währing where he completed his three final, and supreme, symphonies – in E flat K.543; in G minor K.550; and in C major K.551 ('Jupiter'). At the end of June, the Mozarts' six-month-old daughter died and Mozart was writing to his old friend Johann Michael Puchberg begging for a loan of money.

In August, he began to give concerts again – probably at van Swieten's house – and his financial situation improved slightly. Sometime after this, the Mozarts moved back to the centre of Vienna to a house on the Judenplatz. For the remaining months of 1788, their depressing state of impoverishment continued and it was not until the spring of 1789 that new hope appeared in Mozart's life. This came

An 18th-century painting of the dinner given at the palace of Schönbrunn in celebration of the marriage of Joseph II to Isabella of Parma

from Prince Lichnowsky, a son-in-law of Count Thun in Prague and a Masonic friend of Mozart. He was also Mozart's pupil and when, early in 1789, he was obliged to return to Berlin, he invited Mozart to accompany him.

Prince Lichnowsky and he set out on 7th April 1789 and at one of the first roadside halts he wrote to Constanze saying: 'Every moment I look at your portrait and weep, half in joy, half in sorrow.' On 10th April they arrived at Prague and after seeing some friends in the town were back on the road again by nine o'clock in the evening. Two days later, they were in Dresden and in addition to seeing further friends and musical acquaintances, Mozart was bidden to perform for the Elector Frederick August III of Saxony. This was a great honour since the Elector was not in the habit of receiving virtuosos who were simply passing through Dresden. For this concert Mozart performed the D major 'Coronation' Concerto and it must have pleased the Elector for the following day Mozart received 'a very fine snuffbox'.

On 18th April Mozart and Prince Lichnowsky moved on, arriving in Leipzig on 20th April. Here he played the organ in Bach's Thomaskirche for Johann Friederich Doles, who had been a pupil of Bach. Rochlitz, an eye-witness of the occasion, relates that 'Doles was utterly delighted with his playing and thought that old Sebastian Bach (his teacher) . . . had been resurrected.'

After three days, the journey was continued and they next halted at Potsdam. But by 8th May Mozart was seriously worried that he had had no news of Constanze for some time and consequently the travellers retraced their steps to Leipzig. There he found a letter from Vienna and was also delighted to meet the singer Josepha Duschek and his friends the Neumanns of Dresden. Because of them, the stay in Leipzig was protracted until 17th May.

Leaving Leipzig on 17th May a two-day journey at long last took them to Berlin. Within a few hours of their arrival, Mozart went to the National Theatre to hear a performance of *Die Entführung aus dem Serail* which had been put on in his honour. Pausing at the entrance to the auditorium he listened to the performance. Much of what he heard pleased him, but sometimes he was irritated by a wrong tempo or some other misinterpretation. He became more and more worked up until there came a point at which the second violins – perhaps through the fault of a copyist – played a D sharp instead of D. At this he was no longer able to restrain himself and called out loudly: 'Damn it, will you play D!' People turned round, he was recognised and when the news of his presence passed through the house he was greeted by excited applause.

On 26th May Mozart finally achieved the main purpose of his journey to Berlin. He was asked to play for King Frederick William II and Queen Frederike. After this performance he was commissioned to write six string quartets and, for Princess Frederike Charlotte, six 'easy piano sonatas'. But there was no great financial gain from this commission and Mozart wrote to Constanze saying: 'My dearest little wife, when I return you must rejoice more in having me back than in any money I bring.' Two days later

Mozart left Berlin, was in Prague by 31st May and a day later was again on the road for Vienna. On 4th June he was back once again with his beloved Constanze.

Mozart set to work almost immediately on the quartets and sonatas which had been commissioned in Berlin. But general material difficulties and Constanze's ill health began to upset his work. The doctor recommended that Constanze should be sent to Baden for another cure and it was the expenses for this and future cures which drew so heavily on Mozart's finances. He was soon writing to Puchberg, his banker friend, begging pathetically for further loans. Earlier he had attempted to give subscription concerts in his own house but this enterprise had been a total failure. He wrote that he was living 'in such wretchedness that my misery keeps me not only from going out but also from writing.' He went on several occasions to see his wife at Baden but was in Vienna again by the end of July as rehearsals for a new production of *The Marriage of Figaro* were starting.

So, at the end of August 1789, *The Marriage of Figaro* was once again back on the stage in Vienna and was received with the same delight as it had been two years before. Although these performances did little or nothing for Mozart's financial situation, they did bring him to the notice of the Viennese public again and he received several new commissions. One of these was for a new opera. He and da Ponte – who was once again enlisted as librettist – have left us nothing to tell us of the origins of this work, which came to be the celebrated *Cosi fan tutte,* but it seems likely that Mozart made a start on the music at the beginning of October.

The month of November was blackened by the birth and death of another daughter, Anna. Mozart's catalogue shows no entries for this month and he must have been giving all his attention to the opera, but in December he turned aside briefly from it to write twelve Minuets (K.585), twelve German Dances (K.586) and a contradance (K.587). As the payment for the opera was not to be made until it had been completed Mozart continued to be short of money and applied yet again to Puchberg, who generously obliged. The first rehearsal for *Cosi fan tutte* was planned for the last day of 1789 and to this Mozart invited only Haydn and Puchberg. Three weeks later the same two friends were invited to the first rehearsal with orchestra and on 26th January 1790 *Cosi fan tutte* was given its first performance at the Burgtheater. Vienna was soon full of its praises – one critic remarking that 'to say that the music is by Mozart is, I believe, to say everything.'

About a month after the première of *Cosi fan tutte,* the Emperor Joseph II died and there was great speculation in the city as to what changes his successor, Leopold II, would make. In actual fact nothing very much happened for the best part of a year but it was natural that Mozart, and many others, felt hopeful about the imminent and inevitable new appointments. He wrote to Puchberg saying: 'At present I stand on the threshold of my future but will be defeated forever if this time I fail of my goal.'

By the middle of May Mozart's finances had taken a turn for the worse and the next three months brought a string of requests to Puchberg, not only for money but also that he should let people know that he (Mozart) wanted more pupils. One cannot help being astonished that this man who, not so long ago, had been piano teacher to the leading families of Vienna should now have to ask for advertisement in order to find pupils. He again hoped to give a series of subscription concerts during the summer months but this project was stillborn as he could not afford to move into an apartment suitable for such gatherings.

Constanze's health once again required a lengthy cure at Baden and this time Mozart stayed there with her as long as possible. He composed virtually nothing in July and began to complain of toothache, headaches and insomnia. It seemed as though his endless disappointments were beginning to take a serious toll on his health.

When Emperor Joseph II died in 1790, Mozart lost his last friend at Court. Joseph had given him a miserable salary, it is true, but he was dimly aware that Mozart was an extraordinary figure. His successor, Leopold II, who came up from Tuscany to rule the Austro-Hungarian Empire, was no friend of Mozart's. The court protested violently when Prague chose Mozart to write the coronation opera there in 1791; and it was only because the Prague city authorities were just as stubborn as the Viennese Court that *La clemenza di Tito* was staged at all. But the Court arrived an hour late and the Empress Maria Ludovica hissed at the end of it, 'Questa è una porcheria tedesca' ('This is a piece of German swinishness') – not, perhaps, an enlightened description of Mozart's music.

An 18th-century print depicting the festivities to celebrate the coronation of Leopold II (National Gallery, Prague)

The Closing Months: 1790-91

On 19th September 1790 a triple royal wedding was to be celebrated in Vienna. The Archduke Francis was marrying the Princess of Naples, Maria Theresa; his brother, the Grand Duke Ferdinand of Tuscany, was marrying her sister, Louise Marie; and Leopold II's daughter Maria Clementine was being married to Crown Prince Francis of Naples. Four days before the wedding the contingent from Naples arrived in Vienna and there was a series of concerts and operas for the festivities. Mozart had hoped that he would be allowed to shine at these concerts but once again he was disappointed. The main concert was conducted by Salieri and the operas performed were Salieri's *Axur* and Weigl's *La caffeteria bizzarra*.

Five days after the wedding the royal party set out from Vienna to attend the official coronation of Leopold II as the Holy Roman Emperor at Frankfurt. For this occasion fifteen members of the Vienna court orchestra led by Salieri went to play at the celebration concerts but Mozart was not included in this venture. However he still hoped to profit by the assembly of the German-speaking nobility at the coronation and so felt it obligatory that he should go to Frankfurt at his own expense. Pawning his silver to buy a carriage, he set off with Franz Hofer, who was now his brother-in-law, having married Constanze's elder sister, Josepha.

Mozart and Hofer, by all accounts, had a pleasant and leisurely journey to Frankfurt. On 28th September they arrived in the coronation town but were obliged to stay at an inn in the suburb of Sachsenhausen owing to the immense number of the visitors in the town. Two days later they managed to find lodgings in a private house nearer the centre of the town. For the days prior to the coronation, when the town was in a state of ferment, Mozart led a quiet life staying at home most of the time to write. In all probability he was composing the Adagio and Allegro for Mechanical Organ, K.594, for Count Deym. He was bored by this composition and had only accepted the commission in order to 'put a few ducats into the hands of my dear little wife'. More interesting to him than this work was his chance of success with the various opera companies who were in Frankfurt at the time. It was planned to stage *Don Giovanni* on 5th November but this fell through and Mozart's opera was replaced by Dittersdorf's *Liebe im Narrenhause*. However *Die Entführung aus dem Serail* was performed about a week later.

Everything seemed to be against him for when the coronation actually took place in the second week of October, Mozart was only able to give his concert in the Stadttheater after all the main festivities were over. Obviously this was a very bad time since most of the visitors had started to drift off home soon after the ceremony. Once again Mozart had to write to Constanze telling her that the concert had been 'splendid from the point of view of honor, but meager as far as money is concerned.'

Arriving back in Vienna on 10th November, Mozart found a letter from O'Reilly, the manager of the London Opera, inviting him to come to London for six months. For the sum of three hundred pounds he would be asked to write two operas. It was about this time that Haydn had been invited to go to England by the impresario Salomon and at the farewell dinner before Haydn left, Salomon tried to persuade Mozart to go to England with them. Thus, in a short space of time, Mozart had received two invitations to go to England and thus to realise his dreams. But for some reason these invitations could not be accepted and Mozart went back to his depressing life which continued to be punctuated by appeals to Puchberg for money.

Emanuel Schikaneder, who had been Mozart's friend in 1780 and had given him the idea for *The Marriage of Figaro,* had left both his wife and Vienna in March 1786. At the beginning of 1789 he was in Regensburg but when he received a cry of help from his wife, he returned hastily to Vienna. There he and his wife were reconciled and at the end of the summer of 1789 he revived his friendship with Mozart. Mozart spent much of this time – especially when Constanze was at Baden – in the company of Schikaneder and the composers Franz Xaver Gerl and Benedikt Schack. During 1790 Schikaneder and Mozart had set to work on *The Magic Flute.* Mozart had expressed doubts about his ability to compose what he described as 'a magic opera' and in order to speed the work Schikaneder had provided him with a small wooden house near the Freihaus auf der Wieden which proved far more conducive to composition than did Mozart's gloomy apartment in the Rauhenstein-gasse to which he had moved in October 1790.

June and July of 1791 he spent with Constanze at Baden, no doubt working on the new opera When Mozart had to be away from her in Vienna he sent her daily letters with messages like: 'Kisses, 2999 and $\frac{1}{2}$, are flying from me to you and waiting to be caught.' In the middle of June when he was at Baden, he wrote the Ave Verum Corpus, K.618, for his friend Stoll, the choirmaster at the Baden parish church.

When he was away from Constanze, Mozart's spirits were low, a state that was aggravated by the continuing money difficulties. In the middle of July he went to Baden and brought his wife back to Vienna, and not long after, on 26th July, another son was born to them and was christened Franz Xaver Wolfgang.

Back in June of that year Mozart had once again been invited to England, this time by da Ponte, but being involved in the work on *The Magic Flute* he had declined saying that he would reconsider the idea within six months. In September 1791 he wrote to da Ponte, who was now in Trieste, tacitly refusing the invitation. But more important than this is the fact that the letter is full of references to Mozart's premonitions of his own death. He ended the letter by saying that he had before him his 'swan song' and that he must not leave it incomplete. His 'swan song' was that supreme work which he created during the final stages of the composition of *The Magic Flute* – the Requiem. In

July, a mysterious stranger had visited Mozart's house and had left an anonymous letter commissioning a funeral Mass. The author of this commission was identified by Constanze, after Mozart's death, as Count Franz Walsegg-Stuppach. Walsegg, in whose Viennese house Michael Puchberg lived, wanted a Requiem to fulfil his own needs as an amateur composer. It was standard practise among amateur musicians of the nobility at that time to commission a work by a famous composer, to copy it out in their own hand and then to have it performed in front of their friends, who were subsequently invited to guess the composer. Out of politeness the guests always named their host who in his turn would probably not deny this flattery, even if he did not affirm it. Mozart was suggested – possibly by Puchberg – and Andreas Leitgeb, the owner of a factory on one of Count Walsegg's estates, was sent round as the 'mysterious stranger' in order to maintain the secrecy.

During the latter half of the summer of 1791 Mozart had been suffering from general depression and uremic irritation of the brain and there are various accounts which relate the effect which the visit of the 'tall, gaunt man in grey clothes' (Leitgeb) had on the dying composer. Although deathly ill, Mozart undertook the composition. However there was also an added, more practical reason for producing a new piece of church music. Having finally despaired of obtaining the post of court Kapellmeister, Mozart had applied for the place of Leopold Hoffmann as Cathedral Kapellmeister in Vienna. In May, he was appointed unpaid deputy to Hoffmann.

An early 19th-century print of Mozart and Catharina Cavalieri, a singer who performed many of Mozart's compositions (Bertarelli Print Collection, Milan)

Leopold II was to have a separate coronation in Prague on 6th September 1791 as King of Bohemia and it was decided that the coronation opera should be based on Metastasio's celebrated opera *La clemenza di Tito*. The court poet at Dresden, Cattarino Mazzolà, produced a streamlined version of the original text and Mozart was asked to compose the music. There were only a few weeks left for this composition and Mozart had to work furiously, even though the *recitativo secco* (literally 'dry recitative') was delegated to his pupil and assistant Süssmayr.

On 15th August the Mozarts and Süssmayr set out for Prague and all through the three-day journey Mozart worked on *La clemenza di Tito*. Arriving in Prague, Mozart continued his feverish work which was not helped by the fact that he had written the part of Sextus for a tenor, only to find that the cast in Prague necessitated it being scored for a woman, so that it had to be rewritten.

At the end of the month the Emperor and the Empress came to Prague and on the evening of their arrival *Don Giovanni* was performed to the delight of the whole court which attended the opera, according to the official diary of the coronation. The actual coronation day itself was con-cluded by the first performance of *La clemenza di Tito* which was received rather coolly.

However this somewhat cool reception of *La clemenza di Tito* did not worry Mozart too much – especially as he received 200 ducats for it! – and he continued work on *The Magic Flute*. By the middle of September Mozart had left Prague but the strain of producing *La clemenza di Tito* had left its mark and he was reported to be pale and sorrowful and troubled by thoughts of death. *The Magic Flute* was finished by 29th September and the première was fixed for the following day. At the beginning of the first performance, which Mozart was conducting, it seemed that the opera was going to receive the same reaction as *La clemenza di Tito*, but after the second act it went better and by the end the audience was clamouring for the composer.

At the beginning of October Mozart had sent Constanze off to Baden again and he wrote to her several times telling her about the performances of *The Magic Flute*. On 13th October he drove out to Perchtoldsdorf with his brother-in-law Franz Hofer to fetch his son Karl who was at school there. He then took Karl, Hofer, his mother-in-law, Salieri and the singer Cavalieri to hear *The Magic Flute* and was delighted by their enthusiasm for it. The success of this his last opera seems to have done much to stop him falling into despair. Two days later he went to Baden and brought his wife back to Vienna, for the weather was getting cold and winter was not far away.

Still desperately working on the Requiem, Mozart also composed a handful of works which include the Clarinet Concerto, K.622, and a small cantata for the Freemasons, K.623. This cantata was the last work to be recorded by Mozart in his catalogue.

It is remarkable that over these last painful months Mozart managed, through self-discipline and his creative urge, to continue to produce the masterpieces which he did. It was not simply a question of combatting exhaustion for he was also plagued by fainting fits and attacks of enervation. Constanze, on her return from Baden, attempted to distract him from his worries but, during a walk with her in the Prater, he broke into tears as he spoke of his premonitions of death, of his inability to complete the Requiem and of his fear (which proved groundless) of having been poisoned. Constanze finally took away the score of the Requiem to stop him working. By 18th November he had recovered slightly and started work on the Requiem again but a few days later he had taken to his bed. Over the next two weeks his condition began to decline and he was often over-whelmed by unbearable despondency. Things became gradually worse and on 4th December 1791 he went into a uremic coma. Not long after midnight he died and the fight was over.

Constanze was prostrated by grief but was sufficiently calm later on 5th December to write a small obituary of her husband – her 'beloved husband Mozart, who cannot be forgotten by me and all of Europe'. The funeral was held in the Chapel of the Cross in St Stephan's Cathedral but when the coffin was carried out to be buried, the rain and snow deterred the mourners from going further than the city gates. And so Mozart was buried without any witnesses. As a cross was not placed on the grave the exact location has never been known for sure.

The bust of Mozart which stands in the hall of his last house in the Rauhensteingasse, Vienna (Austrian National Library, Vienna)

PROGRAM NOTES FOR THE RECORD

by ROBERT JACOBSON

The Last Symphonies

The 1780s witnessed the rising curve of the Classical symphony. This was the period of Haydn's 'Paris' symphonies and Mozart's masterful last three symphonies, written during 1788. All three were composed within two months and are considered the apotheosis of Mozart's symphonic writing. From here the line travelled to Haydn's twelve 'London' symphonies of the early 1790s and to the nine Beethoven symphonies, extending from 1800 to 1823. That forty-year period yielded incredible musical riches, bringing to fruition a symphonic form that had had its origin earlier in the 18th century.

Despite the fact that Mozart's career was entering a new maturity in the late 1780s, it was a time of increasing debt and despair for him. As a 'free-lance' composer, he had begun writing more and more for his own taste — and less and less for the lighter and more predictable palate of the Viennese. Even the popularity of *The Marriage of Figaro* (1786) and *Don Giovanni* (1787) in Prague did not keep him out of debt. He had been named Imperial Court Composer by Emperor Joseph II of Austria, but his annual salary for this post was not enough to sustain him, being less than half that of his illustrious predecessor Gluck. By June of 1788 Mozart was in dire financial need, and there began a series of letters to his faithful friend and fellow Freemason Michael Puchberg, a well-to-do merchant, in which he sought one loan after another. Mozart dreamed of straightening out his affairs and repaying the loans by writing enough new music. His pleas were pitiful, and the generous and understanding Puchberg responded with the much-needed funds.

During this same difficult time, nevertheless, Mozart wrote his last three and greatest symphonies: No. 39 in E flat (K.543), No. 40 in G minor (K.550), and No. 41 in C major (K.551), the 'Jupiter.' This vigorous and powerful music gives little clue of its composer's sad straits, but rather would seem to reveal him as an assured, happy man. Donald Francis Tovey has written that the Symphony No. 39 'has always been known as the *locus classicus* for euphony; the G minor accurately defines the range of passion comprehended in terms of Mozart's art; and the C major ends his symphonic career with the joyful majesty of a Greek god.' He adds: 'Within these three types each individual movement is no less distinctive, while, of course, the contrasts within the individual symphony are expressly designed for vividness and coherence. Even in the treatment of the orchestra . . . each symphony has its own special colouring; and that colouring is none the less vivid in that it is most easily defined by stating what instruments of the normal orchestra are absent.' That is, No. 40 in G minor is without clarinets, trumpets or timpani (though Mozart later added clarinets to the score); the 'Jupiter' is also scored without clarinets, but with trumpets and timpani.

Wolfgang and Karl—Mozart's two sons in a portrait by Hansen painted in 1798 (Mozarteum, Salzburg)

The cover of an edition of Mozart's complete works, of which this section covered the symphonies (Verdi Conservatoire, Milan)

Symphony No. 40

The G minor Symphony (which Wagner called a work of 'indestructible beauty') does have an air of tragedy, but this is something deeper than any personal travail Mozart himself was then undergoing. The very key of G minor is associated with tragic emotions. In *The Magic Flute*, Pamina's aria 'Ach ich fuhl's' is in that same key of despair as she wishes for death, and such works as the Symphony No. 25, the String Quartet K.516, and the Piano Quartet K.478 share this emotional climate. As biographer F. J. Fétis wrote: 'Although Mozart has not used formidable orchestral forces in his G minor Symphony, none of the sweeping and massive effects one meets in a symphony of Beethoven, the invention which flames in this work, the accents of passion and energy that pervade and the melancholy colour that dominates it result in one of the most beautiful manifestations of the human spirit.' Musicologist Eric Blom states that in this symphony Mozart blended romanticism with the Classical perfection of formal balances so that they meet in perfect equilibrium: 'It is in this respect at least the perfect musical work.'

The Symphony No. 40 in G minor opens *Molto allegro* as the violins play a throbbing, impetuous principal theme over a restless accompaniment by the violas, which concisely sets the movement in motion. This is repeated after sharp chords by the full orchestra. After a pause, the graceful second theme in the winds and strings weaves downwards through the orchestra, conveying serenity and classical beauty. The whole movement is built on these two ideas. With a violent harmonic wrench into a distant tonality, the development section begins. The first theme is chopped up into small pieces, tossed back and forth from one part of the orchestra to another, in a wide range of dynamics. The excitement dies down and the first theme returns, and then the second theme, but this time in a minor key, lending a certain poignancy to that melody.

All through the second movement (*Andante*) there is a restless, brooding undertone which rises to an agonised climax. The first motive is passed from the violas to second violins to first violins. The mood is one of tension and melancholy intensity, ending in pathos. The Minuet section (*Allegretto*) is a long way from the courtly grace and polite charm usually associated with that dance; it is, instead, aggressive and stark, plunging ahead with decisive rhythms. This is contrasted with a graceful, sunny Trio in the middle — the only relaxed, idyllic passage in the work. The Finale (*Allegro assai*) is full of grim, hectic humour, bordering on tragedy. Its main force is again a rhythmic propulsion, conveying a nervous energy. The main theme rockets upwards through the orchestra — at first lightly, but then wild and rushing, moving from the strings on to the other instruments. A second singing theme is soon caught up in the dynamic drive of the first, as harmonies clash sharply and the musical texture becomes more and more complicated. There is a quick climax; the themes return in nearly their original form, and the work closes with insistent reiterations of the dark, severe atmosphere that pervades this symphony.

The 'Jupiter' Symphony

The Symphony No. 41 in C major is music of matchless brilliance and power. The name 'Jupiter' was bestowed on it by the London music publisher J. B. Cramer for what he called the work's 'loftiness of ideas and nobility of treatment.' It opens *Allegro vivace*, contrasting two moods — a virile, heroic figure for full orchestra and a serene, meditative phrase for the strings. The exposition, mainly in a martial mood, concludes with a lilting, dancing melody which Mozart quoted from a comic basso aria, 'Un bacio di mano,' he had composed earlier that year for an *opera buffa*. This kernel becomes an important theme in the dramatic development that follows and, of course, shows the close link between Italian comic opera and the Viennese Classical symphony.

The slow movement (*Andante cantabile*) begins conventionally, but soon a characteristic Mozartean undercurrent of suppressed agitation begins to boil under the charming surface, manifested in strenuous syncopations. Again, the loud-and-soft contrasts are important. The muted violins create a special mood of intimacy and lamentation. The Minuetto (*Allegretto*) is reminiscent of the playful serenity of the first movement, and the droll woodwind phrases of the Trio recall Haydn. Mozart alternates forcefulness and ease in equal balance. The four whole notes that begin the Finale (*Molto allegro*) had been used by Mozart in two of his Masses and in his B flat Symphony (K.319). He then gives this theme to five string sections in succession, and goes on to pursue a richly symphonic, enormously skillful working-out of his materials, in which his dazzling contrapuntal ability serves to emphasise the joyful play of forces that come together in the rest of the Symphony. Mozart fused all these elements to an incandescent, dizzying coda at the climax. Blom has written: 'There is a mystery in this music not to be solved by analysis or criticism, and perhaps only just to be apprehended by the imagination. We can understand the utter simplicity; we can also, with an effort, comprehend the immense technical skill with which its elaborate fabric is woven; what remains forever a riddle is how any human being could manage to combine these two opposites into such a perfectly balanced work of art.'

Printed in the United States of America

Ludwig van Beethoven

His Life and Times 1822-1827 (Part 3)

PROGRAM NOTES FOR THE VIOLIN CONCERTO OPUS 61 AND THE EGMONT OVERTURE

By Robert Jacobson

fw

FUNK & WAGNALLS, INC.
NEW YORK, NEW YORK

The Fruitful Years: Life 1822-25

As we noted before, Beethoven suffered many trials during the last decade of his life. The lawsuit concerning his nephew Karl left him financially in serious straits, he was lonely and deaf, and his health was deteriorating badly. Yet artistically it was the greatest period of his life and produced the last five piano sonatas, the two Cello Sonatas, op. 102, the Diabelli Variations (certainly the greatest variation work ever written), the *Consecration of the House* Overture, the *Missa solemnis*, the Ninth Symphony, the supreme late quartets from Opus 127 to Opus 135, as well as many smaller but far from negligible things. And his head was full of plans to the end – a Requiem, a Mass in C sharp minor, a Tenth Symphony, a setting of Goethe's *Faust;* one would not easily imagine a sick man with such thoughts. He still wrestled with his deafness, not because it interfered in any way with his composition (it was more likely an aid to concentration, for his inner ear was unimpaired), but because he still occasionally felt the urge to take part in performances. The revival of *Fidelio* in 1822 found him in this frame of mind and brought about one of the saddest experiences of his life. Schindler, Beethoven's first biographer, describes the occasion[1]:

'Beethoven asked around among his friends whether he should dare undertake the direction of the opera with the help of his highly esteemed friend, the Kapellmeister Umlauf. We all advised against it, in fact we pleaded with him to resist his own desires and to remember the difficulties that had attended the concert in the University auditorium as long ago as 1819, and again at the Josephstadt Theater performance. After several days of indecision, he finally declared his readiness to conduct the work, a deplorable decision on many counts. At his request I accompanied him to the dress rehearsal. The E major Overture went perfectly, for despite several hesitations on the part of their leader, the bold army of the orchestra moved in their customary disciplined ranks. But in the very first number, the duet between Marzelline and Jacquino, it was apparent that Beethoven could hear nothing of what was happening on the stage. He seemed to be fighting to hold back. The orchestra stayed with him but the singers pressed on, and at the point where knocking is heard at the prison door, everything fell apart. Umlauf told the musicians to stop without telling the master the reason. After a few minutes' discussion with the singers, the order was given: *da capo*. The duet began again and as before the disunity was noticeable, and again at the knocking there was general confusion. Again the musicians were stopped.

'The impossibility of continuing under the direction of the creator of the work was obvious. But who was to tell him, and how? Neither the manager, Duport, nor Umlauf wanted to have to say, "It cannot be done. Go away, you unhappy man!" Beethoven, now growing apprehensive, turned from one side to another, searching the faces to see what was interrupting the rehearsal. All were silent. Then he called me to him. I stepped to his side in the orchestra and he handed me his notebook, motioning me to write down what was wrong. I wrote as fast as I could something like: "Please don't go on. I'll explain at home." He jumped down on the floor and said only: "Let's get out of here." Without stopping he hastened to his apartment in Pfarrgasse in the suburb of Laimgrube. Once there he threw himself on the sofa, covered his face with both hands, and remained so until we went to dinner. During the meal he did not say a word; his whole demeanour bespoke depression and defeat. After dinner, when I wished to go, he asked me not to leave him until theatre time. When I left him, he asked me to go with him the next day to see Dr Smetana, his physician at that time, a man who had gained a reputation in ailments of the ear.

'In the long years of my association with the mighty composer, there was never any experience to equal that day in November. Whatever difficulties, unpleasantnesses, or disturbances to mind and spirit might have occurred as a result of unhappy personal relations or other circumstances, I had always seen the master only momentarily out of sorts or occasionally depressed. Very soon he would regain his composure, carry his head erect, stride ahead with his customary purpose and vigour, once more master in the workshop of his genius as though nothing had happened. But he never wholly recovered from this blow. . . .

'Dr Smetana prescribed medication to be taken internally. This seemed to be an indication that he wished to occupy his patient with something, but that he entertained no hope whatsoever that an improvement in the impaired hearing could actually result. Yet the doctor knew from experience how this impetuous, distraught patient regarded medical prescriptions. The dosage read: "One teaspoonful to be taken every hour." Bah! what good was a mere teaspoonful? The patient went about correcting the order as if it were a copyist's error in one of his musical scores. It ought to say a tablespoonful – that is the way to take medicine. If he remembers to take his medicine at all, the bottle is empty in a few hours, and the prescription must be refilled. So it goes for days, with no indication to the doctor as to the patient's progress unless the doctor himself makes inquiries. Generally the progress is poor, and the patient feels much worse than before starting the treatment for he is forced to drink quantities of water, thereby precluding the slightest chance of any benefits from the medicine.

[1] Schindler, Beethoven as I Knew Him, translated by Constance S. Jolly, Faber 1966

'Such a patient was our Beethoven, when indeed he bothered to go to a doctor at all. It was not without its dangers to the doctor involved, for his cavalier attitude towards prescribed dosages frequently produced detrimental effects for which the physician was held responsible. At the beginning of his hearing difficulties, the master was treated by his Rhenish compatriot, the Emperor's staff-surgeon, Dr von Vering. Accustomed to his patients' strict observance of his instructions and exercising a certain authority over the musician, Vering expected Beethoven to follow his orders precisely. But this patient disregarded the orders and did whatever he wished, and was just as intransigent about having his freedom restricted in the manner of medication as in his personal life. Absolute freedom in the commission or omission of any deed, limited only by the laws of morality: such was the guiding principle of this unique character.

'Hardly had the treatment under Dr Smetana begun when the master remembered Father Weiss at St Stephan's, the capable ear doctor whom the reader met when we first spoke of Beethoven's hearing difficulties. He was consulted again. I accompanied the master on this visit. The priest was moved by what his renowned visitor told him, and though he made no promises, he so encouraged Beethoven by his sympathy that the composer had hopes that his condition would improve. He vowed he would follow all the doctor's orders to the letter and would be regular and persistent in his visits.

'The first phase of Father Weiss's treatment was simply an oil injection which the patient accepted docilely. According to medical law, the cleric was allowed to see patients only in his apartment. Our master was thus instructed to visit his kindly doctor every day. Yet after a few days he stopped going. Father Weiss wrote him a note warning him not to interrupt the treatment, for he hoped for success at least with the left ear. But the 'obstinate donkey' who in the Bonn days had baulked at going to his pupils now found it just as difficult to take himself to the rectory near St Stephan's. Admittedly there was now a compelling reason for the composer's impatience with a prolonged course of medical treatment, namely the pressing work at home on his desk. This alone, however, would not have prevented Beethoven from continuing the treatment if a more personal, far more potent element of his personality had not intervened and silently made him give up all attempts: his impatience and lack of respect for any medical treatment that did not achieve the hoped-for results within twenty-four hours.

'I have now described in full the condition of Beethoven's deafness. The reader now knows what the sufferer did, and what he failed to do, to relieve the great misfortune that with almost no surcease permeated his whole life. The conflict that followed the incident at the opera was the last of its kind. From then on no such attempts were undertaken. Following the example of so many wise men of ages past, the master submitted to his hard fate without uttering another word of complaint.'

Visitors' Impressions: Life 1825-26

Sir George Smart, who conducted the first performance in England of Beethoven's Ninth Symphony on 21st March 1825, visited the composer later the same year. His diary of the event runs as follows[1]:

'Friday, 9th September. . . . We then went to Mecchetti's music shop, they too are publishers, and bought three pieces for Birchall. . . . Mr Holz, an amateur in some public office and a good violin-player, came in and said Beethoven had come from Baden this morning and would be at his nephew's – Karl Beethoven, a young man aged twenty – No 72 Alleegasse. . . . At twelve I took Ries to the Hotel Wildemann, the lodgings of Mr Schlesinger, the music-seller of Paris, as I understood from Mr Holz that Beethoven would be there and there I found him. He received me in the most flattering manner. There was a numerous assembly of professors to hear Beethoven's second new manuscript quartet, bought by Mr Schlesinger. This quartet is three-quarters of an hour long. They played it twice. The four performers were Schuppanzigh, Holz, Weiss, and Lincke. It is most chromatic and there is a slow movement entitled "Praise for the recovery of an invalid". Beethoven intended to allude to himself, I suppose, for he was very ill during the early part of this year. He directed the performers, and took off his coat, the room being warm and crowded. A staccato passage not being expressed to the satisfaction of his eye, for alas, he could not hear, he seized Holz's violin and played the passage a quarter of a tone too flat. I looked over the score during the performance. All paid him the greatest attention. About fourteen were present, those I knew were Boehm (violin), Marx (cello), Carl Czerny, also Beethoven's nephew, who is like Count St Antonio, so is Boehm, the violin player. The partner of Steiner, the music-seller, was also there. I fixed to go to Beethoven at Baden on Sunday and left at twenty-five minutes past two. . . .

'Saturday, 10th September. . . . Previous to this sightseeing I called for the music at Artaria's for Birchall, for which I paid, and on our return found a visiting-card from Earl Stanhope and also from Schlesinger of Paris with a message that Beethoven would be at his hotel tomorrow at twelve; therefore, of course, I gave up going to Baden to visit Beethoven, which he had arranged for me to do. . . .

'Sunday, 11th September. . . . From hence I went along to Schlesinger's at the "Wildemann", where was a larger party than the previous one. Among them was L'Abbé Stadler, a fine old man and a good composer of the old school, to whom I was introduced. There was also present a pupil of Moscheles, a Mademoiselle Eskeles, and a Mademoiselle Cimia, whom I understood to be a professional player. When I entered Messrs C. Czerny, Schuppanzigh and Lincke had just begun the Trio, Opus 70 of Beethoven, after this the same performers played Beethoven's Trio, Opus 97 – both printed singly by Steiner. Then followed Beethoven's quartet, the same that I heard on 9th September, and it was played by the same performers. Beethoven was seated near the pianoforte, beating time during the performance of these pieces. This ended, most of the company departed, but

Schlesinger invited me to stop and dine with the following party of ten. Beethoven, his nephew, Holz, Weiss, C. Czerny, who sat at the bottom of the table, Lincke, Jean Sedlatzek – a flute player who is coming to England next year and has letters to the Duke of Devonshire, Count St Antonio, etc. – he has been to Italy – Schlesinger, Schuppanzigh, who sat at the top, and myself. Beethoven calls Schuppanzigh Sir John Falstaff, not a bad name considering the figure of this excellent violin player.

'We had a most pleasant dinner, healths were given in the English style. Beethoven was delightfully gay but hurt that, in the letter Moscheles gave me, his name should be mixed up with the other professors. However, he soon got over it. He was much pleased and rather surprised at seeing in the oratorio bill I gave him that the *Mount of Olives* and his 'Battle' Symphony were both performed the same evening. He believes – I do not – that the high notes Handel wrote for trumpets were played formerly by one particular man. I gave him the oratorio book and bill. He invited me, by his nephew, to Baden next Friday. After dinner he was coaxed to play extempore, observing in French to me, "Upon what subject shall I play?" Meanwhile he was touching the instrument thus:

to which I answered, "Upon that". On which theme he played for about twenty minutes in a most extraordinary manner, sometimes very fortissimo, but full of genius. When

Right: *A painting by J. Schmid of Beethoven playing the piano at Prince Lichnowsky's house. Informal occasions of this kind gave rise to the famous improvisations which made Beethoven's name in Vienna (Austrian National Library, Vienna)*

4

[1] Beethoven: Impressions by his Contemporaries, edited by O. G. Sonneck, Dover 1968

he rose at the conclusion of his playing he appeared greatly agitated. No one could be more agreeable than he was – plenty of jokes. He was in the highest of spirits. We all wrote to him by turns, but he can hear a little if you halloo quite close to his left ear. He was very severe in his observations about the Prince Regent never having noticed his present of the score of his 'Battle' Symphony. His nephew regretted that his uncle had no one to explain to him the profitable engagement offered by the Philharmonic Society last year. I have had a most delightful day. Schlesinger is very agreeable, he knows Weber and Franz Cramer's family. About seven I took a little walk with Carl Czerny – whom Neate taught, he says, to speak English. I then went to his house and played four or five duets with him; they are clever compositions but not easy. He taught young Liszt. About nine I went home by myself, having promised to go to C. Czerny's on Wednesday evening.

'On Friday, 16th September, at half-past eight in the morning young Ries came and we went in a hired carriage from Mödling to Baden. The distance is about six miles south of Mödling and sixteen miles southwest of Vienna. The journey cost five florins in paper money and took us about an hour. After walking in the little park and looking at the baths we went to Beethoven's lodgings according to his invitation. These are curiously situated, a wooden circus for horsemanship has been erected in a large court before his house. He has four large-sized rooms opening into each other, furnished *à la genius:* in one is the grand pianoforte, much out of tune, given him by Broadwood, in which is written, besides the Latin line, the names of J. Cramer, Ferrari, and C. Knyvett. Beethoven gave me the time, by playing the subjects on the pianoforte, of many movements of his symphonies, including the 'Choral' Symphony, which according to his account took three-quarters of an hour only in performance. The party present, namely Holz, the amateur violin; Karl Beethoven, the nephew; besides young Ries, agreed that the performance at Vienna only took that time; this I deem to be totally impossible. It seems at Vienna the Recit. was played only with four celli and two contra bassi which certainly is better than having the tutti bassi. Beethoven and we deservedly abused Reicha's printed specimen of fugueing. He told me of a Mass, not yet published, which he had composed. We had a long conversation on musical subjects conducted on my part in writing. He is very desirous to come to England. After ordering his dinner with his funny old cook and telling his nephew to see to the wine, we all five took a walk. Beethoven was generally in advance humming some passage. . . . On our return we had dinner at two o'clock. It was a most curious one and so plentiful that dishes came in as we came out, for, unfortunately, we were rather in a hurry to get to the stage-coach by four, it being the only one going to Vienna that evening. I overheard Beethoven say, "We will see how much the Englishman can drink." *He* had the worst of the trial.'

Another visitor to Beethoven in this year was Gerhard von Breuning, the son of Stephan von Breuning. Stephan von Breuning was an old friend, faithful to Beethoven from his youth despite various ups and downs in their relationship. Towards the end of the composer's life Gerhard met Beethoven often and has left us this lively description of his impressions:

A 19th-century print of the first performance of the Ninth Symphony. Beethoven is standing in the middle of the orchestra, by the conductor (Bettmann Archive, New York)

'Once my father told my mother, when she had incidentally said to him that she could not quite understand how Beethoven, since he was neither handsome nor elegant, but looked positively unkept and unkempt, could have been such a favourite with the ladies: "And yet he always has been fortunate with women." Beethoven always, where women were concerned, showed himself possessed of noble, elevated sentiments, whether in his friendships or in his love affairs.

'On one occasion I visited Beethoven in his house in the Ungargasse, near the Escarpment. He happened to be standing at the piano with his hands on the keyboard. When he saw me he brought down both hands on the keys with a crash, laughed and walked away from the piano. With this he probably meant to say to me: "You thought I was going to play something for you, but that is just what I am not going to do!" Nor did I ask him.

'Though all his household affairs were now in such good order [Frau von Breuning had put Beethoven's housekeeping arrangements into shape], the way in which he kept his room continued to be just as disorderly. His papers and possessions were dusty and lay about higgledy-piggledy; and in spite of the dazzling whiteness and cleanliness of his linen and his repeated bodily ablutions, his clothes remained unbrushed. This inordinate bathing may, perhaps, in some past time have been the primary incidental cause and origin of his deafness – perhaps owing to a rheumatic inflamma-

tion – rather than his "predisposition for intestinal complaints", as so often has been taken for granted. He always had been in the habit, after he had sat for a long time at the table composing and this had heated his head, of rushing to the wash-stand, pouring pitcherfuls of water over his overheated head and, after having thus cooled himself off and only slightly dried himself, of returning to his work or, even, in the meanwhile, hastening out into the open for a brief walk. All this was done in the greatest hurry, so that he might not be snatched out of his imaginative flight. How little he thought at the time of the need of drying his thick hair, sopping wet, is proven by the fact that, without his noticing it, the water he had poured over his head would flood the floor in quantities, leak through it, and appear on the room ceiling of the lodgers living beneath him. This, on occasion, led to annoyances on the part of his fellow lodgers, the janitor and, finally, the owner of the house, and even was responsible for his being given notice.

'He liked to have us invite him to dinner, and would often send us a portion of fish, if he had ordered some bought for himself in the market; for fish was one of his favourite dishes and when he himself liked something he liked to share it with his friends.

'Beethoven's outward appearance, owing to that indifference to dress peculiar to him, made him uncommonly noticeable on the street. Usually lost in thought and grumbling to himself, he not infrequently gesticulated with his arms as well when walking alone. When he was in company, he spoke very loudly and with great animation and, since whoever accompanied him was obliged to write down his answers in the conversation note-book, the promenade was interrupted by frequent stops, something which in itself attracted attention and was made more conspicuous by the replies he made in pantomime.

'Hence the majority of those whom he met turned around to look when he had passed, and the street boys even poked fun at him and called after him. For this reason nephew Karl disdained to go out with Beethoven and once told him plainly that he was ashamed to accompany him in the street because he looked such a fool, a remark which Beethoven expressed himself to us in a deeply hurt and wounded manner. For my own part, I was proud to be allowed to show myself in the company of this great man.

'The felt hat then worn, upon Beethoven's homecoming, though it might be dripping wet with rain, after merely giving it a slight shake (a habit he always observed in our house, without concern for what was in the room) he would clap on the very top of the hat-rack. In consequence it had lost its even top and was vaulted in an upward bulge. Brushed infrequently or not at all, before and after it had rained, and then again allowed to grow dusty, the hat acquired a permanently matted appearance. In addition he wore it, so far as possible, back from his face in order to leave his forehead free; while on either side his grey, disordered hair, as Rellstab so characteristically says, "neither curly nor stiff, but a mixture of all", stood out. Owing to his putting on and wearing his hat away from his face and back on his head, which he held high, the hat's hinder brim came into collision with his coat-collar, which at that time shot up high against the back of the head; and gave the brim in question a cocked-up shape; while the coat-collar itself, from its continual contact with the hat brim, seemed to have been worn away. The two unbuttoned coat-fronts, especially those of the blue frock coat with brass buttons, turned outward and flapped about his arms, especially when he was walking against the wind. In the same manner the two long ends of the white neckerchief knotted about his broad, turned-down shirt-collar streamed out. The double lorgnette which he wore because of his near-sightedness, hung loosely down. His coat-tails, however, were rather heavily bur-

dened; for in addition to his watch, which often hung out on the one side, in the pocket of the other he had a folded quarto note-book, anything but thin, besides a conversation note-book in octavo format and a thick carpenter's pencil, for communication with friends and acquaintances whom he might meet; and also, in earlier days, while it still aided him, his ear-trumpet. The weight of the note-books considerably extended the length of the coat-tail containing them and, in addition, the pocket itself because of its own frequent pulling out and that of the note-books, hung down visibly on the same side, turned outward.

'The well-known pen-and-ink drawing [Böhm's drawing, since Lyser's apparently first came into being after Beethoven's death] gives a fair idea of Beethoven's figure, even though he never wore his hat pressed sideways, as the drawing – with its usual exaggeration – presents it. The above sketch of Beethoven's outward appearance had been inextinguishably impressed upon my memory. It was thus that I so often saw him from our windows, toward two o'clock – his dinner-hour – coming from the direction of the Schottentor across the Escarpment where the Votive Church now stands, his body and head, as usual, projecting (not stooping) forward, and bearing down alone upon his own house; or I myself might be walking with him.'

A print by Postl of St Michael's Square in Vienna, looking towards the Royal Palace (Ingo Nebehay Collection, Vienna)

7

Twilight: Life 1826-27

We continue Gerhard von Breuning's reminiscences of Beethoven in the last years of his life[1]:

'In the street, where there was not always sufficient time to write, conversation with him was most difficult, and, that he was absolutely deaf was attested to me by the following striking proof, had proof been needed. Once we expected him for dinner, and it already was almost two o'clock, our dinner-hour. My parents, always suspecting that, lost in composition, he might not remember the appointed time, sent me out to fetch him over. I found him at his work-table, his face turned toward the open door of the room in which stood the piano, working at one of the last (Galitzin) quartets. With a brief upward glance, he bade me wait awhile, until he had set down on paper the thought which preoccupied him at the moment. For a short time I remained quiet, then I moved over to the piano standing nearest at hand, the one by Graf (with the attached resonance-gatherer) and, not convinced of Beethoven's tone-deafness, began to strum softly on the keys. Meanwhile I looked over at him again and again, to see whether this disturbed him. But when I saw that he was quite unconscious of it I played more loudly; then, purposely, very loudly – and my doubts were resolved.

Höchle's drawing of Beethoven's study in his house on the Schwarzspanierhaus in Vienna, where he spent the last years of his life (City History Museum, Vienna)

He did not hear me at all, and kept on writing with entire unconcern until, having at last finished, he summoned me to go. In the street he asked me something: I screamed the answer directly into his ear; but he understood my gestures rather than my words. Only once, when we were sitting at table, one of my sisters uttered a high, piercing shriek; and to know that he still had been able to hear it made Beethoven so happy that he laughed clearly and gleefully, his dazzlingly white and unbroken rows of teeth fully visible.

'Characteristic, too, was the liveliness with which he discussed circumstances that interested him, and at such times it might even chance that walking up and down the room with my father, he would spit into the mirror instead of out of the window, without knowing it.

'On 24th September, 1826 – it was my birthday – Beethoven was again our dinner guest in honour of the occasion. While we were eating, he told us that the Vienna City Council had made him a Vienna citizen, and in this connection had informed him that he had become, not an ordinary but an honorary citizen, whereupon he had replied: "I did not know that there were also scandalary citizens in Vienna." [A pun on "Ehrenbürger" and "Schandbürger".]

'In the afternoon we all went out to Schönbrunn together, on foot. My mother had a visit to make in Meidling (bordering on Schönbrunn) and I accompanied her. My father, Beethoven and my teacher waited for us on one of the benches in the parterre of the Schönbrunn Garden. When we then went walking in the garden, Beethoven, pointing to the leafy alleys trimmed in wall-pattern according to the French style, said: "Nothing but artifice, shaped up like the old hoop petticoats! I feel benefited only when I am out where nature is free!" An infantryman passed us. At once he was ready with a sarcastic remark: "A slave, who has sold his independence for five Kreuzer a day!"

'When we were going home, several boys in the middle of the right-hand park alley in front of the Schönbrunn bridge were playing bowls with a small ball, and the latter accidentally struck Beethoven's foot. Thinking it had been done with malicious intent, to plague him, he at once turned violently on them, calling out: "Who gave you permission to play here? Why do you have to pick out this particular spot for your carrying on?" And he was on the point of rushing on them to drive them away. My father, who feared the brutality of the street arabs, however, soon calmed him, and, besides, the ball which had grazed him had caused him no more than a passing pain.

'It was already dark when, returning over the "Schmelz", we lost our way and were compelled to walk straight across the ploughed fields. Beethoven growled melodies to himself, as he swayed rather helplessly from one hummock to the next, and, in view of his near-sightedness, was glad to have a guide for the time being.

[1]Beethoven: Impressions by his Contemporaries, edited by O. G. Sonneck, Dover 1968.

'I must preface what comes next by telling how now that my ardent desire to enter into close daily communion with Beethoven had been most fully gratified, I nourished the further wish to be able, like my father, to call him "du" [in German the "you" of intimate friendship and affection]. Had I not long since attached myself to him with all my soul, and taken no little pride in knowing he loved me and that I, too, was one among the few chosen ones in this connection? I asked my father how I might introduce the subject and whether he would act for me in the matter. My father replied offhand: "If it will give you pleasure all these circumlocutions are unnecessary; simply address him as 'du', and he will in nowise be offended, but more apt to be pleased. In any event it will not even seem strange to him." Relying on this encouragement, since I was well aware of how entirely at home my father was where Beethoven's mental processes were concerned, I at once made the venture on the occasion of my next visit, when I was alone with Beethoven (this was during the first earlier period of his illness). With a beating heart, it is true, and yet with venturesome boldness I made my attempt and in the first sentence I wrote down of our conversation, I used this form of address. I watched his features with tension when I held up the slate to him. And – it was as my father had foretold – Beethoven never even noticed it, and thus I henceforth continued to address him.

'During his illness (toward the end of February 1827) one forenoon, Handel's complete works – in a handsome bound quarto volume edition – arrived as a present, sent by the harp virtuoso Stumpff. Beethoven had long cherished the wish to own them, and it was in accordance with this very wish, which he had once expressed, that the gift had been made. When at noon I entered his room, as was my daily custom when the clock struck twelve, he at once pointed to the volumes heaped up on the piano, his eyes radiant with pleasure: "See, this is what I have received as a present today; they have made me very happy with these works! I have wished to own them for a long time because Handel is the greatest, the most solid of composers, from him I still can learn something. Fetch the books over to me!" These and other things he said in connection with them, speaking with joyous excitement. And then I began to hand one after another volume to him in his bed. He turned the pages of one volume after the other, as I gave them to him, at times dwelling a while on certain passages, and then at once laying down one after another book to the right, on his bed, against the wall; until at last all were piled up there, where they remained for several hours, for I found them still there that afternoon. Then once more he began to deliver the liveliest eulogies on Handel's greatness, calling him the most classic and thorough of the tone poets.

'Once, as often was the case when I arrived, I found him asleep. I sat down beside his bed, keeping quiet – for I hoped the rest might be strengthening – in order not to awaken him. Meanwhile I turned the pages and read one of the conversation note-books which was still lying ready for use on the little table next the bed, to find out who had lately visited him, and what had been said. And there, among other things, I found in one place: "Your quartet which Schuppanzigh performed yesterday did not appeal to me."

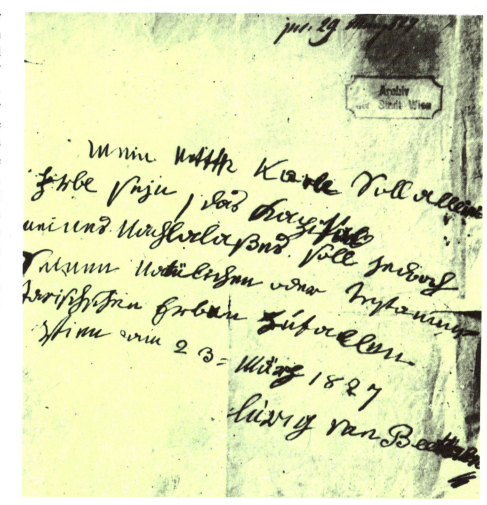

Beethoven's will, dated 23rd March 1827, which was the final proof of his generosity towards his beloved nephew Karl (*Austrian National Library, Vienna*)

When he awoke a short time after, I held the sentence up to him and asked him what he had to say to it: "Some day it will suit them" was his laconic reply. He at once added with legitimate self-confidence some brief remarks to the effect that he wrote as seemed well to him, and did not allow himself to be led astray by contemporary opinion: "I know that I am an artist!"

'I improved an opportunity to ask him why he had written no second opera. He answered: "I wished to write another opera but I found no suitable text-book for it. I must have a text which stimulates me; it must be something moral, elevating. Texts which Mozart could compose I would never have been able to set to music. I never have been able to get into the mood for setting lewd texts. I have received many text-books, but as I have said, none which I would wish to have." And furthermore he said to me: "It was my wish to write many another thing. I wanted to compose the Tenth Symphony, and then a Requiem as well, and the music to *Faust*, and even a piano method. This last I would have done in a way different from that in which others have written them. Well, I shall no longer get around to that, and, anyhow, so long as I am sick, I will do no work, no matter how much Diabelli and Haslinger may urge me; for I have to be in the mood for it. Often I have been unable to compose for a long time and then all at once the desire returned to me."

'Another time I found a sketch-book lying on a piece of furniture in the room. I held it up to him, asking whether he really found it necessary to note down his inspirations. He replied: "I always carry a note-book of the kind about me, and when an idea occurs to me, at once note it down. I even rise at night when something happens to occur to me, since otherwise I might forget the idea." '

The Death of Beethoven

Beethoven's last illness was a complication of troubles that had accumulated throughout his life, culminating in disorders of the liver, intestines, lungs, and kidney with, finally, dropsy; he had to undergo several painful operations. Modern medical opinion varies widely about the exact cause of his deafness, his frequent ill-health, and ultimately his death. Dr Edward Larkin, in a very interesting appendix to Martin Cooper's *Beethoven: The Last Decade 1817-1827,* propounds the persuasive theory that Beethoven suffered from some kind of pathological auto-immunity; i.e. that his system rejected substances necessary to its well-being, with the result that a general and chronic condition developed. He discounts entirely the possibility of venereal disease, often suggested as a possible cause for Beethoven's deafness which, he says, could well have arisen from a general condition.

The composer Ferdinand Hiller gives the following moving account of his visit to Beethoven, very near the end[1]:

'On 13th March Hummel took me to Beethoven the second time. We found that his condition had changed decidedly for the worse. He lay in bed, seemed to be suffering violent pain and occasionally gave a deep groan, although he talked a good deal and with animation. He now appeared to take it to heart that he never had married. Already, on our first visit, he had joked about the matter with Hummel, whose wife he had known as a young, beautiful girl. "You," he said to him on this occasion, with a smile, "you are a lucky man: You have a wife who takes care of you, who is in love with you, while I, poor unfortunate . . . ." and he sighed heavily. He also begged Hummel to fetch his wife to visit him, though the latter had not been able to bring herself to see in his present state the man whom she had known when he was at the height of his powers. A short time before Beethoven had been presented with a picture of the house in which Haydn had been born: he had it near his bed and showed it to us: "I was as pleased as any child," said he, "the cradle of a great man!"

'Not long after our second visit the news spread through Vienna that the London Philharmonic Society had sent Beethoven one hundred pounds sterling, in order to ameliorate his sufferings. It was added that the surprise had made so deep an impression on the poor great man that he even felt himself bodily much relieved. When we once more stood by his bedside on the 20th, his remarks, it is true, showed how much the attention had rejoiced him, but he was very weak and spoke only in a low voice and in broken sentences. "I shall probably soon make my way up above," he whispered after we had greeted him.

'Similar exclamations he uttered frequently, yet together with them he voiced hopes and projects which, unfortunately, were not to be realised. Speaking of the noble action of the Philharmonic Society and praising the English, he opined that as soon as his condition had improved he would undertake the journey to London. "I shall compose a great overture and a great symphony for them." And then he also wished to visit Madame Hummel (she had come with us) and stop, I no longer recall just where, at all sorts of places. It did not even occur to us to write down anything for him. His eyes, which when last we had seen them, still had shown considerable life, had collapsed, and he found it hard, from time to time, to sit up. It was impossible longer to deceive one's self – the worst was to be anticipated.

'Altogether hopeless was the appearance of this extraordinary man when we once more visited him on 23rd March, for the last time. He lay there faint and wretched, at times sighing gently. No further word passed his lips; the perspiration stood out on his brow. Seeing that by some chance he did not have his handkerchief at hand, Hummel's wife took her dainty wisp of batiste and at different times dried his face. Never shall I forget the grateful glance which his broken eyes sent up to her when she did this. While we were spending 26th March in the home of the art-loving Mr von Liebenberg (who formerly had been Hummel's pupil) in merry company, we were surprised between five and six o'clock by a heavy thunderstorm. A dense fall of snow was accompanied by violent thunder and lightnings which illuminated the whole chamber.

'A few hours later guests arrived with the news that Ludwig van Beethoven was no more; that he had died at quarter to five.'

[1] Beethoven: Impressions by his Contemporaries, edited by O. G. Sonneck, Dover 1968

Beethoven conducting his patron Count Rasumovsky's quartet—after a painting by A. Brockmann. Small musical gatherings were extremely popular in Beethoven's Vienna—one patron even used to invite his friends to listen to string quartets before breakfast (Austrian National Library, Vienna)

by ROBERT JACOBSON

The Violin Concerto

Just as Mendelssohn's friendship with the violinist Ferdinand David and Brahms's almost life-long acquaintance with the virtuoso Joseph Joachim led to the creation of their ever-popular violin concertos, so did Beethoven's association with Franz Clement lead him to compose his single, equally sublime Violin Concerto. (The work, incidentally, did not begin to hold a place in the standard repertoire until Joachim took it up later in the century.) From the age of nine Clement toured all over the Continent as a Wunderkind. In 1794 Beethoven wrote to the fourteen-year-old instrumentalist: 'Proceed along the path which you have hitherto trodden so splendidly and so gloriously. Nature and art vie in making you one of the greatest artists. Follow both, and you need not fear that you will fail to reach the great—the greatest goal on earth to which the artist can attain. Be happy, my dear young friend, and come back soon, so that I may hear again your delightful, splendid playing.'

Ten years later Beethoven and Clement found themselves in close union when the composer's opera *Fidelio* was given its first performance at Vienna's Theater an der Wien in November 1805; the concertmaster of the orchestra was none other than Clement, whose ability to devour and memorise scores was widely admired. This renewed friendship resulted in, in 1806, what has been called 'perhaps spiritually the richest of the four or five greatest works for the instrument.' The Concerto was written for Clement, who played its first performance in the same Theater an der Wien late in December of that year. The story is told that Beethoven was so late in delivering the Concerto that Clement had to play the solo part at sight from manuscript at the première. But according to Beethoven's pupil and friend Carl Czerny, the score was finished two days before the date set for Clement's concert, December 23. Furthermore, Clement seems to have had some influence in the writing of the solo part, and this may mean that he saw parts of the composition as fast as they were put down on paper.

Clement was a superb instrumentalist and was also musician enough to have composed half a dozen concertos of his own, in addition to twenty-five concertinos. He was a bit of a virtuoso show-off as well, for at this same concert he performed a work of his own while holding his violin upside down. He was, nevertheless, an artist of distinction, purity and nobility of style. 'His performance is magnificent,' said one contemporary, 'in its way probably unique. It is not the bold, robust, powerful playing of the school of Viotti, but it is indescribably graceful, dainty, elegant.' Another adds that 'gracefulness and tenderness were its main characteristics.' These same qualities are inherent in Beethoven's Concerto. He heaped pages of technical difficulties on Clement, but also paid him the compliment of writing music that placed the violinist's highest artistic gifts in the foreground. Beethoven dedicated the manuscript to him with a dubious bilingual pun: 'Concerto per clemenza pour Clement.'

The Concerto had great popular success at its première, but there were grumblings from the critics—enough to cause the score to lie more or less fallow for several decades. The publication *Theater Zeitung* offered the opinion of one Johann Nepomuk Moser: 'Concerning Beethoven's Concerto, the judgement of connoisseurs is unanimous; its many beauties must be conceded, but it must also be acknowledged that the continuity is often broken, and that the endless repetitions of certain commonplace passages may easily become tedious to the listener.' The work, instead, has long since been found to be far from tedious, and has become perhaps *the* classic among violin concertos because of its radiance, purity, spirituality and dashes of humour.

The D major Violin Concerto is a rare bird in music history, too, for in April of 1807 Beethoven was visited by Muzio Clementi, a composer-turned-publisher, who wished to secure exclusive English rights for publishing a number of Beethoven's works. During the course of negotiations Clementi suggested to Beethoven that he transcribe his Violin Concerto into a more saleable Piano Concerto. The composer agreed to do this and converted the work by the simple means of transferring its solo line, nearly intact, to the piano while leaving the orchestral parts absolutely unchanged. The one major innovation in this conversion was the first movement cadenza; in the piano setting, Beethoven wrote out a cadenza for the instrument that employs a fanciful and highly effective timpani accompaniment. The work has sometimes been billed in performance and recorded as Beethoven's Sixth Piano Concerto.

Beethoven's hands, a painting by Danhauser (1805-45) (Beethovenhaus, Bonn)

This serene Concerto in D major was composed midway in what is probably Beethoven's happiest and most productive period, the first decade of the nineteenth century. It was a period that spanned his Third Piano Concerto (Op. 39) through the 'Les Adieux' Piano Sonata (Op. 81a). It also produced his first six symphonies, including the 'Eroica,' the Fifth, and the 'Pastoral'; the 'Kreutzer' Violin Sonata (Op. 47); such piano sonatas as the 'Waldstein' (Op. 53) and the 'Appassionata' (Op. 57); his opera *Fidelio*; the 'Rasumovsky' String Quartets (Op. 59) and his Piano Trios (Op. 70); and the 'Emperor' Concerto (Op. 73). By 1809 the Archduke Rudolph, Prince Lobkowitz and Prince Kinsky had joined in a financial arrangement designed to keep Beethoven's musical genius in Vienna: ' ... It is, however, clear that only a person who is as free from worries as possible can devote himself exclusively to his profession, and that such single-minded application, without the intrusion of any other concern, is alone able to produce great and sublime works honouring the name of art.' Together the three pledged an annual subsidy of 4,000 gulden to keep the esteemed composer in their midst, and without fear of being 'embarrassed by the necessities of life,' to produce such 'great and sublime' works of art.

Five soft repeated beats on the timpani usher in the serene, almost Mozartean first movement of the Violin Concerto (*Allegro ma non troppo*). This haunting motive—a first cousin to the knocking four-note theme of Beethoven's Fifth Symphony—is to play an important role throughout the movement. As in most concertos of the time, there is a long extended exposition for the orchestra before the soloist enters. After these muffled timpani beats, the oboes introduce the calm main theme, the violins take up the repeated notes, and then the clarinet and bassoon offer a rising scale figure that is followed by a dramatic outburst from the full orchestra. These various themes are pursued until the violins present a closing theme that is answered by the cellos and basses. There is a dramatic hush as the solo violin makes its majestic entry with a cadenza-like ascending octave passage, followed by the principal subject in ornamented form, along with the repeated timpani notes. The woodwinds play the ascending figure, which is then taken up by the soloist. The other themes come back in the orchestra and with the soloist, and the exposition ends with sustained trills by the solo violin above the repeated notes of the orchestra. The principal themes are then developed and recapitulated, as the soloist embroiders a filigree over the orchestral surface. An extended cadenza for the violin brings the movement to a close.

The simple theme of the second movement (*Larghetto*) is first given out by the muted violins. Two horns and a clarinet then take it up tenderly, as the soloist plays a delicate ornamental role. A series of beautiful variations follows. The theme is then repeated by the orchestra alone, after which the soloist introduces a new subject. The first theme returns in the upper reaches of the solo part, accompanied by plucked orchestral strings. At the end the orchestra recalls the dream-like opening, first softly, then more forcefully.

As in his last two piano concertos and some of his sonatas, Beethoven leads directly into the final movement without pause. The soloist has a cadenza that takes us immediately into the brilliant rondo Finale (*Allegro*). The solo violin has the vivacious, dance-like theme at the outset, repeating it an octave higher. It then passes to the orchestra, with a kind of hunting-call subject for the horns. The violin re-enters with a striking new idea. This is elaborated, and the first theme is heard again. The violin then has a new, contrasting episode, repeated by the bassoon over an accompaniment of solo violin arabesques. The first theme returns, and a broad solo cadenza leads to the bravura close.

The Overture to Egmont

In 1809, three years after composing the Violin Concerto, Beethoven was asked by the Burgtheater of Vienna to compose incidental music (an overture and eight set-pieces) for a revival of Goethe's play *Egmont*. For Beethoven this was a labour of love, both because of his veneration for Goethe and because the subject of the heroic drama, set in sixteenth-century Holland, was a passionate affirmation of liberty and a bitter denunciation of tyranny. Count Egmont becomes the leader in a revolt against Spanish despotism. When the ruthless Duke of Alba is sent off to the Low Countries to suppress rebellion, Egmont becomes the champion of independence and pays with his life on the scaffold.

As in many of his overtures, Beethoven here distills the essence of the drama in an urgent, concentrated tone-poem, and this is one of his finest. It opens ominously in the dark key of F minor with strongly accented chords, which can be interpreted as signifying the weight of Spanish oppression. Lyric phrases intrude into this foreboding atmosphere, but there is little respite from the underlying tension. Then the faster main section erupts dramatically, describing the rapidly developing rebellion. A gentler episode for woodwinds tells of the maiden Klärchen's love for the hero Egmont. After a brief development of the themes, the main melodies are recalled. Finally all gloom is dispelled with an exultant and joyous proclamation by the full orchestra, a cry of victory and glad celebration in what Beethoven called a 'Symphony of Victory' for the courageous Egmont and for the cause of human freedom.

Printed in the United States of America

Josephus Haydn

His Life and Times 1732-1809

PROGRAM NOTES FOR THE SURPRISE SYMPHONY
AND THE CLOCK SYMPHONY
By Robert Jacobson

FUNK & WAGNALLS, INC.
NEW YORK, NEW YORK

Early Life: 1732-59

Haydn was not as lucky as Mozart, who was born into a musical family in a thriving cultural centre. Haydn's father was a wheelwright and lived in Rohrau near the border of Austria and Hungary, an unattractive dry place at the mercy of a river which flooded, and a sun which caused fires. Franz Joseph, the composer, was the second of twelve children born to Anna Maria and Mathias Haydn and saw the light of day on 31st March 1732.

At a very early age Sepperl – as he was called in Austrian dialect – showed signs of musical inclinations. As he joined in the evening sing-songs with his father, who accompanied himself by ear on a harp, the boy astonished everybody by the beauty and accuracy of his voice. Not satisfied just with vocal accomplishments, the boy also made a fiddle out of two sticks, which he played in imitation of the local violinist schoolmaster.

All this impressed Johann Mathias Franck, a distant relation and headmaster of the school in nearby Hainburg, when he paid the Haydns a visit. So he suggested that the boy become a pupil in his school, to give him the sort of education he deserved and which he obviously could not get in the village. And after objections from Anna Maria, who had hoped Joseph would become a schoolmaster – or, even better, priest – rather than a musician, the six-year-old Haydn left the village more or less forever.

The training he received in Hainburg was as varied as it was invaluable – reading, writing and religion as well as music. His talents flourished: 'Our Almighty Father had endowed me with such facility in music that even in my sixth year I stood up like a man and sang Masses in the church choir and I could play a little on the clavier and violin!'[1] He also learned to play all the instruments of the orchestra, even the kettledrums. And he readily acknowledged in later life his debt to his relative: 'I shall owe it to this man even in my grave, that he set me to so many different things, although I received in the process more thrashings than food.'[1]

Just at the time when Haydn had learned more or less all this school had to offer, it received a visit from Karl Georg Reutter, Imperial Court Composer and newly appointed choir-master to the important Cathedral of St Stephan in Vienna. He was on the lookout for fresh talent and fresh voices for his choir school. Both these he found in the young Haydn. Reutter was surprised by the 'precision, the purity of tone, the spirit' with which the boy sang at sight, and was charmed by his ability to sing trills with the minimum of tuition from Reutter. For this demonstration the boy was rewarded with a plate of cherries which he had had his eye on throughout the interview (for the rest of his life he said he could not sing a trill without thinking of those cherries).

The consent of Haydn's father to the move was easily obtained, but as the boy could not be admitted to the choir school till he was eight years old, he was urged to spend the intervening nine months practising singing scales – which he did by inventing a solfa system of his own – for Franck was not able to help him.

After these months of eager anticipation, one can imagine the excitement of the boy as he set eyes on the imposing edifice of St Stephan's and the glories of Vienna. But, like Hainburg, it was not all days of wine and cherries. Life was difficult – there was little food. We are told: 'Joseph's stomach had to get used to continuous fasting. He tried to make up for it with the musical academies, where refreshments were offered to the chorister. As soon as Joseph made this discovery, so important for his stomach, he was seized with an incredible love for academies. He endeavoured to sing as beautifully as possible so as to be known and invited as a skilled performer, and thus to find occasions to appease his ravenous hunger.'[1] These concerts and entertainments at the houses of the nobility must indeed have been something of a relief from the daily round of lessons in Latin, religion, arithmetic, writing, playing and singing, and the frequent local occasions they had to take part in.

His training, in fact, was not much help to Haydn the composer-to-be; he received very few lessons in theory from Reutter, who did however encourage to some extent the boy's creative instincts. He studied the important theoretical works of the day with diligence, wrote many exercises and also attempted rather more ambitious compositions for many voices. 'I used to think then that it was all right if only the paper were pretty full. Reutter laughed at my immature output, at bars that no throat and no instrument could have executed, and he scolded me for composing for sixteen parts before I even understood two-part setting.'[1] But Haydn's musical tastes were all the time being shaped, not only by theory books, but by the music he sang and heard – mainly of course, sacred music. 'I listened attentively and tried to turn to good account what most impressed me. Thus little by little my knowledge and my ability were developed.'[1]

But in the life of all choirboys there comes a day when their voices break and they are no longer of any use in the choir. When this happened to Haydn life became more difficult. It was suggested that he should become a castrato, which brought his irate father rushing to Vienna; and comparison and rivalry with his quicker-witted young brother Michael made it appear that his days were numbered.

The actual cause of his leaving the choir school is the well known prank when he cut off the pigtail of the choirboy in the line in front with a pair of scissors. Faced with a public flogging the seventeen-year-old Haydn preferred to leave rather than submit to such an indignity. His offer was welcomed.

As he walked about the streets of Vienna that cold November night, with few clothes and no money, one can imagine what was going through his mind. He could expect no money from his parents, who would suggest his joining the priesthood; determined on music, he was certainly talented but his abilities as composer or violinist were not developed enough for him to earn a living from them. However, that night a chance meeting with a singer he knew, Johann Michael Spangler, who was moved by Haydn's

1. Haydn, A Creative Life in Music, by Karl Geiringer. Allen and Unwin, 1947.

plight, provided him with accommodation in a small attic, with him and his wife and baby.

After this first stroke of luck the composer began to scrape together a miserable living – tiny fees from teaching, playing the organ in church on Sundays, playing at dances and in street serenades. He had to leave his garret when another Spangler baby was on the way, and went on a pilgrimage to the Shrine of Our Lady at Mariazell, where he managed to sing in the choir and so keep body and soul together for a week or so.

Back in Vienna he found a new lodging in the old Michaelerhaus near the church of St Michael (where Spangler was a singer). Strengthened by a loan of 150 florins – an enormous sum, but which he somehow managed to pay back within the year – he went back to his hand-to-mouth existence, the regular pendulum of teaching by day and serenading by night. In his limited spare time he was still attempting to improve his musical technique again by recourse to the famous theory books of the time, mainly Fux's *Gradus ad Parnassum;* but these were probably not much help with the composition of an opera for the 'celebrated harlequin' Kurz (nicknamed Bernardon),which Haydn seems to have semi-improvised in a very short space of time.

But at about this time, while 'I pursued my zeal for composition far into the night', Haydn made the revelatory discovery of the music of C. P. E. Bach, the eldest of J. S. Bach's sons. A volume of the 'Hamburg Bach's' keyboard sonatas served as his strongest influence at that time and for a long time into the future, and on his wretched little piano 'I played them time and again for my own pleasure, especially when I was discouraged or depressed by worry, and always left the instrument cheered and in good spirits.'

It was now, about 1754, that things began to look up for

'The Haydn Family', a copy of a highly imaginative 1837 pen drawing by J. Peter Lyser (Haydn Memorial, Rohrau)

Haydn. For in the very same house where Haydn was, lived the famous poet and opera librettist Metastasio; and through the latter he got a job as accompanist at the singing-lessons which the ten-year-old Marianne Martinez was taking with the famous singer and composer Nicola Porpora. This contact was important for Haydn, who was soon taking lessons from Porpora and repaying him by becoming his regular accompanist and valet. They spent the summer season out of town at the famous spa at Mannersdorf, and during the three months there Haydn both met important composers such as Gluck and Wagenseil and improved his languages as well as his composition.

Such connections as he had by now made were useful to Haydn. As his reputation grew, so he could get more pupils and charge higher fees, and at the same time he managed to hold down many other jobs, such as playing violin and organ at innumerable church functions on Sundays.

He still persevered with his composition – even though by now his brother Michael had become a more immediate success. In the 1750s he wrote his first string quartets at Schloss Weinzierl near Melk, the summer seat of the Fürnberg family; the quartets were soon widely circulated in manuscript. A sonata that Joseph wrote came to the attention of the Countess Thun, who soon began to take singing and harpsichord lessons from Haydn. He had at last made it into 'high society'; and his determination was at last rewarded – for no composer at the time could hope to earn a living without a permanent court position – when in 1759 an introduction to the Bohemian Count Ferdinand Maximilian von Morzin led to Haydn's first regular appointment as director of music and composer of chamber music at Morzin's court.

Wienertor at Hainburg, the town in which Haydn went to study at the age of six (Austrian National Library, Vienna)

Settling Down: Life 1759-80

So at last Haydn's life was settled – no more need to scrape a living by finding and teaching pupils, nor to spend his evenings playing in open-air serenade bands, for in his role as music director to Count Morzin, a position he took up in 1759, his financial problems were resolved. He was given a salary of 200 gulden a month, with free board and lodging. And an existence free of financial worries was also a more relaxed one – his winters were spent in Vienna and summers in Bohemia at Lukavec Castle near Pilsen. Morzin kept a small private orchestra of about sixteen players for which Haydn wrote his very first symphonies.

Haydn was now getting on in life – in his late twenties – and it is evident that his thoughts turned to marriage, even though the Count refused to employ married men. Some years before, he had fallen in love with Therese Keller, one of two daughters of a Vienna hairdresser to whom he gave lessons. She had obviously not fancied him because she had gone off to a nunnery. And so Haydn, presumably against his better judgement, was persuaded to marry the sister, Maria Anna, who at thirty-one was three years older than the composer. They were married on 26th October 1760. It was never a happy marriage – the wife was demanding, shrewish, domineering, bad-tempered, a spendthrift and barren to boot. It is not surprising that Haydn's mind and eye occasionally wandered – 'My wife was unable to bear

children, and I was therefore less indifferent to the charms of other ladies.' Enough said. Soon after this Morzin fell on hard times and had to disband his orchestra. Haydn was not long out of work, however, for he immediately got an appointment as second Kapellmeister to Prince Paul Anton Esterházy at Eisenstadt, who had been impressed with Haydn's early symphonies. Thus began a connection that was to last all Haydn's life (after he had temporarily left the Esterházys the family still gave him a pension).

This was a far better position, for the Esterházys were infinitely richer and grander than the Morzins; the Esterházys, moreover, had always had a vital interest in music, and there had been composers in the family. When Haydn arrived, there was a smallish orchestra which played in church, at concerts and for the opera; Haydn, second-in-command to the Kapellmeister Werner, had complete control of the orchestra. The terms of his engagement are interesting; he was to be 'considered and treated as a member of the household,' had to wear a uniform, abstain 'from undue familiarity and from vulgarity in eating, drinking and conversation', 'shall be under obligation to compose such music as his Serene Highness may command', and so on, for a salary of 400 gulden.

Thus his activities covered a vast range. He played, organised, conducted, composed – he wrote the symphonies

Le Matin, *Le Midi* and *Le Soir* at this time (1761). All this suited his talents, and he attacked every job with equal enthusiasm. He had great respect for old Werner, who however considered the modern young Haydn to be a 'scribbler of songs' and a 'mere fop'.

However, after about nine months the old prince died and he was succeeded by Prince Nicolaus, nicknamed the Magnificent on account of his love of opulence and display. This could be seen both in his splendid manner of dress and his taste for grandiose celebrations for which Haydn had to write a wide variety of types of music, ranging from one-act operas to the more pompous and circumstantial. It is amazing how he kept his head above water with all this work; in addition, he was burdened with family responsibilities after his father died. In order to satisfy the Prince's love for an obsolete instrument – the baryton (a kind of viola da gamba with sympathetic vibrating strings) – Haydn himself spent six months learning it; he demonstrated its potentialities but completely neglected his composing during this interval.

In 1766 he became sole Kapellmeister – which he had been in any case in fact if not in title – and at this time the Esterházy menage moved to the magnificent and grandiose palace which the prince had had built on a swamp in Hungary. Eszterháza, as it was called, imitated the style of the Château de Versailles which had impressed the Prince on a visit to Paris in 1764. It is impossible to describe in a few words the sheer opulence and splendour of this place, but a contemporary description of the opera productions will give a hint:

'In an alley of wild chestnut trees stands the magnificent opera house. The boxes at the sides open into charming rooms, furnished most luxuriously with fireplaces, divans, mirrors, and clocks. The theatre easily holds four hundred people. Every day, at 6.00 p.m., there is a performance of an Italian *opera seria* or *buffa*, or a German comedy which is always attended by the Prince. Words cannot describe how both eye and ear are here delighted. When the music begins, its touching delicacy, the strength and force of the instruments penetrate the soul, since the great composer, Herr Haydn, is himself conducting. But the audience is also overwhelmed by the admirable lighting and the deceptively perfect stage settings. At first we see the clouds on which the gods are seated sink slowly to earth. Then the gods rise upwards and instantly vanish, and then again everything is transformed into a delightful garden, an enchanting wood or, it may be, a glorious hall.'

It was in this setting that Haydn directed his own operas, and between 1768 and 1780 he wrote and produced eight Italian and four German operas. In addition to normal day-to-day music-making there were extravagant festivities, held perhaps more than once a year, of which the visit of the Empress Maria Theresa in 1773 is perhaps typical.

The orchestra and the whole musical establishment had of course grown considerably by this time; Haydn worked hard, demanded the highest standards, but was very popular – he was given the affectionate nickname of 'Papa'. And in addition there were a number of real virtuosos in residence, for whom Haydn wrote concertos – including the violinist Luigi Tomasini, the cellist Joseph Weigl and the horn player Franz.

In a way conditions were ideal. The Prince encouraged Haydn, who could turn his hand to anything, and could also learn from his mistakes.

Yet there was a certain strain: he was not able to travel, so jealous was the Prince of his services, and there was a most arduous daily grind. Yet things were worse for the musicians in a less exalted position than Haydn. Although the palace was huge and spacious, living conditions for the musicians were cramped – so cramped that there was no room for everyone's wives, and as more and more time was spent at Eszterháza, away from Eisenstadt, the orchestral musician felt somewhat deprived. So to draw the Prince's attentions to their complaint Haydn wrote the so-called 'Farewell' Symphony.

'The affectionate husbands appealed to Haydn to help them. Haydn decided to write a symphony in which one instrument after the other ceases to play. The work was executed as soon as an occasion presented itself, and each player was instructed to put out his candle when his part was ended, seize his music and leave with his instrument tucked under his arm. The Prince instantly understood the meaning of this pantomime and the next day he gave the order to leave Eszterháza.'

However, a mere glance at the number and range of his works at this time and their stylistic and technical development shows the artistic assurance and individuality Haydn was attaining by this very isolation (by the early 1770s he had written about fifty symphonies and over two dozen string quartets, including the epoch-making op. 20 set – and by the end of the 70s the influence of the *Sturm und Drang* movement can be seen on the dramatic and impassioned content of some of his music). Life at Eszterháza away from the world was perhaps more desirable than the cut and thrust of Viennese society. In 1775 he was in Vienna to conduct the first performance of his Oratorio *Il ritorno di Tobia*, which was a very great success. However when he was commissioned to write an opera, *La vera costanza*, there was so much trouble and backbiting, and jealous cliquery, that he withdrew the work in disgust.

Nicolaus ('The Magnificent') Esterházy, Haydn's patron, in a contemporary print (Bettmann Archive, New York)

in Vienna prefso Artaria Comp

From Eszterháza to London: Life 1782-90

At the beginning of the 1780s Haydn's fame was slowly but surely spreading throughout Europe. Although his daily life at Eszterháza Castle in Hungary and his annual brief winter period in Vienna hardly changed from year to year, his contacts with the outside world became increasingly important to him. For one thing, printed music was now gradually supplanting handwritten copies, and Haydn soon secured an important Viennese publisher, Artaria & Co., who became his principal publisher for the next ten years; this house also became Mozart's publisher and that of many works by Beethoven.

On 27th May 1781 we find him writing to Artaria about his relations with Paris:

'Now something from Paris. Monsieur Le Gros, *Directeur* of the Concert Spirituel, wrote me the most flattering things about my *Stabat Mater*, which was performed there four times with the greatest applause; the gentlemen asked permission to have it engraved. They made me an offer to engrave all my future works on the most favourable terms for myself, and were most surprised that I was so singularly successful in my vocal compositions; but I wasn't at all surprised, for they have not yet heard anything. If they only could hear my operetta *L'isola disabitata* and my most recent opera, *La fedeltà premiata*, I assure you that no such work has been heard in Paris up to now, nor perhaps in Vienna either; my misfortune is that I live in the country.

'I enclose Herr Boccherini's letter: please present my respectful compliments to him. No one here can tell me where this place Arenas is. It cannot be far from Madrid, however; please let me know about this, for I want to write to Herr Boccherini myself.'

Although Haydn had probably never met Boccherini, the two composers were admirers of each other's music. Boccherini had been in the Vienna court opera orchestra in the late 1750s and early 1760s and had undoubtedly been inspired to write his first string quartets as a result of hearing Haydn's earliest works in that form. Boccherini had written to Artaria from Arenas in February asking Artaria to present his respects to Haydn, and saying that 'I am one of his most passionate admirers . . .'

About this time Haydn and Mozart met in Vienna and became lasting friends — a famous friendship with a literary parallel in that between Goethe and Schiller.

Haydn next entered into profitable relations with the English publishers Forster, to whom he sold some fifteen symphonies, several pieces of chamber music and *The Seven Words*. He also began to have his symphonies printed in Paris, where Boyer, Sieber and Imbault vied with each other to issue his latest symphonies and chamber music.

In 1782 Haydn produced at Eszterháza his opera *Orlando Paladino*, and two years later the last opera he was to write for Eszterháza, *Armida*. On 1st March 1784 he wrote to his publishers Artaria: 'Yesterday my *Armida* was performed for the second time with general applause. I am told that this is my best work up to now.'

He was also sending music regularly to Spain, and there soon came from the faraway port of Cadiz an interesting commission: to write instrumental music on the Seven Words of the Saviour on the Cross. Haydn was told the circumstances under which this music would be played: in a church darkened with black crêpe, the priest was to hold a short sermon on each of the seven last words spoken from the Cross. The authorities at Cadiz specified that they wanted seven slow movements, each to last not longer than about ten minutes. Haydn fulfilled this commission, prefacing the whole with a sombre, slow introduction and completing it with a very short and hair-raising description of the earthquake that followed Christ's death. At the end of this cataclysmic movement, Haydn writes the dynamic mark *fff* for the first time in the history of music. *The Seven Words* made a profound impression on the musical world and was printed both in Paris and London as well as in Haydn's Vienna. In later years, after his second trip to London, Haydn was to rewrite the oratorio to include vocal parts to a text by Gottfried van Swieten, author of the libretti of *The Creation* and *The Seasons*.

Haydn's popularity in Paris – they had been playing his music there for some twenty years and had printed it in 1764, the earliest date of any Haydn edition – brought him a lucrative commission: to write six big symphonies for the Concert de la Loge Olympique, the most fashionable Parisian orchestral society, which boasted a huge orchestra that included forty violins and ten double-basses. The result was the set of six so-called 'Paris' Symphonies, Nos. 82-87, which Haydn composed in 1785 and 1786, working on them at the same time as on *The Seven Words* for Cadiz. How Haydn was able to complete all these compositions in 1786

is an astonishing tribute to his capacity for hard work. In that year, 1786, Haydn also delivered six delightful concertos for *lire organizzate* to King Ferdinand IV of Naples and the Two Sicilies; but, apart from the many compositions, we have to remind ourselves that Haydn was as always running a full-time operatic season at Eszterháza Castle, so that in this year alone, he conducted 125 operatic performances at Eszterháza Castle which included a total of seventeen operas, eight of them premières.

Haydn's 'Paris' Symphonies were perhaps the biggest successes of his career, and the next five symphonies, Nos. 88-92, were written for Paris in the years 1787-89. The last of the works for Paris, No. 92 (1789), later became famous under the title of the 'Oxford' Symphony, when it was conducted by Haydn in the Sheldonian Theatre on the occasion of his receiving Oxford's Doctorate of Music *honoris causa* in July 1791.

Meanwhile the whole establishment at Eszterháza was wearing a little thin for Haydn. He now realised that he was a famous man throughout Europe, and he quite rightly thought that he could employ his mighty talents with more profit to himself and the musical world than by being operatic Kapellmeister in a remote Hungarian castle.

He was longing for freedom, and not even the preparations to stage Mozart's *Marriage of Figaro* at Eszterháza could change the fact that Haydn had outlived his present position. Finally the old Princess Esterházy died, and Prince Nicolaus went into a depression from which he never really recovered. On 27th June 1790 Haydn writes to Maria Anna von Genzinger:

'Again I find that I am forced to remain here. Your Grace can imagine how much I lose by having to do so. It really is sad always to be a slave, but Providence wills it so. I'm a poor creature! Always plagued by hard work, very few hours of recreation, and friends? What am I saying?

The front of Eszterháza Castle, looking north, in an 18th-century print (Austrian National Library, Vienna)

PROSPECT DER FÜRSTLICHEN HAUPT THOR

RESIDENZ ESZTERHAZ VON DEN GEGEN NORDEN

One true one? There aren't any true friends any more – one lady friend? Oh yes! There might be one. But she's far away from me. Oh well! I have my thoughts. God bless you, and may you never forget me!'

Prince Nicolaus 'the Magnificent' Esterházy died on 28th September 1790. Operatic performances ceased when it became apparent that Prince Nicolaus was dying, and it is curious to think of the musicians quietly getting up and leaving after a performance of *The Marriage of Figaro* conducted by Joseph Haydn. The candlelights were darkened in the pretty rococo theatre. Musical life at Eszterháza was finished forever.

The new Prince, Anton, had no interest in music and dismissed the entire orchestra and operatic company, retaining only a small group of wind instruments for the hunt, while giving Haydn and the leader of the orchestra, Luigi Tomasini, handsome pensions. Haydn was now free and quite literally fled Eszterháza in such haste that he left quite a lot of important music behind which he later sorely missed. The famous Esterházy Kapell was disbanded and the musicians went forth all over Europe to find new jobs.

In Vienna, Haydn was surprised one day to receive a visit from the famous impresario Johann Peter Salomon. Born in Bonn, Salomon had gone to England in the 1780s and had soon made a name there as a solo violinist and leader; he had long wanted to lure Haydn to England, and

he happened to be at Cologne engaging singers for the coming season in London, when he read in a newspaper of Prince Esterházy's death. He thereupon rushed to Vienna and burst in upon Haydn with the characteristically to-the-point bluntness for which he was well known and often teased about: 'I am Salomon of London and I have come to fetch you; tomorrow we will settle the agreement.' Haydn had other offers; one from Prince Grassalkovicz to go to Pressburg, and another from King Ferdinand IV to go to Naples. But he wisely chose London as the most interesting of the three possibilities. Salomon also tried to persuade Mozart to come, but Mozart could or would not, and the three had a farewell lunch together just before Haydn and Salomon left Vienna in December 1790. Mozart wept and said the prophetic words: 'We shall never meet again.' A year later Mozart was indeed dead. Mozart also said to Haydn: 'Papa, how can you go to England when you don't even know the language?' Haydn is said to have answered: 'My language is understood all over the world.'

On New Year's Day 1791 Haydn and Salomon boarded the ship at Calais at 7.30 in the morning, and at five o'clock that afternoon they landed at Dover and proceeded at once to London. It was the most important decision of Haydn's life, and it probably resulted in his becoming one of the world's immortal composers rather than remaining an Interesting Historical Figure.

Success Abroad and at Home: Life 1791-1809

Haydn's two visits to London in 1791 and 1794 completely changed his life and brought him out of the isolation in which he had lived since 1761 at Eisenstadt and Eszterháza. During those thirty years he had become Europe's most popular composer; but it was time that he escaped from the provincial court life at Eszterháza and saw some of the rest of the world. From the outset, it was obvious that the financial considerations for the trip would be very inviting, and he was paid in advance to compose a new opera for Sir John Gallini. As it happened, the opera, *L'anima del filosofo (Orfeo ed Euridice)*, was not given due to theatrical intrigues between the two London opera companies and had to await its first performance until the 1951 Maggio Musicale at Florence. Salomon's concerts, although initially postponed, finally took place and with Symphony No. 96, the first of the twelve 'London' or 'Salomon' Symphonies, Haydn won the hearts of the London audiences.

He had brought with him a great many works already composed but not yet performed in London, such as the *Notturni* for the King of Naples, and the String Quartets, op. 64. There were twelve Salomon concerts for each season as well as a benefit concert for Haydn. He also played as a guest artist at the benefit concerts of numerous fellow musicians. For the first season in 1791, Haydn composed two new symphonies, the aforementioned No. 96, and No. 95 in C minor. On 14th March 1791 he writes back to his mistress Luigia Polzelli in Vienna: 'At the first concert of Mr Salomon I created a furore with a new Symphony, and they had to repeat the Adagio. This had never before occurred in London.'

At the end of the 1791 season Haydn immediately agreed to spend the next season as well in London, and during the summer of 1791 he visited friends in the country and prepared the works for the new season. On 17th September 1791 he writes back to Maria Anna von Genzinger, his cultivated Viennese lady friend:
'... during the last two months, ... I have been living in the country, amid the loveliest scenery, with a banker's family where the atmosphere is like that of the Genzinger family, and where I live as if I were in a monastery. I am all right, thank the good Lord! except for my usual rheumatism; I work hard, and when in the early mornings I walk in the woods, alone, with my English grammar, I think of my Creator, my family, and all the friends I have left behind – and of these you are the ones I most value. Of course I had hoped to have the pleasure of seeing you sooner, but my circumstances – in short, fate – will have it that I remain in London another eight or ten months. Oh, my dear gracious lady! how sweet this bit of freedom really is! I had a kind Prince, but sometimes I was forced to be dependent on base souls. I often sighed for release, and now I have it in some measure. I appreciate the good sides of all this, too, though my mind is burdened with far more work. The realisation that I am no bond-servant makes ample amends for all my toils.'

He made many friends in England and soon became a popular figure at the Prince of Wales's (later George IV's) receptions. He was invited to Oatlands to visit the Duke and Duchess of York, and the Prince of Wales ordered Hoppner to paint his portrait (it hangs now in Buckingham Palace). In 1792 another portrait of Haydn's was made by Thomas Hardy, which became even more famous than the Hoppner.

For the second Salomon season of 1792, Haydn composed Symphonies Nos. 93, 98, 94 and 97, as well as the *Sinfonia concertante* and a choral piece which he entitled *Madrigal: The Storm*. By now three or four daily newspapers, even including the reticent *Times*, were reviewing almost every concert. Work after work was applauded and whole movements repeated. The 'Surprise' Symphony, which was first performed at the sixth concert of the 1792 season, became an immediate and lasting favourite.

On the way back to Vienna, Haydn met Beethoven in Bonn and accepted him as a pupil. Their relationship was never a very happy one, although Haydn immediately recognised that Beethoven 'would in time become one of Europe's greatest composers, and I shall be proud to be able to speak of myself as his teacher.' Beethoven came to Vienna to study with Haydn in November 1792 and remained with him until the latter left for England in January 1794. Haydn was a negligent teacher, and Beethoven later got much more accurate training from the famous contrapuntist J. G. Albrechtsberger.

A performance of The Creation at the University of Vienna in the presence of the composer, from a watercolour by Balthasar Wigand (Austrian National Library, Vienna)

Haydn's second trip to London was equally successful. For the season of 1794 he performed Symphonies Nos. 99, 101 and 100, the latter, soon known as the 'Military' Symphony, becoming the greatest single hit of Haydn's symphonic career. The second movement was 'received with absolute shouts of applause . . .' The new quartets of op. 71 and op. 74 for Salomon were equally applauded. For the last season of 1795, a new orchestra with the famous Viotti as leader was formed: it consisted of sixty virtuosi – twenty more than Salomon's band. For this, certainly the finest orchestra at that time, Haydn composed Symphonies Nos. 102-104, all of which entered the permanent repertoire from the very first night they were performed. In the early autumn of 1795, Haydn finally returned to his native Austria a wealthy man. He felt he would not have been able to continue living the high-powered life in London and looked forward to the security and pension that he would receive from his new Prince Esterházy, Nicolaus II, the fourth Prince under whom Haydn was to serve.

Nicolaus had asked Haydn to return to Austria when he was finished with his concerts, and to re-establish the orchestra and vocal soloists. Nicolaus was primarily interested in church music and expected from Haydn only that he provide a yearly mass to celebrate the name-day of the beautiful and vivacious Princess Maria Hermenegild, Nicolaus's wife. Thus we have the great series of six large masses for soloists, choir and orchestra which Haydn composed between 1796 and 1802.

Impressed with the strength of Handel's oratorios, of which he had heard many in England, Haydn decided to compose a modern, large-scale oratorio which should capture the hearts and minds of men in the way that only *Messiah* had been able to do previously. Salomon seems to have dug up an old libretto originally intended for Handel – the author is uncertain but possibly Handel's friend Mrs

Patrick Delany – and Haydn took it back with him to Vienna, where he gave it to his old friend and patron, the Baron Gottfried van Swieten. Van Swieten translated and adapted the work, which was first performed at a semi-private subscription concert in the Schwarzenberg Palace at Vienna in April 1798. *The Creation (Die Schöpfung)*, which was published by Haydn in two languages (German and English), achieved immediate success throughout Europe. Haydn and van Swieten then attempted a new oratorio called *The Seasons (Die Jahreszeiten)* based on the poetry of James Thomson. Haydn was now nearly seventy, and the composition of *The Seasons* proved extremely tiring; but he finished it, and the first performance – again at the Schwarzenberg Palace, on 24th April 1801 – proved that the grand old man of Viennese music had not yet lost his touch. Indeed, *The Seasons* is an astonishingly fresh and youthful composition for a man approaching seventy.

Haydn gradually went less and less to Eisenstadt and settled in a comfortable home at Gumpendorf, a suburb of Vienna: he had bought this house in 1793 and enlarged it. There he lived out the rest of his life in peace and prosperity, his serenity rudely interrupted twice, in 1805 and just before his death in 1809, by the invading French armies under Napoleon. In 1805 Haydn drew up a catalogue of all the works he could remember having written from the age of eighteen on; this was because enormous amounts of spurious works were circulating under Haydn's name – for instance there are more spurious symphonies than the 107 works which we know Haydn to have written. He stopped composing, except for arranging some Scottish songs, after the big *Harmoniemesse* of 1802, and his last quartet remained unfinished.

He died on 31st May 1809, and his death mask radiates an inward peace which was seldom given to any of the other great composers.

The church and convent of Mariahilf in the Gumpendorf district of Vienna, where Haydn spent the last years of his life – a late 18th-century print (Austrian National Library, Vienna)

PROGRAM NOTES FOR THE RECORD

by ROBERT JACOBSON

The 'London' Symphonies

Haydn was fifty-eight when he first arrived in London in 1791, and he was already renowned across the European continent for his symphonies, quartets, operas, oratorios, concertos, sonatas and so on. His new symphonies were regularly received by public and press alike with tremendous anticipation and acclaim. An even dozen symphonies were written to mark the composer's two historic visits to London in the 1790s. The astute London impresario Johann Peter Salomon, who brought Haydn to England, placed at the composer's disposal an orchestra of strings and two each of flutes, oboes, bassoons, horns, trumpets and timpani for the first six symphonies in this set (1791–1792), Nos. 93 through 98. Clarinets were added to the orchestra for his second visit in 1794, for which he wrote Nos. 99 through 104. All were called the 'London' or 'Salomon' Symphonies.

In this last period of composition, Haydn reached the summit of his artistic achievements, summing up his symphonic thought and development. These twelve scores composed between 1791 and 1795 are among his richest and most inventive symphonic works. Biographer Karl Geiringer notes: 'No other of Haydn's scores shows such virtuosity of instrumentation or such delightful unorthodox treatment of musical forms and contrapuntal devices . . . The whole nineteenth century, beginning with Beethoven and ending with Brahms, was able to draw rich inspiration from Haydn's last . . . symphonies.'

The 'Surprise' Symphony

After the première of his Symphony No. 94 (23rd March 1792), the *Morning Herald* wrote: 'Critical applause was fervid and abundant.' *Woodfall's Register* described the music as 'simple, profound and sublime. The Andante movement was particularly admired.' *The Oracle* declared that the second movement was 'equal to the happiest of this great master's conceptions. The surprise might not unaptly be likened to the situation of a beautiful shepherdess who, lulled to slumber by the murmur of a distant waterfall, starts, alarmed by the unexpected firing of a fowling-piece. The flute obbligato was delicious.'

A single loud chord in the sixteenth measure of the second movement of the Symphony No. 94 gives it its famous nickname, the 'Surprise' (in German it is known as *mit dem Paukenschlag*, or 'with the drumbeat'). The oft-told tale is that the chord was intended by Haydn as a kind of prank, to startle drowsy subscribers out of their sleep at his 1791–1792 concert series. No less than three different versions of this story have come down to us from contemporaries who knew Haydn and claimed to have received the explanation from the source himself. The butt of the joke is variously said to have been: (1) late arrivals at the London concerts who, having lingered over large dinners with an aftermath of port, dozed during the soft passages and slow movements; (2) the ladies, who nodded because the programs lasted past midnight; or (3) one lone old man who always sat in the same seat and promptly fell asleep at the beginning of every program.

One of Haydn's more reliable biographers, George August Griesinger, once asked him whether it was true that he had written the Andante with the kettle-drum stroke in order to waken the English public that had fallen asleep at his concert. 'No,' answered the composer, 'rather it was my wish to surprise the public with something new, and to make a debut in a brilliant manner in order not to be outdone by my pupil Pleyel, who at that time [1792] was engaged by an orchestra in London which had begun its concert series eight days before mine. The first Allegro of my Symphony was received with countless bravos, but the enthusiasm reached its highest point in the Andante with the kettle-drum stroke. "*Ancora, ancora!*" sounded from every throat, and even Pleyel complimented me on my idea.'

After a slow subdued introduction (*Adagio*) in the strings and woodwinds, the first movement of the Symphony No. 94 goes on to a quick, dance-like tempo (*Vivace assai*). The violins state the light-hearted principal theme, followed by the full orchestra. A syncopated second theme is then heard first in the violins, making way for a closing theme in the violins, violas and cellos. These ideas are developed and, before this charming movement ends, are brought back in their original form.

The principal theme of the Andante is first heard in the violins—a simple tune in C major taken from a German folk-song about cherries on the trees along a village street. The famous 'surprise' chord—played *fortissimo* by strings, winds, horns, trumpets and timpani—comes after the initial theme has been heard twice. Musicologist Donald Francis Tovey, with a touch of scholarly scorn for this popular episode, observes that in the Symphony the melody 'waddles through the poultry yard in several variations, the first being in the minor and inclined to episodic developments. At the return to the major mode the oboe seems to have laid an egg.' There are four variations on the theme, ending with one for full orchestra, after which the movement ends quietly and poetically.

The third movement (*Allegro molto*) is labelled a Minuet, but is actually a robust Austrian peasant Ländler, or hop-waltz, first played by the flutes, bassoons and violins. The middle Trio, introduced by bassoons and violins, contrasts the weightiness of the main section with lighter material. A sparkling main theme and a very marked second theme dominate the final section. There is abundant sophistication and imagination in Haydn's formal working out of these two ideas, ending with a burst of laughter.

The 'Clock' Symphony

After the première of the Symphony No. 101 (3rd March 1794), the London *Morning Chronicle* recorded: 'As usual the most delicious part of the entertainment was a new grand Overture by Haydn; the inexhaustible, the wonderful, the sublime HAYDN! The first two movements were encored; and the character that pervaded the whole composition was heartfelt joy. Every new Overture he writes, we fear, till it is heard, he can only repeat himself; and we are every time mistaken. Nothing can be more original than the subject of the first movement; and having found a happy subject, no man knows like Haydn how to produce incessant variety, without once departing from it. The management of the accompaniment of the Andante, though perfectly simple, was masterly; and we never heard a more charming effect than was produced by the trio to the Minuet.—It was HAYDN; what can we, what need we, say more?'

The ticking rhythm of the Andante of the Symphony No. 101 has given it the nickname 'Clock'; but Haydn also associated another of its movements with a specific clock. During his return home to Vienna in 1793, he devised twelve short pieces for an elaborate musical clock

he presented, before returning to London, as a gift to his great patron Prince Esterhàzy. The musical clock incorporated a minute pipe organ, with pipes constructed by the Prince's librarian, Father Primitivus Niemecz. The latter enjoyed international fame as a builder of tiny mechanical organs (*Flötenuhren*). One of Haydn's pieces for this 1793 clock is so close to the Minuet of the 'Clock' Symphony that the movement has to be considered simply an elaboration of this piece composed for the mechanical clock.

Geiringer writes that Haydn's interest in musical clocks came from his friendship with Niemecz, who was also a cellist in the orchestra Haydn conducted at Eszterháza: 'Niemecz built three clocks equipped with tiny mechanical organs, the first in 1772, the other two in 1792 and 1793. In these he used only music composed by his friend and teacher, Joseph Haydn . . . The clock of 1792 was built for Prince Liechtenstein. This tiny instrument with its sweet, weak tone plays twelve pieces, one every hour. Twelve numbers also form the repertory of the clock of 1793 which Haydn gave to Prince Esterházy before leaving on his second trip to England.' The great composer mirrored that era's fascination with imitative mechanisms of all kinds.

The Symphony No. 101, too, opens with a slow, solemn introduction (*Adagio*), establishing a romantic mood through chromatic harmonies. The rising scale figure anticipates the principal theme (*Presto*), a lively, lilting subject reminiscent of hunting music, heard first in the violins and then echoed brilliantly by the woodwinds, brass and timpani. The second theme has a similar lift and light touch, followed by a similar outburst. Then both themes are developed, dramatically and energetically, in chamber music fashion. There is a brief climax, after which a playful flute solo leads back to a recapitulation of the two main ideas.

Like the 'Surprise' Symphony, the 'Clock' takes its name from the Andante movement, which opens with a tick-tock rhythm in the bassoons and plucked strings. Above this persistent rhythm, the violins play a delicate melodic line that suggests musical clocks or music boxes. Then the orchestra plunges into an agitated section, the first of three major variations. A return to the original melody closes the movement.

The Minuet (*Allegretto*) is a typically vigorous late-Haydn minuet—more of a folk dance with heavy rhythms—stated at first by the full orchestra. The middle Trio is dominated by a stylised drone, like that of bagpipes, while a solo flute rides above. A repetition of the opening minuet theme concludes the section. The Finale (*Vivace*) begins with a lively ingenuous melody in the violins, after which we are thrown in the midst of some complex, stormy music, in which the little refrain is chopped up and tossed about. It returns, only to be stopped by the churning full orchestra. There is a dramatic pause, followed by a lively whispering passage for strings, and this turns into a full orchestral fugue. The symphony ends, however, with rough good humour. As Geiringer observes, 'Admiring the facets of Haydn's art displayed in these last symphonies, we feel that they fittingly serve as a final point in the gigantic structure erected by the composer's orchestral work.'

The title page of the 'Clock' Symphony in its first edition (Austrian National Library, Vienna)

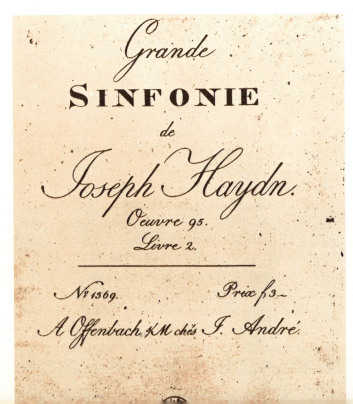

Grande
SINFONIE
de
Joseph Haydn.
Oeuvre 95.
Livre 2.

Nᵒ 1369.   Prix f 3.-

A Offenbach ¼M chés I. André

Printed in the United States of America

THE GREAT COMPOSERS 22
FW-322

Hector Berlioz

His Life and Times 1803-1869

PROGRAM NOTES FOR THE 'FANTASTIC' SYMPHONY
By Robert Jacobson

FUNK & WAGNALLS, INC.
NEW YORK, NEW YORK

Berlioz's Early Life

Berlioz was born in 1803, in the small town of La Côte St André near Grenoble in the south of France. He was christened Louis Hector; the Louis after his father, while the Hector, one may presume, was inspired by the revolutionary spirit of the time which caused parents to grace their offspring with the mantle of a legendary hero. As the local doctor, Berlioz's father was a cultured man who led a prosperous and, evidently, leisurely life; for he was able to afford the time to undertake his son's education single-handed. It is a testimony to the father's expert tuition that, at the age of seventeen, Berlioz passed the examinations necessary to gain entry to the Paris faculty of medicine and went to the capital shortly before his eighteenth birthday to embark on the career his father had planned for him.

Music was part of the liberal education at La Côte, and Berlioz's natural aptitude was allowed to take its course. He learned the flageolet, the flute and the guitar, becoming extremely accomplished on these instruments, and developed enough self-confidence as a composer to offer, at the age of fifteen, several pieces to Paris music-publishers (he got back polite refusals). One of these early compositions, a song called 'Estelle et Némorin', was later incorporated in the introduction to the 'Fantastic' Symphony because it expressed the 'overwhelming sadness of a young heart tortured by helpless love'. This at once indicates something of the intrinsic quality of Berlioz's very early music; but more relevant to our immediate interest is that this song was a consequence of his adolescent love for Estelle, a girl he met at a party when he was twelve and she an imperious nineteen. He never forgot her large shining eyes and her pink shoes, and towards the end of his life, when he was over sixty and Estelle twenty years a widow, he visited her again and awakened in the old lady a tired yet affectionate response to his still deep feelings for her. It is a commonplace of journalism to cite the Estelle episode as evidence of excessive amorousness; but we may regard it rather as symptomatic of the profoundly sensitive nature of a young man brought up away from the rough justice of a normal schooling and with the time and environment for romantic dreaming.

When he arrived in Paris Berlioz at first applied himself conscientiously to his studies as a medical student, even though he was horrified by the smell and the predatory rats and sparrows in the dissecting room. But after a year the medical school was closed by the political disturbances in Paris, and when it was opened again three months later Berlioz had committed himself to a life of music.

He never really intended to take medicine seriously and agreed to study it only because he had promised his father he would do so in exchange for a new flute. Within a few days of arriving in Paris he was at the Opéra, where the works of Gluck (1714-87) made a deep impression on him. Having discovered that the music library of the Conservatoire was open to the public, he was quickly examining scores, copying them out, comparing them—in general acquiring that expert knowledge which accounted for his furious and doubtless alarming outbursts from the auditorium: 'There are no cymbals at that place. Who has dared to correct Gluck?' and 'Why aren't the trombones playing? It's intolerable!' It was Gluck who made him finally decide to give up medicine come what may, and Gluck who was the cause of his first newspaper article. He had been incensed by an article in which Gluck was unfavourably compared with Rossini, and replied in assured and meticulous fashion, demonstrating not only his intimate knowledge of his idol's music but also a remarkably advanced conception of the dramatic possibilities of instrumental music. He was twenty when he wrote the article, his first foray into the world of musical journalism.

By this time he had begun to study composition with the celebrated Conservatoire teacher Jean-François Lesueur, who had accepted him into his composition class. Lesueur regarded Berlioz with kindly encouragement, and even tried to arrange a performance for him of a cantata about the crossing of the Red Sea – although the plans came to nothing. But in 1825 a Mass written under Lesueur's supervision did get performed and its success served to quell the growing opposition from home to Berlioz's activities. But when he failed to pass the preliminary examination for entry for the Prix de Rome – the biggest musical prize in France, which provided for travel in Italy and Germany – his father promptly stopped his allowance and Berlioz had to go home to argue out his position. His father eventually gave in and agreed to let him study music on condition that if he failed further trials he would then choose some other career. His mother, however, regarded music as a disreputable pursuit which would bring shame on the family: Berlioz had to leave home without her blessing.

Back in Paris he was officially registered as a student at the Conservatoire, where he studied fugue and counterpoint with the worthy Anton Reicha (who had been a friend of Beethoven) as well as continuing his composition studies with Lesueur. But although he now appeared set fair on his chosen course, he was living below subsistence level. The performance of the Mass had put him severely in debt and he had to take pupils in singing, flute and guitar. A creditor, however, got wind of Berlioz's troubles and told his father, who paid the debt and stopped Berlioz's allowance again. But at least the debt was cleared, and Berlioz was undaunted. He kept his pupils, got a job singing in the chorus of a new theatre performing comic opera, and continued his frugal existence. On New Year's Day 1827 he regaled himself with dry bread and the poems of Thomas Moore. He began the composition of an opera, Les Francs-Juges, to a libretto by his lifelong friend Humbert Ferrand. The opera was never finished, but the overture is the earliest of Berlioz's works still in the repertoire.

In his famous Memoirs Berlioz explains that he learned nothing about instrumentation at the Conservatoire. He was entirely self-taught. For example, in order to find out whether a passage in the overture to Les Francs-Juges was playable or not, he visited a professional trombone player for advice. Having been assured that it was, he walked home preoccupied with this good news, forgot to look where he was going, fell down and sprained his ankle. 'Now I have a pain in the foot every time I hear that piece.' His fascination with instrumentation was, however, to have more serious consequences. In the summer of 1827 he passed the preliminary examination for the Prix de Rome and wrote the cantata *The Death of Orpheus* as his entry. This work, along with the submissions of the other candidates, was duly played to the judges on the piano. Berlioz's work was deemed 'unplayable'. This in fact meant that the pianist found a work conceived in purely orchestral terms very difficult to play. Berlioz was profoundly discouraged, and fell ill. In his *Memoirs* he writes that he would have died had he not lanced an abscess at the back of his throat himself with a knife. His father evidently heard of this, for the allowance was suddenly restored and now Berlioz could give up his singing job and spend his evenings more congenially in the pit of the Opéra or in the theatre.

Now followed what Berlioz called 'the grand drama of my life'. An English theatre company was in Paris in the autumn of 1827. In the repertoire were *Hamlet* and *Romeo and Juliet*. Ophelia and Juliet were played by a twenty-seven-year-old Irish actress named Harriet Smithson, enchantingly beautiful and remarkably talented. The combination of Harriet Smithson and Shakespeare was overpowering. Berlioz fell in love with his Ophelia; and Shakespeare, in one 'flash of lightning, illuminated the most remote depths of the heaven of art'. He could not sleep, work, or do anything. He wandered about Paris dropping down with exhaustion wherever he happened to be: on one occasion this was at a café where he terrified the waiters, who thought he was dead.

Not long after the shock of his love for Harriet, Berlioz made his first discovery of Goethe's *Faust* in a French translation, and of Beethoven's symphonies, which early in 1828 had been given their first performances in Paris. The effect of Goethe and Beethoven was almost as powerful as that of Shakespeare, and from letters of the period and contemporary observations it appeared that Berlioz was reduced to some Hamlet-like trance. This was, however, only one side of the coin. He was also level-headed enough to undertake single-handed the organisation of a concert of his own music. This was an extraordinarily bold step for a composer still a student and only twenty-four (the only other one-man concerts had been of Beethoven and Weber). The purpose of the enterprise was of course to attract the attention of Harriet, but although the concert did take place, she never heard about it. The musical world, however, was alerted to the presence of the young composer and if he again found himself in debt, at least he had gained an artistic success.

He was therefore confident of winning the Prix de Rome at his second attempt in the summer of 1828. But *Herminie* (a cantata for voice and orchestra) was awarded only second prize. This was a bitter disappointment, hardly mitigated by his parents' surprisingly cordial reception of the news. The importance of the Prix de Rome may seem minimal to our minds, since few composers of consequence have ever won it; but for Berlioz it was vital. Apart from commissions from the Opéra, it was the only means available to a composer of keeping his head above water. It conferred on the winner financial security for five years and considerable public esteem. Berlioz, with typical resilience, now set about gaining an entrée to the Opéra by writing a ballet on *Faust*, a project which did not materialise as planned but which led to the publication of his opus 1, the *Eight Scenes from Faust* (he later withdrew the work, and some of it reappeared twenty years later in the 'dramatic legend' *The Damnation of Faust*). He also took up journalism more seriously, in order to augment his income. In 1829 his third attempt at the Prix de Rome with *Cleopatra* was a further blow – no prizes at all were awarded that year. A student now for eight years, Berlioz had still to wait. There was no need, however, for stagnation on any other than the academic front. He promoted another concert, this time containing – as well as his own music – the first performance in Paris of Beethoven's 'Emperor' Concerto played by Ferdinand Hiller, a teacher at the school where Berlioz himself now taught the guitar. And he was planning an immense instrumental composition which would be performed in London in the presence of Harriet.

He still had not met the elusive and unattainable Miss Smithson, although she had by now learned of his existence and of his strange and rather terrifying passion. His feelings for her continued to torture him. In February 1830 he was ready to begin the new work, which was to depict the course of 'this infernal love of mine'. It was all in his head, but he could write nothing. Then in April he must have heard rumours giving him cause to suspect Harriet's virtue, for in the latter part of that month he wrote to Ferrand saying that some 'horrible truths' had begun to effect a cure: he had just finished the work, whose subject would be set out in a programme to be distributed to the audience at the first performance. Berlioz then announced the 'Episode in the Life of an Artist – a grand fantastic symphony in five parts'. He had hoped to produce the work shortly before the Prix de Rome for 1830 and thus force the judges' hands. But the concert had to be postponed, and Berlioz finally won the prize with his *Death of Sardanapalus*. Meanwhile he suddenly found himself in love with one Camille Moke, who was to inspire another work, *The Tempest,* for chorus and orchestra, which was heard a month before the first performance of the 'Fantastic' Symphony on 5th December 1830 in Paris.

The Moke affair is a strange little episode. She was the love of Berlioz's friend Hiller, and was so stung by Hiller's remark that Berlioz was blind to any woman save Harriet that she determined to capture him, which she did by the simple expedient of declaring herself in love with him. There is no reason to suppose that Berlioz for his part was not genuinely in love with her, for doubtless the company of the pretty eighteen-year-old pianist was precisely what he needed after the years of pining for Harriet. When Berlioz left Paris in late December to begin his two years' study at the French Academy in Rome (one of the conditions attached to the Prix de Rome), the two were engaged.

Berlioz's Life 1830-46

The success of the 'Fantastic' Symphony in December 1830 and the prospects that it opened up for a career in music naturally made Berlioz reluctant to leave Paris. Furthermore he did not want to desert Camille Moke, to whom he had just become engaged. But he could not avoid his commitment, as winner of the Prix de Rome, to spend two years' study at the French Academy in Rome, and in late December he set out. He spent two months with his parents, en route for Rome, becoming ever more anxious as he heard nothing from Camille. When he finally arrived in Italy he found letters from friends containing thinly veiled hints that Camille was not missing him too much.

Berlioz decided forthwith to return to Paris to find out what was happening. At Florence, where he stayed for a week recovering from a feverish cold, he heard what he had perhaps been expecting. Camille was married – to Camille Pleyel, publisher and piano maker, twenty-two years her senior. Berlioz was seized with fury. He bought a chambermaid's outfit and some pistols, planning to disguise himself, settle his account with his fiancée and her scheming mother, and then kill himself. Passport difficulties detained him in Genoa, where he momentarily lost his resolve and made an amateurish attempt to drown himself, and he had to go to Nice, then part of Italy (Nizza), to get an entry visa for France. These delays, however, gave him time to think and at Nice he recovered his *sangfroid* and went on to enjoy there the 'twenty happiest days of my life', as he later described them in his *Memoirs*. He basked in the sun, swam, revelled in the beauties of the landscape – and composed. The overture *King Lear* and another overture inspired by Scott's *Rob Roy* were written there and a third was sketched – which later became *The Corsair*.

In June 1831 Berlioz was back in Rome, where he settled down to his life as prizewinner. He could do virtually what he liked. What he sent back to Paris by way of evidence of application to studies were works he had written earlier.

Although he found it difficult to compose, his period in Italy proved eventually to have inspired many of his later works, notably the symphony *Harold in Italy*. Walking holidays in the mountains, friendships with villagers, the Italian climate and the sea gave him a store of ideas and experiences to draw on.

But his anxiety to return to Paris, where his battles had to be fought, got the better of him and he was allowed to leave Rome after having spent little more than half the stipulated time there. On his return to France his first thoughts were to plan for a large concert including both the 'Fantastic' Symphony and its sequel *Lélio*, which consisted of a number of monologues by Lélio (the 'young musician' of the 'Fantastic' Symphony) interspersed with musical numbers of widely varying character. For Berlioz it was both a means of rescuing a quantity of earlier pieces too good to waste, and of providing an occasion for voicing his personal and aesthetic aspirations and priorities.

Another important feature of this concert was that Harriet Smithson – to whom Berlioz's thoughts returned after the failure of his engagement – was persuaded to attend it through the efforts of Berlioz's publisher. Hearing the words of *Lélio*, she was suddenly aware of the depth of feeling the passionate young composer still had for his Ophelia. Two days after the concert Hector Berlioz and Harriet Smithson met for the first time. In a very short time there were plans for marriage. After several stormy months of difficulties with his and her relations, and Harriet's own vacillations and misgivings (aggravated by a fall from a carriage when she broke her leg), the two were finally married at the British Embassy in October 1833.

Despite the fact that Berlioz had acquired with his bride a huge financial burden (Harriet was deeply in debt), he was happy. Undoubtedly the most prominent French composer of his generation, already a celebrated musical journalist and soon to be a father, inordinately proud of young Louis Berlioz, he was not depressed by the weight of material cares. He gladly accepted a request from the famous Paganini for a composition for his new viola, although it put a severe strain on his time. Within six months he had written *Harold in Italy,* a symphony with viola obbligato. Paganini had refused to play it even before it was completed, dissatisfied with the sparsity of notes for the viola. But the work was successfully performed in November 1834 with Chrétien Urhan, a friend from Conservatoire days, taking the solo part. It is worth mentioning here that following the conductor's incompetence in an encore of the second movement, Berlioz decided that the time had come for him to take conducting seriously himself.

The title of the Symphony has caused some confusion because neither in its character nor in the titles to the individual movements has it much in common with *Childe Harold's Pilgrimage,* other than evoking with its viola part the 'melancholy dreamer' of Byron's poem. *Italy* is the operative word: the work is a marvellous evocation of Berlioz's Roman holiday.

His next step was the obvious one of getting a commission from the Opéra. The text of *Benvenuto Cellini* was submitted, depicting the life, struggles and ultimate triumph of the famous goldsmith whose autobiography had recently been published. Meanwhile Berlioz received a government commission for a large-scale Requiem to be performed at the annual service commemorating the victims of the July Revolution of 1830. The work was to be completed in three months and Berlioz was to receive reasonable financial recompense. But the Requiem encountered the obstacles which Berlioz had by now come to accept as an inevitable part of his life. The proposed performance was cancelled. Then a new setting was conjured up (a memorial service for the French dead after the capture of Constantine in Algeria) and after further intrigues the Grande Messe des Morts was finally performed in December 1837. The government official responsible congratulated himself on providing Berlioz with an occasion for 'displaying his talent'.

The Requiem certainly did provide a spectacular display of Berlioz's musical imagination, and also a fine demonstration of how he adapted the proportions of a work to its acoustical setting. Its most celebrated feature (though in fact not typical of the work as a whole) is the presence of four brass choirs which sound out to magnificent effect in the Tuba Mirum; it was at this point during the first performance that the conductor Habeneck, according to Berlioz's *Memoirs,* opted to stop conducting and take a pinch of snuff – the situation being redeemed by Berlioz himself, who had prudently taken a seat behind the conductor.

In August 1838 *Benvenuto Cellini* was finally produced at the Opéra, the only one of Berlioz's three completed operas to receive that distinction. It was a failure – the result partly of its advanced musical style, partly of an organised cabal,

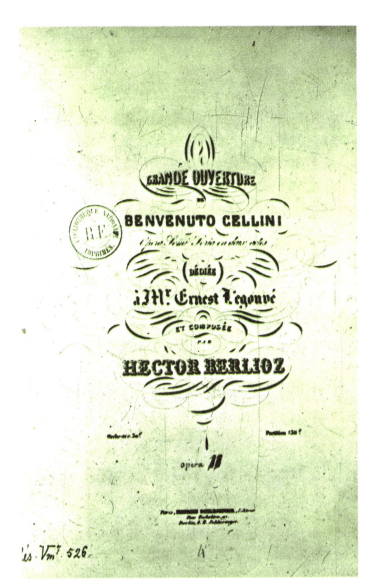

Frontispiece to the first edition of Benvenuto Cellini, **edited by Schlesinger, Paris 1838 (Music Section, Bibliothèque Nationale, Paris)**

Below:
The Italian opera in Paris—a 19th-century print **(Bibliothèque Nationale, Paris)**

partly of the uncooperative tenor who sang Cellini. But although Berlioz had not been able to win enough admirers to fill the opera house, he still had substantial and vociferous support in the concert hall. It was at a concert in December of that same year that Paganini, hearing 'his' *Harold in Italy* played in public for the first time, knelt down and kissed Berlioz's hand. Two days later Berlioz received a letter from him beginning 'Beethoven is dead and Berlioz alone can revive him' and continuing with a request to accept the sum of 20,000 francs (well over $7,000 in present-day terms).

Berlioz was moved quite as much by the gesture of a great artist as by the sum itself and resolved to write a work worthy of Paganini's munificence. For the first time in his career he had the financial security to devote himself entirely to composition. Within a year the Symphony *Romeo and Juliet* had been performed three times, and with unprecedented acclaim – this despite the novelty of a work which must to its first hearers have seemed to be linked to the conventional idea of the symphony by only the most tenuous of threads. Its influence on the future course of music can be gauged from Wagner's remark that it was the 'revelation of a new world of music'.

In 1840 came another government commission, and again in connection with the July Revolution. A new Bastille column was to be erected and Berlioz was to provide music to accompany the celebrations. The *Funeral and Triumphal* Symphony was thus written for a large 'military' orchestra. The first performance was drowned out by the shouts of the crowds lining the streets and by the tramping of the troops. But for the concert performance which followed there was wild enthusiasm.

These successes did not divert Berlioz from his main purpose. His sights were still set on the Opéra. He tried to persuade the famous librettist Scribe to write for him, and though Scribe did eventually agree and produce some of what was called *La Nonne Sanglante*, the opera was never finished. Meanwhile Berlioz got a foot inside the door. He was asked to supervise the productions of Weber's *Der*

Freischütz (for which he orchestrated some of Weber's other music for the additional ballets and wrote recitatives, both of which features were obligatory at the Opéra). He also had hopes of becoming chief conductor there. Cherubini had died, bequeathing his position at the Conservatoire, as Berlioz thought, to Habeneck, conductor at the Opéra, and thus leaving the Opéra position vacant. But the strength of the opposition in the musical establishment was too much for him and he got neither job. It was at this time that he realised that he had no choice but to further his career elsewhere. In 1842 he embarked on the first of his many conducting tours abroad.

In the autumn of 1842 Berlioz gave two concerts in Brussels and at the end of the year began an extensive tour of the major centres in Germany – the start of a way of life, if not a pilgrimage, that was to last until two years before his death. During this first visit to Germany he wrote back the open letters documenting his observations and experiences which now form part of his *Memoirs*. They were designed not only to be entertaining and instructive but also to emphasise his success abroad and thus advance his reputation at home. Back in Paris in the early summer of 1843 he found the situation much as before; he still had to keep up his journalism, and chances of an important musical position there were no better. He was the unchallenged leader of musical Romanticism but had no firm base to work from. He continued to give concerts and left no doubt of his pre-eminence as an orchestral virtuoso, comparable to Liszt and Paganini in their own fields; but he still had to embark on further concert tours to keep himself solvent. In late 1845 he left for Austria, Bohemia and Hungary, where his reception was even more encouraging than it had been in Germany. During this tour he wrote the larger part of *The Damnation of Faust*. It was first performed in Paris in December 1846 and was a miserable failure. Nothing hurt Berlioz more than the indifference of the Paris public to this work, based as it was on a subject which had been close to his heart for nearly twenty years.

In a sense Berlioz's foreign tours were an admission of defeat, rendered only more poignant by the disaster of *Faust*. Certainly he never knew again in his own country the full flush of victory he so often experienced during the 1830s, when the audience overflowed into the corridors for *Romeo and Juliet*, and both that work and the *Funeral* Symphony had to be performed three times to satisfy public demand. But in another sense his travels were a victory of will, and a defiant acceptance of his destiny as a composer. He *had* to spread his music abroad whatever fate might decree. He was not unknown in Europe before he began these tours. He had made friends in Paris and Rome with many of the leading musicians of the day, and it is significant that, although some regarded his music with extreme suspicion, they all respected and liked him as a person. While referring to Berlioz as a 'caricature without a shade of talent', Mendelssohn was kindness itself when Berlioz came to Leipzig, contributing in countless ways to the success of his concerts there. And Berlioz's reputation had been furthered in Germany by articles in Schumann's music magazine.

But it is one thing to have valuable friends and another to win the support of foreign audiences for music of decidedly unfamiliar character. Berlioz took good care to prepare

Two of a series of lithographs by Eugène Delacroix illustrating Goethe's Faust, *the first part of which had been translated by the French poet Gerard de Nerval and published in Paris in 1828. Berlioz's first contact with* Faust *made a deep impression on him and he chose it as the subject of two important works (Bibliothèque Nationale, Paris)*

these audiences for his own music by including much Weber and Beethoven in his concert programmes. He had a resounding success in some cities, a less sympathetic welcome in others; but there was no doubt that the successes outweighed the non-successes (failures would be the wrong word), and Berlioz returned to Paris confident that his pioneer work as a travelling virtuoso conductor-composer had reaped its rewards.

Domestically, it had been none too easy to launch these foreign tours. Harriet had developed a deep and passionate attachment to him; but she was aggressively possessive and, after having finally given up hope of recapturing her popularity on the stage, became increasingly embittered. She was also jealous and suspicious of her husband. Finally she took to drink. Before his first foreign tour Berlioz had to devise an elaborate subterfuge to get his suitcases out of the house. In 1841 he formed an attachment to a young singer called Marie Recio, who provided him with the tender affection notably lacking in Harriet. In fact his marriage had broken down, although he did not leave Harriet until 1844 and then continued to support her until she died in 1854 – a pitiful creature tortured by several strokes, paralysed and incoherent. Marie accompanied him on most of his concert tours, though she was often something of an embarrassment since her vocal accomplishment did not measure up to her pretensions and her indiscreet remarks often compromised Berlioz. But she was devoted to him and was an able organiser. He married Marie a year after Harriet's death. Marie herself died of a heart attack in 1862.

Berlioz was not fortunate with his love-affairs. He sought perhaps an ideal rather than a person and, tenacious in defence of his ideals, he was loath to admit a disparity between the two. That he should have gained the reputation of a great romantic lover is not surprising in view of the publicity attached to the Harriet story. But this was a single episode, and, as has been seen, it was a one-sided affair at the time when it affected him most deeply. Indeed he had affairs with very few women – Harriet, Camille, Marie, two brief idylls in the later part of his career and the almost sacred vision of Estelle which framed his life. And his music suggests that he can hardly have been a Don Juan. If that had been the case there would have been little need to pour out so ardent and tender a personality in music. His finest romantic music, the love scene from the *Romeo and Juliet* symphony, was written at a time when relations with Harriet were deteriorating rapidly.

The Struggle Continues: 1846-69

The two disastrous performances in 1846 of *The Damnation of Faust* marked a turning point in Berlioz's career. If they had been successful he might finally have gained a respectable footing in French musical life and the security to devote himself more fully to composition. (At least, this was theoretically possible: but one surmises that had he obtained an important position – musical director of the Opéra, professor at the Conservatoire, or conductor of the Conservatoire Concert Society – the chances are that he would have addressed himself to the advancement of his triumvirate of musical deities – Beethoven, Gluck and Weber – quite as much as the advancement of his own music.) But the performances were failures, deeply wounding to his ambition and his self-esteem. He had now to continue the hand-to-mouth existence of the professional composer/conductor, accepting whatever engagements seemed practicable and launching whatever of his own enterprises seemed least likely to fall flat, all the while relying on the spoils of journalism for some sort of regular income. A lesser man might have given up the struggle at this point. And indeed in the coming years, whenever his creative energy broke out with uncontrollable power, Berlioz would often ask himself whether it was worth the effort. One of the saddest passages in his *Memoirs* describes an occasion when he did manage to suppress his inspiration: he had conceived the first movement of a Symphony in A minor in a dream, and, while remembering it clearly the following morning, refused to allow himself to be swept away by the project, knowing what heartbreak and financial embarrassment it would bring him.

Frontispiece of the first edition of Berlioz's Harold in Italy, published in Paris in 1834. This work was largely inspired by Berlioz's trips to the countryside around Rome during the months he spent there as a Prix de Rome prizewinner (Bibliothèque Nationale, Paris)

Now, however, with a heavy load of debt and a wife, son and mistress to support, he had more pressing matters to attend to than thoughts of thwarted ambition and wounded pride. Having borrowed from friends and squared the debts, he set out for Russia, fortified by Balzac's assurance that he would gain a fortune there. He did not do that, but concerts in St Petersburg and Moscow certainly retrieved his financial position and he was able to say later 'Russia saved me.'

Back in Paris he found himself duped by two rogues who promised him the musical directorship of the Opéra if he would put in a good word on their behalf. They became joint directors of the Opéra; he remained as he was. He summed up the situation in the *Memoirs* with a variation of a phrase that runs through the book like an *idée fixe:* 'The promises freely given by these gentlemen have been no better kept than so many others, and from that time no more has been heard of it.' Later he reproached himself for having failed to take the two gentlemen to task in the cause of Art. But we may ask whether it was a failure when he had four lives to sustain and when every undertaking on the home front seemed doomed to failure. 'Was it? I am conscious of having been human, that is all . . .' Berlioz's explanation for not having written the A minor Symphony could well have applied here.

At the time however he could regard the Opéra affair with some indifference since in November 1847 he was in England, having accepted an offer from the impresario Jullien to become conductor, at an enormous salary, of a newly formed opera company at Drury Lane. Again his luck turned against him. The grand plans of Jullien had little substance. For the director of an English opera house the main considerations were the poster, and the need for extravagant costumes: everything else was of secondary importance. Within a couple of months the company was ruined and the unscrupulous Jullien had made off with what proceeds there were.

Under this growing weight of misfortune Berlioz must have felt cast in the role of plaything for the whims of fate. Almost every venture attracted awkward or insurmountable obstacles like a magnet. It was not surprising that the impetuous youth was now giving way to the more cool and detached man of middle age, no less meticulous and idealistic than before but protected by a layer of ironic reserve. At any rate this was his public image. With friends and kindred spirits he was still as eloquent and wryly humorous, as vulnerable to expressions of real feeling and as incapable of vindictiveness as he ever had been. (It is worth mentioning here that several years later, when Jullien was in the bankruptcy court, Berlioz spoke up for him and enabled him to continue as an impresario.) This is the tone of his *Memoirs*, written for a 'small number of artists and music lovers'.

Berlioz began compiling the book in London, during the hiatus following the collapse of the opera company. He was without permanent employment and, since the 1848 revolution had broken out in Paris, probably without the employment which he had had in France. The proprietor

19th-century print caricaturing Berlioz and his colourful orchestration (Bettmann Archive, New York)

of the *Journal des Débats*, the newspaper for which Berlioz was music critic, was a supporter of the monarchy and with the rise of republicanism was likely to go under with his paper. With these bleak prospects in view Berlioz imagined himself in the position of the 'Indians of Niagara' who, after giving up the attempt to fight against the current, 'gaze steadfastly at the short distance which separates them from the abyss, and sing, until the moment when they are tossed into infinity.'

However, life was not so grim as he had imagined. He managed to put on two highly successful concerts in London and to make many warm friends and admirers there; and when he returned to Paris he found that his newspaper had survived (although now offering half-pay) and that he had retained his one permanent position, as deputy librarian of the Conservatoire. And despite the worsening health of his wife and the death of his father, he did begin to sing, abyss or no abyss.

In 1849 he wrote his *Te Deum* for tenor, three choirs, organ and orchestra, an awe-inspiring masterpiece which proudly rebukes the period of artistic drought from which it sprang. Berlioz hoped that Louis Napoleon would sanction a performance; but on acquainting himself with the disinterest of the new president of the republic he decided that there was no longer any point in awaiting help from the state. Music must support itself. Accordingly in 1850 the first concert of the new Philharmonic Society, Berlioz's solution to the problem, took place. Lack of adequate finance and the opposition that seemed to spring out of nowhere as soon as his name was mentioned ensured that the Society lasted only eighteen months, and it never gave a performance of the *Te Deum*. It did however give a performance of a short work called the 'Shepherd's Farewell'. This was announced as the composition of a 17th-century master, Pierre Ducré, and was received most favourably. Berlioz had written the piece for the album of

The Salle Musard, Paris. Although the Salle Musard had originally been founded for dances and concerts of light music, Berlioz presented several of his own works there (Bibliothèque Nationale, Paris)

the architect Pierre Duc to amuse himself while friends were playing cards, an activity he disliked, and his little hoax afforded him distinct satisfaction, especially since most of the critics fell into the trap. It became the germ of *The Childhood of Christ*, a work which has received universal acclaim because of its popular subject matter and the appropriately tender and rapturous music. Berlioz was somewhat irritated by the success of its first performance in 1854 which he regarded as an insult to its elder brothers, but at any rate it encouraged him to launch the *Te Deum* which had now lain unperformed for nearly five years. Its first performance, by an array of nine hundred musicians on the eve of the Paris Exhibition of 1855, was another resounding success.

During this period he continued his travels. He went four more times to London (on one of these occasions to conduct the New Philharmonic Orchestra which had been created especially for him, and on another to mount *Benvenuto Cellini* at Covent Garden where it was hissed off the stage, the presence of Queen Victoria notwithstanding). And he made numerous visits to Germany, and especially Weimar where his friend Liszt promoted his music in princely fashion. As it turned out, the mid-1850s were the high-water mark of his career. Certainly without the international prestige he enjoyed at that time he would not have had the confidence to embark on the vast project which was now occupying his mind. While staying at Weimar for Liszt's performances he had told Liszt's mistress, Princess Carolyne Sayn-Wittgenstein, of his plan to write an opera based on Virgil's *Aeneid*, and for the next three years he was continuously occupied with what was to become *The Trojans*. The encouragement of the princess (his correspondence with her tells in fascinating detail how the work was completed) was bolstered by the strictly practical advantage of being elected a member of the French Institute. This distinction carried a small annual income ('What a farce! I don't despair of becoming pope one day.').

Berlioz encountered all the usual difficulties when it came to performing *The Trojans*, and if he had thought a few years earlier that his fortunes were improving, now he found

life running true to form. It was not until 1863 that the work was performed, and then in a theatre far too small, and Berlioz was obliged to sanction its mutilation (it was reduced to almost half its size). Before this, he had written and seen performed another opera, *Beatrice and Benedict*. This had been commissioned by one Bénazet, who purveyed an adroit mixture of gambling and music at Baden-Baden, and who gave Berlioz almost ideal conditions of performance. *Beatrice* was to prove his last work.

The Trojans performances did at least provide him with enough income from royalties to dispense with journalism. But in his final years, when he was tortured by the pain of intestinal neuralgia (the disease which was eventually to kill him has not yet been properly diagnosed: it could have been psychosomatic, an ulcer, or even cancer) and, with the death of his wife in 1862, more and more dependent on the affection of his son, he never became resigned to not hearing the first part of his opera. His bitterness ('If I could only live to be 140, my musical life would end by being distinctly interesting') was allayed somewhat by the correspondence and the occasional meetings with his beloved Estelle. The death of his son Louis from yellow fever in Havana, in 1867, was the final blow. Although Berlioz had neglected Louis during the boy's childhood, in later years he proved a model father and was deeply attached to his son. He managed somehow to gather the strength for a second visit to Russia in late 1867 but when he returned to Paris he was exhausted and knew well that he hadn't long to live. He died on 8th March 1869.

Posterity has been reluctant to accord Berlioz the accolade happily conferred on his contemporaries Mendelssohn, Schumann, Chopin, Liszt and Wagner—reluctant, that is, until quite recently. Since the 1939-45 war he has become known as the composer not only of the ever-popular 'Fantastic' Symphony and a few overtures, but also of (for example) *Romeo and Juliet, The Damnation of Faust*, the Requiem and the Te Deum, *The Trojans* and the Gautier songs *Nuits d'été* —in short, the author of an imposing list of exciting, tender and profound compositions which demand and get regular hearings because they are great music.

PROGRAM NOTES FOR THE RECORD

by ROBERT JACOBSON

The 'Fantastic' Symphony

Perhaps no other composer has deserved restoration to the highest rank of the musical pantheon more than Hector Berlioz. Generations of music-lovers grew to maturity believing him to be merely a 19th-century curio—a mad genius whose music seemed to fit nowhere into the classic sequence of Beethoven, Schumann, Liszt, Wagner, Brahms et al. But in the last decade or so, this lingering judgement has changed significantly. With revivals of such grandiose operas as his *Les Troyens* and *Benvenuto Cellini* and with repeated hearings of his highly dramatic and programmatic symphonies, overtures and choral works, Berlioz suddenly fell into place as one of the major, daring innovators of the Romantic period, without whom Liszt, Wagner, Mahler, Strauss and Debussy might not have achieved such heights of inspiration.

Berlioz was a mere twenty-six when he completed one of the key works of his *oeuvre*, the astonishing 'Fantastic' Symphony, which the composer entitled an 'Episode in the Life of an Artist,' a work that broke all the rules of the prevailing Classical symphony of its time—and yet is a disciplined masterpiece. Seen in retrospect, it is a fitting monument to the flamboyant, volatile world in which it was conceived, a revolutionary age in which long-accepted patterns of behaviour, outdated political doctrines and worn-out artistic traditions all came tumbling down. The year 1830, in which the 'Fantastic' Symphony first stunned a Paris audience, saw three related revolutions: Louis-Philippe, the 'Citizen King,' took the throne of France; Victor Hugo conquered French literary and theatrical circles with the triumphant performance of his Romantic drama *Hernani*; and Hector Berlioz—with his gifts of highly original orchestral colour, extravagant sensitivity, poetic awareness, rhythmic animation and imaginative descriptiveness—stimulated a musical revolution that still reverberates today. This was indeed the music of the future.

Out of the composer's turbulent feelings for the Irish actress Harriet Smithson grew his autobiographical 'Fantastic' Symphony, one of the earliest mentions of which occurs in a letter written to a friend in February 1830: 'I am again plunged in the anguish of an interminable and inextinguishable passion, without motive, without cause ... O unhappy one! If she could for one moment conceive all the poetry, all the infinity of a like love, she would fly to my arms, were she to die through my embrace. I was on the point of beginning my great symphony in which the development of my infernal passion is to be portrayed.' The macabre psychological program he conceived for his symphony is a masterwork of vivid exhibitionism and self-pity; but it was, after all, a time when an artist had to suffer with grand passion. Berlioz hoped that the 'wretched woman' would be present for the first performance. 'But I do not believe she will,' he declared.

'She will surely recognise herself in reading the program of my instrumental drama, and she will take care not to appear.' The première took place on 5th December 1830, at the Paris Conservatoire—but was not attended by Miss Smithson, who heard a performance only two years afterwards.

Franz Liszt—then nineteen and already a famous piano virtuoso—was in the audience at the first performance of the 'Fantastic' Symphony. His enthusiasm was so great that he persuaded Berlioz to forsake his friends after the concert and spend the evening with him instead. Liszt made a piano transcription of the Symphony—which was Schumann's guide when writing his famous article about the work which introduced Berlioz to Germany. Both these musicians were, of course, concerned with the music. But the work gained its initial success in part from its program, whose element of self-dramatisation aroused wide interest. Berlioz, by 1830 aware of the merits of an advertising campaign, had taken care that its contents were well known before the concert. The program itself was sensational enough, but the young composer's curious relationship with the Irish actress was public property and added spice to an already tasty dish. Berlioz wrote in the first version of his program that he had developed from 'certain scenes what they contain that is *musical*.' Let us examine what these 'certain scenes' are.

The composer first explains, 'A young musician of abnormal sensitivity and ardent imagination poisons himself with opium in a paroxysm of amorous despair. The dose

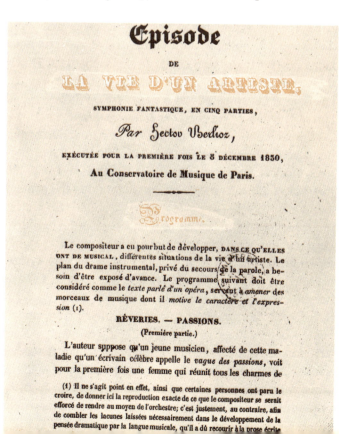

The beginning of the descriptive programme distributed at the first performance of the 'Fantastic' Symphony —it was intended as a text to explain the Symphony (Opéra Library, Paris)

11

is too feeble to kill him and plunges him into a heavy sleep accompanied by the most strange visions, in which his sensations, feelings and memories are translated in his sick mind into musical thoughts and images. The loved one herself becomes for him a melody, a fixed idea [*idée fixe*] which keeps coming back to him and which he hears everywhere.'

Berlioz then goes on to describe each of the five movements: 'I. *Reveries: Passions.* First he remembers that weariness of the soul, that void of passions, that melancholy, those aimless joys he experienced before having seen his beloved; then the volcanic love she suddenly inspired in him, his delirious anguish, his furious jealousy, his returns to tenderness, his religious consolations. II. *A Ball.* He finds his beloved at a ball, in the midst of the tumult of a brilliant festival. III. *Scene in the Countryside.* One summer evening in the countryside he hears two herdsmen calling one another with a *Ranz des vaches*; this pastoral duet, the surroundings, the delicate rustling of the trees gently swayed by the wind, some symbols of a hope he has little known before, all conspire to fill his heart with an unaccustomed tranquillity, to give his ideas a more pleasing colour; but *she* appears again, his heart freezes, painful imaginings assail him . . . will she deceive him? One of the herdsmen resumes his simple melody, the other does not reply. The sun sets . . . distant thunder . . . solitude . . . silence. IV. *March to the Scaffold.* He dreams that he has killed his loved one and that he is condemned to death and is being led to execution. The procession advances to the sounds of a march, now dark and wild, now brilliant and solemn, in which the dull sound of heavy footsteps gives way to noisy outbursts. At the end, the *idée fixe* reappears for a moment like a last thought of love cut short by the fatal blow. V. *Dream of a Witches' Sabbath.* He sees himself at a witches' sabbath, in the midst of a hideous crowd of spirits, sorcerers and monsters of every description gathered for his burial. . .

'Strange sounds, groans, shrieks of laughter, distant cries to which others seem to respond. The melody of the beloved appears again; but it has lost its noble and timid character; it is nothing but a cheap, trivial and grotesque dance tune; it is *she* who comes to the sabbath . . . Howls of joy greet her arrival . . . She joins the diabolical orgy . . . The funeral bell, a parody of the *Dies Irae*. Witches' round dance. The dance and the *Dies Irae* together.'

Without doubt these strange, hallucinatory ideas and the narrative form in which they are cast stimulated Berlioz's musical imagination. Berlioz himself regarded the program as a means not so much of clarifying the content and course of the work (as such, it would be useless duplication of the music) as of filling gaps in the narrative which could not be filled with music. This at least is what he wrote for the first performance. After he had written its sequel *Lélio,* he decided that there was no need to have the program at all unless both parts of the work were played. For the symphony alone, the titles of the movements would suffice. In fact, even these are barely necessary, for the work is far more symphonic than fantastic, planned as a comparatively straightforward symphony in C major.

The first movement, marked *Largo*, begins passionately with an extended slow introduction in the violins and solo horns, suggesting that 'weariness of the soul' the composer experienced before meeting his beloved. The tempo then changes to *Allegro agitato e appassionato assai*, after which the haunting, almost despairing first theme—the 'fixed idea'—is presented by the flute and violins. This theme embodies the adored Harriet Smithson, noble and timid, ethereal, unobtainable. A fiery transitional passage is heard, leading to a second theme derived from the fixed idea. These materials are developed, then the initial theme returns forcefully in the winds. Following an exhilarating outburst of the full orchestra, the music grows increasingly softer and slower, ending in a devout mood.

The second movement—the Ball—is in a graceful dance tempo, a lyrical waltz marked *Allegro non troppo*. Now the *idée fixe* returns in 3/4 time and is heard first in the flute and oboe and later repeated several times. At the end, the waltz turns brilliant and vigorous.

The third movement (*Adagio*) opens with a duet between the English horn and oboe. (The oboist is directed to play his part behind the scene, to evoke a feeling of open space, the outdoors.) The strings tremble under the two voices, followed by the flute and first violins, which offer the main theme and then the second theme. These are succeeded by a closing theme in the violins alone. The initial theme returns in the cellos, with ornamentation in the violins. A desperate climax is reached with trembling upper strings, a dramatic statement by the cellos and the *idée fixe* recurring in the flute and oboe. Further variations of the main theme are followed by a return of the fixed idea in the solo winds, calmly and quietly, set against the principal theme in the violins. A brief epilogue brings back the opening rustic tune for English horn, now unanswered, while the timpani suggest distant thunder fading off into lonely silence.

The grotesque, even savage march music of the fourth movement (*Allegretto non troppo*) is a highly pictorial rendering of Berlioz's program, opening with the heavy tread of footsteps and ending with final thoughts of his love sounding in the clarinets, then a loud chord describing the fatal fall of the axe and a fanfare with percussion.

The Finale (*Larghetto*) opens with nightmarish harmonies in the strings and strange calls in the woodwinds. The *idée fixe*, which returns in a clarinet solo, is now reduced to something ignoble. The orchestra then literally howls as the dance passes to a high clarinet. A descending phrase in the bass instruments leads to the funeral knell, sounded by the bells. Berlioz then brings in the familiar melody of the *Dies Irae* ('Day of Wrath'), a part of the Roman Catholic Mass for the Dead said to have been composed in the 13th century by a disciple of St Francis of Assisi. Here, however, it is mockingly played by the tubas and bassoons and is immediately repeated by the upper brass an octave higher. Then, jumping two more octaves higher, it is plucked out by the violins in a syncopated rhythm. When the *Dies Irae* has run its course, there follows a wildly demonic witches' dance, spreading through the orchestra and being intensely developed. This is later combined with the *Dies Irae*, now shouted by all the winds, and the Finale whirls feverishly to a bold, imaginative conclusion.

12

Printed in the United States of America